ALSO BY ANTHONY BRANDT

The People Along the Sand: Three Stories, Six Poems, and a Memoir

Reality Police: The Experience of Insanity in America

(EDITOR)

The Pushcart Book of Essays

The Journals of Lewis and Clark

Thomas Jefferson Travels

The Tragic History of the Sea

The Adventures of Theodore Roosevelt

The North Pole: A Narrative History

The South Pole: A Narrative

THE MAN WHO ATE HIS BOOTS

THE MAN WHO ATE HIS BOOTS

THE TRAGIC HISTORY OF THE SEARCH FOR THE NORTHWEST PASSAGE

Anthony Brandt

ALFRED A. KNOPF NEW YORK 2010

THIS IS A BORZOI BOOK
PUBLISHED BY ALFRED A. KNOPF

Library of Congress Cataloging-in-Publication Data
Brandt, Anthony.
The man who ate his boots : the tragic history of the search for the
Northwest passage / Anthony Brandt.
p. cm.
"A Borzoi book."
Includes bibliographical references and index.
ISBN 978-0-307-26392-6
1. Northwest Passage—Discovery and exploration—History.
2. Arctic regions—Discovery and exploration—History.
3. Explorers—Northwest Passage—History.
4. Explorers—Arctic regions—History.   I. Title.
G640.B73 2010
970.9163'27—dc22   2009038835

Manufactured in the United States of America
First Edition

To Lorraine

THE WESTERN ARCTIC

0 — miles — 500

North P

Bering Sea

ST. LAWRENCE I.

Chukchi Sea

WRANGEL I.

Bering Strait

Kotzebue Sound

Icy Cape

Point Barrow

Norton Sound

ARCTIC OC

Yukon River

Beaufort Sea

BORDEN I.

PRINCE PATRICK I.

HE Is

MELVILLE I.

BATHURST I

Cape Bathurst

BANKS ISLAND

Viscount Melville Sound

CORNWALLIS

Barro

Gulf of Alaska

VICTORIA ISLAND

PRINCE OF WALES I.

SOM Is.

BOOTH PEN.

PACIFIC OCEAN

Mackenzie River

KENT PEN.

KING WILLIAM I.

Coppermine River

Great Bear L.

Bathurst Inlet

Great Fish (Back) River

Chesterfield Inlet

Great Slave L.

Lake Athabasca

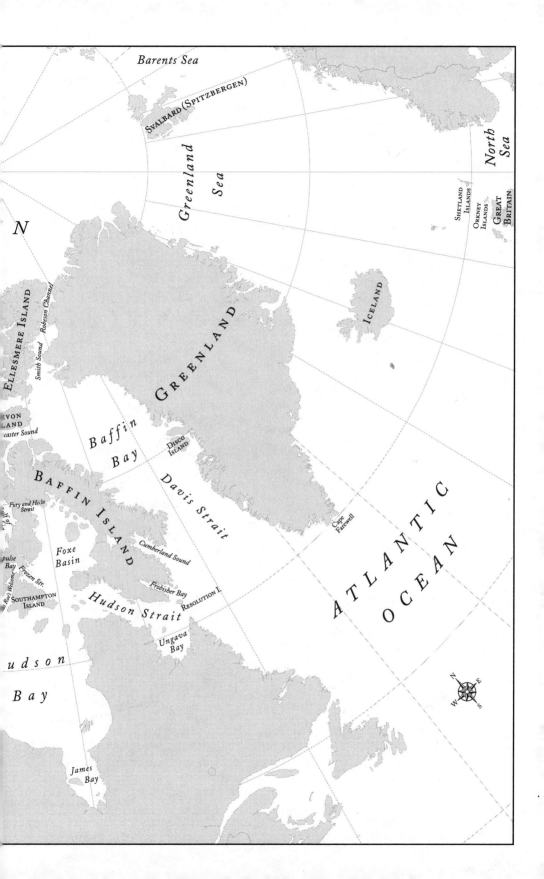

CONTENTS

IV. PROLOGUE TO TRAGEDY

V. TOWARD NO EARTHLY POLE

EPILOGUE

A Chronological List of Arctic Explorations, 1818—1880: The Explorers and Their Ships Who Went in Search of the Northwest Passage and of Sir John Franklin

1818 David Buchan, *Dorothea*, and John Franklin, *Trent*

To the seas north of Spitzbergen (now Svalbard) in search of a passage over the North Pole to the Pacific. Failed to find a route through the ice.

1818 John Ross, *Isabella*, and William Edward Parry, *Alexander*

To Davis Strait and Baffin Bay, in search of the presumed Northwest Passage over Canada to the Pacific. Rediscovered sites first discovered by Baffin two hundred years earlier; turned back from exploring Lancaster Sound.

1819–22 John Franklin, first Arctic land expedition

To northern Canada and the shores of the Arctic Ocean at the mouth of the Coppermine River, for the purpose of mapping the north coast of North America and in search of the Northwest Passage. Discovered Bathurst Inlet; stopped at Point Turnagain on the Kent Peninsula.

1819–20 William Edward Parry, *Hecla*, and Matthew Liddon, *Griper*

To Baffin Bay, Lancaster Sound, and the Canadian archipelago in search of the Northwest Passage. Sailed through Lancaster Sound and Barrow Strait, discovered Prince Regent Inlet, the Parry Islands, Melville Island, Banks Island.

1821–23 William Edward Parry, *Fury*, and George F. Lyon, *Hecla*

To upper Hudson Bay in search of the Northwest Passage. Explored Repulse Bay, Frozen Strait; discovered Fury and Hecla Strait.

1824–25 William Edward Parry, *Hecla,* and Henry Hoppner, *Fury*

To Prince Regent Inlet in the Canadian archipelago in search of the Northwest Passage. Made no new discoveries.

1824 George F. Lyon, *Griper*

To Repulse Bay, in the upper reaches of Hudson Bay, to send an exploring party overland to the Kent Peninsula on the northern Canadian coast. Beset in the ice in Sir Thomas Roe's Welcome; never reached Repulse Bay.

1825–27 John Franklin, second Arctic land expedition

Overland to upper Canada and, via the Mackenzie River system, to the mouth of the Mackenzie; from there proceeding westward along the coast of northern Canada toward Point Barrow (and eastward, under John Richardson, to the mouth of the Coppermine River). Got as far west as Return Reef.

1825–28 Frederick W. Beechey, *Blossom*

To Bering Strait, in support of Franklin and Parry, to await their arrival. Explored the west coast of Alaska from Icy Cape to Point Barrow.

1827 William Edward Parry, *Hecla*

To Spitzbergen, in an attempt to reach the North Pole. Failed.

1829–33 John Ross, *Victory*

Private expedition to Prince Regent Inlet in search of the Northwest Passage. Crossed Boothia Peninsula, discovered King William Island, wrongly thought it to be part of the mainland, explored its north shore to Cape Franklin, and discovered the North Magnetic Pole.

1833–35 George Back, Arctic land expedition

Down the Great Fish River in northern Canada to find and rescue the John Ross expedition, gone four years. Discovered and mapped the Great Fish River; reached Chantrey Inlet at the mouth of the river.

1836–37 George Back, *Terror*

Into Hudson Bay, to send explorers overland from Wager Inlet to Arctic Ocean coastline, to map the coastline from Fury and Hecla Strait to Point Turnagain. Beset in the ice; never reached Wager Inlet.

1837–39 Thomas Simpson and Peter Dease, Arctic land expedition

Hudson's Bay Company expedition to complete survey of Canada's north coast from Point Barrow to Boothia Peninsula. Reached Point Barrow on western leg, Castor and Pollux River on lower Boothia Peninsula on eastern leg. Crossed to the south coast of King William Island and Victoria Island. Discovered Simpson Strait.

1845–48 John Franklin, *Erebus*, and Francis R. M Crozier, *Terror*

To Lancaster Sound and the Canadian archipelago in search of the Northwest Passage. Ships sailed to Beechey Island at the mouth of Wellington Channel, wintered there in 1845–46, sailed north up Wellington Channel and south around Cornwallis Island to Peel Strait, down Peel Strait to Victoria Strait. Beset in the ice north of King William Island in September 1846; ships were abandoned in April 1848. Survivors trekked south toward Chantrey Inlet and Great Fish River. None lived. May have completed one leg of Northwest Passage.

1846–47 John Rae, land expedition

To Repulse Bay in northern Hudson Bay, overland to bottom of Prince Regent Inlet, then to west coast of Boothia Peninsula. Added to knowledge of coastline there.

1848–49 James Ross, *Enterprise*, and Edward Bird, *Investigator*

To Lancaster Sound and Barrow Strait in search of Franklin expedition. No trace found.

1848–52 Thomas Moore, *Plover*

To Bering Strait and Kotzebue Sound, in search of Franklin expedition. A supply ship, it did no exploring.

1848–50 John Richardson and John Rae

Overland expedition to north coast of Canada in search of John Franklin. No trace found.

1848–50 Henry Kellett, *Herald*

To Bering Strait and Kotzebue Sound, in search of Franklin expedition. For resupply of the *Plover*.

1849 Robert Shedden, *Nancy Dawson*

Private expedition to Bering Strait in search of Franklin expedition and to assist the *Herald*.

1849–51   William J. S. Pullen and W. H. Hooper

By small boat from Point Barrow east to Mackenzie River, in search of Franklin expedition. In two summers reached Cape Bathurst. Stopped by ice.

1849–50   James Saunders, *North Star*

Resupply ship for James Ross's attempt to search for Franklin expedition. Ice prevented ship from reaching Ross.

1850   Charles Forsyth, *Prince Albert*

Private expedition, financed by Jane Franklin, in search of Franklin survivors in Prince Regent Inlet. Stopped by ice.

1850–51   H. T. Austin, *Resolute;* Erasmus Ommanney, *Assistance;* John Cator, *Intrepid;* and Sherard Osborn, *Pioneer*

To Lancaster Sound and Barrow Strait in search of Franklin expedition. Discovered site on Beechey Island where Franklin spent first winter. Sledge parties discovered Prince of Wales Island, explored Bathurst Island and parts of Melville Island.

1850–51   William Penny, *Lady Franklin,* and Alexander Stewart, *Sophia*

To Lancaster Sound and Barrow Strait in search of Franklin expedition. Sledge parties explored in Wellington Channel, discovered various islands.

1850–51   John Ross, *Felix,* and yacht *Mary*

To Lancaster Sound and Barrow Strait in search of Franklin expedition. Helped with search of Beechey Island.

1850–51   Edwin De Haven, *Advance,* and Samuel Griffin, *Rescue*

American expedition to Lancaster Sound and Barrow Strait in search of Franklin expedition. Helped search Beechey Island. Beset in ice in September; drifted with the ice in Baffin Bay throughout winter.

1850–51   John Rae, Victoria Island

To Victoria Island by dog sledge, then small boat, in search of Franklin expedition. Explored southern coast of Victoria Island and determined it was one piece of land, not two.

1850–54   Robert McClure, *Investigator*

To Bering Strait, past Point Barrow, into straits off northern Canada, in search of Franklin expedition. Discovered Prince of Wales Strait between Banks Island and Victoria Island. Sailed around Banks Island to west and north. Discovered one of the Northwest Passages and traversed it walking on the ice.

1850–55 Richard Collinson, *Enterprise*

To Bering Strait, past Point Barrow, into straits off northern Canada in search of Franklin expedition. Separated from McClure. With sledging parties covered areas previously explored by McClure and Rae.

1851–52 William Kennedy, *Prince Albert*

Private expedition, financed by Jane Franklin, in search of John Franklin. To Prince Regent Inlet and across North Somerset Island by sledge, to Peel Sound, to Prince of Wales Island, then north to Cape Walker. Discovered Bellot Strait separating North Somerset from Boothia Peninsula.

1852 Edward Inglefield, *Isabel*

Private expedition, financed by Jane Franklin, in search of John Franklin. To Baffin Bay and Jones Sound. Penetrated Smith Sound and mapped coastline there.

1852–54 Edward Belcher, *Assistance;* Sherard Osborn, *Pioneer;* Henry Kellett, *Resolute;* Francis L. McClintock, *Intrepid*

To Lancaster Sound and Barrow Strait in search of Franklin expedition. Belcher and Osborn to Wellington Channel area; Kellett and McClintock to Melville Island. Sledge parties traced unknown coasts of islands in and above Wellington Channel to Melville Island. McClintock discovered Eglinton and Prince Patrick Islands west of Melville Island. Rescued McClure and crew from Bay of Mercy on Banks Island. Ships abandoned.

1852–54 William J. S. Pullen, *North Star*

Depot ship for Belcher expedition (above), in search of Franklin expedition. Based at Beechey Island.

1853–54 John Rae

Overland to Boothia Peninsula, to complete survey of Boothia west coast. Discovered fate of Franklin expedition.

1855 James Anderson

Hudson's Bay Company expedition down Great Fish River, to search for Franklin relics and records.

1857–59   Francis L. McClintock, *Fox*

Private expedition, financed by Jane Franklin, to search for Franklin relics and records. To Prince Regent Inlet; sledge parties to King William Island.

1864–69   Charles Francis Hall

Private expedition to Repulse Bay and King William Island in search of Franklin survivors, relics, and records.

1878–80   Lieutenant Frederick Schwatka

American Geographical Society expedition overland to King William Island in search of Franklin relics and records.

THE MAN WHO ATE HIS BOOTS

INTRODUCTION

When Lieutenant Edward Parry of the Royal Navy climbed a small hill on what he believed to be the southwest corner of Melville Island in the summer of 1820, he gazed out upon an apparently endless sea of ice stretching west to the horizon. The same ice filled up the strait between Melville Island and land he could just make out in what sailors called the offing, far away, to the south, perhaps fifty miles distant. It was August, yet there was no trace of a lane of open water anywhere within sight. The surface of the ice was as hummocky and ridged as the wrinkled surface of a glacier, while the floes close to shore were as thick as a four-story building is tall. If this was the Northwest Passage, he could plainly see, it would never be navigable. Ice that thick, that old, that hard could not possibly melt in the brief Arctic summer, and no ship could penetrate it.

In the summer of 2007, for the first time in history, this particular route through the Canadian archipelago, the complex maze of islands lying north of the North American continent and east of the Mackenzie River delta, opened to ship traffic. The following summer it opened again. All that ice was gone. Thanks to global warming it is beginning to seem likely that the Northwest Passage will open for longer and longer periods each year, until, perhaps by the end of this century, ice will have vanished from the world altogether and the ancient dream of a Northwest Passage will have been, unexpectedly and inadvertently, realized.

The potentially apocalyptic consequences of such an event are too well known to need comment: drowned islands, drowned seacoasts, massive storms, cycles of flood and drought, the reconfiguration of the world's ocean currents, and accelerated species loss. In the immediate time frame, however, there are advantages to global warming, and the opening of the Northwest Passage is one of them. By ship, via the Panama Canal, the distance from New York to Tokyo is 11,300 miles. Via the Northwest Passage it is nearly 3,000 miles shorter. The savings to European shipping would be comparable. And it isn't only a question of shipping costs. If there turns out to be enough oil and natural gas in the Arctic to justify large-scale extraction, it will be much cheaper, and perhaps ecologically safer, to take it out by tanker than by laying pipe across the Arctic tundra.

The opening of the Passage, in fact, has energized a dormant political conflict over both the extraction of resources from the Arctic Ocean seafloor and the shipping lanes themselves. Canada claims the islands of its archipelago as its own but lacks the means and the will to occupy them and maintain its claim; nevertheless it regards the straits and channels that divide the islands as internal waterways with the same status as rivers and streams. The United States, Great Britain, and other countries have always disagreed with this position, insisting that the Northwest Passage is an international waterway free to all, like the oceans. To make its point, the United States sent a Coast Guard icebreaker through the Passage in 1985, before global warming had become an issue, without asking permission from the Canadian government. Canada responded by announcing its intention to build more icebreakers of its own and to enhance security in the Far North, plans that it subsequently abandoned because of the expense. The issue remains unresolved.

Ownership of the seafloor in the Beaufort Sea north of Alaska and the Canadian Northwest Territories has also been in question; with the advent of global warming the question has become more acute. In 2003 the United States tried to auction off drilling rights to an area believed to hold major natural gas reserves that Canada also claims. Energy companies backed off, not wanting to become involved in the dispute. In 2004 the Canadian military conducted exercises on Baffin Island designed to familiarize itself with Arctic conditions. Canada does not, however, maintain permanent bases in the archipelago and has no way to stop nuclear-powered submarines from operating under the Arctic ice, and no stations to detect their passage. In 2007 the increasingly assertive Russians used a submersible to plant their flag on the bottom of the Arctic Ocean at the North Pole. The Danes for their part are claiming rights to oil and gas reserves in the narrow channel that divides Greenland, which is a Danish dependency, from Ellesmere Island, where the Canadians have nailed bronze plaques claiming sovereignty to the bare rocks.

These developments no doubt would have amazed Lieutenant Parry. The industrialization of Europe and the United States that would set global warming in motion was certainly well under way by 1820, but England was still primarily a rural nation. Ships were made of wood, and the age of sail was not yet over. The first passenger railways were a decade in the future; in 1820 railways were used to transport coal and ore. Steam engines had only just begun to appear in a few coastal ferries. It would have been difficult, if not impossible, for Parry to imagine massive icebreakers hundreds of feet long weighing thousands of tons plowing through the frozen waters he surveyed. For Parry, the Northwest Passage was a geographic puzzle to be solved, and his mission was basically scientific. He spent much of his time his first winter in the Arctic measuring temperature, barometric pressure, and compass variations; recording the appearance and frequency of the aurora borealis; collecting specimens of rocks, plants, and animals; and making maps. There were dreamers—there are always dreamers—but few sensible people had any hope that the Northwest Passage might become a commercially viable route to the Pacific. One of those dreamers, to be sure, happened to be the second secretary of the Admiralty, and it was he who had engineered this voyage, and would engineer many more. But for Parry, staring in wonder over this alabaster sea, in awe of what he was looking at and mindful of his own growing experience of sea ice, the idea that it all might one day melt away like so much ice cream would have been incomprehensible. Throughout his lifetime, and the lifetime of the second secretary, during the half-century or so the search for the Northwest Passage engaged British ambitions and thrilled the British public, the ice never melted. It remained intractable, impenetrable, and, for those who challenged it, a kind of fate.

It was a tragic fate in the end. We use the word *tragic* carelessly these days to describe any sort of disaster that kills people, from the space shuttle *Challenger* exploding in the sky to Hurricane Katrina devastating New Orleans. In its original Greek sense, however, the word refers not to straightforward natural disasters but to tragic drama, in which it was hubris, an all-too-human arrogance and pride, that triggered a particular calamity. Historical events are tragic in a looser sense; history is messy, it lacks the tight construction of classic drama, and things can go wrong in a thousand ways that have no connection to human motivation or human action. The study of ice cores in the Canadian archipelago has revealed that the years from 1810 to 1860, during which the British pursued the quest for the Northwest Passage that is the subject of this book, had summers that were the coldest on record, four full degrees below the seven-hundred-year average, and the ice melt during those summers was consequently the lowest. No one could have predicted such an eventuality.

Yet instances of hubris in history abound and the consequences are often fatal. In the case of the quest for the Northwest Passage, a nation pursued an enterprise that met with repeated and often deadly failure over a period not just of years but of centuries, persisting in tempting fate until fatality became inevitable. And fate arrived in the form of sea ice. For generations, as we shall see, men deluded themselves into believing that sea ice did not exist, or that if it did, it occurred only in shallow water, in the vicinity of land, while in the open oceans it could not form because of the action of the waves. Some scientists even theorized that salt water could not freeze at all. The seeds of tragedy are to be found in just such delusions, coming in this case from the minds of men with no experience in the ice, men who had never watched a harbor freeze over or felt the terror of ice floes a mile or two across and ten feet thick bearing down on them in Baffin Bay or the whale-rich waters around Svalbard. In the half-century after the end of the Napoleonic Wars, this tragic folly came to its climax when the British tried to force the Northwest Passage once and for all, no matter what. They believed it their peculiar destiny to do so, to triumph over the ice and add this exclamation point to the great victories at Trafalgar and Waterloo, underlining in the process British command of the world's oceans. In the end two lavishly equipped ships and 129 men fell victim to the ice. Their deaths were ugly, a scene of horror out of a Gothic novel or Dante's *Inferno*. There was no trace of dignity in the record left by their bones, which had been broken open by the last survivors for their marrow.

Yet tragedy can be the scene of heroism as well as arrogance and folly. Men suffered and died in the Arctic in a great cause, to open an entire region of the globe to science and human traffic, however unreal it was at the time to envision sailing through water frozen to a depth of forty feet. Should they have stayed home and waited for global warming? No easy answer suggests itself. To behave nobly and heroically in an obviously hopeless cause is a kind of folly, but it can also constitute a kind of greatness. Despite the wrongheadedness of the enterprise, an air of transcendence arises from their sufferings. It was in vain that they died, but their deaths raised them up, as it were, and made them emblems of whatever it is in human beings that can seem sublime.

John Franklin, known after his disastrous journey along the north coast of Canada as "the man who ate his boots," was just such a hero. Short and tending to corpulence, he was almost excessively pious—but it was a pious age—and so kind that he would not swat mosquitoes but blew them off his skin, telling the astonished Yellow Knife Indians who saw him do this that these pestiferous insects, which in their swarms could blot out the sun on the Arctic tundra, drain a caribou dry, and drive a man insane, had as much right to live as he did. This exaggerated kindness is part of his legend, along with his courage, his sufferings, his persistence, and the mystery of his disappearance in the icy wastes of the North. Within sixty years of his death one short and three full-length biographies appeared. As recently as 2002 there was another. He became a model for the chivalric revival of the mid- to late nineteenth century in England. He seemed to embody the chivalric virtues at their best; he was a gentleman and a gentle man, pious and pure but at the same time brave and indomitable. This book is not a biography of Franklin, but he is its natural focus, because it was he, not Parry, who became the central, the emblematic figure in the quest for the Northwest Passage in the nineteenth century. He was present at the beginning in 1818 and again at the end, when he commanded the last expedition the British sent on this quest in 1845. It was the long, exhaustive search for this expedition that ultimately mapped most of the Arctic and finally solved the riddle of the Northwest Passage.

He was in most respects perfectly ordinary, not in the least heroic in the standard sense of the word, not the swashbuckling naval officer of boys' adventure stories or a moody grand Byronic hero. It is hard to imagine him brandishing a sword. He was socially shy and uneasy at large parties, and being treated as a hero made him extremely uncomfortable. It is his bronze statue, nevertheless, that stands in Waterloo Place in London, honoring not only him but all the men who died with him in the unforgiving Arctic ice; and it is his monument with its portrait bust that is embedded in the wall in Westminster Abbey, with its neat little epitaph by Tennyson:

NOT HERE! THE WHITE NORTH HATH THY BONES, AND THOU,
HEROIC SAILOR SOUL,
ART PASSING ON THY HAPPIER VOYAGE NOW
TOWARDS NO EARTHLY POLE.

Had Franklin been capable of irony he might have smiled, not at the words but at the fact that Tennyson wrote them. Tennyson had married one of Franklin's many nieces, and Franklin had met him once and hadn't approved of him. The young, tall, long-haired poet had sprawled across no fewer than three chairs after dinner and lit a pipe in the presence of the ladies. Franklin was nothing if not proper. But it was precisely the fact that he was not capable of irony that made him such a perfect candidate for heroism. The making of heroes is one way of transcending the ubiquitous irony of history; it is what demonstrates that we are a great people after all, that our hopes and dreams are not foolish and futile, that we can rise above defeat. The hubris was Britain's, not Franklin's. He sailed for the Northwest Passage to redeem a somewhat damaged reputation and to cap his long career with a triumph. But by his death he suffered a sea change. Kind, avuncular, overweight, and too old to be leading an expedition into the Arctic, his death and the death of his companions transformed him from a well-known Arctic explorer into an avatar of British greatness. He actually died before the tragic denouement of that final voyage. No matter. As the leader of the expedition, it was he who was declared to be the discoverer of the Northwest Passage, he was the one to whom the statues were erected. It was Franklin who gave the story its tragic dimension and the nation its catharsis: he, and the tireless work on behalf of his memory of his extraordinary wife, Jane.

But if Franklin was not in fact the great man his wife, and a grieving nation, made him out to be, the personal nobility of the enterprise he was engaged upon is undeniable. Great Britain's Arctic explorers sailed eagerly into the bitter seas of the far North, testing themselves against the deadliest climate in the world, in the service of something they believed in. The conclusion was tragic, but tragedy gives depth and meaning to death. Where would mankind be if it did not take risks? If it were not proud? The story that follows is replete with folly, official and otherwise, but the story as a whole is stirring. Things may have ended very badly indeed, yet it is impossible not to feel that the monuments and memorials were deserved.

It is just this tension, finally, between the nobility and the folly of the enterprise that makes the story so rich and has inspired so many efforts to tell it. And now we have its climactic irony, the melting of the Northwest Passage. It was plain early on in the search for the Passage that it would never be of any practical use. Now it is. Global warming has given the search a whole new context and its history one more twist. In the scramble for seafloor and rights-of-way in the Arctic that is already beginning, Canada is counting on the Franklin expedition's presumed discovery of the Passage in 1848 to establish ownership, and every summer now Parks Canada is sending underwater archaeology teams into the area of the Canadian archipelago where Franklin's ships disappeared in the hope of finding their remains. So far they have come up with some pieces of copper sheeting. The muse of history must be smiling. She has become relevant again, in a way no one could have expected.

John Barrow
(National Portrait Gallery, London)

A NATIONAL OBSESSION

You cannot contest the inestimable benefit which I shall confer on all mankind to the last generation, by discovering a passage near the pole to those countries, to reach which at present so many months are requisite.

—Captain Walton to his sister in
Mary Shelley's *Frankenstein; or the
Modern Prometheus*

CHAPTER ONE

THE CROKER MOUNTAINS

The four ships cast off one by one from their moorings in the new canal connecting the maze of Royal Navy docks at Deptford, just below London, with the Thames, and moved toward the river and the beginning of their journeys. It was mid-morning, April 4, 1818, and a crowd had gathered to cheer them on. With the tide on the ebb, however, two of the ships, the *Trent* and the *Alexander,* did not reach the canal gates before they closed and were forced to lay over one more night. This gave still more "parties of ladies and gentlemen," as Alexander Fisher, assistant surgeon on the *Alexander,* described them, a chance to come aboard to wish them well and say good-bye.

Parties of ladies and gentlemen had in fact been visiting the four ships for weeks, sending their visiting cards below to the officers, asking to be led on a tour. Lieutenant John Franklin wrote his sister, "It would be quite impossible for me to convey to you the amazing interest our little squadron has excited. Deptford has been covered with carriages and the ships with visitors every day since they were in a state to be seen." Franklin had as a result been introduced to a great many people, "some of them persons of considerable rank and all men of scientific eminence." The Duke of Clarence, King George III's youngest son and later King William IV, who had served his own apprenticeship in the Royal Navy, paid an official visit to see them off. We do not know if he met them then, but among the people who visited the ships were the two women who would later become Franklin's first and second wives. The expedition had aroused a great deal of excitement in England. The visitors "all appeared," Alexander Fisher remarked, "to be as much interested in the success of our undertaking, as we could possibly be ourselves; but, *by way of comfort,*" he added, "they frequently expressed their concern for our safety in such a hazardous enterprise."

Hazardous indeed. All four ships were on their way to the Arctic.

They were not heading, however, to the same region. The *Dorothea* and the *Trent,* under the overall command of Captain David Buchan, R.N., with Lieutenant Franklin in command of the latter, the smaller of the two ships, were bound to Svalbard, then called Spitzbergen, an archipelago lying a few hundred miles to the east of Greenland about fifteen degrees north of the Arctic Circle. Their mission was to test the theory, widely credited at the time, that the Arctic Ocean was in fact not frozen except around its edges. Within its tonsure of ice it was an open sea and it ought to be possible, if the theory were correct, to penetrate this frozen rim and sail to the Pacific over the top of the earth, right across the North Pole, cutting thousands of miles off the usual routes around Cape Horn and the Cape of Good Hope.

The other two ships, the *Isabella* and the *Alexander,* had orders to sail to Baffin Bay to search for the entrance to the Northwest Passage. If they found it they were to go on through the Passage, wintering over if necessary in some sheltered spot on the northern coast of Canada, then proceed to the Hawaiian Islands. They had supplies on board for twenty-eight "lunar months" (a little over two years), enough canvas to cover the decks with a tent if winter caught them in the ice, plenty of warm clothing, a surgeon and his assistant on each ship. They also carried trade goods for the natives that included, among the brass kettles, 350 yards of red, yellow, and blue flannels, butcher's knives, scissors, two hundred mirrors, cutlasses, thread, snuff, gin, and brandy in abundance, no fewer than forty umbrellas.

One native was already aboard, an Inuit from southern Greenland, John Sacheuse, who had been saved by an English whaling ship in a storm, come to live in England, learned the language, and converted to Christianity. Sacheuse had volunteered to join the expedition because the southern Greenland Inuit believed that a lost tribe of Inuit lived in the far north of Greenland, an area no ship had approached since William Baffin, who had sailed around the perimeter of the bay named after him two hundred years earlier. Sacheuse said that he hoped to find them and convert them to Christianity.

Of the first expedition, under Buchan, there is not much to say. The Admiralty, the Royal Navy's administrative arm, normally required commanders to publish accounts of exploring expeditions, but this one had little worth recording, and no account of it appeared until 1843. Like the expedition to Baffin Bay, it was prompted by the fact that in the summer of 1817 the seas around eastern Greenland had unexpectedly cleared of ice. Under normal circumstances it was impossible to sail close enough to the eastern shores of Greenland above seventy-five degrees north latitude even to see land. These conditions had prevailed for four centuries. During all that time some eighteen thousand square miles of ice had barred all access to the east coast of Greenland from its southern tip all the way to the top of the island, the edge of this ice shelf describing a great arc stretching north by east, trending away from Greenland toward the coast of Spitzbergen. This ice was old, thick, and impenetrable. Nobody had landed on the eastern coast of Greenland since the Middle Ages. There were rumors that Danish colonists had settled there then. Nobody knew, if that were true, whether their descendants had survived.

Then in the summer of 1817 the whalers who hunted in the seas around Spitzbergen noticed that this ice had simply vanished. Pack ice still lay above Spitzbergen but to the west and south of it, along the Greenland coast, it was gone. William Scoresby, Jr., who regularly hunted whales in these waters but was as much a scientist as a whaler, made the fact of the ice's disappearance known through the newspapers. Sir Joseph Banks, the longtime president of the Royal Society, England's premier scientific organization, promptly wrote him and asked for details. Banks and Scoresby already knew each other. Banks made it a point to know everyone in Great Britain with serious scientific interests. Scoresby's father, a whaler himself, had once given Lady Banks polar bear skins, which she used in the winter, Banks told Scoresby, "to her great comfort." Scoresby replied that the ice had indeed broken up and drifted away to oblivion, that he had been able to sail along the east coast of Greenland and could have landed, and that this had never happened before in the memory of anyone living. Banks forwarded Scoresby's letter to John Barrow, the second secretary of the Admiralty, and suggested that this could be the time to pursue exploration in the Arctic. With ice conditions having changed so radically off east Greenland, it stood to reason that the ice above Spitzbergen had also thinned out, even the ice elsewhere in the Far North. The rim of ice, if that was all it was, that had protected the high Arctic from the eyes of humankind through all of previous history might be penetrable. This then could be the moment when explorers, *English* explorers, finally discovered that great foggy shortcut to the Orient, the Northwest Passage, or perhaps even reached the North Pole. The *Dorothea* and the *Trent,* like the *Isabella* and the *Alexander,* had provisions for two years, but if the polar seas were indeed open, neither expedition would need them. Hawaii might lie only a couple of months away. There umbrellas might come in handy as trade goods after all.

Of course no one had actually seen this polar sea or knew for certain that it existed. All that blank space at the top of the globe could very well be solid land. Greenland might extend all the way to the northern coast of Asia, as some mapmakers speculated. There was evidence for a northern water route of some kind between the Atlantic and the Pacific, but it was not decisive. A whaler had found a sawn mahogany plank near Disco Island, which lies off the west coast of Greenland; huge mahogany tree trunks had also been found. Mahogany is tropical in origin and these pieces of wood might, speculation ran at the time, have been borne up the west coast of North America through Bering Strait and across the top of the continent through unknown straits—through the Northwest Passage—to Greenland. This drift of ten thousand miles would have required ocean currents that followed that particular route. A current was known to run north through Bering Strait. Another ran south down Baffin Bay, taking the ice with it every summer. (The iceberg that sank the *Titanic* in 1912 was carried south from Baffin Bay on this current.) Conceivably these two currents were one and the same.

Whales also seemed to know the way across the top of North America. Whalers talked of finding harpoons in the native Greenland style in the bodies of whales caught in the Pacific Ocean, and vice versa: "Whales with stone lances sticking in their fat, (a kind of weapon used by no nation now known)," wrote Scoresby, had been found in the bodies of whales killed off Spitzbergen and in Davis Strait. But what route the whales used was anybody's guess. Above eighty degrees of north latitude, everything was white space on the map of the earth. In other parts of the Arctic the geography well below eighty degrees was equally mysterious. Samuel Hearne and Alexander Mackenzie, exploring in northern Canada for the fur companies, had reached the mouths of the Coppermine and Mackenzie Rivers in 1771 and 1789, respectively—both rivers empty into the Arctic Ocean—and found open sea, but their accounts were not entirely clear about exactly how much of this sea they had seen, and no other white man had ever been to the coast of northern Canada in any other part of the continent.

As for Baffin Bay, no one had been to its northern reaches since William Baffin himself in 1616, and his maps had vanished when Samuel Purchas, who first printed Baffin's account of the voyage, decided he could not afford to print the maps and stored them away, to be forever lost. So there was nothing to go on but Baffin's verbal description of what he saw and his latitude readings. The whalers operating in Davis Strait, south of Baffin Bay, never sailed north of about seventy-one degrees north latitude. The head of Baffin Bay lies 550 miles to the north of that. A few geographers doubted that Baffin Island existed, doubted indeed that Baffin had even sailed where he claimed he had sailed. And if Baffin Island did exist, no one knew what waited for the first explorers who might find a passage through it.

Not that the speculative geographers of the time didn't have ideas about what the Arctic contained. In some Renaissance maps the North Pole turns up as an actual protuberance (the Inuit, when it was explained to them what the North Pole was, came to call it the Big Nail), a great pyramid or mountain of iron, the iron explaining why magnets point north. Other early maps showed a Strait of Anián north of North America, sometimes through it, that connected the Atlantic and the Pacific. The idea for this strait seems to have come from the writings of Marco Polo; it first appeared on an influential map drawn in 1566. Thereafter it became a fixture on maps of North America and its environs.

But by 1818 the Strait of Anián had vanished from the maps. John Barrow, second secretary of the Admiralty, in his *Chronological History of Voyages into the Arctic Regions,* published that year, mentions the strait and Spanish attempts to find it in the sixteenth century, but his map of the Arctic does not show it, does not in fact indulge in any untoward speculation about what might exist in these unexplored areas of the globe. The east coast of Greenland, where the ice had slipped away so unexpectedly the previous year, trails away on Barrow's map into nothingness just before it reaches eighty degrees north. The west coast of Greenland, which forms the eastern shore of Baffin Bay, vanishes at a point well south of eighty degrees. Barrow was one of those who did not believe Baffin Island existed. He called the southern half of what we now know as Baffin Island by another name, Cumberland Island. It does not extend on his map above that known southern half. Spitzbergen appears on his map, but north of it is only white space. In Alaska the coast east of Icy Cape, which Captain Cook had discovered and named on his third voyage in 1778 when he was trying to find the western outlet of the Northwest Passage, is a dotted line to the Mackenzie River, hundreds of miles away. The two expeditions sailing from London that April day were hammering at the unknown.

In Spitzbergen the hammer nearly broke on the ice. Buchan and his two ships, the *Dorothea* and the *Trent*, reached the island in June, where he found that ice conditions had returned to normal. The east coast of Greenland was once again unapproachable. The sea above and to the west of Spitzbergen was frozen solid. The two ships took refuge in Magdalena Bay on the west coast of Spitzbergen and were promptly frozen in, unable to move for several weeks. One day a few men decided to walk across the ice toward shore, three or four miles away, only to have a sudden fog envelop them when they were halfway across. Nothing is so dense, or so common, as an Arctic fog. Arctic fog will turn the man walking next to you into a vague gray form; the man next to him will disappear. They turned around to retrace their steps, but the floes they had crossed, and therefore their own tracks across them, were spinning slowly in the currents, making it impossible for them to determine what direction they had actually come from. They fired their muskets, hoping somebody on the ships would hear them and fire back, letting them know where the ships were. The men on the ships did fire back, but the fog must have swallowed the sound. Any one of the floes they were standing on might at any time break free and drift away. Finally two men still on board ship volunteered to venture out on the ice and try to find them. Luckily they did. This adventure lasted eighteen hours. The men on the ice had no shelter of any kind. Another eighteen hours and it is doubtful any of them would have lived.

The Arctic is full of this kind of danger. Storms come up quickly, without warning. Mist freezes on ropes and sails and makes them too stiff to manage. Fog can last for days, for a week, two weeks. Ice floes six, eight, ten feet or more thick and two or three square miles in area drive implacably on ships. Ice can wedge a ship right out of the water. The animals can be dangerous. Polar bears will attack people, drag them off, and eat them. A group of angry walrus attacked one of the ship's boats off Spitzbergen, lunging over the sides at the men inside, and nearly capsized it.

After the ice broke up, the two ships left Magdalena Bay and headed north to try their luck in the pack, to see if it was in fact only the frozen edge of a liquid polar sea, a white crown circling gray waters. Following narrow leads of open water in the ice that appeared, then disappeared, the crew walked on the ice down these leads, hauling the ships with ropes, by hand; they found themselves in early July locked into the pack some thirty miles from the edge of it, unable to go on. The leads had vanished, the pack closed up. They had achieved a latitude of eighty degrees and change, as far north as any human being except William Scoresby and his father had ever sailed. From their mastheads they could see nothing but ice to the north, stretching to the horizon. Then the weather suddenly turned cold. It took them nine days, working night and day, for the sun never sets in the Arctic in July, to make it out of the pack back to the open waters around Spitzbergen.

As soon as the ice released them, a sudden storm came up from the southwest, forcing them back against the pack. Now their situation was truly desperate. If they could not stand off from the pack, and they could not, the ships would be pushed broadside by the wind and waves into the violent chaos at the leading edge of the pack, where huge broken floes tossed in the heaving water and smashed into each other with enormous force. That level of battering would have turned the *Dorothea* and the *Trent* into driftwood. They had only one chance to survive, and that was to sail back with the storm through the chaos and try to find refuge in the pack, an opening, a lead, a cove of ice where the conditions were not quite as hopeless. It was as risky a maneuver as sailing ships could try in an Arctic storm, but they made it. These were men of high courage; most of them had seen service in the Napoleonic Wars.

The storm died down as quickly as it had come up. The *Dorothea* was so heavily damaged, however, that it could not proceed. John Franklin, commanding the *Trent*, wanted to go on alone, search to the west along the edge of the pack for a better opening to the north, take his chances and sail into it, but Buchan overruled him. Lieutenant Franklin, then in his early thirties, had sailed with Matthew Flinders on his 1802 mapping expedition to Australia and had been shipwrecked on the return voyage. He had been in the thick of the action at Trafalgar, where an officer standing right beside him had been shot and killed by a French sniper. At New Orleans in 1815, during the War of 1812, a bullet had hit him in the shoulder on a raiding party. No other word but *intrepid* will do for him. He was always ready to go on.

It was the usual practice, however, that two ships were sent on exploring expeditions and they stayed together if they possibly could. If Franklin lost his ship, there would be no other ship present to save his crew. In the end the two ships limped home. They had accomplished nothing. If there were an open polar sea, they had not reached it. They had not even caught a glimpse of it. To the north everything was ice, nothing but ice.

The other expedition put Baffin Bay and Baffin Island permanently back on the map, but it too failed to achieve its goals. Its leader was Captain John Ross, a native of southwestern Scotland, born and raised on Loch Ryan in sight of the sea. Ross was ruddy, stout, opinionated, and a strong believer in the rectitude of his own judgments. He was also a veteran of the Napoleonic Wars who joined the Royal Navy when he was nine years old. To join so young was not unusual—it was customary in the eighteenth and well into the nineteenth centuries for boys to join the navy. He had been wounded in the wars thirteen times, and not lightly, like John Franklin. In a boarding operation he had been run completely through with a bayonet, and both legs and one arm had been broken. Ross too was clearly brave; he was also at least familiar with ice. Buchan and Franklin, sailing to Spitzbergen, had no experience in the ice whatsoever. (The navy hired whaling captains familiar with the ice to serve as pilots, or "masters," for all four ships; at least one ship, Ross's *Isabella*, was a leased whaler.) But Ross had sailed north of Europe into the White Sea, which lies east of Lapland, and he had spent years fighting in the Gulf of Bothnia, the northern bulge of the Baltic, which freezes every winter, so he was at least familiar with the ice.

Commanding the second ship, the *Alexander*, was a young lieutenant named William Edward Parry. Ross was on board the larger, speedier *Isabella*. Both ships had been reinforced with extra planking on the outside and oak braces on the inside to withstand the pressure of the pack. Nearly every year the ice sank one or more whaling ships. In mid-July 1818 two large floes caught the *Three Brothers*, a whaler out of Hull, in what is known as a pinch. The ship, says Alexander Fisher, "was cut right in two." Even reinforced ships could seem fragile in the ice. "Let any one consider the violence of the shock which must ensue from the meeting of two floes," Fisher wrote in late June, "each perhaps several miles in circumference, and three feet thick, and these moving in contrary directions, at the rate of a mile, or of a mile and a half, an hour, and he will readily conceive the little chance a ship would have of withstanding the enormous pressure which would be upon her, were she to be caught in such a situation."

Three weeks later Ross almost lost both ships when that very thing happened. The *Isabella* and the *Alexander* were moving up a lead between two floes that were "passing each other with a velocity of at least two miles an hour." The ships came "unavoidably alongside of each other" and were squeezed together so violently that they thought they were lost. The ships survived but not without damage. Pieces of the *Alexander,* including two ship's boats, were carried away. The beams in the *Isabella*'s hold, says Ross in his account, began to bend, doors sprang open, and the whole ship was lifted several feet by the pressure. Ross says the floes were six feet thick. One floe curled back on itself up the side of the *Isabella.* Chain plates were torn loose. Anchors were broken. At any moment they expected the masts to go. In the end the ships escaped, but only, says Ross, by the "interposition of Providence."

Despite this incident the process of working through the ice was not so much risky as tedious. Much of the voyage was tedious. The two ships reached the Shetlands on April 30, where they took on fresh meat and water and established baselines for their scientific instruments, then left on May 3. They saw their first iceberg on May 26, by which time they had reached Davis Strait, the broad passage, two hundred miles wide, between Greenland on the east and Baffin Island on the west. For the next two months they worked their way slowly up the coast of Greenland, in company with as many as forty-five whaling ships.

Up the coast of Greenland was the only way to get into upper Baffin Bay. Usually some open water lay between the coast and the bay, which was almost always clogged with icebergs and pack ice drifting south during the short summer. Even near the coast ships would often be stopped for days at a time, mooring to icebergs, waiting for the wind to come up and blow the pack apart. Ross took advantage of every opportunity, every promising lead, to break through into open water, but he could seldom sail free more than a couple of dozen miles before ice or icebergs barred his path. At Disco Island, a major stopping point for whalers, Ross counted more than seven hundred icebergs within his view.

Frequently there would be no wind and only a narrow lead, and the men would get onto the ice and "track"—grab the ropes and haul the ship manually, just as Buchan and Franklin had done north of Spitzbergen. "Warping" was another common process of moving through ice: ice anchors would be set in the ice, then the rope attached to them would be wound about the capstan and the men would winch the boat forward through a lead. It was backbreaking, miserable work. Some-times the ship's fiddler would play as they were tracking, a pied piper leading his children across the ice. Once he fell through a hole into the freezing water, fiddle and all, amusing everyone except himself.

As they moved north the whalers fell off one by one to hunt whales. By the end of July the expedition had worked its way past the farthest north the whaling fleet had ever gone and was seeing land that only William Baffin before them had seen. Ross occupied himself naming features on the coast that Baffin had neglected to name: Melville Bay, after Lord Melville, first lord of the Admiralty; Cape York, after another lord; Capes Alexander and Isabella, after his ships; and Cape Sabine, for Edward Sabine, an artillery officer who had been assigned to the expedi-tion as one of its scientists. (Sabine would go on to become the president of the Royal Society years later and a prime mover in scientific explo-ration.) It was new territory to all of them, and a new experience to those who had never been in the Arctic before—everyone, in short, except Ross and the whaling masters. Alexander Fisher was stunned by the number of "rotges" on the water. "Rotges" were a species of small auk, close kin to dovekies, and they arrived in clouds. Fisher said they saw "several million" of them in one day. They proved good to eat and were so plentiful that men killed dozens of them with a single blast of their guns. They saw narwhals, the unicorns of the sea. They shot at polar bears and generally missed them. One they did kill amazed them by its size: paws a foot and a half long; weight, more than a thousand pounds.

And on August 9 they came upon Sacheuse's lost tribe of Inuit. These extraordinary people fascinated Ross and he spent as much time with them as he could, asking them questions through Sacheuse about their customs, beliefs, and surroundings. He might have made a good ethno-grapher. The natives fled when they first saw the ships but returned the next day, and eventually, after the gift of a knife, Sacheuse was able to make contact. Fisher describes them as being in a state of nature. Unlike almost all other Inuit they had no kayaks, they had never seen a ship before, and they thought the *Isabella* and the *Alexander* were alive. "They first pointed to the ships," says Ross, "eagerly asking, 'what great creatures those were?' 'Do they come from the sun or the moon?' 'Do they give us light by night or by day?' "

Sacheuse explained that they were houses made of wood, but the natives refused to accept this. "No," they said, "they are alive, we have seen them move their wings."

Eventually they came aboard the *Isabella* and were given a tour. They mistook glass for a form of ice. The wood in the ship astonished them; no wood of any kind grew that far north. They pilfered whatever they could, one man running off with a hammer, another trying to steal Ross's best telescope. They had iron of their own, interestingly enough; it came from meteorites some twenty miles inland that Robert Peary would, less than a century later, steal from this very same tribe and deposit in the American Museum of Natural History in New York. Ross gave them hand mirrors, a traditional gift for native peoples, and their own reflections held them spellbound. He discovered that they had no idea there were other people in the world. They thought they were the only human beings. They had no gods, only shamans, and no idea of an afterlife. The shamans had the power to call seals and birds to the tribe, they claimed, or else drive them away, and a wise man, no doubt a shaman, had once said that they might after death go to the moon. But no one believed this anymore. They lived in stone huts half buried in the earth and lined with skins.

They were filthy, Ross added; "their faces, hands, and bodies, are covered with oil and dirt, and they look as if they never had washed themselves since they were born." Most subsequent English explorers in the Arctic made similar comments about Inuit dirt, but of course the Inuit had nothing with which to make soap, and cleanliness is a relative thing. Louis XIII of France, born in 1601, was not given his first bath until he was almost seven years old. Despite their dirtiness they seemed to be quite content with their lives. When Ross tried to explain the concept of war to them, they could not understand it. In the end he found them so interesting he was reluctant to leave, even when the ice conditions changed and he had to leave, and he devoted a whole chapter of his book to them and gave them what was, in effect, a Scottish name: Arctic Highlanders. For Ross, without question, meeting them was the best thing that happened to him on this voyage.

But duty called. Ross had sailed to find not unknown Inuit tribes but the Northwest Passage, and they were nearing places that, as Baffin had described them, might offer a way through. The Arctic Highlanders lived close to the top of Baffin Bay, and at the very top Baffin had discovered a sound extending to the north that he named Smith Sound, after one of the sponsors of his voyage. Ross approached Smith Sound and saw the opening to it, he said, from forty miles off shore. The entrance, framed on each side by magnificent capes that he named after his ships, was, he says, "completely blocked by ice." From what he could see he decided that it bottomed out about eighteen leagues north of the entrance (that would be about fifty miles) and never tried to approach it. "Even if it be imagined . . . that some narrow Strait may exist through these mountains, it is evident, that it must be for ever unnavigable," he wrote, "and that there is not even a chance of ascertaining its existence, since all approach to the bottom of these bays is prevented by the ice which fills them to so great a depth, and appears never to have moved from its station."

Half a century later Elisha Kent Kane would sail into Smith Sound and discover within it the basin he named for himself, Kane Basin, and beyond that Kennedy and Robeson Channels, the door to the North Pole. The fact that Ross didn't even try to approach Smith Sound disturbed some of his junior officers, especially William Edward Parry. When Parry wondered out loud why Ross had backed off, he got a curt note from Ross explaining that he was accustomed to making his decisions without regard to the opinions of others. It was a formal rebuke. Parry raised no more questions after that—not, that is, to Ross's face.

The two ships were now skirting south down the coast of Ellesmere Island. Ross passed Jones Sound, named by Baffin for another of his sponsors, once again making no attempt to explore it. Jones Sound as it happens is also a strait, dividing Ellesmere Island from Devon Island, though its western outlet is narrow and generally closed by ice.

Then on August 29 Ross reached Lancaster Sound, and here at last he had no choice but to sail into it, for it was completely free of ice. Rugged high mountains stood on the south side of it, forming the northern coast of Baffin Island, while the mountains on the north were somewhat lower, and the entrance to the sound itself was forty-five miles wide. You could have sailed the entire Royal Navy into it. Baffin, who had named it after still another of his expedition's sponsors, had described it as a sound and made no attempt to enter it himself, but it looked as if it stretched to the west indefinitely, as if it were a strait, not a sound. It looked indeed as if it might be what they were looking for.

We cannot say with complete confidence what happened next. When Ross wrote his account of the voyage—in record time, by the way; the ships reached England in early November, and Ross's book was published the following March—he clearly knew that he would be attacked by the reviewers, and regarding Lancaster Sound he was writing on the defensive. He says that over the next two days, August 30 and 31, he sailed into the sound some eighty miles (another account says it was only thirty miles), with the *Alexander*, the slower boat, consistently about eight miles, "hull down," behind. All morning on the thirty-first, says Ross, he caught glimpses of land at the bottom of the sound, but it was raining off and on, fog obscured the view, and he could not be sure. At half past two in the afternoon he went below to dinner. At three the officer of the watch came down for his dinner, having been relieved by Mr. Lewis, the whaling captain who was the ship's master, and reported that the fog seemed to be lifting up ahead. Hearing this, Ross went on deck, alone, "and soon after it completely cleared for about ten minutes," he says, "and I distinctly saw the land, round the bottom of the bay, forming a connected chain of mountains with those which extended along the north and south sides." Lancaster Sound was a dead end. These mountains, he goes on, seemed to be about eight leagues, or twenty-five miles, away. He also saw ice barring his path seven miles away. He asked Mr. Lewis if he, too, had seen the mountains ahead. Mr. Lewis, according to Ross, said yes.

Ross named this new mountain range the Croker Mountains, in honor of the first secretary of the Admiralty, John Wilson Croker. Then the fog settled in again. At three thirty Ross ordered both ships to turn around and sail east, out of the sound.

That's Ross's story, but he embellishes it. He reminds the reader that his orders specifically said he was to look for telltale currents that would indicate a strait, and he had found no currents. If Lancaster Sound were a strait, connecting two large bodies of water, there would have to be currents. His orders said that he was supposed "to leave the ice about the 15th or 20th of September, or at latest the 1st of October," and that left him a month at the most to explore the rest of Baffin Bay, "a distance of above four hundred miles." He quotes Captain Sabine, the artillery officer, to the effect "that there was no *indication* [Ross's stress] of a passage." The *Alexander*, Lieutenant Parry's ship, was too far behind, he says, to have seen the ice barring the way. He refers to the general opinion on board his ship that Lancaster Sound was not the Northwest Passage. To nail it home, he drew a picture of the Croker Mountains and printed it in the book. He was a good artist. It is a remarkable likeness of a mountain range.

What he does not mention is that nobody else besides himself and Mr. Lewis on the *Isabella* saw the Croker Mountains, and there's some doubt about Mr. Lewis, for later on Ross would admit more than once that he was the only person to see them. Nobody on the *Alexander* saw them. Alexander Fisher, the assistant surgeon on board the *Alexander*, says:

> On the morning of Sunday, the 30th, the wind being from the eastward (by compass), we stood into the inlet above-mentioned, and the more we advanced, the more sanguine our hopes were that we had at last found what has been for ages sought in vain. Every thing, indeed, tended to confirm this our belief: at noon we tried for soundings with two hundred and thirty-five fathoms of line, without finding bottom; and in the evening, when the sun was getting low, the weather being remarkably clear, we could see the land on both sides of the inlet for a very great distance, but not any at the bottom of it.

They sailed on, he says, through the night and into the next day, August 31, and

> every thing tended, if possible, to increase our hopes. Not any ice was to be seen in any direction . . . But, alas! The sanguine hopes and high expectations excited by this promising appearance of things were but of a short duration, for, about three o'clock in the afternoon, the Isabella tacked, very much to our surprise indeed, as we could not see any thing like land at the bottom of the inlet, nor was the weather well calculated at the time for seeing any object at a great distance.

Fisher took the trouble to append to his account a copy of the ship's log for that day. It indicates that the weather was a little clearer at three in the afternoon, when Ross turned back. It does not mention seeing any land to the west. The *Alexander* was at that time, according to the log, four miles, not eight, behind the *Isabella*.

The journal kept by the purser on board the *Alexander*, a man named Hooper, is even more vivid. "The weather was so thick," he reports, "we could see very little of the land, and very heavy rain the whole afternoon." The men on board the *Alexander* were stunned that Ross had turned around. "To describe our mortification and disappointment," Hooper goes on, "would be impossible at thus having our increasing hopes annihilated in a moment, without the shadow of a reason appearing." Nobody was satisfied with Ross's explanation that he had seen mountains.

Ross's troubles began as soon as they arrived home in England. Lieutenant Parry, for one, believed that Lancaster Sound was a strait and he would report as much to John Barrow. Only a month after they returned, a letter appeared in *Blackwood's Magazine*, written by an officer on the expedition who did not sign his name, insisting that there was no reason whatsoever to believe "that there is no passage from Baffin's Bay into the Pacific. I am perfectly certain that no officer employed on the expedition ventured to hazard such an assertion." It was clear what he meant: Ross had not gone far enough into Lancaster Sound. A few months after Ross's book appeared, Sabine, the artillery officer, attacked Ross's account of the voyage in a pamphlet. Sabine was upset not only because Ross had claimed his, Sabine's, scientific work on geomagnetism as his own, but also because he had alluded to his, Sabine's, opinions about Lancaster Sound twice in the book, "obviously for the purpose of supporting the propriety of his conduct in not prosecuting the examination of the Inlet." Sabine wrote that his own opinions had had no influence on Ross, and he reminded the world that he was an artillery officer—a landsman. "Captain Ross was accustomed to act solely from his own judgment; he formed his plans and executed them without a reference to any person; he certainly at no time placed his confidence in me."

Ross replied to Sabine's attack but it was Barrow, not Sabine, who was his real enemy, and it was Barrow who mattered. John Barrow, second secretary of the Admiralty and its chief administrator (the first secretary's role being more political, to represent the Admiralty in Parliament), was not someone a naval officer wanted to cross. And Barrow was furious. Barrow had thought that Baffin Bay did not exist. He was sure the Arctic Ocean was an open sea. It was he, much more than Croker, who had persuaded the Lords of the Admiralty to pursue this dream of a Northwest Passage. He could accept that Baffin Bay did indeed exist, but he could not tolerate a naval officer who had probably found the entrance to the Northwest Passage and failed to investigate it.

He and Ross seem to have first had words when Ross reported to the Admiralty on what he had found, or not found. We have no record of what was said but it was evidently not pleasant. Ross had had provisions for two years, his own experience in the ice was extensive, and everybody else on the voyage was convinced that Lancaster Sound was their best possibility. Why had he not gone on?

That conversation was only the beginning. When Ross's book came out, it was John Barrow who reviewed it in *The Quarterly Review*, that great monument of ruling-class opinion, a publication only slightly less influential among government circles than *Debrett's Peerage*. Barrow went after Ross like a pack of hounds after a fox, in full throat. It was an odd circumstance to begin with that the man who had written Ross's orders and sent him to Davis Strait and unknown points north and west should be reviewing Ross's account of the voyage. It was even odder that Barrow himself had ordered Ross to write his book. The whole thing has the appearance of a setup.

Then came the knockdown. Barrow attacked Ross for wasting so many pages on the Arctic Highlanders. He sneered at him for his naming of capes and headlands, noting that Ross "has transferred one half of Scotland to the shores" of Baffin Bay. He pointed out that Ross could not possibly have seen the bottom of Smith Sound at the distance he describes, eighteen leagues (which is close to sixty English miles). He could not possibly have known whether ice was blocking the entrance to it.

But it was Ross's explanation of what happened at Lancaster Sound that aroused Barrow's greatest wrath. "Captain Ross," he grumbles, "talks of danger in Lancaster's Sound, and of the bad sailing of the Alexander. A voyage of discovery implies danger; but a mere voyage, like his, round the shores of Baffin's Bay, in the summer months, may be considered a voyage of pleasure." He finds it incredible that Ross would think he could see the Croker Mountains stretching all the way across Lancaster Sound at a distance of twenty-five miles when,

> to bring the matter home to ordinary readers, . . . there is not a *reach* in the Thames that to the eye does not appear to terminate the river; and in many of them . . . it is utterly impossible to form a conjecture, at the distance only of two or three miles, what part of the land is intersected by the stream.

He points out that Ross had already admitted that his eyes were bad. How could he have been so irresolute as not to sail on? To find out?

Barrow contrasts Ross's lack of perseverance in Lancaster Sound with Magellan's courage in passing through the straits named after him; with "the fortitude of Columbus"; with Captain Cook braving the ice and the gales for thousands of miles in the high latitudes of the Southern Hemisphere, searching for the great continent some geographers believed to be there. "Reputation and risk," he writes, "are almost inseparable in the life of a naval officer; at least the former is rarely acquired without a large portion of the latter." Barrow was disgusted. He already had plans afoot for another voyage. When Ross wistfully applied to lead it, he was summarily refused. The assignment was given to Lieutenant Parry, who had become Barrow's protégé. Ross never again received an assignment from the Admiralty, and Barrow continued to attack him, in print and out, until the end of his life.

We shall never know what John Ross actually saw at the bottom of Lancaster Sound. The Arctic is peculiarly prone to refraction, that trick of light by which the appearance of distant landscapes seems to bend around the curve of the earth and become visible hundreds of miles away. Earlier in the voyage they had seen landscapes that they later discovered were 140 miles distant. But refraction is an unlikely event in weather as foul as the rain and fog they were sailing through in Lancaster Sound. Ross's "imperfect vision" may also have been a factor. Fog seen from a distance is often mistaken for land. It must remain a mystery.

But Barrow may have put his finger on the problem in his review. "There occur," he writes, "unfortunate moments in the history of a man's life when he is himself unable to account for his actions; and the moment of putting about the Isabella would appear to be one of them." Ross may have been tired, or bored. He may not have believed as fervently in the existence of a Northwest Passage as Barrow and the English public did; in fact, he came away from his experience convinced that there was no Northwest Passage. "Had he continued to advance," Barrow went on, "even supposing there was a continuity of land or ice, three *hours* more," that would have decided the issue. If there had been no land, no ice, then three days more would have brought him "very near to the meridian of the Coppermine River." That would have made him one of the great heroes of Arctic exploration, instead of its goat.

Barrow's review appeared in June 1819. Parry was already back in Baffin Bay, navigating the pack on his way to Lancaster Sound. On the first day of August, with a fresh breeze behind him and half the men on his two ships crowded into the rigging or out on the yardarms, staring ahead, he sailed right through the Croker Mountains. Ross's mountain range did not exist. John Wilson Croker, first secretary of the Admiralty

and sharp-tongued Tory orator, whose ambitions lay as much in literature as in politics, would be remembered not as the namesake of a
mountain range in the Arctic but as the reviewer who wrote one of the
cruelest, snidest, most damning of the reviews that so spoiled the last
year of John Keats's life. Lancaster Sound is a strait. Parry named the
western end of it Barrow Strait, in honor of "my friend," John Barrow. It
is also the only entrance to the Northwest Passage that could remotely
be described as practical for ships.

In the end, though, in what we like to call the light of history, it
might have been better for all concerned if John Ross had been right.

CHAPTER TWO

THE SECOND SECRETARY

In a way John Ross was right. There is a Northwest Passage; in fact there are several sea routes through the islands of the Canadian archipelago, as the huge cluster of islands north of North America is known. But only with global warming has it become possible to use the main route for shipping, and the Arctic winter still shuts it down. Before global warming kicked in, it took Roald Amundsen, the great polar explorer who beat Scott to the South Pole, three years, 1903 to 1906, to sail his little converted herring boat, the *Gjøa*, through the Northwest Passage. He was the first to make the trip. A Russian icebreaker now makes it most summers carrying a cargo of tourists wealthy enough to pay the freight.

But while the Passage does exist, what does not—not yet—is an open polar sea. The ice cap is thinning, yes, and sea ice that in the past averaged eight to ten feet thick now averages closer to four. But over the Pole ice does still last throughout the summer, and it still piles up in the many straits and channels of the northern half of the Canadian archipelago and blocks the narrower straits, if not permanently, then for most months of the year. The prevailing wind and current patterns in the Beaufort Sea, which is that part of the Arctic Ocean that lies above western Canada, reinforce this blockage. A clockwise flow of ice known as the Beaufort Gyre pushes ice directly against the northwestern sides of the Canadian archipelago. Within the archipelago wind patterns blow ice down these straits and jam them up. Before global warming took effect these same patterns jammed up the southern straits as well, making the southern routes through the archipelago chancy most summers except for icebreakers. Not until 1944 did a Canadian icebreaker, the *St Roch*, make the trip in one season. Ice conditions in the northern Arctic were difficult enough in the recent past that new islands were still being discovered in the Canadian archipelago after World War II, and then only by flying over them.

None of this was known, of course, in 1818. The Inuit had mental maps of their own local regions and they were remarkably accurate, but their knowledge extended only a few hundred miles in any direction. No one had been in—or on—the Arctic Ocean, so it was still possible to entertain the idea that offshore, toward the Pole, it was an open sea. This was in fact an old idea that dated as far back as 1527, to an essentially prescientific age. In the 1660s it gained a certain scientific veneer when the hydrographer to King Charles II, a man named Joseph Moxon, promoted it. Moxon believed that the ice in polar waters formed near landmasses—and *only* near landmasses. The nonstop daylight of the Arctic summer must, he reasoned, melt any ice that might form on open water. Sail far enough north of the landmasses, then, and you would find yourself in an open sea.

The idea proved amazingly long-lived, surviving into the late nineteenth century, right through the end of the British search for the Northwest Passage in 1860, a search that accumulated a vast amount of experience with sea ice. In the 1760s Samuel Engel, a Swiss geographer, agronomist, mathematician—in short, one of those Enlightenment figures who lusted to know everything there was to know—adopted the idea as his own, producing a treatise purporting to demonstrate that seawater cannot by its nature freeze. The influential French naturalist the Comte de Buffon agreed. In the 1770s a French mapmaker named Robert de Vaugondy based his charts of the polar regions on Engel's ideas and Buffon's agreement, and those charts found their way into Denis Diderot's great and authoritative *Encyclopédie*. In them the polar seas are open. It would be an easy sail to the Pacific, once you broke through that outer carapace of ice. In England yet another would-be polymath, Daines Barrington, bought into the notion. Barrington was a lawyer, but more than that he was a member of the Royal Society and a scientific enthusiast best known for his examination of the eight-year-old Mozart, whose father had brought him to England to perform; Barrington duly declared him a prodigy. In 1775 Barrington published a short treatise called *The Probability of Reaching the North Pole Discussed*, basing his arguments not just on the idea that sea ice cannot freeze but on the stories that Dutch whalers from a century before told in the taverns of Amsterdam and Rotterdam. The North Pole? Why yes, we've been there, or close enough. One claimed to have been within half a degree of latitude, perhaps thirty miles, of the North Pole. He saw no ice at all. Joseph Moxon first published these tales in his own treatise on the subject. It was more than a trifle credulous on Barrington's part to believe them, but then Barrington was known to be credulous. He once argued that a watch from the seventeenth century had belonged to Robert Bruce, king of Scotland. Robert Bruce died in 1329. The first pocket watch made its appearance around 1500.

John Barrow clearly had some of that same willingness to believe, for he accepted Barrington's arguments at face value and he, too, was convinced that the Arctic Ocean was free of ice. The interesting thing is that evidence to the contrary lay, so to speak, right before his eyes. When William Scoresby, Jr., sent his explanatory letter to Sir Joseph Banks in the fall of 1817, he enclosed with it a copy of his paper "On the Greenland or Polar Ice," which he had written in 1815 and published in the *Memoirs* of the Wernerian Society, a scientific organization based in Edinburgh and not unlike the Royal Society of London. (The Wernerian Society later morphed into the Royal Physical Society.) Banks had passed the letter on to the Admiralty, specifically to John Barrow, who not only had the power to make something happen but was also a Banks protégé, and it is highly unlikely that Banks did not also enclose with it Scoresby's paper. He was always eager to spread information around.

Surely, then, Barrow had read Scoresby's paper. Scoresby had made his first whaling voyage north with his father at the age of ten and had been sailing into Arctic waters for fifteen years; he was scientifically inclined and a superb observer. He described quite clearly the process by which sea ice froze, a process he had witnessed many times. He had seen the sea freeze even in rough weather to the thickness of a foot. He knew perfectly well that sea ice did not form only near landmasses. No such theory could account for the "immense fields" he had seen in the seas around Spitzbergen every year. "These evidently come from the northward," he wrote, "and have their origin between Spitzbergen and the Pole."

Scoresby's evidence made no impact on John Barrow. He continued to believe in an open polar sea for the rest of his long life.

Based on his considerable experience with ice, Scoresby was skeptical about the possibility of navigating the Northwest Passage, assuming it existed, but he hoped nevertheless to command at least one of the two expeditions that Barrow sent out in 1818, Ross's or Buchan's; he spoke to Banks about it and went to see Barrow to apply for the job. Barrow was evasive. In the end he asked Scoresby if he would accept the position of master on one of the ships; the master was the officer who managed the actual sailing of the ship. Scoresby might have known more about ice than anyone in the Royal Navy, but the navy was not about to put its officers and seamen under the command of a civilian. Indignantly, Scoresby declined, and other whaling captains assumed the role.

It was a pity. Not only would Scoresby have been able to put his knowledge of the ice to good use, but he would almost certainly have sailed farther into Lancaster Sound than John Ross did. In 1806 he and his father reached a latitude of 81 degrees 30 minutes north, which for years remained the farthest north anyone had reached by sail. In 1820 Scoresby published *An Account of the Arctic Regions,* in two volumes (the second volume is a history of whaling), one of the founding classics of polar science. In 1828 he suggested a method of reaching the Pole across the ice, not by ship but by dogsled, in the Inuit style of travel. He was the first to do so. He invented devices to measure the temperature of seawater at different depths. His drawings of snow crystals—snowflakes—revealed their crystalline structure in detail for the first time.

Others besides Scoresby were skeptical of the possibility of navigating the Northwest Passage, assuming it existed, and John Ross did have his defenders. The London *Times,* the voice of upper-middle-class England, printed a piece on Ross's book and quoted at length from his description of the Arctic Highlanders, then remarked about the controversy over Ross's actions in Lancaster Sound:

> Whoever may be right in this case, no direct charge has, so far as we hear, been brought against Captain Ross; and in a narrative which he has published of his voyage, though he evidently writes with the spirit of a man who thinks himself ill-used, he makes no reply, but endeavours only to be particularly clear and definite upon those points on which he knows he has been thought, or described as remiss, and on the whole shows the blunt courage of an English seaman.

The Edinburgh Review, the Whig rival of the conservative, Tory *Quarterly,* came even more unequivocally to Ross's defense. No less a personage than Sydney Smith, the well-known wit ("I never read a book before reviewing it," he once remarked; "it prejudices a man so"), reviewed Ross's book and took the tack that if Ross had not found a Northwest Passage or a "Polar Basin," why should the powers that be grow angry with him over the fact? And if there was no open polar sea and no Northwest Passage, why should this be regarded as a loss to mankind? Even if there were such a Passage, he pointed out, it would work no benefit to mankind. There was just too much ice. "The condition of Baffin's Bay, to a late period in the summer, is such, and the uncertainty of effecting a passage through that Strait, if it existed, so great, as plainly to make it impossible that any advantageous commerce should ever be carried on by such a route with the Pacific Ocean." A year earlier John Leslie, the Scots mathematician and scientist, had said much the same thing in the *Edinburgh* in a review of various other polar books. Leslie thought it, nevertheless, "befitting the character of a great maritime nation" to look for the Northwest Passage, useless as it was. The scientific community as a whole, from Sir Joseph Banks on down, believed that the nation's reputation for discovery was at stake, and that the geographical information that would result was worth the effort involved. The example of Captain Cook lay before them. Geographic discovery was an English tradition. The question of its usefulness missed the point.

Here Leslie found himself in full agreement with John Barrow. The renewed British interest in Arctic exploration that sprang up after the Napoleonic Wars and continued into the 1840s was in large part the result of Barrow's enthusiasm and his ability as second secretary to inspire the Admiralty to send out explorers. But the public was enthusiastic as well. The Napoleonic Wars were over, and the British had beaten their ancient rivals the French so decisively on the seas that no other nation in Europe for many years thereafter dared to challenge them. In 1809 the British had as many warships in service as all the other naval powers in the world put together. The historian Élie Halévy quotes a writer to the effect that the British victory over Napoleon's armies had demonstrated nothing less than "the inherent superiority of the British race," a sentiment that would be repeated many times over the course of the nineteenth century and drive the growth of the British Empire. It can be heard as well in the shouts and cheers of the crowds that lined the wharves whenever an Arctic expedition left the docks, and also in the more refined tones of the endless "parties of ladies and gentlemen" who came to visit the officers on board and wish them well. In

1824, when William Edward Parry left on his third voyage to the Arctic, six thousand people signed the visitors' book of one of his ships.

Dissenting voices were few. This was the heyday of satirical cartoons; they hung in every shop window; and there's a George Cruikshank engraving from 1818 of a fat, ludicrous John Ross returning from his expedition leading his crew of sailors through the streets. The men are carrying a dead polar bear, which is also a stand-in for the northern constellation Ursa Major; stars stud its sides. Someone displays an ivory stick, which is, of course, the North Pole. They have samples of rock, a bucket of the red snow that Ross found on a Greenland bluff, and a seagull on the point of a bayonet. Inuit dogs follow behind. Off to the side stands one of those English types, short, round, and hearty, who could have sat for a portrait of John Bull. He mutters that "we have bears, gulls, savages, chum wood, stones & puppies enough without going to the North Pole for them." What was the point, in short, of sailing into these barren regions of the earth?

But this was the attitude only of the dour, or of satirists like Cruikshank, who specialized in making fun of the navy. William Edward Parry would become a famous man. John Franklin, after leading his own expedition to the Arctic, would become even more famous. People would stop and point him out on the street to their companions. The Arctic enterprise caught the heart of the nation; it was inspiring; it was heroic.

It was also pure. If there were an open polar sea or a Northwest Passage, it might serve as a boon not only to Great Britain but to every European power, and the enterprise was advertised that way, as a kind of gift to mankind. It would have been impossible in any case to prevent the ships of other nations from sailing over the Pole across an open sea, and as for the Northwest Passage, England had declared the seas everywhere to belong to no one nation as early as the reign of Queen Elizabeth I. Canada was already part of the British Empire, so it could not be said that Great Britain was seeking land, and trade with the Inuit of the North was not an especially attractive prospect to any English merchant, for the natives had little to sell. Sealskins, perhaps, and narwhal and walrus tusks. A competitive motive did develop when it became known in 1818 that Otto von Kotzebue had explored the northwestern coast of Alaska, then Russian territory; it was feared the Russians would continue to explore in the area, pass Icy Cape, and continue east along the northern coast of Alaska into Canada. Barrow used this possibility as a reason for the British to get there first. It became a factor in selling Parry's third voyage in 1824–25 to the Admiralty. But otherwise British exploration in the Arctic was, relatively speaking, disinterested, if we can speak of the hope of glory and greatness as disinterested. The whaling industry was well established, so that was not an object. The snowy wastes of the islands lying north of Canada had no commercial value. Only mosses and grasses grew there. Only the Inuit knew how to survive there. There was no profit in this enterprise. But even the practical men of this practical nation fell in behind it.

It helped that the first lord of the Admiralty, Robert Dundas, second Viscount Melville, was in favor of the search for the Passage and was himself deeply interested in science. (Thus it is that the Melville name is found attached to sounds, bays, islands and capes all over northern Canada.) And the scientific problems that exploration in the Arctic might help solve were indeed pressing. One of the biggest scientific questions of the day was geomagnetism. Scientists had been trying to understand the earth's magnetic field and its variations since the early 1600s, and nowhere were those variations greater than in the Arctic. In some places in Baffin Bay the compass pointed not north but west, making navigation difficult, to say the least. Because there was no night in the Arctic summer, ships could not navigate by the stars. It was thought at the time that there might be more than one magnetic pole in the North. And were there, indeed, open seas beyond the ice? Was Greenland an island, or did it extend right across the Arctic to Asia? These were real questions. John Barrow devoted one of his numerous articles in *The Quarterly* (he wrote 195—all of them, including the attack on Ross, unsigned, as was the custom) to demolishing, with only modest success, an argument advanced by several respected scientists at the time that Bering Strait, the sixty-mile gap that separates Asia from North America, opened up not on an ocean but on an inland sea like the Mediterranean. They argued, in other words, that a bridge of land stretched across the Arctic connecting Asia and North America. We know this not to be the case, but without any explorer having yet found, or failed to find, this hypothesized bridge, its existence remained a possibility. Barrow could not eliminate that theoretical possibility with the few facts at hand. Too much was unknown.

Besides the scientific value of the voyages, the Admiralty also had a compelling practical reason to promote exploration. The Napoleonic Wars were over, and the Royal Navy was now idle. At the height of the wars, in 1813, the navy had had 147,087 men and officers in service. By 1815 the number had been cut almost in half. By 1817 it stood at about 20,000. Demobilization had thrown thousands of men on the streets, a contributing factor in the serious economic depression that followed the war, while hundreds of ships lay, slowly rotting away, at anchor. Economic depression led in turn to labor unrest and riots. Patrick Colquhoun's *Treatise on the Wealth, Power and Resources of the British Empire*, published in 1815, devoted a chapter to the question of what to do with demobilized sailors and soldiers. He proposed immigration to the colonies as a solution. Some naval officers did, in a sense, immigrate; they wound up in other countries, especially in South America during the wars of liberation, fighting each other in the service of these countries' navies.

Officers who had made the navy their career had a particularly hard time dealing with demobilization. Officers who were not on active duty received half-pay from the Admiralty. A navy lieutenant, for example, who might well have command of a ship, received a little over a hundred pounds a year, which was enough to provide a home and support for a family, his own support while at sea being absorbed by the navy. He also had the chance of sharing in the prize money for any enemy ships he and his men were able to capture. But on half-pay, with no chance at gaining prize money, living at home with all its attendant expenses, he and his family would be close to starvation. One of Cruikshank's illustrations of naval personnel shows a midshipman, the lowest of officers, working the streets of London after the war, polishing other people's boots.

At the upper levels, captains and above, most officers had other resources to fall back on. A few were the second or third sons of peers. Many were from the families of professional men, lawyers and the like. Others had independent means, usually from modest pieces of inherited land. Captain Wentworth, a character in Jane Austen's novel *Persuasion*, had accumulated a fortune in prize money during the wars; he was a rich man. After the debacle in Lancaster Sound Captain John Ross went home to Scotland to restore his pride as best he could and built himself a house at Loch Ryan. He called it North-West Castle and lived there on half-pay with his wife.

But whether they had independent means or not, most of them would have preferred to be at sea. Officers on active duty were promoted faster than those on half-pay. Most of them were ambitious. Active duty in the Arctic had the further inducement that an officer might become famous. Nothing broadens a military officer's horizons, socially and financially, so much as becoming a hero. Nor was that all. As early as 1745, Parliament had passed a law granting "to any subject, or subjects of His Majesty, a reward of twenty thousand pounds for discovering a North-West Passage through Hudson Strait." Confining it to Hudson Strait was unnecessarily limiting, so the law was amended in 1786 to broaden the scope. Now the passage had only to lie above the 52nd parallel. Then in 1818, just as Ross and Buchan were getting under way, Parliament amended the law once more. It was no longer necessary to sail all the way through the passage to collect prizes. The prizes were now graduated. The officers and men of the first British ships to cross the 110th meridian, which at the latitude of Lancaster Sound is only six hundred miles from its entrance, would win five thousand English pounds—a good deal of money at the time—while crossing the 130th meridian; another four hundred miles, would bring them ten thousand. The money would be divided according to rank, with the officers taking the bulk of it. Even a partial victory, in other words, would constitute a bonanza, while the prize of twenty thousand pounds for reaching the end of the Passage still stood. For British naval officers, the Northwest Passage was now a place where they might find a future.

Exploration obviously held benefits for the Royal Navy as well. After the Battle of Trafalgar in 1805 the navy had had little to do except to escort trading convoys here and there around the world and to blockade the coast of Europe to keep Napoleon's defeated navy out of the oceans. Trafalgar had been the signature victory of the Royal Navy; it had made national heroes out of any number of officers, and it had given the nation a martyr in Admiral Nelson. But the next ten years were an anticlimax. When the allied powers defeated Napoleon in 1814 and again in 1815, it was on land, and the British Army and its generals, most notably the Duke of Wellington, gathered most of the glory. The navy had had Nelson, but no one since Nelson. Coastal blockade work offers little opportunity for the making of great national heroes. The Admiralty surely understood that achieved glory constitutes a strong argument for increases in budget appropriations; and what could be more glorious than to discover, at last, the Northwest Passage? Lord Melville could always find money in his budget for northern exploration.

Put all these factors together—unused ships and personnel; no war to wage; the need for some naval heroics; great gaps in the world's geographical knowledge—and they added up to both an opportunity and real reasons to send out explorers. Barrow was interested not just in the Far North but in Africa as well, where he had spent four years of his life and had done some exploring himself. The sources of the Nile remained unknown. No white man had been to Timbuktu. The course of the Niger was a mystery; Barrow believed that it joined the Nile somewhere south of the legendary Mountains of the Moon. It seems odd that naval officers should lead expeditions south across the Sahara or east into the interior from the west coast of Africa, but not to Barrow. They weren't expeditions in any case; they were two- or three-man operations piggy-backing on Berber trade caravans. And Barrow clearly saw no reason not to use navy men to do this work. For the previous half-century exploration had been a Royal Navy tradition, firmly established by the great Captain Cook, who had himself gone in search of the western out-let of the Northwest Passage.

From a utilitarian point of view, attempts to penetrate the ice and find the Northwest Passage made little sense, but Barrow had only scorn for skeptics. The spirit of the times was romantic, expansionist, triumphal-ist, and, when it came to defying the elements, even a little Byronic. Interestingly enough, it was John Barrow who suggested sending Napoleon into exile this time not to Elba, in the Mediterranean, but to distant St. Helena, in the South Atlantic, where his supporters could not reach him. With Napoleon safely out of the way, the future belonged to England. What was a little ice to English seafarers, men with "hearts of oak"? What were difficulty and danger? Barrow was no Romantic, not with a capital R, but he breathed the same air as other men of his times, an air full of possibilities. A great war had been won. The world was England's to conquer. If the ice was impenetrable, if the odds were impossible, no matter: they were *Englishmen*, members of a superior race, the children of destiny. The search for the Northwest Pas-sage was not strictly speaking an imperial enterprise, but it grew out of this self-same imperial attitude. That attitude would reach its apotheo-sis in Antarctica with its most famous martyr, Robert Falcon Scott. Shortly thereafter it would die en masse in the trenches of World War I.

At the same time, this new enterprise into the ice would likely not have gotten started at all if John Barrow had not been second secretary of the Admiralty. The title hardly does justice to his power and influence. Since the mid-1790s the role of the first secretary had been divided between administrative duties and duties in Parliament. He was a member of Parliament (as were some or all of the seven Admiralty lords), and he and the first lord became the Admiralty's principal representatives in Parliament. John Wilson Croker, the first secretary through much of Barrow's tenure as second secretary, was a major voice of the Tories as well. Croker was deeply involved in naval administration, but when Parliament was in session Croker had to be in attendance, had to defend the Admiralty's budget against the opposition, had to work the corridors of power.

Barrow, who outlasted Croker in office by fifteen years, thus ran the Admiralty's daily affairs and wielded almost equivalent power. In the matter of naval exploration, he wielded more. Barrow became one of Britain's first pure civil servants. He and Croker earned, during wartime, the remarkable salaries of £2,000 and £4,000, respectively, £1,500 and £3,000 during peacetime.

These salaries were more than the Admiralty lords made, but the workload justified them. The first secretary, or more likely the second, read every single piece of correspondence that came into the office, and one or the other of them answered it the same day. This was no small task. The Admiralty received thousands of letters on Admiralty business each year. There were reports to prepare, promotion lists to maintain, and a constantly shifting and often hostile relationship with the Navy Board, which handled the material needs of the navy, to negotiate. Thanks partly to the efficiency and professionalism with which Barrow performed his work, the administration of the Royal Navy, despite its inherently unwieldy nature, became even more stable during his tenure than it had been in the past. Barrow was wise enough to stay out of politics, which Croker by the very nature of his job could not do, and to keep politics out of the navy's administration as far as that could be done. He was a lifelong Tory, but when the Whigs took power in 1830 after nearly fifty years of Tory rule, they kept Barrow in office. He was first appointed in 1804. After a brief hiatus in 1806–7, when a reform government took power for a year, he remained in office until 1845. In 1832, the year of the Reform Act in Great Britain, which changed the way members of Parliament were elected in much of the country, he himself brought reform to the administration of the navy. He was in his eighties when he retired, boasting that only once had he had so much as his pulse taken. He had survived thirteen changes of administration. By that time his official title was not second secretary but permanent secretary.

Barrow was far from the dull civil servant type. A woman who had taken him up socially in South Africa, before he came to the Admiralty, described him "as one of the pleasantest, best-informed and most eager-minded young men in the world about everything curious or worth attention." As we have seen in the case of John Ross, he was also capable of towering rages and could hold a grudge his entire life. He came from a poor family; his father was a Lancashire smallholder—a farmer one step above a day laborer—and he had had little formal schooling. He was assiduous about educating himself, however, and by the time he was fifteen was teaching mathematics at a school in Greenwich, where he lucked into a position tutoring the son of Sir George Staunton. To rise in England, as everybody knew, one needed an aristocratic patron. Barrow had found his in Staunton. Staunton was himself a friend and adviser to Sir George (later Lord) Macartney. In 1792 Macartney led an embassy to China that hoped to open the country more widely to British trade. Staunton went along and took his son, and his son's tutor as well. Staunton's son, interestingly enough, was an amazing boy. He could speak five languages, including Chinese, by the time he was twelve.

Barrow distinguished himself on this trip and in subsequent work in South Africa, where he became private secretary to Lord Macartney and explored much of the country, which was little known. He spent a year in the bush, covering three thousand miles all told, made extensive notes, became a crack shot, and ended up knowing more about South Africa than any other British subject. Barrow married the daughter of a Boer in South Africa and stayed on when Macartney returned home. He was in his mid-thirties by this time and had bought land, and possibly he might have considered staying in Africa if the English had not transferred the colony back to the Dutch in 1803, during the Peace of Amiens, which interrupted the Napoleonic Wars for a couple of years. Barrow left the cape then. He had already begun his writing career. Lord Macartney and Sir George Staunton had already seen to the London publication of the first volume of his book about his travels through South Africa. Soon after Barrow arrived back in England the second volume appeared. It was the first of Barrow's many books, and his map of the countryside was the first reliable map of the interior of South Africa. The book attracted the attention of Sir Joseph Banks, among many others, and Banks and Barrow became friendly. The book, and Barrow's now-broad experience of the world, led to Barrow's becoming the reviewer of choice for *The Quarterly* when it came to the literature of travel and exploration.

And to his becoming second secretary. When he returned to England in 1803 Macartney introduced him to Henry Dundas, the first Viscount Melville, father of Robert Dundas and soon to be first lord of the Admiralty, and to William Pitt, soon to be prime minister—in short, his new patrons. Barrow had climbed remarkably high for the son of a small-holder. Lord Melville was a powerful man; he was Pitt's good friend and a Scottish grandee who controlled thirty-seven of Scotland's forty-five seats in Parliament. There were members of the Dundas family highly placed all through government. Henry Dundas's nephew had been commander of British forces in South Africa and must have known Barrow there. Henry Dundas's son Robert would become first lord of the Admiralty after him. Barrow's career could not have been in better hands.

Our few personal glimpses of him are not terribly revealing. His biographer says, "What he did is more important than what he was." He was certainly a stubborn man, never submitting his idée fixe of an open polar sea to critical scrutiny. Fergus Fleming in *Barrow's Boys*, an account of the expeditions Barrow sponsored both in the Arctic and in Africa, has hardly a kind word to say about him. Barrow was not only stubborn, he was often wrong. The Arctic Ocean is not in fact free of ice, and the Niger does not empty into the Nile but into the Gulf of Guinea. Barrow never gave up either idea. Jane Griffin, who was John Franklin's second wife, met Barrow at a dinner party in 1824 and noted that "he is said to be humourous & obstinate & exhibited both propensities." He shared a house for years with John Wilson Croker, and Barrow's son George would marry Croker's adopted daughter Nony. Croker was very much more on display than Barrow, not only because he was in Parliament but because of his personality. Sydney Smith called him "the calumniator general of the human race," and the great Whig historian Thomas Macaulay hated him "more than cold boiled veal." Croker made enemies; Barrow did not. Barrow was the survivor in the Admiralty.

Over the years he would go on to acquire yet more power. His very longevity in office, not to mention his abilities, guaranteed it, and his abilities were considerable. Barrow helped Sir George Staunton prepare the official account of the embassy to China; then he wrote his own, more entertaining account of the trip. It sold well. On the basis of this book Barrow became one of England's resident experts on matters Chinese as well as South African. His scientific curiosity—he had described wildlife in his book on South Africa that was entirely new to Europe—brought him membership in the Royal Society.

Banks would become his ally and his mentor. Banks was old, fat, and gout-ridden when John Ross set sail for Baffin Bay in 1818. In two years he would be dead. Since accompanying Captain Cook on his first voyage to Tahiti in 1768 to observe the transit of Venus, Banks had served as chief scientific adviser to the Admiralty; indeed, no scientific or exploring expedition had left England since without Banks suggesting it or approving it, setting its scientific goals, and advising it on the makeup of its scientific instruments and personnel. After Banks, that role fell to John Barrow. And John Barrow was obsessed with the Northwest Passage.

CHAPTER THREE

A Passage to India

In becoming so deeply committed to finding the Northwest Passage, the second secretary joined a long and persistent tradition. European merchants, navigators, adventurers, and geographers had been sporadically seeking the Northwest Passage ever since the first half of the sixteenth century, when it slowly began to become clear that North and South America were one continuous landmass and that the Pacific Ocean did not conveniently lie just to the west of the Outer Banks, as Verrazano believed, or the Massachusetts coastline. How were they to get around all this acreage to the riches of the Orient? Perhaps they could find a way over the top of it. The Spanish and the Portuguese dominated the newly discovered southern routes to Asia, the former through the Straits of Magellan, the latter around the Cape of Good Hope. Alexander VI, a Spanish pope, had complicated the matter by drawing a line down the middle of the Atlantic Ocean in 1493 and granting everything west of it to the Spanish and everything east to the Portuguese.

This left nothing for the northern European powers, and, because the southern routes were, after a fashion, taken, no way to get to the East in any case. In 1493 the issue was still moot. Magellan had yet to make his voyage and find his straits; the known world hardly extended beyond Europe and the Mediterranean; the import of Christopher Columbus's discoveries the year before was not yet understood. But as the sixteenth century grew older and the world began to unfold, it became increasingly urgent to the French, the Dutch, and the English to find their own way to the Far East. The Spanish were conquering Mexico and Peru, building ports along both coasts of South America, and bringing home the kind of wealth that had in the past been the stuff only of wild fantasies. Little Portugal was establishing a thriving trade in silk and spices, precious stones, and other luxury goods, spreading that trade into the East Indies as a whole, while simultaneously cornering the market in slaves and gold along the coast of West Africa. The most profitable parts of the world were being snapped up. All that remained to northern Europeans was the unknown mass of North America and its apparently unbroken coastline. This coast was occupied by illiterate savages dressed in skins who had no gold, no precious gems, no spices, silks—nothing, in short, of value. Could there be a route through it or around it to the Pacific and the magnificent fortunes to be made in Cathay, or in legendary remote Japan?

The French sent Verrazano in 1524 to find out. He sailed up the east coast of North America and "discovered" the Pacific across a narrow isthmus that subsequently appeared on a number of maps, making the continent look like it was badly pinched at the waist, like a wasp. He was actually looking at Cape Hatteras, in future North Carolina; his would-be Pacific Ocean was nothing more than Pamlico Sound. Henry VII of England had sent John Cabot west in 1497, and he had discovered the island of Newfoundland but no passage. The St. Lawrence, for which there were early hopes, proved to be a river, not a strait through the continent. The French would eventually give up on the search for a Northwest Passage, contenting themselves with the soft gold of the fur trade; they explored up the St. Lawrence into the interior of North America and no longer tried to sail around it. The Dutch pursued the route over the top of Asia, the Northeast Passage, into the early years of the seventeenth century, but gave up after the ice stopped them one too many times just to the east of the aptly named White Sea. Only the British would continue the pursuit and become, over time, obsessed by it. Only the British would come to see it as peculiarly their problem to solve.

The source of this national obsession lies, perhaps, in the dangerously vague but insidiously seductive idea of the English national character. National character is an idea that sets most contemporary historians to grinding their teeth, as it is more or less impossible to describe the national character of any people without bumping into numerous examples that contradict it. But it is not completely unreasonable to suggest that an island people will consistently, necessarily seek first to find water routes to the places they want to travel, and come to think of themselves as adept at finding them. Nor is it unreasonable that a northern people would consider northern routes as something natural to them, even reserved to them in God's plan; this argument was in fact advanced as early as the 1520s.

But a more specific source lay in a conviction that simply refused to die—that the Northwest Passage *must be there*. It *had* to exist. Scientific method has taught us not to draw this kind of premature conclusion about the nature of the world or of anything else. We hypothesize, we investigate, and then we make our maps. This was not the case in the Renaissance. Sixteenth-century geographers did not hesitate to postulate the existence of landforms or water routes that had yet to be found, basing their conclusions not only on the accounts, real and imaginary, of actual (and fictional) voyagers but on ancient Greek and Roman thought and on medieval traditions about the nature of the world. The medieval traditions were symbolic, interested less in the actual placement of landmasses and bodies of water and their proportional sizes than in the religious meaning of places. Medieval geographical thought, as it came to expression in the *mappae mundi* of the time, shaped the continents in the rough form of a cross, as if the surface of the world were yet another representation of the passion of Christ, and placed the center of that cross in Jerusalem. In these same maps Ocean—the world ocean—encircled the world.

The fifteenth-century rediscovery of Ptolemy's description of the world and his world map, along with the growing influence of Aristotle's ideas about the world's layout, began to dissolve medieval influence on geographical thought in the Renaissance, but it did not eliminate the tendency to speculate about the world, even in the absence of evidence, and the notion that water circled the world, and thus the continents, survived in the belief in a Northwest Passage. Aristotle too was a principal source of geographical speculation. Because he believed that the landmasses of the world had to be balanced—that is, there had to be as much land in the Southern Hemisphere as the Northern, otherwise the world would wobble on its axis—maps of the world included, for more than two centuries, an enormous continent in the high latitudes of the Southern Hemisphere, a *terra australis,* that did not vanish from globes until Captain James Cook sailed through those same high latitudes and found a few small islands and a great many icebergs. Theories, in short, fueled speculation. Speculative geographers drew maps.

For all anyone knew the Northwest Passage was just such a ghost in the world's landscape, but the fact that no one did know made it all the easier to believe that it had to be there, waiting to be discovered. The first English attempt to find it may be dated, tentatively, to Sebastian Cabot's voyage to the west and north along the coast of North America in 1507—tentatively because, while most historians believe the voyage took place, no contemporary records of it survive. We have only Cabot's oral testimony to affirm it, and Cabot was notoriously careless with his facts. Henry VII sponsored this voyage, as he had sponsored John Cabot's ten years earlier, but by the time Sebastian returned, the king had died, and Henry VIII took only occasional interest in further voyages. This last Henry's interests lay in Europe at the time; he still entertained designs on the French crown. England was not yet the maritime power it would become and, deeply preoccupied by the religious disputes of the English Reformation, it was slow to develop an interest in expanding its trade to a wider world.

A few English merchants were interested, however, and grew more so after Queen Elizabeth came to the throne in 1558. As early as 1527 an English merchant named Robert Thorne had suggested that England pursue a northerly route to the Far East. Living in Seville at the time, Thorne was impressed by how rich Spain and Portugal were becoming by their trade with the East, with its "gold, Rubies, Diamondes," its "Cloves, Nutmegs, Mace, and Cinnamom." He knew, he said, two Englishmen who were "somewhat learned in Cosmographie" and in speaking with them he may have come to understand that from England it would be shorter by nearly two thousand leagues, or six thousand miles, to sail to the Orient over the North Pole.

He wrote a short discourse addressed to Henry VIII's ambassador to Spain, the merchant Edward Lee, promoting exploration to the north, over the Pole, including a map drawn up to show the ambassador what the route would be.

The map is crude, but the idea is plain enough—South and North America, he points out, form a continuous landmass from Tierra del Fuego to Labrador. The pope has given the world, Thorne reminds Lee, to Spain and Portugal. But what precisely were the boundaries of this extraordinary grant? The Spanish and the Portuguese are arguing about it as we speak, he noted. If we were to sail over the North Pole, we would cut six thousand miles off a voyage to the equator in the Pacific from the Spanish route through the Straits of Magellan. There must be many more islands undiscovered, rich islands full of treasure. It would be thousands of miles shorter to Cathay. The very word *Cathay* called up images of fabulous wealth in the Western mind. Since Marco Polo, it had been the dream of Europe to reach it and to trade with it, wherever it was. (The name *China* did not appear in English until 1555.) Nothing in the pope's edict said anything about giving the rights to Cathay to Spain or Portugal.

Then Thorne brought up the question of ice. He admitted that cosmographers had universally believed that "passing the seventh clime [i.e., the Arctic], the sea is all ice, and the colde so much that none can suffer it." But the cosmographers had also believed that the lands around the equator would be uninhabitable for just the opposite reason, because of the heat, and it turned out that people lived there comfortably. Indeed, he went on, "no land [is] so much habitable nor more temperate . . . I thinke the same should be found under the North, if it were experimented. For as all judge, Nihil fit vacuum in rerum natura." You do not find a vacuum in nature. "So I judge," he wrote, "there is no land unhabitable, nor Sea innavigable." If people can live on the equator, in other words, it follows that people can live around the Poles, and the polar seas must therefore be free of ice. This spectacular piece of illogic is the origin of the idea that the polar sea is open.

Thorne wrote to Henry VIII proposing that the king sponsor a voyage to the North. As it happened, the king, uncharacteristically, had already approved a voyage, the only voyage of exploration he sponsored, but it was to the West, not the North, and nothing came of it. Thorne's vision of England's destiny to the North lay fallow for quite some time, and Thorne himself died in 1532. His words were not forgotten, however, and by the second half of the sixteenth century English merchants were looking once again at the idea of reaching the East by way of the North. In 1553 a group of merchants calling themselves the Muscovy Company sent three ships in search of a Northeast Passage, to sail over the top of Europe and Asia to the Far East. These waters were as unknown as the waters north of Labrador. The question of a Northeast Passage was as unsettled as a Northwest. One of the ships made it to Archangel before winter settled in. From there the captain, Richard Chancellor, traveled overland to Moscow, where he obtained trading agreements with the then tsar, Ivan the Terrible. This was something of a coup. Until then the Hanseatic League in the Baltic had dominated trade with Russia. Subsequently English mariners in the employ of the company would make occasional attempts to penetrate the Arctic Ocean beyond Archangel, but always without success. The Dutch did persist in this direction, sending various expeditions in the next sixty years over the top of Norway and Lapland to the White Sea. They all came to grief on the pack ice east of Novaya Zemlya. The best the Dutch could do in the end was to name the waters west of Novaya Zemlya after their great navigator William Barents, who died of scurvy on one of these voyages.

Merchant adventurers, not governments, were behind most of these early expeditions to the North. In contrast to Spain and Portugal, which were building empires, and where exploration was under the control of their respective crowns, English exploration was a mercantile project. Explorers did not sail without royal approval, but the ships were merchant ships, the financing was largely private, and profit was the goal. The government merely gave its stamp of approval, in the form of a monopoly on trade. Assuming the initial exploration was successful, no other company would then have the right to trade in the area discovered; after 1553, for example, only the Muscovy Company could trade with Russia. When the East India Company was formed in 1600, it enjoyed a monopoly on English trade with Asia. And when the search for the Northwest Passage reopened in 1576, it was a company, a consortium of merchants, that reopened it.

Merchants and men of affairs, but the group was not large. The English as a whole remained slow to take an interest in opening trade to faraway places, and Queen Elizabeth had no imperial ambitions except in the British Isles. In the 1550s, however, shortly before she came to the throne, intellectual interest in the new discoveries around the world began to grow rapidly in England. Spanish accounts of their discoveries were translated into English, and a few enterprising men of affairs began to discuss the prospect of England becoming actively involved. They were mostly landed gentry, many of them from the West Country, Devon and Cornwall; they formed around the Gilberts, Adrian and Sir Humphrey. Sir Walter Raleigh, later a great promoter of schemes of colonization, was their half brother. A couple of prominent men in government had developed an interest in the idea too, most notably Sir Francis Walsingham, secretary of state in the queen's Privy Council and her spymaster, and Lord Burleigh, in effect her prime minister, who was even more powerful than Walsingham. A Welshman named John Dee, who had been educated in Europe and was deeply learned in mathematics, cosmography, and the art of navigation, provided the intellectual context, the ferment, that sets such projects going. Dee strongly believed in the existence of a Northwest Passage. The queen once went to Dee's house just to see his library, which was, it was said, magnificent.

A circle developed around these men. Meetings were held. Sir Humphrey Gilbert in an audience with the queen debated the advantages of a Northwest Passage over a Northeast one. His opponent was Anthony Jenkinson, a mariner for the Muscovy Company who had not only sailed to Russia but had traveled by land from Moscow as far south as Persia. Sir Humphrey had no doubt that the Northwest Passage existed. In 1566 he wrote a treatise on the subject, published ten years later, which is much more substantial than Thorne's letters, and he does give reasons where Thorne did not for the viability of a route.

He argues first of all, in proper Renaissance fashion, from authority. Plato had brought up the existence of a great island civilization called Atlantis that had disappeared into the sea in deep antiquity, and it was likely the islands of America were the remains, and they were islands, not an unbroken landmass, so there had to be a way around them.

He gives us more plausible reasons as well. If America is not an island but connected to Asia, why isn't it full of Asians? He refers to sea currents, beginning a train of argument that will last to Barrow's day. The currents run, he says, out of the Pacific around the tip of Africa westward, then turn north along the east coast of the Americas and from there pass west around the top of North America into the Pacific again. Lacking any actual evidence for this pattern, he has no way of knowing whether this line of reasoning is true, but the currents *must* run this way, he says, because the currents of the world's seas, it is well known, run east to west generally, and if there were no exit over the top of North America, they would be forced back to the east, onto the coast of Britain, and they are not. Only the existence of a strait above North America can explain the way the currents run.

He then refers to travelers who somehow know the Passage exists, or have heard that it does from other travelers, or from Chinamen, or Sebastian Cabot, who told Sir Humphrey personally before he died that he had seen the entrance to the Northwest Passage in 1507 and would have sailed to Cathay if he had not been threatened with mutiny. Indians, he goes on, had been forced onto the Baltic shores of Germany by contrary winds, and they could only have come there through the Northwest Passage. "Indians" was a loose term then, impossibly inclusive. He was referring to an incident, possibly real, in which people who were probably Inuit plausibly could have been, and maybe were, blown by a storm out of Greenland and crash-landed somewhere in the Baltic. But Gilbert seemed to think that they were actually Indians from India, that fabulous land located someplace in an only vaguely understood East. He argued that these "Indian" Indians could not have come from the north of Asia, along the coast of Russia, because there was no passage that way. He was sure of that. They could only have come from "India." And why, by the way, are there no Asian animals in the Americas—camels, perhaps, or tigers—if the Americas and Asia are connected?

There *had* to be a Passage. We, the English, must find it. That way "we may safely trade without danger or annoyance of any prince living, Christian or Heathen, it being out of all their trades . . . It were the onely way for our princes, to possesse the wealth of all the East parts . . . of the world, which is infinite."

Gilbert was arguing from the best geographical knowledge of the day, and we cannot dismiss him even though he was wrong on most counts. The native people of the Americas are indeed Asiatic in origin. Ocean currents do not run in the directions he says. But he was working from a globe John Dee had brought from the Continent made by the brilliant Flemish cosmographer Gemma Frisius, and Frisius was highly respected. Frisius had invented the surveying method called triangulation. He had also solved the biggest problem in navigation, the determination of longitude. (The solution depended, unfortunately, on having an exceptionally accurate clock; that would take another two hundred years.) Mercator studied under Frisius. Frisius published his first globe in 1530 and a second in 1537 that showed North America not as a continent but as a group of islands, with a strait to the north separating it from the landmass of Asia, which reaches out over the top of the Pacific all the way to Greenland. Frisius used the writings of Marco Polo; reports of the voyages of the Corte-Real brothers, two Portuguese mariners who had explored the waters off Greenland and Labrador in the early 1500s; and "unspecified Spanish and Portuguese sources" to come up with this configuration. One of the Corte-Real brothers is supposed to have passed through this strait to Asia. Sebastian Münster adopted this strait in his own world map of 1540. Some of the greatest authorities of the time, in short, would have agreed with Gilbert. Gilbert was an enterprising, forward-looking man. He was up to date.

He was also persuasive enough to talk a prominent London merchant named Michael Lok into backing an expedition to search for the Northwest Passage. Lok had spent time in Spain and Portugal and had seen firsthand the wealth that was being produced by trade with the Orient and the Spanish New World. He was the London agent of the Muscovy Company. In the 1550s he had traded in the eastern Mediterranean on his own account. Lok was just the man to assemble a company of merchants to help with the financing, organize the expedition, and launch a few ships. They would sail to Asia, acquire some of that "merchandize of an inestimable price," and great wealth would be theirs. The group called itself the Company of Cathay.

To lead the expedition Lok chose one of England's chanciest men, the semiliterate privateer Martin Frobisher, a sea dog not unacquainted with jail who made little distinction between friendly and unfriendly ships when he was seizing them. Frobisher had an old connection with the Lok family and had sailed for them before, and he had also sailed for the queen. In 1572 he had served with Sir Humphrey Gilbert in Ireland, crushing one of Ireland's many rebellions against the English. A few years later he was working for the Irish, then for the Spanish, in situations that were provocative, to say the least, and probably treasonous. He plowed through the fortunes of two widows he married in succession and then abandoned. He was a freelance, pursuing opportunities wherever they were to be found. He claimed to have been interested in finding the Northwest Passage for a long time. It was, he told one chronicler of his expeditions, "the onely thing of the Worlde that was left undone, whereby a notable mind mighte be made famous and fortunate," that is, rich.

Under Michael Lok's sponsorship—Lok provided half the funds; other merchants the rest—Frobisher sailed with three ships in 1576 toward the tip of Greenland, from there to sail west. The voyage did not begin well. The ships were so small they would hardly qualify as yachts today. The smallest, a mere pinnace, for use only in coastal waters, vanished in a storm with its crew of four somewhere east of southern Greenland. That was enough for the second ship, which turned back soon after. Frobisher himself in the *Gabriel* almost came to grief when another storm knocked the ship on its side; only Frobisher, clambering over the decks of the tilting ship, cutting ropes, spilling wind from the sails, acted quickly enough to save them.

When they did reach land their fortunes seemed to change. There before them lay a wide inlet between two bodies of land, and this inlet stretched to the west and seemed to have no bottom. Frobisher leaped to his conclusion—this had to be it, the Northwest Passage. He identified the land to the north of his inlet as Asia, the land to the south as America, just as it was on Gemma Frisius's globe, and sailed west down its reach. His strait narrowed as he sailed west and he fell into a tangle of islands, but climbing a mountain he looked out to the west and saw more water, and it seemed to be open, with no end to it, and he concluded that this was definitely it, the "West Sea," the Pacific, "whereby to pas to Cathay and to the East India." At that moment he had his first contact with the natives. A small group of them were approaching in their kayaks.

Eventually nineteen of them would come aboard the *Gabriel*, and they would trade with the English for the next several days, but trouble found the English in the end. The ship's boat took an Inuit ashore, with five of Frobisher's seamen rowing. They swept around a point toward the Inuit village and were never seen again. Frobisher had arrived in his strait with eighteen men; now he had thirteen. It was August, and it was beginning to snow. Frobisher tried for two days to find his men, then gave up. On August 25 he sailed for home. He had for a guide to the behavior of strange peoples only one book, *The Travels of Sir John Mandeville*, a fourteenth-century farrago of imagined voyages to such excellent places as the land of Prester John and the front gates of the Earthly Paradise. At the time the book was thought to be an account of actual travels. It describes the wonders of the East in truly vivid terms. In some countries lived people with the heads of dogs, in others people who were perhaps sixteen inches tall and lived a mere six years; and of course there were cannibals. It would have been perfectly natural for Frobisher to assume that the Inuit were yet another of these strange alien races, and that they had eaten his five men. He seized an Inuit of his own to take back to England. This unlucky person died soon after he arrived in London.

Frobisher did have something to show for his efforts, however, besides the open water he glimpsed at the end of his strait. He had brought back a stone as a token of possession and Michael Lok had it assayed. Two English assayers told him it was worthless. But a Venetian came to a different conclusion—it was shot through with gold, he claimed, so much gold, indeed, that it would yield a return of 2,400 percent on an investment in another expedition. Gold, as it tends to do, trumped all other considerations. The Northwest Passage suddenly faded into the landscape. Over the next two years Michael Lok would finance two more expeditions, both under Frobisher's command. The first was to locate the ore and bring back enough to establish a definitive assay, and then came a truly ambitious, much larger expedition with fifteen ships, a large group of miners, and materials with which to build houses where they could spend the winter. This aspect of the scheme ended when ice stove in the ship carrying these building materials and it sank. There would be no wintering over. But such was the enthusiasm for Frobisher's enterprise that Queen Elizabeth herself invested substantial amounts of money in both these expeditions. When the ships returned in late 1578, they brought back fourteen hundred tons of what they all believed was rock laced with gold. Here was a chance for England to compete with Spain in the gold rush that exploration had become.

It was not to be. In 1581 it was finally established that Frobisher's ore held small amounts of marcasite, a form of iron pyrites—fool's gold. Some of this ore is still to be seen on Priory Road in the English town of Dartford, where it was used to build a wall. On Baffin Island the trenches Frobisher dug to extract his ore are also still visible. The native Inuit, who lost four of their own, kidnapped back to England, maintained their memory of Frobisher's fleet of ships in oral tradition for three hundred years and in remarkable detail; the American explorer Charles Francis Hall heard the story from them in the 1860s, when he spent a winter with them. The passage Frobisher thought he had discovered comes to a close about eighteen miles from the small mountain he climbed to see the Pacific Ocean to the west. It is now called Frobisher Bay. Michael Lok went bankrupt and was jailed eight times for debt in the subsequent years. Sir Humphrey Gilbert set his heart now on colonizing attempts, but he disappeared in the Atlantic Ocean in a voyage meant to establish a colony in New England in 1583. The queen, twice burned, had refused to invest in this enterprise. Sir Humphrey had "not good hap at sea," she remarked. Indeed.

Only Martin Frobisher survived the affair with a certain degree of honor. The queen continued to employ him on various missions and in 1588 he proved to be one of the most recklessly brave of the outgunned English sea captains who defeated the Spanish Armada; he was knighted for his exploits. He died in hand-to-hand combat while leading a force of marines in an assault in Brest.

The first serious English effort to find the Northwest Passage concluded, then, in a tale of fool's gold, bankruptcy, and geographical farce. But Frobisher's expedition had been a grand adventure that absorbed England's attention. Not one, but four, accounts of it were published. The quest was by no means over; it had only just begun. Humphrey

Gilbert might be dead, but the circle around him remained active. His brother Adrian, John Dee, and another enterprising mariner, a man named John Davis, were still determined to find the Passage, as was Sir Francis Walsingham, and in 1585 Davis set out on the first of his three voyages to the west of Greenland. He was backed by William Sanderson, a London merchant undaunted by Michael Lok's experience. Davis was an altogether different sort of person from Frobisher. Davis sailed in ships called *Sunshine* and *Moonshine* and he took musicians along to entertain his seamen. Not only did he not kidnap Inuit, there is a charming moment during his first voyage when his musicians played and a group of native Greenlanders danced alongside the ships' crews. A day or two later they held wrestling matches with these people. Davis sailed from Greenland across the strait that now bears his name to Baffin Island, found only barren land, and sailed home in September. He made two more voyages in the two years following, exploring Cumberland Sound on Baffin Island on the third and rediscovering the bay where Frobisher had dug his ore. Sailing south, he passed by Hudson Strait without entering it.

Davis, too, fought the Spanish Armada and made enough money from the Spanish ships he captured to try again for the Northwest Passage in 1591—from the Pacific side. But foul weather aborted his attempt to sail through the Straits of Magellan and reach the Pacific. His map of Davis Strait and the pieces of Baffin Island he had explored, however, was used on the so-called English globe of 1592; and in 1595 he wrote a book called *The Worldes hydrographical description,* an account of the world's waters as they were then known, in which he argued for the same proposition Robert Thorne had advanced—there was no part of the world that was not habitable and no seas that were not navigable. Davis was a believer, the first in a long line of Englishmen whose faith in the Northwest Passage remained unshaken despite numerous failures to find it. These first northern voyages seemed to breed believers in the Passage, and they seeded England with their faith.

English interest in North America had shifted by the 1590s, however, to colonizing activities. The defeat of the Spanish Armada in 1588, furthermore, and the success of English raids on Spanish shipping in the West Indies, had given the English a new confidence in themselves as a sea power. After the voyage of Sir Francis Drake around the world in 1577–80, they no longer regarded the Straits of Magellan as belonging to the Spanish; nor did they think of the Pacific as a Spanish lake. It was now official English policy to regard the seas as belonging to everyone, the common property of mankind. In 1600 the queen granted a charter to the East India Company, which intended to trade around the Cape of Good Hope to India and the spice islands. Early on in its history the company tried unsuccessfully to annex the area around Table Mountain on the cape to ensure English control of this route to the Orient—an initial step in the creation of the British overseas empire.

The long voyage to India was expensive, to be sure, not only in money but in lives, and the East India Company did make a brief sally to the northwest in 1602, when it sent George Waymouth in command of two small ships to look once again for that elusive shortcut to the Far East. Waymouth may have sailed for a little way into the entry to what is now known as Hudson Strait, but it was a bad season for ice and he failed to make any other major discoveries. The company tried again in 1606, but this voyage was even less successful, and by this time the company had begun to make significant profits in India. The Portuguese and the Dutch would fight the growing English trade in the Far East, but they could not stop it. English merchant adventurers still believed in the Northwest Passage, but the sense of urgency about finding it had begun to fade.

But while English interest in the Passage might sleep, it could always be aroused. The voyages of Frobisher and Davis, while not successful, had been exciting, and published accounts of them were available. They had had a pronounced effect on English perceptions of their opportunities as mariners and their role in the exploration of the world. The second edition of Richard Hakluyt's enormous folio collection of English voyages, *The Principall Navigations,* came out in 1600; it included the printed accounts of the Frobisher and Davis voyages, and it gave voice to Hakluyt's own uncritical enthusiasm for exploration. The findings of the Waymouth voyage were promising. Davis too had talked about coming to a great strait with powerful currents and strong tides surrounding it, and Waymouth had gotten partway into this strait. In 1610 Henry Hudson, backed by twenty-three merchant adventurers, both the Muscovy and East India Companies, and with the personal blessing of the Prince of Wales, sailed through it. It bears his name: Hudson Strait. The great bay beyond is, of course, called Hudson Bay.

With Hudson's voyage we enter a new phase in northern exploration and the hunt for the Passage. All previous voyages had come and gone to the Arctic and Subarctic in the same short season, reaching Davis

Strait and the lower reaches of Baffin Island usually in July, staying for six or eight weeks, and then turning for home before the ice embraced them. Hudson was the first to spend the winter there deliberately, according to plan, with what he believed would be enough provisions to survive in relative comfort.

But things seldom go as planned in the Arctic. Hudson had not in fact brought enough food. He chose the southernmost, presumably the warmest, corner of Hudson Bay to spend the winter, but while he was a bold navigator and a resourceful sailor, he was neither a good leader nor a good judge of men. His ship was full of troublemakers, and a quarrel over a coat descended into a mutiny. It left Hudson adrift in a dinghy the following spring with eight others, including his young son, as the ship sped away without them. As so often in Arctic experience, the fate of Hudson and his companions, and the subsequent fate of those who abandoned him, reads like tragedy—Jacobean revenge tragedy in this case; John Webster might have written it. One justification for the mutiny was the belief that Hudson had been hiding food in his cabin for himself. When the mutineers searched his cabin, they found charts, his journal, and clothing, but nothing edible. Hudson, his little boy, and the men loyal to him were never seen again. Then, on the way out of Hudson Bay, as they were hunting along the shoreline for birds, the cruelest of the mutineers died at the hands of Inuit who unexpectedly ambushed them. Hunger ruled. Men stole bread from each other. When the few survivors left Hudson Strait for England they had nothing left but a cache of birds they had killed for food before the Inuit massacre. They ate everything edible from these birds, including the skins, "and as for the garbage, it was not thrown away." They ate candles when there was nothing else, one pound of candles per man per week, and considered it "a great dainty." The men were so weak they could hardly manage the sails.

But they had wintered over, that was the significant fact; they had sailed down the eastern shore of Hudson Bay, and they had not died of the cold. Men could survive in the Arctic. (No one mentioned that the natives had been surviving in the Arctic for millennia.) What, then, lay to the west? Was the eastern shore of Hudson Bay the western shore of North America? Was Hudson Bay part of the Pacific Ocean? In 1612 the same merchants who had sponsored Henry Hudson sponsored another expedition, this one under the command of Captain Thomas Button. He and his crew also spent and survived the winter, and he reached the western shore of Hudson Bay and coasted it far enough south to determine that it was a bay, and not an arm of the Pacific.

Yet parts of the bay remained unexplored—the northwest portions beyond Southampton Island. There, perhaps, lay the entrance to the Strait of Aniàn, the Northwest Passage. Hudson Bay remained a possibility. Button came home to discover that enthusiasm for finding the Northwest Passage had grown while he was gone. A new company had been formed to exploit it and there were now 388 subscribers. Yet another voyage was sent west. This one failed even to enter the strait, which was blocked with ice. In 1615 Robert Bylot, one of the mutineers who had left Hudson to his fate, commanded a fourth voyage to Hudson Bay, with William Baffin as his navigator. This voyage charted as much of the bay as it could reach, but Bylot and Baffin did not spend the winter. Baffin had come to believe that Hudson Bay was not the entrance to the Passage, and on the final voyage of this series, still sponsored by the same merchants, he and Bylot avoided it, sailed north through Davis Strait, and made their famous voyage around the rim of Baffin Bay. They came back with the map of the bay and Baffin Island that Samuel Purchas lost, the map that, had it survived, might have changed John Barrow's mind about the feasibility of the enterprise he was sending men and ships to pursue.

Baffin's final voyage brought this new series of voyages to the northwest to a close, but it was clear from the numbers of sponsors—not only the Muscovy Company and the East India Company, but 388 independents—that interest was no longer confined to a few visionaries like the Gilbert family and Walsingham and John Dee. The Passage had become more than a business venture. It had entered the culture, become familiar enough to serve as a common source of metaphor, a term of reference everybody recognized. It was as difficult to understand melancholy in all its forms, wrote Robert Burton in his *Anatomy of Melancholy* (1621), as to find "the creeks and sounds of the north-east or north-west passages." The poet John Donne refers "to the heat of a lover's eyes" that "The passage of the West or East would thaw, / And open wide their easie liquid jawe / To all our ships." The Northwest Passage had come "to stand for all that was heroic and venturous and difficult," writes R. R. Cawley in his book *Unpathed Waters*. England had come late to the game; all the major geographic discoveries belonged to other powers. That left them the North, which had become England's particular heritage, its destiny. The English might pause, might give up the search, but not indefinitely. It had become by this time not only a route to the Orient but one of the great geographical problems, the solving of which promised wealth, yes, but glory too, fame for him who solved it equal to Drake's, say, or Columbus's. The fact that the problem was intractable only made it more seductive.

No one attempted to follow Baffin into Baffin Bay until John Ross made the trip in 1818, although British and Dutch whalers were hunting whales in Davis Strait by the 1650s. A Dane, Jens Munk, persuaded the Danish king to send him into Hudson Bay for fame and wealth and the way to the East, and they wintered over—and all but Munk and two of his sailors died of scurvy. A hundred years later the bones of the others still lay on the ground where they were left. This was another of those stirring adventure tales, three greatly weakened men making it back to civilization somehow across the Atlantic Ocean; it was the kind of deadly adventure that paradoxically inspires other men to want to do the same. In 1631 the English made one more attempt to break through the ice in Hudson Bay and follow its coastline. Two ships, one under Luke Foxe, the other under Thomas James, one with the support of the king, the other financed by merchants from Bristol, sailed from England two days apart. Foxe discovered the basin north of Southampton Island in Hudson Bay that bears his name, but could not enter it for the ice; nor did he winter over. He had solved no problems, only complicated them. Thomas James did winter over, sinking his ship to protect it from the ice at Charlton Island, in the same bay where Henry Hudson had spent the winter. The bay is named after him. He raised the ship in the spring of 1632, sailed north and tried to pass through Foxe Channel into Foxe Basin, but he too failed to find a route through the ice. He returned to England to write an account of his voyage that his publisher titled *The Strange and Dangerous Voyage of Capt. Thomas James*. Strange indeed, for how many captains would sink a ship to save it? John Barrow called it, scornfully, a book of "lamentation and weeping and great mourning." Englishmen are not supposed to complain about difficulties. James has been thought of ever since as a bit of a wimp.

But no one who has not been to the country of thick white ice has any right to question what those who have lived through a winter in it have had to endure. James's gunner's mate, out hunting, fell through the ice in a pond, the ice closed over him, he was lost. They had built themselves a small cabin for protection against the cold, but they woke every morning with their beds covered with frost. Most of the men had scorched or even burned their shoes by standing too close to the fire when they were outside; as a result they had no shoes, only rags to wrap their feet. Exposed skin froze instantly. All their axes were broken trying to cut down trees frozen hard as cement. They cut wood for their fires with pieces of hatchet attached to handles made to fit the broken fragments. Everything liquid froze, including oils. Snow covered their cabins to the roof lines. "Thus we lived," James writes, "in a heap and wilderness of snow."

Worst of all was the scurvy:

> We had three sorts of sick men. Those who were so sick that they couldn't move or roll over in their beds, but must be looked after like infants; those who were crippled as it were, with the aches of scurvy; and finally those who were sick with scurvy, but not yet crippled . . . [O]ur surgeon . . . would be at work early in the morning, picking the men's teeth, and cutting away the dead flesh from their gums.

All but the first sort of sick, those too weak to move at all, had to work, however long it took just to get out of bed. When they raised the ship they had to cut the ice out of the inside of it by hand. Four of the twenty-two men aboard died.

Again and again expeditions had begun in hope. Thomas James carried with him a letter from the king of England to the emperor of Japan, in case he found the Passage and sailed through to the Pacific. Again and again they ended in failure. Yet the enterprise was not abandoned. Only the first phase was over. Arctic winters might kill the men who braved them, but they did not kill English expectations for ultimate success. The Passage *had* to be there. National pride, in a sense, now demanded it.

Thomas James, to be sure, did not agree. "In all probability," he wrote at the end of his book, "there is no northwest passage to the south sea," that is, the Pacific, at least not through Hudson Bay. Tides and ice, he pointed out, move only into and out of Hudson Strait, and not in any other direction. Hudson Bay attracted no whales. James was one of those rare voices, the voice of experience. The prevailing winds were contrary, from the west. As for the ice, "it is easier," he said, "to sail 1000 leagues to the southward, around the Cape of Good Hope where the winds are constant, than 100 in these seas where you run the daily risk of losing your ship and your life." Above all, what would be the use of such a dangerous route as the Northwest Passage must clearly be? How often could ships get through, even if it were there? Even in the two best months for sailing, August and September, storms were common.

As for Hudson Bay, it was barren and worthless as far as James was concerned: "There are certainly no commercial benefits to be obtained in any of the places I visited during this voyage." On this point James was wrong. The next ship to enter Hudson Bay came in 1668, not to search for the Northwest Passage but to trade for furs with the local Cree. Two years later Charles II granted a royal charter to the Hudson's Bay Company, which went on to become one of the great monopolies of all time, a consistently profitable enterprise that still exists and still thrives.

CHAPTER FOUR

AN OBJECT PECULIARLY BRITISH

After Thomas James's voyage, Great Britain lost interest in the Northwest Passage for close to a century. One reason may have been James's own pessimism about whether there was such a passage. But other reasons are more likely. Even though the seventeenth century saw an enormous expansion in English travel and trade, the drive to explore faded away in England, as it did all across Europe for that matter. Partly this was a consequence of the very expansion in trade. Up to 1630, especially among the northern European countries, exploration had been a product of commercial interests looking for trading opportunities. Now the success of the East India Company and the growth of British colonies in North America opened up those opportunities. British sailors now freely ranged global trading routes, and books of voyages and travel became one of the most popular genres in British publishing. It was no longer necessary to worry about the lack of access to the Orient; access had been won. The East India Company was competing with Dutch traders in Indonesia and Malaysia and founding a trading settlement at Surat in India. Britain was gaining a foothold in the slave trade. British colonies in the West Indies and along the North American coast were growing rapidly. It could hardly have seemed pressing to go off on expensive, unprofitable quests into the ice.

Great Britain was being pulled apart as well by religious turmoil. In the seventeenth century Britain witnessed the decapitation of its king and a civil war. Protestant was ranged against Roman Catholic, the Church of England against Dissenters of all kinds. There were wars to fight with France, with Spain, with the Dutch. A large and tumultuous history was hurrying forward. In 1662 Charles II granted a charter to the

Royal Society, the nation's first scientific organization. Isaac Newton published his studies in the calculus. At the end of the century the English astronomer Edmund Halley made the world's first voyage for purely scientific purposes, sailing a small ship known as a "pink" and named the *Paramore* into the South Atlantic to chart magnetic variations. The only sign that anybody was paying attention to the Northwest Passage during this period was the aforementioned notice by Joseph Moxon, Charles II's hydrographer, published in the *Transactions* of the Royal Society in 1675, arguing for a free and open sea at the North Pole.

Only the Hudson's Bay Company was on the scene, so to speak, where it might have made sense to keep up a search for the Northwest Passage, but the company showed no interest whatsoever in exploration. It did not even explore its own lands: by its charter the HBC owned all the land draining into the bay. Was it curious about this land? Not at all. After establishing trading forts along the south and west coasts of Hudson Bay, it settled into the business of trading furs and making money. Supply ships came once a year, bringing trade goods and taking out furs to be turned into hats and coats in Europe. Some of the traders, or factors as they were called, wintered over; and every "factory" had its resident Indians, living outside the posts on the largesse of the company. In the spring, when the rivers opened up, the Cree and other tribes brought their furs to the factories to exchange for blankets, shirts, iron pots, axes, guns, knives. Occasionally the company sent men into the interior, but not far. "To be allowed to trade in comfortable obscurity," says historian Glyn Williams, "was the height of their ambition." The HBC wanted only to grow rich.

When exploration did resume toward the end of the seventeenth century it was conducted not by explorers per se, men bent on filling in the huge empty spaces on the map of the earth, but—in England at least—by pirates and buccaneers, men like Shelvocke, Clipperton, Woodes Rogers, and the most famous of them all, William Cecil Dampier. Dampier operated mostly in the little-known Pacific, trying to intercept the Spanish treasure ship that sailed annually between Manila and Acapulco, but he was as much an explorer as a pirate, he had an excellent mind, and he circled the world three times. He wrote well too, and his accounts of his exploits became best sellers and did much to spark a resumption of the old English enthusiasm for exploration.

In the North, in somewhat the same spirit, a man who also had treasure on his mind proposed in 1719 to the HBC that the company sponsor a voyage to look once more for the Northwest Passage—and also to follow up on rumors of gold lying on the ground for the taking in the virgin wilds of northern Canada. This would-be explorer was one James Knight, then sixty years old, who had been an HBC employee, captaining HBC ships making the run between England and Hudson Bay every year. Since it was still totally uncharacteristic of the company to sponsor exploration, it is a testimony to Knight's powers of persuasion that it agreed to become involved. But gold may have had something to do with it. During his years at the company, Knight had listened perhaps too many times to a Chipewyan woman who told him about the yellow metal to be found along a river that was also the site of copper deposits—presumably the Coppermine, which empties into the Arctic Ocean east of the Mackenzie. This metal "is very Yellow Soft & heavy and . . . they find Lumps so bigg sometimes that they hammer it betwixt Stones and make dishes of it." Here was an idea to stagger the imagination of any European, even a stuffy, conservative HBC director: illiterate savages eating their caribou steaks off gold dinner plates.

Knight left the mouth of the Thames in June 1719 in command of two ships, the *Albany* and the *Discovery*, and forty men, including a group of miners. Two company supply ships sailed with them to Hudson Bay, then turned south to the company factories. Knight continued to sail west, in the direction of the bay's west coast. That was the last anybody saw of them. Pieces of masts, an ice pole, a medicine chest, and other items of European make were found in subsequent years on a small island known as Marble Island, just south of Chesterfield Inlet. The HBC never made any attempt to search for survivors and wrote off the expedition. Glyn Williams quotes an early company critic to the effect that "some of the Company said upon this occasion that they did not value the loss of the ship and sloop as long as they were rid of those troublesome men." An Inuit informant told the explorer Samuel Hearne in the 1740s that the last survivors had spent their final days at a lookout scanning the horizon for a sail—a touching story, if true. Modern searches have discovered the remains of a building and numerous artifacts on Marble Island, making it clear that the expedition had probably spent at least one winter on the island. The search for bones stretched into the 1990s. What happened to Knight and his men still ranks as one of the great unsolved mysteries of the Arctic. The HBC had tried to keep Knight's expedition a secret before it left England. It did not inform the public of the fact when it vanished. The artifacts subsequently discovered on Marble Island do not include any journals, or an inscribed plank or piece of wood, or a record of any kind.

Knight's attempt to find the Northwest Passage must be regarded as a quixotic adventure with little more behind it than one man's overactive imagination. Within a decade or so, however, the dream of finding it would arise again, and decisively this time. The dreamer was altogether unexpected, not a mariner like Knight or an English merchant, and certainly not the Admiralty, but a member of the Irish Parliament named Arthur Dobbs. Dobbs was Anglo-Irish, one of the landed gentry, ambitious and smart and the author of a highly respected tract on Irish trade. In 1730 he engineered an introduction to Sir Robert Walpole, the powerful and notoriously Machiavellian prime minister, who took an interest in him.

Shortly after that Dobbs turned his attention to the Northwest Passage, for reasons that remain obscure. He made a study of the literature of the Passage, reading the expedition accounts of a hundred and more years earlier. From this, he wrote, he developed "a very strong reason to believe there is a Passage." The spirit of *it has to be there* clearly had not died. Dobbs wanted to revive British interest in the subject and thought the British should sponsor a voyage of discovery. It would forestall, he said, French expansion in northern Canada, which might lead to the French discovering the Passage. He sent his proposal to Walpole, having already secured the support of the lord-lieutenant of Ireland, the British government official who ran the country. The Board of Trade, a governmental organization, decided to support the idea and forwarded the proposal to the Admiralty with its blessing. Lord Wager, first lord of the Admiralty at the time, smiled on the proposal and referred it to the Hudson's Bay Company. Wonderful idea, Sir Bibye Lake, director of the HBC, told Dobbs. According to Dobbs's biographer, Sir Bibye "promised Dobbs he would use his influence and request the Company to undertake a voyage of discovery as soon as conditions and circumstances permitted."

It need hardly be added that "conditions and circumstances" never seemed to permit anything like an exploring expedition at the HBC, but Dobbs was a persistent man. The fate of the Knight expedition, which the HBC told him about at this time, did not discourage him. Repeated visits to the HBC offices in London finally elicited a promise that the company would send its trading sloops farther up the west coast of Hudson Bay than it had in the past and scout out the coastline for a possible entrance to the Passage. Doing so was in fact dangerous, however, and Sir Bibye's promises were basically a stall. The coast was little known and seldom entirely free of ice even in summer, while the Inuit to the north were thought to be unpredictable and possibly violent. The company may have seemed recalcitrant to the point of cowardice, but with three-quarters of a century of experience in the field it understood the difficulties and the cold in a way that somebody like Dobbs could barely imagine. The only window of opportunity for a voyage of any kind was the months of August and September. In the event, company sloops never did make a meaningful attempt to explore to the north; nor did any of the factors handling affairs on the ground at their posts along Hudson Bay show any interest in pursuing the idea.

While he waited Dobbs maintained contact with a group of prominent London merchants and discussed with them the possibility of creating a second company to search for the Passage in Hudson Bay, in partnership, they hoped, with the HBC. Dobbs contacted Christopher Middleton, a captain in the HBC's service, and asked him if he would be interested in leading an expedition to find the Passage. Middleton was supportive of the idea but declined the chance, so Dobbs took things one step further. Convinced by now—he had been pursuing this subject since 1731, and it was now 1739—that the HBC would never undertake an expedition, he attacked the company publicly. It was, in fact, an easy target. Despite the company's obsessive secrecy, the leading London merchants were well aware that the HBC was making large amounts of money from its monopoly, and there could be no doubt that French fur traders were becoming more and more active in the Canadian North. The company's failure even to venture inland, not to mention up the coast above Marble Island, was indefensible.

In the end Dobbs got what he wanted, not a company but an Admiralty expedition. Early in 1740 Lord Wager, nearing the end of his tenure as first lord, mentioned the project to the king, George II. "His majesty," he reported, "seemed to approve it very well, and said that the Expence was such a Trifle, that it should not be obstructed on that Account." In 1741 Christopher Middleton, the same HBC captain Dobbs had approached some years before, left the HBC, was given a commission in the Royal Navy, and set out with two small ships for Hudson Bay purely for the purpose of searching once more for the Northwest Passage. Only twice before had the Royal Navy taken an active role in exploring the world.

Middleton's voyage was like so many previous exploring voyages to

the North, and so many to follow: unpromising. As a Royal Navy captain he had the authority now to press seamen off the streets or out of
taverns or wherever he found them, but he had trouble putting a crew
together nevertheless and left late in the season. By the time he got to
Hudson Bay it was too late to explore, so he wintered over at a Hudson's
Bay Company post. The Admiralty had ordered the company to cooperate, which it reluctantly did, but food supplies were low and the winter was severe. By the end of it ten of Middleton's men had died the
horrible death of scurvy. The ships had been frozen into docks cut out of
the permafrost along the shore. The ice surrounding them was ten feet
thick. The snow on top of the ice was thirteen feet deep. It took more
than two months in the spring to hack them free. This had to be done
by hand, with hatchets, the men lying full length on the ice chipping
away at it under the hulls. Then the mosquitoes came. They were as
thick, as inescapable as fog. Says Glyn Williams, describing the circumstances, "A bushel of mosquitoes might be swept off a hunter as he
emerged from the woods, and [then] they had to be shoveled off the
ground before a door could be opened."

Not until July could the ships actually leave Fort Churchill for the
north. They sailed four hundred miles up the west coast of the bay into
a funnel-shaped strait, Sir Thomas Roe's Welcome, that separates
Southampton Island from the mainland. It was clogged with ice. They
came to a headland that Middleton named after Arthur Dobbs, then
took refuge in a large inlet he named for Sir George Wager. Large
inlets raised questions. Was this one perhaps the entrance to the Passage? They sent boats up to find out. Although they did not actually
reach the end of the inlet, the water toward what they presumed to be
the end was fresh. The Pacific Ocean, of course, was salt water, so they
turned around. The tides, furthermore, rose and fell only a few feet.
Tides would rise much more than that, they believed, in an oceanic
environment. They left the inlet and sailed farther north, where the
strait got narrower and narrower. They reached another headland and
beyond it saw open water. The sea! The sea! The next day the haze
cleared and the open water turned out to be another bay. Repulse Bay,
they named it, their disappointment obvious in the name. They
climbed a high hill to investigate the landscape. To the north lay land
that came to bear the name Melville Peninsula. To the south and east,
Southampton Island, already named. Along its north shore lay another
strait, separating it from land that might have been more islands visible

in the distance. It was frozen solid, so they called it Frozen Strait. It was now early August. Half of Middleton's men were sick with scurvy again. Wisely, he backed out of Sir Thomas Roe's Welcome and set sail for England.

Only a man obsessed could have turned such a pronounced failure into victory, but that is what Arthur Dobbs had become, obsessed, John Barrow *avant le lettre,* so to speak, and he did to Middleton something like what Barrow did to John Ross in 1819. In Dobbs's eyes Middleton had not sailed *all the way* into Wager Inlet. He had not thoroughly investigated the coast on his way north. Dobbs found or bought men among Middleton's crew who were willing to testify that Middleton got the tides wrong and that Frozen Strait, the iced-up body of water between Melville Peninsula and Southampton Island, did not exist. Dobbs forced the Admiralty to investigate Middleton, who was not, after all, one of its own. Dobbs took to his pen and waged a pamphlet war against him that went on for well over a year. He offered the public a map of the region, based partly on vague Cree accounts of the territory, Cree tales of a great sea to the west, and wishful thinking of his own, that had the "unknown coast" of an ocean—the Pacific Ocean—waiting to be explored within a few hundred miles of Hudson Bay. The map was worthy of a Renaissance geographer, just as fanciful, just as wrong. The northwestern coast of North America dropped precipitously to the southwest from the top of Hudson Bay and became "Part of California." Between Hudson Bay and the top of this coast were several vaguely delineated straits. One of them was the not quite fully explored Wager Inlet. Another was at the head of Repulse Bay.

Propaganda once more trumped experience and Dobbs's ceaseless efforts to belittle Middleton's findings and promote his own had their effect. He was, after all, an able man. He had a successful political career, becoming Surveyor-General of Ireland and a major figure in Irish trade. He would become governor of colonial North Carolina in the 1750s. Like John Barrow after him, he had studied the history of attempts to find the Northwest Passage and seemed to know what he was talking about. Whatever experienced mariners might think of the possibility of a Northwest Passage, Dobbs managed to turn the public and the merchant class in his favor. In 1745, at Dobbs's urging, a group of London merchants submitted a petition to Parliament asking the government to establish a reward for discovering the Northwest Passage. A committee was formed to investigate the idea, and it duly heard witnesses and filed a report. The report largely repeated Dobbs's arguments for the existence of the Passage in Hudson Bay. Parliament said yes, to the tune (or rather the symphony) of twenty thousand English pounds. This was the reward that John Barrow was able to have renewed, under expanded terms, in 1818.

An Act of Parliament put a stamp on things. If Parliament approved of an enterprise, surely it was worthwhile. Its immediate effect was to enable Dobbs to get up another expedition, this one financed by subscription, the subscribers to receive the benefits of the new reward in proportion to their contribution. Two ships, again, were to make the voyage. Dobbs wrote their sailing instructions himself, telling them to try Wager Inlet again, or some other opening they were sure to find. If the tide flowed from the west "you may depend on having an open and large Passage, as the Ocean cannot be far distant." Once through to the ocean, they were to spend the winter on some "Part of California" in ease and warmth, then spend the next summer exploring the California coastline. That his instructions depended on huge assumptions for which there was no evidence whatsoever never seemed to occur to him. No European in the 1740s knew anything at all about the Pacific coast north of Baja California. News of Vitus Bering's expedition to Alaska had yet to reach Europe. Asia might extend all the way to North America, might connect with it. There might not be a Northwest Passage.

No matter. The English public found the enterprise quite exciting. Glyn Williams quotes John Campbell, a compiler of voyage accounts, who said that the enterprise was "the Topic of common Discourse, and of almost universal Expectation." The craze for the Passage spread to Europe, which followed the developments with great interest. Dobbs had pulled this rusty old gun out of the cabinet of British maritime history, and it still worked.

The expedition left London in May 1746. There were, as always, two ships, the *Dobbs Galley* and the hopefully named *California.* It took them a full month to get through Hudson Strait, which is only two hundred miles long. Ice. They had little time left for exploring and did little of it. They spent the winter, once again, at a company fort, this one York Factory, farther south than Churchill. This time seven men died of scurvy. The captains of the two ships quarreled; relationships between the two crews deteriorated. The two captains continued their quarrel all through the explorations of the following summer. Once more men climbed hills to look for open sea to the west and saw only lakes. They found another inlet, Chesterfield Inlet, but failed to sail to the end of it, leaving open yet another possibility for the Passage. They did, however, reach the end of Wager Inlet. It was a cul-de-sac. With the cold approaching, their crews sick, and absolutely nothing accomplished, they gave up. They sailed for England.

One would think this outcome would have been decisive. There was no Passage here. Hudson Bay was a dead end. But it was not decisive. Henry Ellis wrote one of the two accounts of the expedition and concluded that, although they had not discovered a Northwest Passage,

> yet were we so far from discovering the impossibility or even improbability of it, that, on the contrary, we returned with clearer and fuller proofs, founded on the only evidence that ought to take place in an inquiry of this nature,—plain facts and accurate experiments, that evidently shew such a passage there may be.

When John Barrow came to write his history of the search for the Northwest Passage in 1818, this cheerfully hopeful, completely unwarranted conclusion was the only part of Ellis's account that he quoted at any length. The "plain facts" consisted primarily of tidal measurements, which were, since the nature of tides was so little understood at the time, meaningless.

But a die had been cast, a corner turned. It happens sometimes that events gather momentum and then cannot be stopped, even under the most discouraging circumstances. We may have reached that point in the history of the Northwest Passage, here in the 1740s, when Parliament established its reward and the voyages Arthur Dobbs inspired were being talked about so widely. Continuous failure can be explained away when the underlying drive to succeed is strong enough. The fire that flickered out in 1631 had been reignited. The British people were once again warming their hands at the prospect of a Northwest Passage.

But not in Hudson Bay. Interest shifted now to the Pacific Ocean, for if there was a Northwest Passage it would have to exit in the Pacific somewhere on the west coast of North America, and that coast was completely unknown. For all anyone knew Dobbs could have been right—the Pacific coastline might indeed lie a mere couple of hundred miles west of Hudson Bay. The publicity given Dobbs's second set of voyages to Hudson Bay had excited all maritime Europe. Finding the western exit to the Passage now became a race among empires. If the British found it first, the threat to Spain, with its overextended claims in the Pacific, was obvious. Spain claimed the western coast of North America as far as it went, however far that might be. If the Spanish found the Passage first, they could conceivably enforce their claim, send ships to this western entrance, build forts, and close it off to other powers. The French for their part were almost as eager to find it as the English, as a means of expanding their North American fur trade to the shores of the Pacific. The great European empires could no longer ignore this ancient geographical problem.

As for Hudson Bay, not for another sixty years would anyone sail into it again specifically to look for the Passage, but it was not forgotten as a potential route. Even the Hudson's Bay Company had been startled out of its torpor. It began to send its own men into the interior more frequently, and to greater distances, not so much to explore but to persuade tribes farther inland to trade. Meanwhile the French fur trappers who had been moving north and west aggressively since the early 1700s continued to do so until the end of the Seven Years' War in 1763, when France lost Canada to the British.

Vitus Bering's discoveries upped the ante still further. Bering came to North America from a totally unexpected place—Asia. A Dane who was sailing for the tsar, he discovered Alaska in 1741, and over the next decades small numbers of Russian fur traders set up posts there, then gradually moved farther down the Pacific Coast. News filtered out of Russia slowly, but when Spain found out what was happening, it grew alarmed at this encroachment. In the 1780s the Spanish began to send expeditions north to intercept the Russians. They were worried for two reasons now—the French or British might discover the Northwest Passage; and Russia might lay claim to the Northwest Coast. They continued to send ships north up the coast to the end of the eighteenth century, exploring it, searching for signs of the Northwest Passage, and trying to defend what they thought was theirs even though they lacked the manpower to occupy it.

They were too late; the Spanish Empire was fading away. On Captain Cook's last voyage in 1778 he explored the west coast of Canada in search of the back end of the Northwest Passage and stumbled across the sea otter trade. The Chinese would pay large sums for sea otter pelts, and the Haida and other Northwest Coast tribes were eager to trade them for a nail, a knife—any piece of iron. Spectacular profits were there to be made, and were made. Many a Boston magnate owed his Back Bay mansion to the trade in sea otter skins.

After Cook, then, came the merchants, and after them the explorer George Vancouver. Setting sail in 1791, Vancouver made a detailed survey of the entire Northwest Coast. The Royal Navy was now conducting these explorations. Trade was always the goal, but it was now seen as a national goal, a function of empire, not something to be left to individual merchants or merchant companies. Vancouver established to almost everyone's satisfaction that no Strait of Anián or any facsimile thereof cut across the North American continent, emptying into the Pacific below Alaska. The coastline was full of bays and inlets, some of them large, but none led deep inland. Alaska was not an island. Cook had sailed far enough north through Bering Strait to establish as well that the northern coast of Alaska stood above the Arctic Circle. A detailed outline of North America was on the charts at last. Only the northern coast of Canada lay undiscovered, and Samuel Hearne and Alexander Mackenzie had reached the Arctic Ocean via the interior of northern Canada at latitudes comparable to Cook's farthest north in the Bering Sea. It was now apparent that if the Northwest Passage existed, it would have to be in the polar basin, and that anyone who discovered it would have to sail around the top of Alaska, where ice had stopped even the great Captain Cook.

This was the world, then, as John Barrow understood it at the end of the Napoleonic Wars. Barrow's book about the history of Arctic exploration, *A Chronological History of Voyages into the Arctic Regions,* came out in 1818, just as the Ross and Buchan expeditions were leaving to explore those regions. On the map he printed in his book it's all there, the known and the unknown—white space above eighty degrees north everywhere, while below eighty degrees only parts of the Arctic have been sketched in. He had read all the polar exploration accounts to write his book, and he knew the record of continuous failure quite well. Repeatedly, invariably, for the previous three hundred years, ships had come to the end of their voyages at the edge of the ice. The "seventh clime" of the ancients was a forbidding place; the ice was as hard as stone and as sharp as steel. It could tear right through a ship's sides. It spread to the horizon.

But Barrow was the second secretary of the Admiralty; he had the power to make things happen, so it was the map inside his head that counted—that, and his ambition, and his attitude toward ice. In the last respect his book is quite revealing. Not only did he believe in an open polar sea, he tended to think that previous explorers had lacked the fortitude to discover it. At the same time that he attacked Thomas James for complaining too much about the hardships he and his men endured in James Bay in 1630–31, he came down heavily on Luke Foxe for not exploring northward in Foxe Basin that same year, calmly ignoring the fact that ice had prevented Foxe from getting into Foxe Basin. Throughout the book he belittled every failed voyage, every calamity, every piece of evidence that would have persuaded a more disinterested observer that the Arctic was impassable. Explorers in Barrow's book shamefully lose heart. They do not go far enough, are not persistent enough. He ended the book with a brief account of an 1815 voyage by the Russian explorer Otto von Kotzebue, who looked for the western entrance of the Northwest Passage above Bering Strait and discovered instead Kotzebue Sound. For Barrow this was calamitous. How could it be that a *Russian* had picked up this sword? That could not be allowed to happen. "It is sufficiently evident," he wrote, from the history of Arctic exploration he had just summarized, "that the discovery of a north-west passage to India and China has always been considered as an object peculiarly British."

"There is," Robert Thorne had written in 1527, "no land unhabitable, nor Sea innavigable." Thorne's self-assurance on the matter had survived; it was one of John Barrow's core beliefs. Ice formed in bays and along coastlines, but in the open sea ice could not form. The constant motion of the water, the ocean swell, and the salt in the water, which lowered its freezing point, would prevent ice from forming. Never mind that William Scoresby had *watched* it form. What did William Scoresby know? He was a mere whaler, not a geographer.

Scoresby amused his sailors from time to time by taking clear pieces of polar ice out of the water and shaping them into lenses, then using these lenses to concentrate the rays of the sun and light their pipes, set fire to wood, even melt lead—without affecting the lens itself, which remained cold to the touch. In his 1820 book *An Account of the Arctic Regions,* Scoresby, who knew the history of Arctic exploration perhaps as well as Barrow, remarks, "It has been advanced as a maxim, that *what we wish to be true, we readily believe:*—a maxim which, however doubtful in general, has met with a full illustration in the northern voyages of discovery." He does not say so, but it is highly likely he was referring to John Barrow's book.

To a situation so pregnant with ironies, the temptation to add more is difficult to resist. In the same year, 1818, that John Ross and David Buchan set out on the first two expeditions to renew the search for a northern route to the Orient and that John Barrow published *A Chronological History*, Mary Shelley published her first novel, *Frankenstein, or the Modern Prometheus*. It is written in the voice of an English explorer named Walton who at the outset of the book is mounting his own private expedition to the North Pole, hoping to find the passage to Asia and confident he is sailing toward paradise. "I try in vain," he writes his sister,

> to be persuaded that the pole is the seat of frost and desolation; it ever presents itself to my imagination as the region of beauty and delight . . . I will put some trust in preceding navigators—there snow and frost are banished; and, sailing over a calm sea, we may be wafted to a land surpassing in wonders and in beauty every region hitherto discovered on the habitable globe.

By the end of the book, after Walton has encountered Dr. Frankenstein and his monster pursuing each other across the ice and they have each, separately, told him their dreadful story, the situation has changed dramatically. The ice now has Walton in its claws and is about to destroy him. "I am surrounded by mountains of ice," he writes his sister again, "which admit of no escape, and threaten every moment to crush my vessel. The brave fellows, whom I have persuaded to be my companions, look towards me for aid; but I have none to bestow. . . . If we are lost, my mad schemes are the cause."

First Secretary of the Admiralty John Wilson Croker, his name about to be temporarily bestowed on the mountains made of fog and pusillanimity that Captain Ross saw at the bottom of Lancaster Sound, reviewed the book for *The Quarterly*. Croker conceded that the writing had vigor but called it in other respects "a tissue of horrible and disgusting absurdity." Poor Croker. He was as wrong about Mary Shelley as he was about John Keats. He does not comment in his review on the fact that Shelley used an Arctic voyage as a frame for her story, but it is evident what Shelley was thinking. She had grown up in an intellectual household surrounded by books, she had read deep into books of voyages and travel, and she had taken from them quite a different lesson from the lessons John Barrow took. Men start out, blithely and idealistically, without thinking of the consequences, on enterprises fraught with danger and rich with the potential to go horribly wrong. Dr. Victor Frankenstein's all-too-successful attempt to reanimate dead flesh was one such enterprise. Expeditions to the Arctic were another.

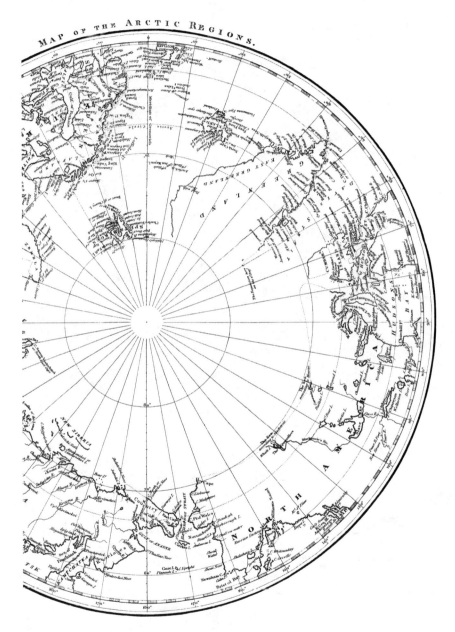

John Barrow's 1818 map of the known Arctic

(Source: John Barrow, *A Chronological History of Voyages Into the Arctic Regions*, 1818.)

Sir John Franklin in the 1830s
(Scott Polar Research Institute)

II

Northern Gothic

No fear can stand up to hunger, no patience can wear it out, disgust simply does not exist where hunger is, and as to superstition, beliefs, and what you might call principles, they are less than chaff in a breeze.

—Joseph Conrad, *Heart of Darkness*

CHAPTER FIVE

O CANADA

John Ross's voyage had made it plain that Lancaster Sound was the door to the Northwest Passage if there were such a door, and Barrow lost no time in opening it. Hardly had the two initial 1818 expeditions returned before he ordered Lieutenant Parry to sail back to Lancaster Sound the following year. He was to proceed to the sound directly, without wasting time on the straits to the north that Ross had said were iced up.

Parry had his problems crossing Davis Strait, which is often clogged with pack ice drifting south until quite late in the season, but he did reach Lancaster Sound a month earlier in the summer than Ross had. It was at the end of July, not the end of August, 1819, that Lieutenant Parry sailed through the "Croker Mountains," which left him plenty of time to continue west and see where these waters led.

But Barrow was not content to launch just one expedition to search for the Passage. The very possibility of a route depended not only on the polar seas being free of ice but also on the location and nature of the north coast of Canada. Only two white men had ever seen this coast, Samuel Hearne in 1772 and Alexander Mackenzie in 1793, at the mouths of widely separated rivers, and their accounts of their discoveries were thought to be not terribly reliable. Barrow wanted to explore that coast and map it. He saw his pair of expeditions as a kind of pincer movement on this unknown geography. He would send Parry by sea, approaching it through Lancaster Sound, while the second expedition, under the command of John Franklin, would come by land; it would start from one of the Hudson's Bay Company forts on the west coast of Hudson Bay, follow whatever the best route might be to the mouth of the Coppermine

River, then turn east to map the coast. Or else, conversely, Franklin might travel up the west coast of Hudson Bay to find the northeastern corner of North America, and then sail west to the Coppermine.

William Scoresby believed all along that the best way to find the Passage was to send a mapping expedition to northern Canada, and Barrow may have gotten the idea from him, although he would never have deigned to acknowledge the debt. Barrow went so far as to express the hope in the instructions he wrote for both expeditions that at some point along this coast the two of them would meet, Parry arriving by sea, Franklin along the Canadian shore. It is a pretty thought, two British sailors meeting in a wilderness of cold thousands of miles from civilization. Failing that, they could at least set up cairns for the other to find.

Parry was a natural choice to lead another voyage into Baffin Bay and through Lancaster Sound. It was Parry who had told Barrow that Ross had been wrong, that there had been no Croker Mountains and no need to turn for home, Parry whom Ross had reprimanded for questioning his judgment earlier in the voyage. Parry and Barrow had become allies; it was close to inevitable that Barrow would call upon Parry to lead ships back to Lancaster Sound.

John Franklin was another matter. Heavyset and not very fit, he had no known qualifications for leading a land expedition across some of the most brutal terrain in the world. He was by all reports a nice, charming, likable man, he had performed well off Spitzbergen with Buchan, and he had demonstrated in battle that he was brave. Matthew Flinders had taught him the art of navigation and his skills were first rate. But David Buchan had led an expedition into the interior of Newfoundland, and Buchan, senior to Franklin, was not offered the job. His career subsided into obscurity, while John Franklin would become one of Great Britain's most famous men.

Franklin's charm could have had something to do with the choice. It does not emerge from his correspondence, where he expresses the most conventional sentiments in the deadest prose, but people did like him and used the word *nice* about him frequently, not a common epithet for a military man. The occasional need to punish seamen under his command, according to one of his biographers, left him full of anxiety. He had difficulty watching when someone was flogged. Much more important than his charm, however, would have been the fact that Franklin was enthusiastic about exploration. The son of a successful grocer in Spilsby, a village in Lincolnshire, and one of twelve children, he had shown an early aptitude for the sea and joined the navy at fourteen as a "volunteer," a rank below midshipman and the first step on the career naval officer's ladder. He was the nephew by marriage of Matthew Flinders and via that connection landed a place on the *Investigator*, sailing with Flinders on his exploration of the southern coast of Australia in 1802 and his subsequent circumnavigation of that continent which demonstrated that it was a continent, and not a group of islands.

That was an exciting trip. Flinders ran aground on the Great Barrier Reef, marooning the expedition on a sandbar that was fifty feet wide and nine hundred long, two hundred miles from land. Sydney, the only place from which they could hope for rescue, was eight hundred miles away. Flinders left for Sydney in a six-oared ship's boat with thirteen men while the rest of the crew made camp as best they could, living on the provisions they had been able to rescue from the ship. Six weeks later Flinders was back to the rescue on a merchant vessel headed for Canton, China, accompanied by two cutters. Franklin found himself on the merchant ship, while Flinders headed for England on one of the cutters. Flinders had monumentally bad luck. On its voyage home the cutter stopped in Mauritius, which was held by the French, for repairs. The Peace of Amiens had failed, France and Britain were at war again, which Flinders did not know, and the French commander detained Flinders as a prisoner for the next six years and confiscated most of his papers. This was extremely bad form. Nations at war normally left explorers and scientists alone. Plagued with bad health, it took Flinders four years, after he at last got back to England, to prepare his charts and his account of the voyage for publication. He died in 1814 on the day the book appeared.

Franklin by then had long since returned to England. He had good luck, a knack for being in the right place at the right time. On his return from Canton he had traveled in a convoy of lightly armed merchant ships that bluffed, engaged, and finally chased off a heavily armed French squadron on patrol in the Strait of Malacca. This coup got triumphant attention in the British press. Franklin had no sooner joined the Navy as a boy than he found himself on the *Polyphemous*, a ship of the line under the command of a Captain Lawford and sailing in Nelson's squadron, in the middle of the Battle of Copenhagen. This was one of the fiercest naval battles in the Napoleonic Wars. Nelson added to his legend in this battle when Sir Hyde Parker, the admiral in command of the fleet, advised him by flag signal to retire from the action. The one-eyed Nelson clapped his telescope to his blind eye and "failed" to notice the message, carrying on the fight for another hour until all the Danish ships engaged were taken or destroyed.

Twelve hundred British seamen died in that battle. Franklin himself was not injured. Years later he told a relative that he recalled looking into the clear and shallow waters of the sound and seeing dead bodies littering the bottom.

He had no sooner returned from Copenhagen than he was transferred to Flinders's exploring expedition to Australia; he had hardly returned from Australia before he was on board the *Bellerophon*, on blockade duty along the coast of France. Franklin was eighteen in 1804 and still a signal midshipman. Blockade duty was famously dull, but after a year of it, in October 1805, Nelson was able to engage the combined French and Spanish fleets at Trafalgar off the coast of Spain in the decisive naval battle of the war. The *Bellerophon* sailed into the thick of it, fighting at close quarters with four French and Spanish ships, so close that its spars entangled with those of *L'Aigle,* a French seventy-four-gun ship of the line. *L'Aigle* had taller sides than the *Bellerophon,,* allowing French soldiers to line the rails of their ship and climb into the shrouds to fire on the British sailors below. Forty of the forty-seven men on the quarterdeck of the *Bellerophon* were wounded or killed, including the captain. On the poop deck, Franklin's station, another midshipman was shot dead while Franklin was talking to him. Franklin, seeing that the same sniper was now aiming at him, stepped behind a mast just before the bullet hit the deck beside him. The two ships were so close that the cannon crews could grab each other's ramrods. With swords and axes English sailors chopped at the hands of French soldiers trying to board over the rails and sent dozens of them into the sea to drown. The noise of the cannons made Franklin half deaf for the rest of his life. But otherwise Franklin was intact. Men had died all around him and hundreds had been wounded, but not him.

It was an impressive record for such a young man: exploration, shipwreck, and two of the major naval battles in English history. He was promoted to lieutenant in 1807 at the age of twenty-one and spent most of the rest of the war, as did the Royal Navy itself, on blockade duty, with an interval in Brazil, where his ship danced attendance on the exiled prince regent of Portugal, that nation being in Napoleon's hands. In December 1814, at the end of the War of 1812 between Britain and the United States, he saw action in the Battle of New Orleans, where he was wounded in the shoulder. A year later, in the fall of 1815, the wars over, he was paid off, along with most of the rest of the navy, and went home to live with his family. By this time he had made first lieutenant and was nearly thirty years old. He would now have to live on half-pay.

Why Franklin? Why was he chosen to take command of the *Trent* and sail under Buchan toward the North Pole in 1818 over hundreds, thousands of other navy officers living poor and eager for assignments? Since joining the navy he had performed well; he had sailed to Australia with Flinders; he had fought in historic battles; and he had learned the arts of navigation and command. But many others were just as qualified. He was likable, but that by itself would never have been enough. What counted most in obtaining assignments was "interest"— a man's connections. (This system survives in the United States in the requirement that applicants to the national military academies obtain a letter of recommendation from a congressman.) Franklin apparently had connections. Flinders was dead and could not help him, but in 1814, soon after Flinders died, he had written his friend Robert Brown, the naturalist on the Australian expedition, that he would welcome an assignment on an exploring expedition, with the hope, he added, that it would be "accompanied by promotion." He had already applied to the Admiralty for promotion on his own and been turned down. It was no use to apply again. He waited three long, idle years in Spilsby. Then came 1818 and salvation: the command of the *Trent*. When it was about to depart he wrote one of his sisters about the many scientists who were visiting the ships with all kinds of questions they wanted answered on these explorations. "It really seems quite ridiculous to find myself among these parties, when I consider how little I know of the matters which usually form the subject of their conversations," he said. "At present, however, the bare circumstance of going to the North Pole is a sufficient passport anywhere. What a fortunate person must I . . . consider myself to be to have it, and thankful indeed to my good friends who procured it for me!"

Who his good friends were, alas, he does not go on to say, but Robert Brown was almost certainly one of them. Brown was close to Sir Joseph Banks, and the Franklin family was known to Banks. If Banks was behind Franklin, that would have been all the recommendation John Barrow needed.

It was probably his go-for-it attitude on the *Trent* that got him the second assignment. Barrow liked spirited, ambitious men; he liked his explorers to be enthusiastic. Barrow clearly believed that being an officer in the Royal Navy qualified a man all by itself to explore by land or by sea. Having won total command of the seas, the officers of the Royal Navy were, men like Barrow and most Britons believed, qualified to do just about anything. In 1805, when the first lord handed Admiral Nelson a list of officers and asked him to choose among them, Nelson handed it back and said, "Choose yourself, my Lord. The same spirit actuates the whole profession. You cannot choose wrong."

No record survives of the send-off Franklin received on this expedition to northern Canada. Probably there was none. Parry had left with the usual crowds lining the wharves several days earlier, but Franklin and the five men with him were sailing on the first of the annual supply ships that the Hudson's Bay Company sent to York Factory, their post at the mouth of the Hayes River on the southwestern coast of Hudson Bay. The routine departures of company ships attracted little or no attention. Franklin was already a public figure of sorts, however. In 1819, at the Leicester Square Panorama in London, Henry Aston Barker had mounted a panorama celebrating the voyage of the *Dorothea* and the *Trent* the year before to Spitzbergen. Panoramas were the IMAX theaters of their time, huge paintings covering all 360 degrees of the inside of a circular room; the viewers stood in the middle of the room to see it. This one showed Franklin and Buchan on a beach at Spitzbergen talking over their situation after the storm that nearly destroyed both ships. Franklin must have posed for his portrait, because he mentions in a letter that he had seen the painting when it was half-finished. But he had no appetite for public notice of the vulgar sort. "I shall not venture," he wrote his sister Isabella, "to approach very near Leicester Square, for fear the passers-by should say, 'There goes the fellow in the panorama.'" But then he adds, clearly pleased, "I have just heard that Sir Joseph Banks has seen it, and approves of it highly." That was all the public attention Franklin wanted.

Franklin had only five men with him when they left but it was not planned as a small expedition. He expected to hire more when he got to Canada, men to man canoes and carry supplies, and men to guide him. Three of the five were officers—John Richardson, a surgeon, who was Franklin's age, thirty-three, and would become one of his closest friends; and George Back and Robert Hood, both midshipmen in their early twenties. Richardson was also a trained naturalist, an avocation physicians often took up in the eighteenth and nineteenth centuries. Franklin may have asked for Back, who served under him on the *Trent*. Hood and Back were both competent artists; that was one reason they were chosen. It was common in the days before photography to send artists with explorers in order to record the landscape and draw animals, plants, and native inhabitants. Wealthy peers did the same, taking their own artists with them on the Grand Tour. The Royal Navy school that trained officers gave courses on drawing, as did the school for army officers. The Admiralty also assigned him two seamen, John Hepburn and Samuel Wilkes; the latter, picked for his skill as a gunsmith, did not play much of a part. Franklin sent him home from Cumberland House, their first stop on the trip into the interior. Wilkes could not handle the rigors of Subarctic travel.

These were considerable. In a terrain without roads of any kind, travel was by water in the summer, in winter by dogsled, usually up frozen riverbeds. The weather controls everything. Summers are brief, starting in mid- to late June; the first snow falls in late August or early September, although snow can and does fall from the sky any month of the year. Temperatures run to the extremes; they can soar into the eighties and nineties in July on the Canadian tundra, then drop to forty or fifty below zero, and sometimes lower, in the winter. The country to the west and north of Hudson Bay, between the bay and the Arctic Ocean, is laced with lakes, thousands of them, and the rivers and streams that connect them. Geologically the area is known as the Canadian Shield. It is a relatively flat granite upland made up of some of the oldest continental rock on earth. On top of this rock in the Far North lies permafrost, in a few places frozen to a depth of a thousand feet. Because the permafrost never melts, the water that falls on the shield cannot drain down into the ground. Thus the lakes and the multitude of rivers. Where there are no lakes or rivers, there are swamps.

And everywhere, mosquitoes. Arctic and Subarctic mosquitoes are famous, and with good reason. In 1912 a mathematician visiting the coast of James Bay, the southern arm of Hudson Bay, trying to quantify what he was experiencing, guessed that "there were fifteen million mosquitoes per cubic yard of free air" in the area. It sounds impossible, but people talked about clouds of mosquitoes blotting out the sun. Mosquitoes have been known to kill caribou, literally sucking them dry. The tiny biting insects known as black flies, sand flies, or no-see-ums are even worse. Said James Knight of the HBC in 1711—the same James Knight who vanished in 1719—"where they light is just as if a spark of fire fell and raises a little bump which smarts and burns so that we can- not forbear rubbing of them as causes such scabbs that our hands and faces is nothing but scabbs. They fly into our ears nose eyes mouth and down our throats as we be most sorely plagued with them." The Indians dealt with them by coating their bodies with bear grease, and stank in consequence. White men learned to live with them.

Franklin would never have had to endure such conditions in any of his previous travels. But he was also entering a war zone. The two fur companies that ranged the Canadian interior were not merely in com- petition with each other; they were at each other's throats, arresting and detaining the other's personnel, stealing their furs, doing whatever they could to destroy each other, flouting the law in the process. Law means little in such a wilderness in any case. Franklin and his little party of men were about to ask bitter enemies to pause in the midst of a battle and cooperate in helping him cross the battlefield.

In its original 1670 royal charter the Hudson's Bay Company had been granted an enormous piece of property, namely all the land that drained into Hudson Bay from any direction. The HBC owned, in effect, half of Labrador, most of the Canadian Shield, lands running up to the Rocky Mountains in the west, and the Red River Valley in the south, which includes parts of Minnesota—in all, 1.5 million square miles, half the size of Australia. For more than a hundred years the HBC had slept at the watery edge of this huge ice machine and, without doing anything more than occupying its posts on Hudson Bay, reaped large profits from the furs the Indians brought in.

So much unoccupied land positively invited competition. In the early 1700s largely French fur trappers and traders began moving deeper and deeper into the Canadian West and North, going where the furs were and wooing the Indians away from their dependence on the HBC. The French traders often lived with the Indians and kept Indian wives, and the Canadian West was therefore full of half-breeds, or métis, as they were known. They got their trade goods from Montreal, creating a sup- ply line that stretched twice as long as the HBC's, but they were enter- prising where the HBC was not. In the 1780s they joined together in a loose confederation known as the North West Company. By the time Franklin showed up in northern Canada in 1819, the North West Com- pany controlled 78 percent of the fur trade of northern Canada, the HBC only 20 percent. The other 2 percent belonged to a few freelancers.

To survive, the HBC had little choice but to rouse itself at last and do what it had never done before: venture into the interior and set up its own competing posts. The decades preceding Franklin's arrival saw increasingly aggressive competition between the two companies; the HBC built posts seldom more than a few miles from the NWC posts, each rival trying to keep track of "its" Indians, making sure there were no defections. Because they were so close to each other it was easy for them to harass each other, and they did so continually and savagely, which only intensified the rivalry. The situation reached a bloody climax when the Earl of Selkirk, a Scottish noble, bought a controlling interest in the HBC and used his power in the company to establish a settlement in the Red River Valley south of Lake Winnipeg. Selkirk was trying to make a home for thousands of Scottish crofters dispossessed by the enclosure of the great estates in Scotland. The settlement lay directly across the supply lines of the North West Company. In 1816, only three years before John Franklin arrived in Hudson Bay, métis from the NWC ambushed a party of Red River settlers and killed twenty of them, then stripped and mutilated the bodies and left them to the crows.

The Admiralty was aware of the antagonism between the two companies but may not have known how bitter the rivalry was or how thinly stretched the companies were by it. Admiralty officials called on both of them to cooperate with Franklin's expedition, to help with men, supplies, guides, and translators, and the companies agreed to do what they could, sending directives from London to their men in the field to that effect. But the reality on the ground was always going to govern what happened. The warfare between the two companies had exhausted their resources; at the posts in the interior both were short of supplies. The HBC employees who sailed with Franklin on the supply ship were the first to apprise him of how bad things were. He would not be able to hire men at York Factory. Everyone in company employ would be busy off-loading the ship and preparing for their own inland journeys in their big birchbark canoes. The HBC was a business, and it was all business. Lines of communication and supply in the Canadian interior were fragile. The weather was unpredictable. Supplies had to reach the trading posts to keep the business going. As far as personnel were concerned, Franklin was on his own.

It would have helped Franklin to know this before he set out. As it was he had had little time to learn about conditions in Canada, and little time to prepare. Barrow's formal minutes on the proposed expedition are dated late February 1819, and Franklin was to depart in late May. In those three months he had to consult the available maps of northern Canada; they were inadequate, since the fur traders did not see it as their duty to make maps. He had to figure out in detail what supplies he would need and requisition them. He had to learn to use the various scientific instruments he would be taking. He visited the aging Alexander Mackenzie to learn how he had managed the logistics of the trip he made on the river named after him to the Arctic Ocean. Mackenzie wrote him a letter making suggestions. Get as far into the interior as possible before freeze-up, he advised, as far as Île-à-la-Crosse; then as soon as the weather allows go farther, to the Athabasca country. Take clothing with you to trade with the natives, and spirits. Take an Inuit who can translate for you when you reach Inuit country. Take as much pemmican as you can carry. Pemmican is the staple of northern travel, a calorie-rich mixture of two-thirds dried and pounded buffalo meat and one-third caribou fat, mixed with some berries. Voyageurs who normally eat eight pounds of meat a day can manage on one and a half pounds of pemmican. Someone from the Earl of Selkirk's Red River settlement advised him to take portable soups, flour, chocolate, arrowroot, biscuit, fishhooks, nets, and flannel underwear reaching to the ankles. Bacon is better than pork, he was told—Franklin ordered seven hundred pounds of it. Most of all, the man advised, get inland. Get inland right away. Waste no time on the coast of Hudson Bay.

In late April Franklin sent his want list to Barrow: three hundred pounds of preserved beef, two hundred of mutton, a hundred pounds of the best portable soups, the bacon, a hogshead of rum in eight-gallon casks, a hundred pounds of arrowroot, two hundred of ship's biscuit, a hundred each of tea, coffee, and sugar, two hundred pounds of tobacco, the scientific instruments (most of them having to do with measuring magnetic variation and dip), a small library, reams and reams of paper, weapons and ammunition in abundance, the supplies necessary for preserving animal and plant specimens, surveying equipment, and more food, with everything divided into packages of ninety pounds each. On portages around rapids or falls it was customary for men to carry one, sometimes two ninety-pound packages at a time.

Would this be enough? Who knew? The real question was, how was he going to get all this tonnage upriver and into Canada? He needed more than his two seamen, that was obvious. HBC ships normally left London and skipped up the east coast of Great Britain to the Orkney

Islands at the northern tip of Scotland, where they paused to take on fresh water and beef and possibly hire employees before they sailed west for Hudson Bay. On the way north company officials explained to Franklin for the first time why no men would be available at York Factory. He would have to hire help in the Orkneys, just as the HBC did. (Eighty percent of HBC employees were Orkney men.)

In an expedition where timing was everything, Franklin's would prove to be consistently bad, for the most part through no fault of his own. The herring fishery in the north was unexpectedly booming. The manpower required for it had tripled in the past year. A year earlier and it would have been easy to hire men. Told to post a notice on the church door in Stromness, the Orkneys' main port, Franklin did so, appointing a time for men to come to apply. Only a few showed up, and they were less than enthusiastic. None would take the job on the spot; they would think about it and give him an answer the next day. Franklin was "extremely annoyed"; the ships were scheduled to leave the next day. Four men signed on, but only to go as far as Fort Chipewyan on Lake Athabasca. Franklin "was much amused," he wrote in his expedition account,

> with the extreme caution these men used before they would sign the agreement; they minutely scanned all our intentions, weighed every circumstance, looked narrowly into the plan of our route, and still more circumspectly to the prospect of return. Such caution on the part of the northern mariners forms a singular contrast with the ready and thoughtless manner in which an English seamen enters upon any enterprise, however hazardous, without inquiring, or desiring to know, where he is going, or what he is going about.

Wise men, these four: they were Orkney men, they *knew* northern Canada. Franklin would find the same attitude among the Indians he recruited to hunt for him and guide him to the shores of the Arctic Ocean. They were all cautious. They could read the seasons, they knew the caribou routes, they knew how to stalk and kill game in a treeless country, they could travel quickly, and yet for all their knowledge and skill they sometimes starved. Like the Orkney men, they understood the risks. Franklin had little idea what he was getting into, and the luck that had sustained him all those years before was beginning to drain away.

Franklin and his party, which now, with the addition of the Orkney men, numbered ten, arrived at York Factory at the end of August. It was already late in the season and time was of the essence. He briefly considered taking Barrow's suggested northern route inland, first up the coast to the HBC fort at what is now Churchill, then striking cross country toward the Arctic coast, but this route was unknown, it led into the aptly named barren lands, and there were no trading posts in that direction. Its only advantage was that it was shorter. The HBC officials advised him to take the usual, roundabout route up the Hayes River and its tributaries to the HBC post called Cumberland House, then go on from there the next summer. This is the great circle route to Great Slave Lake and the Coppermine area. It is a lengthy, difficult trek, and in no sense direct. But there were trading posts all along the way, and the route was known.

One wonders how company officials reacted to Franklin when he arrived. In the account of his expedition that he published when he returned, he speaks again and again of his "demands" on fur company officials for help and supplies, and the word has a ring of imperiousness to it. But in fact he was a beggar, in no position to demand anything. And this rank amateur of the North was trying to do what only two other white men, Hearne and Mackenzie, had ever done, reach the Arctic Ocean across the barren lands, above the tree line, and come back alive. He had tons of supplies but no canoes and not enough men. The companies were waging an undeclared war with each other. Three partners of the North West Company, indeed, were in detention at York Factory, prisoners of the HBC. Franklin spoke to them, sought their advice too, and asked for help. Follow the route up the Hayes, they said. Get to Cumberland House as fast as you can.

The HBC did what it could, giving him not canoes but a York boat, a river craft pointed at both ends, like a canoe, for easier management in river conditions, and one steersman or guide. That was all they could spare. Franklin now had a crew of eleven, one boat, and seven hundred miles to go before the rivers and lakes froze. It was already September. Not to make Cumberland House, to have to spend the winter in the open, was unthinkable. The alternative was a long winter at York Factory, twiddling frostbitten thumbs. The nights were already getting chilly.

They left on September 9, using a sail on the seven-mile stretch before they came to the first rapids. Because of the shortage of help, half

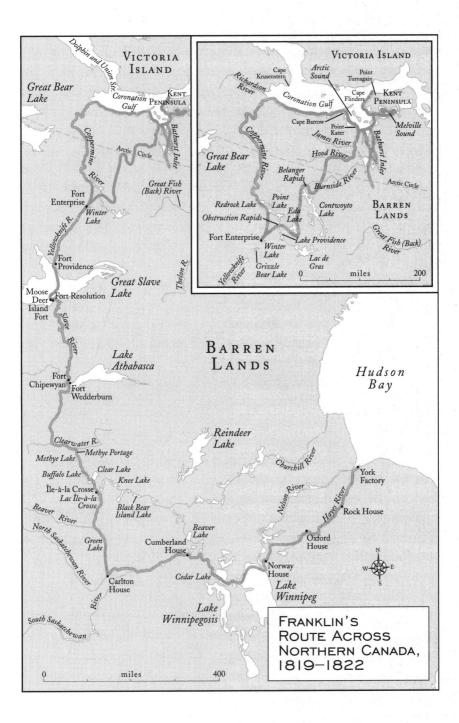

Inset map (Victoria Island detail):

VICTORIA ISLAND

Richardson River · Cape Krusenstern · *Arctic Sound* · Point Turnagain · KENT PENINSULA

Coronation Gulf · Cape Flinders · *Melville Sound*

Cape Barrow · Point Kater · *James River* · Barhurst Inlet

Coppermine River · *Hood River* · Arctic Circle

Great Bear Lake · *Belanger Rapids* · Burnside River

Redrock Lake · Point Lake · Eda Lake · *Contwoyto Lake* · BARREN LANDS

Obstruction Rapids

Fort Enterprise · Lake Providence · *Great Fish (Back) River*

Yellowknife River · Winter Lake · Grizzle Bear Lake · Lac de Gras

0 · miles · 200

Main map:

VICTORIA ISLAND

Dolphin and Union Str.

Great Bear Lake

Coronation Gulf · KENT PENINSULA

Coppermine River · Arctic Circle · Barhurst Inlet

Fort Enterprise · Great Fish (Back) River

Winter Lake

Yellowknife R.

Fort Providence

Moose Deer Island Fort · Fort Resolution · Great Slave Lake

Slave River

Thelon R.

Lake Athabasca

Fort Chipewyan · Fort Wedderburn

BARREN LANDS

Hudson Bay

Clearwater R.

Methye Portage

Methye Lake

Buffalo Lake · Clear Lake · Knee Lake

Reindeer Lake

Île-à-la Crosse · Lac Île-à-la Crosse

Beaver River · Black Bear Island Lake

North Saskatchewan River

Churchill River

Nelson River · Hayes River

York Factory

Rock House

Green Lake · Beaver Lake

Cumberland House

Oxford House

Carlton House · Cedar Lake

Norway House

River

South Saskatchewan

Lake Winnipeg

Lake Winnipegosis

N · W · E · S

FRANKLIN'S ROUTE ACROSS NORTHERN CANADA, 1819–1822

0 · miles · 400

the supplies had to be sacrificed before he could even begin. Four or five more Orkney men and he would have been able to man a second York boat and carry everything. He had to leave thirty-five packages behind—all his seven hundred pounds of bacon, perhaps half his rum, the equivalent of three barrels of flour, two cases of preserved meat and soup, two cases of powder, and three bags of shot. Franklin was learning in a hurry about the difficulties he faced. He already understood that, given the distances and the shortness of the summer traveling season, the expedition would take three years to complete, not the two he had originally expected. The resident governor of the HBC, William Williams, who traveled into the interior with Franklin with his own small flotilla, assured him that they would forward his abandoned supplies the following spring. Franklin relied on this promise; he had no choice but to rely on promises. But perhaps he sensed already that it would never be fulfilled.

The Hayes, like almost all northern rivers, was full of portages. They tracked their York boat through the first, dragging it with ropes through the rapid. As the river progressively narrowed and the rapids became shallower, they would more and more often have to unload the boat, then not just drag but lift it over the stones. The length of portages determined the speed of travel. Some days they made only a couple of miles; one day, a mere mile and a half. Other days they could make twenty or more.

It is astonishing how much labor was involved. On a long portage— and they might run as long as a mile—the men would have not only to drag the boat the length of it but frequently to empty it, then carry the packages the length of the portage, only to come back for more packages until all of them had been carried ahead. Since so much of the work involved dragging the boat through or over shallows, the men were in the water, their clothes wet, a good part of the day. The water was primarily meltwater, and quite cold.

All this effort burned calories at a prodigious rate. It is no wonder that the standard fare was eight pounds of meat per man per day. Lewis and Clark on their trek up the Missouri allowed nine. Officers carried only their own personal belongings, their portmanteaus—journals, combs and brushes, weapons and ammunition, a change of boots and socks. The officers did not share in the physical labor unless it was absolutely necessary, but Midshipman Hood was always on duty; it was his job to map the route, which meant taking angle measurements where the rivers changed direction, estimating distances, and drawing the shape of lakes and the location of landscape features. The maps Franklin published with his expedition account were largely Hood's. The land was generally flat, but there were a few low waterfalls. The Hill River was marked by one solitary six-hundred-foot hill in otherwise flat country. They climbed it and saw lakes everywhere. Franklin allowed himself a few comments on the scenery in his journal. It was the fall, the trees were turning, and "the light yellow of the fading poplars," he wrote, "formed a fine contrast to the dark evergreen of the spruce, whilst the willows, of an intermediate hue, served to shade the two principal masses of colour into each other." An occasional dogwood lent the scene "bright purple tints."

Other aspects of the voyage were not so pretty. All along the route they encountered Cree Indian families dying en masse from whooping cough and measles, and the epidemic was spreading north and west—that is, in the same direction Franklin and his men were heading. The natives had no natural immunity to these European diseases. The expedition ran into occasional dangers as well. Once, walking along a bank, Franklin slipped and fell into the river. It was unlikely that he could swim; very few people could swim in 1819, and that would have included naval officers. Another time, when they were tracking up a rapid, the rope broke and everyone in the boat, including the officers, had to leap out and steady the boat in the stream so she wouldn't be swept broadside into the rocks. Hood remarks in his journal on the strength required to drag a boat up a rapid against a current running seven miles an hour. Worst of all, on September 17, eight days after leaving York Factory, they had to leave sixteen more packages at a place called Rock Depot because they were still overloaded. That was almost fifteen hundred pounds of supplies. William Williams again promised to forward these supplies to Franklin in the spring. That night it snowed heavily, although in September the snow seldom lasted. Five of the packages they left behind did eventually reach the expedition, but as it happened they contained the least useful of the items they had been forced to abandon.

Early in October they arrived at Lake Winnipeg and crossed the cloudy waters around the north end of it into the mouth of the Saskatchewan. Here they passed a route used by the North West Company voyageurs, and the little HBC contingent went on the alert for an ambush. Geese and ducks were flying south now in huge flocks, and the night frosts lasted all day. It snowed heavily on October 21. As they crossed one small lake in a storm, the spray froze to the oars, making them so heavy they were extremely clumsy to manage. On the twenty-third they reached Cumberland House. The lake was frozen two hundred yards out from the edges and they had to break through the ice to reach the landing place, but they had come 690 miles and had beaten winter. By the end of November the ice was thick enough to cross the lake on sledges.

Cumberland House had no facilities for a large party of guests, so Franklin had his men build their own building on the grounds. As they were unskilled at the task, it was drafty, and so cold that they kept fires going night and day in every room, broiling on one side of their bodies, freezing on the other. Northern winters were new to all of them but the Orkney men. Pens and brushes froze to the paper inside the house when they tried to write or draw. They had plenty to eat, living on salted (i.e., preserved) geese, fish, buffalo, and moose meat. "We have no reason to complain of our fare," wrote Hood. The fish were tittameg and sturgeon, he added, "and are, perhaps, the best in the world." They wrapped their feet in several layers of cloth, then covered them with rawhide moccasins made of moose skin and tied with thongs above the ankle. In the North ordinary leather boots froze, and nobody wore them. Exercise kept them warm when they were outside, but Hood was amazed nevertheless by the stark intensity of the cold. "It is scarcely to be credited," he noted,

> that natural cold is ever so great as to cause sensations instantaneous and violent. No good conductor of heat can be touched without severe pain. A piece of metal put into the mouth inadvertently immediately freezes all the moisture about it, and the part in contact loses its skin. Large pike and trout, which when taken struggle with great strength, are thrown on the ice and become motionless in a minute, and before they are carried to the house might be pounded to powder.

The cold contracted the metal in their scientific instruments and made them useless.

The education of John Franklin, meanwhile, continued. He was still a long way from the Athabasca region, a long way from knowing what he would find at Fort Chipewyan hundreds of miles to the north. He had decided not to try to talk the Orkney men into going any farther than Fort Chipewyan. They didn't want to go, for one thing, and he thought they might be better employed by returning to York Factory in the spring, bringing up the supplies he had left behind, then trekking back to York Factory and taking the last ship home. But could he hire men at Fort Chipewyan to do the work the Orkney men were doing now? He didn't know. He didn't know whether the Copper Indians—also known as Yellow Knives, a subtribe of the Chipewyan and the same people who had taken Samuel Hearne down the Coppermine River to the Arctic Ocean—could be induced to hunt for them and guide them north. Would supplies be available there? How far had the whooping cough and measles advanced into the Arctic? He grilled the HBC agents at Cumberland House, then walked across to the North West Company fort and asked the same questions. Nobody could give him answers. Each man had his own territory to worry about, his own Indians, and his rivals were within sight.

In the Arctic gloom of December Franklin decided he would have to go north himself to get answers to his questions. He had sent letters to the factors at Fort Chipewyan, but the chances of getting replies in the middle of winter were slim. He would leave Richardson and Hood at Cumberland House to bring up the Inuit interpreter the HBC had promised they would recruit for him, and the supplies left behind at York Factory, when the ice broke up in the spring. He understood now that he was more than a year away from the chief object of the expedition, to reach the coast. Fort Chipewyan was itself still hundreds of miles from the Arctic Ocean. The traveling season was short. He would have to build his own fort, as close to the Coppermine as he could, and spend the next winter there. His progress after that would depend on unknowns—the following summer's weather; the cooperation of the Yellow Knives; the configuration of the coastline it was his job to map. And supplies. Most of all supplies. He had had no idea of how difficult it was to keep men fed in the Arctic.

The first stage of the route led to the southwest again, to the HBC post called Carlton House on the Saskatchewan. From there it took its first turn north into the Beaver River and the posts at Île-à-la-Crosse, named for the game of LaCrosse that the Indians gathered there to play. Franklin had George Back with him, and seaman John Hepburn, who was tough and strong. They traveled by dogsled. In an unusual moment of cooperation, each of the fur companies had provided sleds, drivers, and dogs. This would be Franklin's first experience with French voyageurs on the trail, but George Back spoke fluent French, so language was not a problem. They had three sleds, each one loaded with three hundred pounds of provisions and equipment. Officers did not ride on the sleds. They all walked, on snowshoes three feet long. They traveled with a party from the HBC, their four sleds following the same route. They left Cumberland House on January 18, 1820, in serious cold. The temperature was forty-two degrees below zero. The day after, the mercury in the thermometer froze in the bulb at fifty below.

Franklin and Back both kept journals, but the most vivid account of this trip is Back's letter to his brother written in May at Fort Chipewyan. "One days march on snow shoes," he writes,

> will give you a clear idea of the whole—and will be quite sufficient to enable you to reflect on your own happiness when compared to mine in North America—It is customary to start as soon as there is sufficient light to direct the party on its way—the dogs are harnessed and attached to the sledges—each person puts on his snow shoes and one goes before, to beat a track through the snow which is seldom more than six inches deep—the whole party follows, the dogs always adhering to the track . . . In this manner you go on following the track and this has been generally 40° below zero or the quicksilver frozen which was the case with us—you are compelled to walk fast to prevent being frozen—but it is almost impossible to do so and few there are who escape. In the early part of the morning a person feels brisk and after four hours thinks it no little comfort to make a meal of pemmican and a tin pot of tea—(which by the way if removed two feet from the fire though the tea be quite hot will adhere firmly to the lips) . . . an hour passes in eating—and you proceed—an Englishman always feels satisfied after eating and three or four leagues pass by unheeded—but continued exertion of the muscles depresses the spirits and however firm the mind yet nature can but do her utmost, and the languor of the body is soon seized by fatigue—you soon feel the thongs of the snow shoes chafing your feet particularly the toes, both under and above, and this evil cannot be remedied—weak and tortured with oppressive pains you drag your listless form

along (far behind the rest) till dark . . . and bless God that
repose is near—the fire being made the snow is cleared away
and branches of the Pine laid in even order forming the travellers carpet—a blanket and the skin of the buffalo serves for
your covering in the coldest winter's night . . . the party melt
snow and prepare a meal, and take off their shoes (already
frozen) to dry—Tea and a pipe are inseparable companions . . . Those who are frozen feel it on approaching to the
fire and immediately rub the place with Snow, but the skin is
certain of being penetrated and much pain endured—you lay
with your feet to the fire, and your head entirely covered not
daring to look out and equally heedless about the Wolves
which are constantly howling around you and make frequent
excursions in search of prey—your Gun, Pistols and dagger
are by your side and this is a most necessary precaution—In
the morning chilled with excessive cold and stiff with laying
in the same position little relieved by rest—merely nominal—
you prepare for the journey of the day in the same manner as
before.

Back took pride in traveling easier and faster than Franklin, "who had
never been accustomed to any vigorous exertion[;] besides his frame is
bulky without activity," and Franklin himself, who never entirely lost the
self-pitying note in all that was to come, was convinced that he "had
Suffered more than any other." Back conceded, however, that by the end
of this trek Franklin had grown used to the constant exertion "and was
as lively as any." Back had been plagued with corns; the snowshoes
rubbed them out of his toes. The snowshoes tortured them all, but the
covering of blanket and buffalo robe at night actually kept them relatively warm, even in temperatures far below zero. The dogs usually slept
among them, preferably on top of them. Back woke up one morning
aware that he was actually hot, only to find that it had snowed during
the night. Snow, he had discovered, is a natural insulator, an additional
blanket.

A few days into the trip a runner passed them, searching for a group
of Indians. This man, Back observed,

had a certain quantity of provisions with him [i.e., for his
own sustenance; voyageurs commonly traveled light, Indian
style, with just enough provisions on their backs for a few

days, a buffalo robe for sleeping, a hatchet, a gun]—it was of little consequence when it was expended—as he would continue the search to starvation itself—such men look at three day's fasting as nothing—I cannot learn the secret.

He would have to in the year to come. Back noted a few days later that they were running low on provisions, and there was almost nothing left of the dog food. "The men," he wrote, syncopating the text with his characteristic dashes,

> began to be impatient—some of their provisions were already expended and there remained a distance of five days march to perform [to Carlton House]—This was entirely the fault of themselves—for they are always averse to take provisions— and when they have sufficient, the extravagant use they make of them at the commencement of the journey is certain of leaving them deficient in the end.

The Indians, Back would learn, were the same. This was the style of living in the north, and the English officers never understood it. Men lived day to day; they did not think ahead. They preferred traveling light, with a light load, and moving fast, to the more elaborate, deliberate, heavily laden, slower English style. The difference was almost philosophical. The voyageurs saw life as a matter of chance. Unpredictable blizzards, an all-too-sudden access of winter, accidents to equipment they could not survive without, lack of game where there had always been game, empty fish nets where fish were always abundant—all these things could kill you, but they accepted that. There was no margin of safety in nature, they knew, and precious little comfort. Risk was built into their lives. At the same time they trusted to their considerable wilderness skills to live off the land and to survive most eventualities. And they scorned to store food. Only farmers stored food, and they looked down on farmers.

By January 29 food for the dogs was gone and "several of the party were stupefied by the frost," drunk with cold, moving like automatons. It got so cold that when they tried to drink their tea it froze in their tin cups before they could get it to their lips. Two days later they reached Carlton House. In eleven days they had come 240 miles. Back's and Franklin's legs and feet were swollen and their joints stiff and sore from the snowshoes. They were exhausted; so were the men; so were the dogs. They decided to rest for a week or so. Back was grateful for a shave and a wash, the "only one in fourteen days," he noted. "Our pemmican and dried meat had so hardened our jaws," he added, "that I verily believe it would have been of little consequence whether our next meal had been granite or limestone," but it was steak, and he declared it "the sweetest meal I ever tasted."

They were on the edge of buffalo country now, on the great plains of western Canada, moving out of Cree country into the homelands of the "Stone Indians," known more generally as the Assiniboine, who were great thieves fond of stealing horses, which they thought of as the common property of mankind, meant for human use and therefore to be taken whenever and wherever found. The Assiniboine were semihostile, blaming the white man, with some justice, for bringing measles and whooping cough into their territory. About three hundred of the Cree and Assiniboine in the area had died of the two diseases within the last year. That had a major effect on the operations of the fur company posts located there. They were provisioning, not trading, posts; they existed to make pemmican out of buffalo meat and deer fat, and the Assiniboine and Cree who lived around them hunted for a living. With fewer Indians to hunt, there was less pemmican. The two posts together had put up between three and four hundred ninety-pound bags of pemmican that year. That was considered low. Franklin bought ten bags for himself for the trip to the Arctic coast, and he sent a note back to Richardson to pick them up when he came north in the spring.

The next stages were like the first, a hard slog with dogs and sleds on snowshoes, sleeping in the open, eating pemmican or the occasional hare or partridge, and stopping at small posts along the way. At the first such post a Mr. McFarlane told them that because of the Indian epidemic and their consequent inability to hunt, they could barely muster up enough food to feed themselves. At another they caught up to the letters Franklin had sent north to Fort Chipewyan. On February 23 they reached Île-à-la-Crosse and dined on the delicious tittameg. They left there on March 5. All along there were signs of the epidemic—Indian numbers reduced, the survivors half starved, in miserable condition; posts short of provisions. It was the Indian custom to grieve extravagantly when close relatives died. They would rip their clothing to shreds, destroy their weapons, tear apart their tents. The territory had lost a third of its Indian population. Franklin, good Englishman that he was, with European attitudes toward property, found it impossible to understand this level of grief and the destruction of goods that went with it. And of course it only made his plans shakier as he went along.

Everything seemed to be falling apart the farther north he got. With more than half of his own provisions left behind at York Factory and Rock Depot, he had been forced to throw himself and the fate of his expedition on the mercy of the land—on the ability, that is, and the willingness of Indians to hunt for him. The land was turning out to be merciless. He would need voyageurs to make his trip down the Coppermine and along the coast, and one trader told him it would be hard to hire them no matter what he paid, partly because the voyageurs were terrified of the Inuit, and partly because they would be traveling on the sea. The Yellow Knives were also terrified of the Inuit, considering them their lifelong enemies. The help of the Yellow Knives was essential to his enterprise, and when he reached the coast he would need Inuit help. He had heard nothing yet about the Inuit interpreter the HBC was supposed to hire for him.

With the unknowns only multiplying, Franklin and his party reached Fort Chipewyan on March 26. They had walked 857 miles by his reckoning from Cumberland House, in an unusually cold winter, at temperatures Franklin guessed lay at thirty below zero a considerable part of the time. It had taken two months and eight days, and it was a genuine feat. In all Franklin had traveled some fifteen hundred miles since leaving York Factory. Fort Chipewyan was a North West Company post and larger than any other post in northern Canada, and it housed the equivalent of a small village. It was located on the north side of Lake Athabasca, about a mile from the HBC post, Fort Wedderburn, which was much smaller. As fur posts went, it was comfortable and well built and relatively warm. At last he met men who knew what the country to the north was like. Now he could get his questions answered. But they were still six hundred miles shy of the Arctic Ocean.

CHAPTER SIX

WINTER LAKE

At the end of May Franklin called the chief traders at Forts Wedderburn and Chipewyan to a tent he had erected on neutral ground between them. He needed their help, he told them. He needed not only supplies, men, and canoes; he needed a plan. "They were unanimous in the following opinions," he wrote Barrow in London,

> 1st, "That the party must pass the next winter on the border of some Lake well stocked with Fish . . . 2nd. The Party must be of sufficient force when approaching the Sea to overawe the Esquimaux (about Twenty) but they do not suppose the Tribes we may meet on the Coast are either so numerous or hostile as near to the Mouth of Mackenzie's River. 3rd. The Indians who know that part of the country best and must accompany the Expedition as Guides & Hunters are called Red Knives [more often, Yellow Knives] . . . The NW Company alone trade with these and have promised to procure them."

Franklin would go north, then, in the summer season that was coming on, build a post in which to spend the winter of 1820–21, and solidify the arrangements to use the Yellow Knives whom the North West Company people would hire to guide him and his party to the Coppermine and downriver to the sea. When he reached the coast he would turn east and spend the summer of 1821 mapping it, searching for the northeastern corner of North America, and—even if everything was taking much longer than expected, one could always hope—connecting up with Parry in his ships.

"Three Canoes will be required," he went on,

to convey the necessary supplies to the Wintering ground manned by five men each including Guides & Interpreters. These men together with the Indian Hunters will keep the Party amply supplied with Provision & Fish. On the first opening of Water next spring, I propose leaving that Establishment in two Canoes fully manned, the whole party then to consist of twenty persons.

He would send the third canoe and any excess men back to Fort Chipewyan. Each company would contribute equally to his supply and manpower needs. Franklin had only to wait now for Richardson and Hood to arrive with the Inuit interpreter, if he was available, and more of the supplies they had been forced to leave behind before proceeding north.

It was a reasonable plan and it was the product of the best advice Franklin could obtain—Franklin was no pigheaded John Ross, unwilling to listen to the opinions of others—but it depended on too many variables to be foolproof. The biggest was provisions. Franklin had no way of knowing whether the provisions he had left behind were on the trail someplace, speeding his way. He could only wait and see. Whether the Yellow Knives would find enough game the next spring to feed them all on the trek to the Coppermine and downriver from there was a major variable—assuming, of course, that the Yellow Knives would be willing to work for Franklin at all. Twenty men were a lot to feed. Twenty men would go through a ninety-pound bag of pemmican in three days. He would be sixty days on the coast alone, if all went well. Anyone could do the math. He needed a minimum of twenty bags of pemmican, thirty if he counted the march back across country. He had bought ten in the south. Because of the epidemic, it was an open question whether he could acquire more.

So many men, so much food. Franklin was used to naval expeditions, big ships stocked with two or three years' worth of salt pork and beef, condensed soups, potatoes, ship's biscuit, lemon juice, and big stoves to prepare it. Traveling light was not a Royal Navy talent. The navy never went anywhere without taking all it thought it would need, plus more, to make sure.

Franklin could not travel as light as the voyageurs in any case. The old hands at Fort Chipewyan had told him he needed twenty men, which was the minimum required for a show of force to the Inuit. That spring he hired sixteen French-speaking voyageurs, most of them half-breeds,

one a full-blooded Iroquois, paying them double what the fur companies paid. Now that they were in his pay, he had to feed and clothe them.
Like all the other posts, Fort Chipewyan had no food to spare, or clothing. The people at Fort Chipewyan had been living entirely on fish.
Franklin told the men he had hired to spread themselves among the
fishing posts on the lake. He would give them clothing, he said, as soon
as Richardson and Hood came up with some.

Richardson and Hood arrived in mid-July. The ten bags of pemmican
that Franklin had bought at Île-à-la-Crosse had gone bad. Properly
made, pemmican lasted for years. This pemmican must not have been
made properly. "Thus were we unexpectedly deprived," wrote Hood, "of
the most essential of our stores." Nor was there enough fresh clothing
for the voyageurs. Their other stores consisted of two barrels of flour,
some chocolate, arrowroot, portable soups, and dried meats, none of it
plentiful. All of it had to be saved for the winter ahead. They had also
brought ten more men, making twenty-six Franklin had to maintain,
plus his own party of four officers and Hepburn, the seaman. "The fort
could not provide them with food for a single day," Hood noted; the
men ate fish when they could catch it, went hungry when they could
not, and grew more and more "disgusted at so unpropitious a commencement of the enterprise." It was their first real crisis. Franklin had
to whittle their numbers quickly. Richardson and Hood had hired three
Orkneymen from the HBC. They quit, "deterred by the dread of famine
and fatigue, which they thought we were doomed to encounter."
Franklin got rid of three others equally unenthusiastic about the
prospects. The party now consisted of the four navy officers, Hepburn,
twenty voyageurs (two of whom understood the language of the Yellow
Knives and received extra pay as interpreters), and an uncertain number
of voyageur wives (possibly two, possibly three)—Franklin gave the total
as twenty-seven people. The wives seemed to come and go, but it was
still a lot of bellies to fill.

Now they had to move north, and right away. It was mid-July and
they had to leave the comforts of Fort Chipewyan, canoe to Great Slave
Lake, the fifth largest lake in North America (and the tenth largest in
the world), cross it to reach the North West Company post Fort Providence, the northernmost trading post of all, and meet and negotiate an
agreement with the Yellow Knives who were waiting for them there.
Then they had to move still farther north into the barren lands, find a
spot where there were trees to build with, and build themselves a
home—all before winter, perpetually just over the horizon this far

north. Richardson and Hood had traveled hard, endured temperatures that soared above a hundred some days, and fled swarms of mosquitoes so thick and so persistent that they traveled at night to escape them; but they got no chance to rest. On July 18 the entire party set out down the Slave River. They had food for only seven or eight days, but that seems not to have bothered the men, says Franklin, and they departed in "high glee," singing "a lively Canadian Song." (George Back would publish a volume of these songs when he returned to England.)

The singing, and the departure, seem to have taken Franklin's mind off his problems. At this stage he was more hopeful than he had reason to be. At least they were on their way. He was glad the scenery was "too uninviting to attract much attention or divert the mind from the full enjoyment of pleasing anticipations and agreeable conjectures." It's unlikely these happy thoughts lasted very long. They camped in a swamp that first night. A "most violent" thunderstorm blew down their tents and it rained for two hours, flooding the campground. Then the mosquitoes drove them back to the canoes and at a little before midnight, in the white night of the Arctic summer, they paddled on.

They were fortunate that the river was high; they could run some of the rapids, rather than having to carry everything around them all. On July 20 they reached the Portage des Noyées, the portage of the drowned, where some years before a brigade of canoes had come and the leader had run the tricky rapid but had left instructions that no one should follow him until hearing a gunshot from downstream, which would be the signal that it was safe. He barely escaped the rapids with his life and was about to walk back upstream to warn the others not to embark when one of his men, seeing birds overhead, impulsively took a shot at them. The leader broke into a run, trying to reach his companions before they launched their canoes, but it was too late. They were already launched into the rapid. Everyone in them drowned.

There was another thunderstorm. There were more huge swarms of mosquitoes. One day a buffalo crossed the river just ahead of them. It took fourteen shots to kill it, but now they had enough meat to sustain them for a few days. By July 24 they had reached Great Slave Lake and the competing company posts on Moose Deer Island—260 miles in about a week. No supplies were available there, either, but on the twenty-fifth some Chipewyans arrived with four hundred pounds of dried meat for the expedition. Four hundred pounds would last only four or five days, but at this point Franklin was grateful for anything. Many Indian families had fled to the Chipewyan lands because of the epidemic moving north. Not enough hunters were left in the area to keep the fur posts supplied, much less Franklin's party. On the twenty-seventh the expedition left for Fort Providence, which lay across Great Slave Lake, more than thirty miles away over open water. The Yellow Knives were waiting for them at Fort Providence, anxious for their arrival. Willard Wentzel was waiting there too. Franklin had hired Wentzel, a NWC employee with two decades of experience in the area with the Yellow Knives, a man who spoke their language, to serve as a liaison with the Indians. Time was short. They island-hopped across the lake and arrived at Fort Providence on July 29.

A great deal depended on the impression Franklin made on these Indians, and he was grateful for the fact that they were out hunting when he got there. The fate of the expedition, it was now obvious, depended on them. He had done his best to save what he could of the English salted meats and the flour and soup he had kept in reserve for the coming winter. He had twenty-seven people with him more or less completely dependent on his ability to impress the Yellow Knives. They pitched the tents, said Hood, "and decorated ourselves with remnants of our European apparel." They raised a silk ensign on a pole before the camp.

Then the Indians appeared in a flotilla of small canoes. Their leader, Akaitcho (Gros Pied to the voyageurs, or Big Foot in English), stepped ashore first and strode forward to greet them. He wore a capot, a kind of hooded jacket, and a blanket over his shoulders. They led him into a room prepared for the parley. Before they could begin to talk they had to smoke, which was an Indian ritual. Then Franklin distributed a small quantity of spirits, probably rum, to Akaitcho's companions. Only then did Akaitcho speak. According to Franklin, he merely told them that he was prepared to fulfill the bargain he had made to go with them to the mouth of the Coppermine. George Back's version was much more thorough. Akaitcho spoke, says Back, of "the great pleasure he felt in seeing us." He had heard, he said, that we had a "Great Medical Chief—whose powers were so superior—as to enable him to cure the sick, and raise the dead." That would have been John Richardson, who had been treating Indians throughout their journey. This had given him hope, Akaitcho went on; he had recently lost two relatives, and he thought perhaps Richardson could bring them back to life. "Now I find it false," he said, "and am as miserable as if they had just died." Then he changed the subject. "The season was far advanced," he said, and "we cannot proceed far this year . . . but I will take you to a land where there are plenty of animals—It is true I have been unfortunate—starvation has haunted me—but the Great Lake—the waters gave me life—It is but a short time ago—since my canoe upset and I had nearly sunk—but now I am well—I am in my strength." Then he added, "I have been always considered as an old man—I have some reflection—and am not without ideas."

Franklin seems only to have heard that they were ready to hunt for him. He seems not to have heard the words "the season is far advanced" and "we cannot go far this year." He had been nursing an ambitious plan to do more than merely set up a winter camp. He wanted to go all the way to the coast, right away, this summer, run a reconnaissance down the Coppermine, build a cairn for Parry's expedition to find, and discover all he could about the route and what to expect at the mouth of the river before he settled anywhere for the winter. It is not clear that he told Akaitcho of this plan then. He did tell the Indians about the Northwest Passage, and how beneficial it would be for them if large ships came to their territory to trade with them. He also told them their Great Father in England wanted them to live at peace with the Inuit and with all other tribes. It was the same speech whites gave Indians all over North America: Keep the peace. We will make you rich.

That night Franklin gave the voyageurs their last jug from the stores and they danced for Akaitcho and his band, and the Indians reciprocated with two of their traditional dances. Hepburn in the meantime had set some embers down in Franklin's tent to drive out the mosquitoes with the smoke. When he fell asleep the tent caught fire. The tent and part of the silk ensign were destroyed. It was a bad omen, and they tried to conceal it from Akaitcho, who was not happy when he heard about it. He did not want things kept from him. He wanted to be treated with respect.

But other than the fire, things had gone well. Akaitcho had sealed the bargain, and Franklin was impressed by his intelligence. The propensity was to think of Indians as hopeless savages with changeable minds and unstable loyalties, but it was clear to everyone that Akaitcho was no fool. He knew how to survive in one of the worst climates in the world. He was also much too smart to sacrifice himself or his people to the wild enterprises of inexperienced English explorers.

It was in the area of Fort Providence that the present town of Yellowknife was founded, and it was up the Yellowknife River that they proceeded north on August 2 toward what would become the expedition's winter quarters. Akaitcho had gone ahead with his hunters the day before. Their destination was only about 140 miles north, but they were moving upstream on the Yellowknife, which flowed south; the river was swift and shallow, rocky, full of portages; and they were bringing everything they had. At each portage the canoes had to be unloaded, their contents borne ahead to the next launching site. It took four trips to carry everything; thus each portage was, in effect, four portages rather than one. They moved slowly and painfully. The Indians, who carried little, moved quickly. Franklin's canoes were big, one of them thirty-four feet long, a miniship. The Indian canoes were small and light.

Once again, food became a problem. The party was numerous and the portage work only increased the appetites of the men. By the fifth the fresh food was gone; they still had the portable soups and a few pounds of preserved meat, but nothing else. They fished whenever they stopped, but fish were scarce on the river that year. One day George Back fished with a fly rod, to the astonishment of the Indians. Back showed the Indians his flies, and Akaitcho "laughingly said the fish were not such fools as to catch at feathers," whereupon Back proceeded to catch twelve Arctic grayling without moving from the spot. "'Ah!'" said they, 'the Whites could live where we could not.'" By this time Back should have known that it wasn't true.

He could certainly not supply the whole party by fly-fishing. They put out nets at night, and in the morning the nets came up empty. "The disappointment was more severely felt," writes Franklin,

> because we had commenced upon the last case of preserved meats (brought from England) and it was evident if some supply of Provision was not soon procured the Men would be unable to support much longer the increasing labour of bearing their burdens across the Portages, which now followed in quicker succession than before.

The next portage was more than a mile long over rocky, uneven ground. Every portage risked laming one or more of the men. There were no paths, only a rock-strewn arid landscape where nothing but grass and moss grew, or an occasional stand of willow or stunted firs.

The nets still came up empty and by the eighth Franklin was dipping into his precious arrowroot and his portable soups to feed his men, some of whom had swollen feet from carrying so much weight. It rained some days, and the air was cool. By the twelfth the Yellowknife had dwindled to the size of a brook, and the route was now nothing but long portages between small lakes. In hollows in some places there were still occasional groves of spruce and thus firewood; but in many places it looked like a desert. The land itself was broken up into rough hills a couple of hundred feet high, while the valleys between were strewn everywhere with boulders and loose stones, glacial debris from the Ice Age. On August 13 they traveled for thirteen hours across this cruel landscape, paddling where they could, more often carrying the canoes and their burdens. That evening the hunters arrived with food, but only enough for an evening's meal and breakfast the next morning.

For the men that was the last straw. They had been hoping, waiting for food; now it came; it was not enough. They refused to go on. Franklin was circumspect about this incident in his journal, but George Back made it clear what happened. "Mr. Franklin told them we were too far removed from justice to treat them as they merited—but if such a thing occurred again—he would not hesitate to make an example of the first person who should come forward—by 'blowing out his brains.'" He could be hard when he needed to be. The men returned quietly, said Back, "to their duty—the night was cloudy—with hard gales and rain." Not until the sixteenth did the Indian hunters, to everyone's relief, start bringing meat in every day. Then on the nineteenth, after a seven-hour portage, they finally reached their goal, a lake Franklin promptly named Winter Lake, because it was where they would spend the winter. It had taken them more than two weeks to struggle a mere 140 miles north.

The person who found this the most remarkable was Akaitcho.

He returned on August 26. By that time Franklin's men had begun work, chopping down a small stand of pines, one of the very few spots at this latitude where the trees were big enough to use as building material, and constructing their fort—Fort Enterprise. Akaitcho was supposed to have been hunting, but he had not. He had just found out that his brother-in-law had died. For days he had mourned, and not hunted, Franklin reported in disgust; they had brought only fifteen caribou for Franklin. Worse, this death had prompted the Indians among whom the dead man lived to withdraw from the banks of the Coppermine River, where they were supposed to be drying and caching food for Franklin's descent of the river the next year. They had all retreated to Great Bear Lake.

As for descending the Coppermine then, as Franklin had hoped to do, Akaitcho flatly refused to go. It was too late in the year to think of such a thing, he told Franklin. The cold had already begun. Lives would be lost. He would not go; nor would any of his hunters. It was six days to the Coppermine, "and five more, before any wood would be found. Until the expiration of this time, the Party could not expect to have Fires, because we should find no trees after quitting the borders of this lake." This was a season of heavy rains, making it impossible to light fires with the wet moss and the twigs they might find. Beyond that it would take forty days to reach the sea, and much longer to return upriver. Akaitcho had now seen how slowly Franklin's party moved. Franklin argued with him, said he had instruments "which would infallibly point out cold weather and when it was about to set in severely." He said that he wanted to go as far north as possible to observe a coming eclipse of the sun.

"It appears," Akaitcho replied, "as if you wished to lose your own lives, and those Indians who might accompany you. However if you are determined to go," he added, "since we brought you hither, it shall not be said that we permitted you to die alone. Some of my Young Men shall also go, but the moment they embark in the Canoe, we who remain, shall suppose them all devoted to death, and begin in conse-quence to mourn and deplore their loss."

Then he pointed out that this was the season for hunting caribou; their skins were now in "the best condition for making clothing, and . . . his Party must not only prepare their Winter dresses, but pro-vide skins to furnish the Canadians who could not live here without them, and he remarked, perhaps justly, if the opportunity be now lost, it could not be regained, and some of the men, might in consequence be starved to Death, especially the Indians who were not strong or capable of bearing cold or Fatigue like the Canadians." Then he told Franklin he would leave him after the hunting season. "Because his advice was not followed, he said he was useless here." He declared, according to Hood's account, "that he had always believed us to be wise and experienced chiefs; instead of which, he was convinced by our obstinacy and rash-ness, that we resembled all other white people."

This threat finally killed Franklin's plan. He needed Akaitcho far more than Akaitcho needed him. If Akaitcho and his hunters left the vicinity of the fort it would mean almost certain starvation for Franklin and his party, and he knew it. He had to admit as well that the season was indeed growing late. Both air and water temperatures had dropped dramatically in the previous several days. The snow geese were deserting the Arctic for their winter quarters in Texas; long skeins of them flew high overhead toward the south. It proved to be a mild winter, but it did come early.

So Franklin compromised. He sent Back and Hood north with a guide to find the Coppermine, a trip, it transpired, of under fifty miles. A week later he and Richardson set out themselves to walk to it. Both parties were caught in sudden snowstorms but returned without any problem. When the eclipse came the sky was dark with clouds. Willard Wentzel was directing the men who were building Fort Enterprise, and they worked fast. The caribou were moving south too, toward the tree line; they wintered in the northern forests, not in the open. By early October they were arriving around Fort Enterprise in large numbers. On October 9 six men killed forty-five of them. On the tenth Franklin went outside to count them. He saw two thousand caribou pass by in the two hours he watched. By the end of the month he had enough meat to last the winter—or so he hoped, because he had nearly run out of ammunition. The lakes, meanwhile, were freezing up. Had Akaitcho let him go Franklin and his men would have been out there, in the open, one or two hundred miles down the Coppermine from the Fort, without means to build a fire, when the Coppermine itself froze up and the Arctic winter set in for real. Franklin still had much to learn about the North.

But it was a mild winter for northern Canada, one of the mildest the Yellow Knives could remember. That's not to say that it wasn't cold. The lowest recorded temperature was fifty-seven degrees below zero, but runs of forty below were common enough, and during January and February the thermometer never once rose above zero. Nor was the cold kept safely outside. The men used clay to close up the chinks between the logs in their buildings; but the clay froze and cracked and the cracks let in the wind. During December, which was their coldest month, the temperature inside Fort Enterprise just sixteen feet from the fire stood even during the daytime at fifteen below zero. In the mornings it dropped more than once to forty below. Sunlight, of course, was scarce. Fort Enterprise lay three degrees of latitude below the Arctic Circle. In the days around the winter solstice, the sun rose, if that's the word for it, around eleven thirty in the morning and set at two thirty in the afternoon, just peeping above the horizon "in a limited circuit not exceeding four points of the Compass." There was no warmth in it.

But the gloom was not unremitting. Franklin, with his occasional aesthetic feel for the natural world, noted that "the resident in these regions has an ample gratification in witnessing the resplendent beauty of the Moon, which appears in all its lovely grandeur, and frequently, as at this time, passes round in full brilliancy, scarcely disappearing from the view during the twenty four hours." The stars too were brilliant in the unpolluted clarity of the atmosphere, and the aurora borealis, the northern lights, brightened the darkness as well.

One of the expedition's missions was to record the influence, if any, of the aurora on the compasses and dip needles they had brought with them. It was widely believed that the aurora made a sound, an odd rustling in the air, like a breeze moving through curtains at a window, and that was another part of their mission—to listen for it. The deep silence of an Arctic winter was certainly the place to hear it if it existed. Franklin's notebooks are full of descriptions of the aurora, night after splendid night, but neither he nor anyone else in the party could be sure they heard the sounds they were listening for. They did hear things, but it was usually just the ice on Winter Lake stirring and cracking in the cold. The connection between the aurora and the earth's magnetic field had been known about since 1741, but to this day geophysicists do not fully understand it. In any case when the aurora appeared the compasses were affected so reliably that on cloudy nights the officers could infer from the movements of the compass needles that the aurora was present even if they couldn't see it.

Franklin has little to say about the domestic arrangements in the fort. They had built three buildings, one for the officers, one for the men, and a storeroom. Hepburn, the English sailor, was forced to sleep with the voyageurs even though he did not speak their language. That was typical of the Royal Navy. It was quite strict about preventing fraternization between officers and sailors, and Franklin was not the type of officer who would have made an exception to that rule. The fort had other occupants as well. Akaitcho with his hunters and their families camped outside the fort into December, eating the dried meat they had provided to the expedition; Franklin finally had to ask him to leave and live elsewhere. But he left behind his elderly mother and two female attendants for Richardson to care for, plus another relative, an Indian guide named Keskarrah who was too old to hunt and whose wife was ill, an ulcer eating away at her face.

Keskarrah's fifteen- or sixteen-year-old daughter, a beauty they

named Greenstockings, was also living with them. Hepburn, reminisc-
ing many years later, said that Hood and George Back were rivals for
her affections, and the rivalry quickly became so intense in the confines
of the fort that the two men challenged each other to a duel over her.
Hepburn took the bullets from their pistols surreptitiously before one of
them got killed. In October Back volunteered to make a trip south to
Fort Providence to look for more supplies and, perhaps, to take himself
out of the picture. When he was gone Hood took Greenstockings into
his bed. She delivered herself of his child after the expedition had left
for the Arctic coast the following summer. Nobody knows whether
Hood knew he had made her pregnant.

Otherwise Hood occupied himself drawing the maps of their route
from York Factory to Fort Enterprise, while Richardson worked on his
collection of plants and animals. Richardson was a Scot and a veteran
like Franklin of the Napoleonic Wars. The word *surgeon* was the name
given medical doctors at that time; it does not imply that Richardson
was what we think of as a surgeon. Richardson's natural history work on
this expedition would lead ultimately to the publication, beginning in
1829, of a magisterial four-volume work on Arctic wildlife that became
the foundation of all subsequent work on the subject. He was an excellent botanist as well as zoologist. In the first days at Fort Enterprise,
before winter settled in, he identified forty-two separate species of
lichen, the favorite food of caribou. Four of them grew "in consort," he
noted, covering "the surfaces of most of the larger stones which strew
the barren grounds." The voyageurs had given these four species a common name, *tripe de roche*, rock tripe, possibly for their velveteen texture,
and probably all of them had eaten it at one time or another. Samuel
Hearne had written years earlier that it had "a gummy consistence . . . It
is remarkably good and pleasing when used to thicken any kind of
broth, but it is generally most esteemed when boiled in fish-liquor."
Hearne must have had steam pipes for guts. George Back called it "very
nauseous," and it gave most men severe intestinal cramps and diarrhea.

George Back's trip south was the most interesting event of the winter,
and the most important, for he went to ask for more supplies from the
North West and Hudson's Bay Company posts at Great Slave Lake, and
to pick up the expedition stores that had been abandoned at Rock
Depot nearly a year before, which the two companies had promised to
forward north when the chance came. By late November Franklin was
out of ammunition and powder and at one point was reduced to melting

pewter mugs to convert into lead balls. The Indians had used up most of their ammunition when they hunted for him while the caribou were migrating south. The hunters had killed hundreds of caribou and dried the meat, but by staying around Fort Enterprise they had eaten a good part of these stores. Franklin reduced his own men to five pounds of meat a day, from eight. More than anything he needed ammunition, and tobacco for the Indians. These supplies lay in bales and kegs and boxes at Rock Depot and York Factory. Without them the outcome of the expedition now depended entirely on the generosity of the fur companies.

Back's trip south was an effort to draw upon that generosity. It was another link in the chain of ordeals that the expedition had become. He left on October 18 with Willard Wentzel, plus two of the voyageurs and two Indian hunters and their wives. Franklin in his notes called the voyageurs simply "two men," but Back would have known not only their names—Gabriel Beauparlant and Jean-Baptiste Belanger—but something more personal about them. Back and Richardson were alike in that they both took an interest in the individuals who worked for them, Richardson in the Indian hunters and their families, whose names he struggled to transliterate, and Back in the French Canadians. Back had joined the Royal Navy in 1808 at the age of twelve; at thirteen the French had captured him during a raid when his ship was attacking the Spanish coast and he spent the next five years as a prisoner of war at Verdun, where he learned French and also how to draw, and saw enough of life in the raw, in prison, to toughen him both physically and emotionally.

The walking was the worst of it. Not only was the landscape uneven, all hills and valleys, but large stones lay on the ground everywhere, and the ground was wet and slippery. Only the shallower lakes had frozen, and even on those the ice was too thin to cross. And there were lakes in virtually every valley, so they had constantly to detour around them, doubling or tripling the distance they had to travel. It was slow work, and the Indians made it slower, running off to hunt every time they saw a caribou. Within five days they were down to eight lead balls, and the animals had disappeared. Nine days after leaving Fort Enterprise they were nearly out of food, and when an Indian woman caught a fish the Indians themselves did not partake of it. "We are accustomed to starvation," one of the Indians told Back, "but you are not." After it snowed the ground became even more difficult to walk on, the snow covering the stones, making it slipperier than ever underfoot, especially on snow-shoes. By October 28 the women were lame and the whole party was out of food. On the night of the thirtieth "the hunters," Back wrote his brother, "brought us a small quantity of pounded meat fat and a greater proportion of deer and Indian hair than either." They had collected it from the remains of an old skin bag that had been used to carry provisions. Fat and hair: "though it may not appear very enticing to a person in England," Back went on to his brother, "it was thought a great luxury—after three days starvation in America."

On November 2 they arrived at Fort Providence, which was being run over the winter by a man named Nicholas Weeks, an apprentice clerk, and his news was bad. They had been expecting sixteen packages, all they had left behind at Rock Depot, but there were only five. They were stored at the Hudson's Bay Company post at Moose Deer Island, across Great Slave Lake, and they consisted of the least useful articles: flour, sugar, three kegs of watered-down rum, one roll of tobacco, and only forty pounds of ammunition. Weeks said he had been ordered not to give them anything from his supplies. Back had no choice but to go on, but he had to wait for the lake to freeze before he could cross it. In the meantime he tried to sort out what had happened. The North West Company partner whose responsibility it would have been to pick up his share of the expedition's stores at Rock Depot, it turned out, had refused to do so. His canoes were full. He would not jettison NWC supplies in favor of the expedition's.

Back knew the five bales would be of little help. He would have to go farther, to Fort Chipewyan and higher authority. The situation was actually worse than he knew. Weeks had been telling tales to the Indians about the unreliability of the expedition's leaders. He was advising them not to supply them with meat. Where this animus came from is not known, but Weeks was obviously no friend. Later in the winter Franklin, unable to reward his Indian hunters for their work or supply them with ammunition, sent them to Fort Providence with notes, written on the running account the expedition kept with the fur companies, instructing Weeks to issue them the supplies they had earned. Weeks refused to honor these notes. Both fur companies had pledged to support the expedition in any way they could, but those pledges were breaking down on the ground, where fur company factors had to worry about their own survival, the health of their business, their profit margins, and the war between the two companies. Franklin and his officers could not grasp that the fur companies operated at the maximum of efficiency with the minimum of waste. The companies never sent more supplies to the wilderness posts than they thought they would need for a single season. They had nothing to spare for an enterprise like Franklin's. Franklin could not have come north at a worse time.

Back spent five months of that winter on foot traveling between the posts, walking a total of eleven hundred miles. At the end of December he found himself on the Slave River trying to keep leather shoes on the dogs' feet, which were so raw from pulling sleds down the rough river ice that the men had to drag the sleds themselves. On New Year's Eve they were navigating down the frozen river and "our journey this day was the most annoying we had yet experienced," with "vast masses of ice" piled on one another on the river, interrupted by open rapids they had to maneuver around. A gale was blowing out of the northwest and freezing their faces, which they had to rub constantly to keep the blood circulating, pulling off one mitten to rub in one place, quickly putting that hand back in the mitten before it froze, too, then rubbing another part of the face with the other hand. One man rubbed his face almost raw. Back himself could hardly walk from a recent sprain.

Yet overall the trip was a success. Two Inuit interpreters had arrived at one post and he was able to send them north to Fort Enterprise. At Fort Chipewyan he was able to cadge a significant quantity of supplies from the North West Company, enough to make sure the expedition could proceed. The HBC was less helpful, but in the end both companies had in fact done their best to help with the limited means available to them. Back reached Fort Enterprise in late March. Franklin asked him when he returned if he wanted to retrace his steps all the way to York Factory, take a vessel from there, sail to Wager Bay, and wait for them to show up. Wager Bay is on the west coast of Hudson Bay, well above Churchill; it is the inlet Christopher Middleton failed to explore all the way to the end. It was also where Franklin hoped his own exploration would lead him. Wisely, Back said no. Whether he could find a ship that would take him there was doubtful. The HBC schooner, they knew, was in disrepair. Men might be, once again, in short supply, and there just wasn't enough time. Back remained with Franklin instead and helped save his life.

Franklin had enough ammunition now, and enough supplies to trade for food with the Inuit he expected to meet; he had three big birchbark canoes for the trip down the Coppermine and along the coast. He had his Inuit interpreters, one named Augustus, who spoke a "tolerable" English, the other a younger companion to him named Junius who spoke only Inuit. He thought he was ready. They were still short of food at the fort, but at critical moments Indians showed up with meat. The season advanced into April and May, snow still two feet deep on the ground, but ducks and loons were appearing in small numbers and on May 14 they saw a robin.

A week later Akaitcho arrived with his party. All but Akaitcho and one hunter came with their faces painted, for a formal visit. Akaitcho wanted guns fired in salute in his honor as they approached the fort. He was in a decidedly bad mood.

To Franklin it must have seemed like the last straw. All winter he had fretted and worried, sent letters via Back remonstrating with the factors at Fort Chipewyan, to Weeks at Fort Providence, reminding them of their promises of supplies, of their patriotic duty to help the expedition proceed. He had taken pains to reassure the Indians that the rumors that ran wild around northern Canada—one rumor had them all killed by a party of raiding Inuit—were false, that their plans were firm and they were doing fine. The Great Father in London would honor all debts to them. He thought he had headed off all the rumors, had secured the cooperation of the Indians, had begged and cadged enough supplies to make this expedition a reality. Just a few months before Akaitcho had been so taken with Augustus, his newly arrived Inuit, that he had invited him to come share his camp with him. Augustus had accepted.

Now here he was, the Leader, as Franklin and the other officers called him, surly, uncooperative, ready, he announced, to abandon them to their own devices. He had a long list of complaints. The keg of spirits that had been kept for him was not as large "as he had been accustomed to receive." If he accepted it, it would be an insult to his dignity. He was upset by Weeks' action in refusing to honor Franklin's chits on the North West Company. He feared the same thing would happen to the larger rewards Franklin had promised for his help. He was disappointed that he had not been given "a Chief's dress" that spring. He could see that Franklin had trade goods now, and when Franklin explained that they were for the Inuit they expected to find on the coast, he was not mollified. This conversation continued, off and on, all day long.

Nor was Akaitcho the only problem. Franklin suspected that his interpreters, not Wentzel but the voyageurs, a man named St. Germain in particular, might have planted doubts in Akaitcho's mind, on purpose, to sabotage the expedition. St. Germain denied doing anything of the kind, but he had told Akaitcho, he admitted to Franklin, that he had himself received less rum at this post than at any other in the past.

The voyageurs were, indeed, afraid of what was coming. They feared the Inuit most of all. Not many years before, the Inuit had massacred a party of Dogrib Indians, whose lands bordered those of the Yellow Knives. They were deeply worried about the lack of provisions. Voyageurs knew what it took to feed them; they had years of experience carrying supplies around portages, driving canoes up and down rivers and across the wide lakes of northern Canada, doing the grunt work for the men who ran things. But none of them had taken a canoe into the open sea. None of them had ever even seen the sea. There was much to fear.

While all this trouble brewed Franklin was trying to arrange his stores and get ready for the journey down the Coppermine that they had come for, and the great pioneering reconnaissance along the coast. On May 25 Akaitcho's brother showed up with his band. One hundred and twenty-one Yellow Knives were now encamped around the fort. Franklin counted them: thirty hunters; thirty-one women; the rest children. Akaitcho continued to sulk and still refused to commit himself to hunting for them down the Coppermine to the coast. Franklin dealt out the few goods he could spare to Akaitcho's hunters, ammunition and clothing. Akaitcho kept to himself and refused to cooperate in this distribution.

Then suddenly the sulking was over. The Leader could see that he was beginning to lose authority with his own people, most of whom were only too glad for whatever goods Franklin could give them. All at once he was smiling, even friendly. He would help. He would send his men down the Coppermine to hunt, just as he had agreed to do.

Franklin came to think that all this trouble had arisen because Akaitcho wanted the goods reserved for the Inuit, and he may have been right, but Akaitcho was not merely greedy. He held his position in his tribe not as a hereditary leader, not as a king in any sense of the word. He led because he had shown himself more effective than any rival. And one thing a leader does is provide for his people. His position depended in part on his ability to cadge goods out of white men, the maximum quantity possible. If he had gotten more, he would only have been doing what he conceived as his job. He was a businessman and this was a business arrangement. He wanted better terms. When he saw that he wasn't going to get them, he gave up the fight and agreed to abide by the original deal.

But Franklin was shaken. He had come this far, held things together such a long way, a long time, only to find that his success depended entirely on his relationship with a man he regarded as a savage. In his journal he warned future travelers about "the fickle disposition and avaricious nature of these Indians, and how little reliance can be placed on their most faithful promises, when your views on proceedings jar in any way with their Interests, the mainspring of all their actions." It seems not to have occurred to him that "their Interests" are the driving force of most people's actions. Unfortunately for Franklin, he had no choice but to rely on a man he believed to be unreliable. He knew he might not make it to Hudson Bay. To make sure that food would be waiting for him if he had to return, he asked Wentzel to tell Akaitcho before the entire tribe that he wanted Fort Enterprise stocked with food while he was gone in case they had to come back. Wentzel did so. He understood now that nothing was certain this far from civilization and he had to provide for every possible contingency, even if it meant asking somebody he no longer trusted to make a promise.

Akaitcho made the promise. But he did not tell Franklin that he had very serious doubts about the feasibility of what these obstinate, rash white men were about to do. He did not expect a single one of them to survive.

CHAPTER SEVEN

DE QUOI À MANGER

Now that Akaitcho was cooperative again, Franklin and his party were free to leave—only winter was not quite over. The canoes had suffered the kind of damage that a winter in the Arctic will do to most man-made objects, but the weather remained too cold to work the tree gum that was used to repair them. On June 4 Franklin sent John Richardson north to the Coppermine with fifteen of his voyageurs, two Indian hunters, and most of the supplies, while he, Hood, Back, and Hepburn stayed behind to wait on the three canoes. The going was hard, as always. Seven men dragged their own small sledges; five carried burdens of eighty pounds on their backs, plus their personal gear, which Richardson guessed to weigh forty pounds each; and three men managed dog sledges. The dog sledges were double-loaded. Their food supplies consisted now of two bags of pemmican and five bags of fat with which to make more pemmican along the way. They had dried meat, portable soup, arrowroot, sixty-four pounds of gunpowder, sixty-eight pounds of ammunition, all the scientific instruments (which were heavy), metal tools for the Inuit, two tents, the sails and masts for the canoes, a bale of trade goods for the Inuit, fishing nets, ropes. They were well above the tree line, so that wood for fires was a sometime thing. On the first night, Richardson noted, "the want of fuel prevented our voyageurs from eating," and it was too cold to sleep. "They passed their time miserably enough."

The word *miserable* could describe this whole trip—little food, deep snow, wildly varying temperatures. The season only sixteen miles north of the fort was two weeks behind. On the night of June 6 it rained, softening the snow; the next day "we sink at least two feet at every step."

The men were quickly exhausted, but when the snow melted it was worse, for now there was water everywhere. It took six days to reach Point Lake, a fifty-mile-long widening of the Coppermine, and only fifty-four miles north of the Fort. Here they stopped and camped to wait for Franklin. Richardson sent thirteen of the voyageurs back to pick up the canoes and the rest of the supplies, and he stayed at the lake. It was June 11. The return trip to the fort, without their burdens, took only two days.

It would take them more than a month to reach the mouth of the river, where their expedition work could properly be said to begin. They had been close to two years just getting to that point. Dragging sledges and the heavy canoes down the string of long, narrow lakes that led to the actual river—Point Lake, Red Rock Lake, Rock Nest Lake—was an ordeal like the others. Three canoes were too many, too much weight; they left one behind. Sometimes caribou were abundant, sometimes scarce, and Franklin had to dig into his precious pemmican to feed the men, who were not only burning thousands of calories a day but suffering. They broke again and again through rotten ice, cutting their feet and legs on the stones beneath. They were always wet and usually cold. The men's legs became sore and inflamed from the burdens they were pulling or carrying. The lake ice was increasingly difficult to cross, open here and there, in other places only thinly frozen. "The recent rain," Back noted, "had damaged the ice so much, that it was now formed into innumerable spikes which not only gave excessive pain but actually penetrated the feet . . . the poor dogs suffered the most—and left tracks of blood at each step." Mosquitoes were as always a plague. By mid-July, according to Back, they "were so numerous and tormentingly troublesome, that it was with difficulty we could see a few yards before us." They wore gloves, wrapped handkerchiefs around their necks, tried to veil their faces, but it was no use. They were usually hungry. It took two caribou a day to feed them; seldom did they take two caribou a day. Franklin suspected that Akaitcho was more interested in hunting for his own people than for him. They continued to chip away at the pemmican.

The descent of the Coppermine proper, once the river emerged from the string of lakes, was easier but also more dangerous. By early July, the river was no longer frozen and they were in open water, running downstream, but the rapids were numerous, the river full of shoals. The current ran from three to six knots an hour, Back estimated, and the river was littered with moving ice now, "so that we had to contend with shoals, rocks, and ice, either of which (had we struck against) would have destroyed all our hopes at once." Only the great skill of the voyageurs in the canoes kept them safe. When they entered musk oxen country they were able to kill enough game to strip and dry meat beyond their daily needs. This meant cutting it into thin strips, then exposing it to the sun or to the heat of a slow fire, after which it would keep. One of Akaitcho's brothers, the Hook, gave them enough dried meat to make two and a half bags of pemmican. Franklin gave him a medal in return. On July 12 Akaitcho killed a grizzly bear and gave the meat to Franklin. The Yellow Knives did not eat grizzly meat because they regarded it as tainted. Grizzlies occasionally attacked, killed, and ate members of their tribe. It would have felt like a cannibalistic act to them to eat of the same animal.

The next day, July 13, they reached the Bloody Falls of the Coppermine, where the river cut through a range of hills, dropping through steep rapids down to the Arctic Ocean. The rapids take their name from the massacre that Samuel Hearne had witnessed fifty years before, his Yellow Knife guides killing a band of Inuit camped out there. Akaitcho would go no farther. They were in Inuit territory and he was already nervous. Memory was long in the North. The party halted above the falls and Franklin sent the two Inuit interpreters, Augustus and Junius, ahead to make contact with the Inuit they expected to find there. This was a crucial moment for Franklin. He was relying on the Inuit to help him in the same way Akaitcho and his band had helped. He would give them the usual presents, knives, hatchets, clothing, and they would hunt for him along the way and keep the expedition fed. It was important to be friendly, not to frighten them, not to show up in too much force.

Augustus and Junius did not return all day. On the second day Franklin and the entire party, anxious for their safety, set out to find them, the officers walking along the shore. Junius appeared that evening. They had made contact, found four Inuit lodges, had some conversation, conversing with them across the river. Augustus "shewed the presents he had [and that they were unarmed]—and told them the white people were come with plenty for them." But this news had only frightened them. They refused to land from their kayaks where Augustus and Junius were standing. That night they left their lodges and took refuge on an island farther downriver. "Next morning," wrote Richardson, "they returned and threw down their lodges, as if to give notice to any of their nation that might arrive, that, there was an enemy in the neighbourhood." That afternoon, when the rest of the expedition approached the falls on foot, they fled, leaving their possessions behind. It was a small group, four men, as many women. That night the expedition camped on the very site where the massacre had occurred so many years earlier. Bodies can be buried in the Arctic only with great difficulty because the permafrost lies just below the surface. Thus "the ground," noted Richardson, "is still strewed with human skulls."

On July 16 some of the voyageurs came upon other members of this small Inuit clan and approached them, but they fled too. An old man among them, however, was unable to get away, and they were finally able to find out a little about these people. The old man's name was "the White-fox" and he and his tribe had never seen white people before, although they had heard of them. They spent their winters a little to the west in igloos and came to the mouth of the Coppermine in the summer to fish for salmon, which they dried. The officers gave him gifts—hatchets and other metal "instruments," probably ice chisels—and he was pleased with them and promised to try to persuade the young men to come and talk, but they learned from an old woman who appeared that night that the entire band had disappeared. The next day, when other Inuit showed up near the mouth of the river, they fled as soon as they saw the expedition tents. This in turn spooked Akaitcho and his men. He decided to leave the next day, fearful of being surrounded, his retreat cut off. Franklin tried to persuade one or two of the Yellow Knife hunters to follow them along the coast and hunt game for them. None would agree.

That day, July 18, the expedition reached the Arctic Ocean. With the Yellow Knives leaving, Willard Wentzel had no reason to continue, and he left with them. Franklin discharged four voyageurs and sent them back with Wentzel and the Indians. He had planned to cut his party to twenty men when they reached the coast. More would have gone back if they could. "Our voyageurs seem terrified at the idea of a voyage through an icy sea in bark canoes, and have had frequent debates on the subject," Richardson observed. "The two Interpreters in particular express their fears with the least disguise and have made many urgent requests to be allowed to return with Mr. Wentzel." It was not only the sea they were afraid of. The expedition now had provisions for a mere two weeks of travel. They were about to set out on a journey of hundreds of miles along an unknown coast where they would have to live off whatever bounty the land and the sea produced. But the officers were happy. They were on their element, the ocean, for the first time in two years, and the first day they covered some thirty miles. It must have been a euphoric feeling after all they had endured to get there. Back wrote in his notebook that they speculated "about being in time for the homeward bound ships—in Hudsons Bay."

But this was the Arctic, and while the ocean was not frozen solid, there was ice everywhere in the water—pack ice, brash ice, floes, an occasional small iceberg—and they were in bark canoes. Depending on which way the wind was blowing, pack ice moved offshore, leaving them room to maneuver, or, if the wind was from the opposite direction, closed in on them. They could set sails when the wind was light, but when it blew hard and the waves were too high they had to stay put and watch a precious day or two of progress, maybe even three, vanish. They took chances, squeezed through channels in the ice where channels hardly existed. The coast was rocky and barren, high cliffs lined the shore, and there were chains of islands offshore. From day to day they saw Inuit encampments, but they were all abandoned. They could not depend on Inuit hunters when there were no Inuit to be found. The voyageurs continued to be afraid. "We overheard them stating their fears of starvation or of being crushed amongst the ice," wrote George Back. They had, he went on, to "be treated and humoured exactly like children—that is when you are short of provisions—for as long as the article lasts—you may lead them anywhere—it is quite indifferent to them whilst there is *de quoi à manger.*"

Enough to eat. That had been the issue from the beginning two years before. Occasionally they shot a caribou, but mostly they hunted without success. The land was barren, growing nothing but lichen, moss, and occasional patches of grass, and the voyageurs lacked the hunting skills of Indians. The caribou could see them coming from a long way off. They set out fishing nets whenever they camped for the night, but the catch was usually small. Supplies were dwindling fast. On July 24 they reached a rough headland on a day so foggy they could not see the tops of the hills. They named it Cape Barrow. They named every feature of the land as they went along, capes, bays, islands. Hepburn had an island named after him; Wentzel a river. Spreading names over the landscape is the peculiar privilege of explorers. Being in canoes, low in the water, they had trouble distinguishing islands from the mainland. They could tell their bearings but could not tell whether they were on the north side of islands that could take them away from the coast without their know-ing. After they rounded Cape Barrow the coast trended southeast, then south.

Without knowing it, they had entered a huge inlet which they even-tually named Bathurst Inlet, after Lord Bathurst, who ran the Colonial Office. It took them into a smaller body of water they called Arctic Bay, around a projection of land they called Banks Peninsula, after Joseph Banks, and then north again, day after day spent following the coastline. They were obliged to do so. They were mapping the coast; that was their job. But it was not taking them east, toward Hudson Bay. It took them south, it came to its narrow bottom, and then it took them north. Finally the land veered to the east again. They could see more land to the north, but they thought it was just more islands. It was not. They were pushing east into another inlet. They named this one Melville Sound and were forced to turn west again along its northern shore and around another peninsula, and it was now well into August.

They shot a bear one day that was so lean the voyageurs thought it was ill and, hungry as they were, would not eat it, but the officers boiled the paws and found them delicious. Sometimes they found driftwood for a fire. When wood failed them and they could not cook their food they had to dip into the pemmican. They had wasted days, weeks, in Bathurst Inlet, in Melville Sound. Fog, rain, gales of wind grounded them on other days. By August 9 they had two bags of pemmican left and a "small bundle of dried meat," wrote Richardson. There were twenty of them, twenty hardworking men who had to be fed every day. "The men began to apprehend the approach of absolute want, and we have for some days had to listen to their gloomy forebodings of the deer [i.e., caribou] entirely quitting the coast in a few days."

They had yet to see any of the Inuit they had been hoping to trade with for food, and they never did.

They attained their farthest east at the closed end of Melville Sound; then they were traveling back the way they had come. "Paddled the whole day along the northern shores of Melville Sound," Richardson reported. "They are flat and invisible from the opposite side of the sound, otherwise a short traverse might have saved us some days of time." On August 15 they came to the open end of Melville Sound again and bad weather drove them ashore. The weather indeed was beginning to fall apart. A year earlier on this date they had almost reached the site where they would stop traveling north and settle in for the winter. The voyageurs were close to panic. From the shortness of the provisions, the coldness of the nights, they deemed "any attempt to proceed farther as little short of madness." The canoes were suffering serious damage from the stress of ocean travel. On one of them fifteen of the seventy-odd ribs were broken, one of those in two places. Franklin and Richardson began to suspect the voyageurs of intentionally not killing game, in order to force Franklin to turn around.

He was not ready to do so. The exploration of Bathurst Inlet had killed all prospects of reaching Hudson Bay, but Franklin wanted to make sure the coast turned east again. John Ross had ruined his career by not going far enough. Risk and danger, Barrow had written, were of the essence of success in a naval career. Magellan had not turned around and sailed home. Columbus had been fearless in the face of the unknown.

On the fifteenth, after talking with his officers, Franklin told the men he would turn back as soon as they saw the coast trend eastward. That cheered them up. But the weather stayed bad for the next three days. On the eighteenth, pinned down by storms, some of the officers walked ahead ten miles and saw in the distance that the land did turn east. Point Turnagain, they called it. Dinner was a fox that night, and a portion of an unwary caribou that Augustus had managed to kill. On the twentieth they began eating their last bag of pemmican. It would last three days with care, longer if they could bear the hunger.

That night it was squally with frost and snow. Out hunting, Augustus lost his way in the vastness of this landscape and wandered all night. He saw caribou, plenty of them, but could not get close. On August 22 they got into the canoes and turned south. Richardson added up the mileage. They had covered only five degrees of longitude from the mouth of the Coppermine River, a little more than a fifth of the distance, he calculated, to Hudson Bay. But they had gone 550 miles all told, both along the coast and in and around the folds and intricacies of Bathurst Inlet. That was a little less than the straight-line distance to Hudson Bay from the Coppermine River—if they had been able to travel in a straight line.

Now it began, the race home, back to Bathurst Inlet, running south into it, to where a river (which they had named Hood River) emptied into its west coast, then up that river into the barren grounds, across these to Point Lake, that is, back to the Coppermine at the point they had started from, and from there straight south again to Fort Enterprise. That was the plan. They were trying to stretch the last of the pemmican, doling out small amounts to the men each day. The caribou had begun their own retreat from the coast toward the tree line. The caribou and the geese had a line on the weather, and they were leaving. The distance from the mouth of Hood River, which they reached on August 24, to Fort Enterprise was a little over two hundred miles in a straight line, but they could not travel in a straight line. They were crossing unknown country, a blank on the map. There would be unknown rivers and lakes to cross, hills, obstacles. Twenty men, two hundred miles, deteriorating weather, no wood, and food an enormous if. The Indians had told Back the previous winter what they were all now learning firsthand: the Indians knew how to starve, but the whites did not.

They paused at the mouth of the Hood for a few days so that the men could take the damaged canoes apart and rebuild them on a smaller scale. They would need canoes to cross the lakes in their path and to navigate up the Hood (which proved unnavigable), but at their current length and weight they were too bulky. Franklin distributed clothing from the stores to the men who needed it and cached some, but not all, of the hatchets and ice chisels that had been reserved for the Inuit. They took with them ammunition, nets, the scientific instruments, the two tents, their bedding, some spare clothing, the canoes, cooking utensils, and whatever food remained, which still included some portable soup. The loads were heavy, says Richardson, and when they killed three musk oxen late on the afternoon of August 31, the day they left, they could carry only a small amount of meat with them because of the weight of their loads.

The men carrying the canoes had it the worst. They bore them on their backs and it was like carrying a heavy sail; in a wind they were constantly being knocked over. And the weather was bad. The first night wind blew down the tent the officers were sleeping in. It rained, then it snowed. When they woke up the thermometer read two degrees above freezing. The first three days they were lucky and shot enough game to feed themselves, and they built fires out of the dried moss that covered the ground. But by September 4 they were consuming the very last of the pemmican. On the fifth it rained, then snowed heavily. Now they had nothing to eat, so they stayed in bed, "but the Covering of the blanket was insufficient to preserve us from feeling the severity of the frost and suffering in consequence the drifting of the snow into the Tents," wrote Franklin. This storm lasted three days. "We suffered much from the Cold, but more from hunger." Outside the tent the drifts were running to three feet. Winter had come all at once, like night in the tropics, and the wind was relentless. Franklin ordered them to set out anyway, but the tents were frozen and could not be folded. So were the bed-clothes, and "no one could keep his hands long out of his Mittens." When he stepped outside his tent Franklin fainted from hunger. A little "piece" of soup—no doubt itself frozen, because they could not light a fire—revived him. They struggled on. It was only September 7, they had come only a little way, but already they were in deep trouble.

It got deeper that afternoon when the man carrying the best of the two canoes fell down under his load once too often, and the canoe was "so much broken as to be rendered entirely useless." They burned it that noon and used the fire to cook the very last of their portable soup and the remaining arrowroot. That night they ate a few partridges they had killed, boiled with *tripe de roche,* which now became their principal food. It was the first of many meals that would consist mostly, if not entirely, of the nearly indigestible lichen.

Good days followed bad. Sometimes they came upon game and were able to kill an animal. When they killed a musk ox the entire party swarmed over it like wolves or hyenas and ate the intestines raw. They proved, said Franklin, to be excellent. Snow covered the rocks on the stony ground and they fell down again and again. It was hardest on the men carrying the heavy loads. "The whole party complained more," wrote Franklin, "of weakness & fatigue than they had ever done before." On September 13 they abandoned some of the scientific instruments and anything else that was not absolutely necessary for survival. Franklin started promising rewards to the hunters who went out ahead searching for game. On September 14 one of the voyageurs, a man named Ignace Perrault, surprised the officers by giving each of them a small piece of meat he had saved out of his own rations. This unex-pected act of generosity brought the officers to tears. Franklin was usu-ally dismissive of the voyageurs; he regarded them as employees at best, children at worst. This was one of the few times Franklin actually used a voyageur's name in his narrative.

The same day one of these voyageurs almost drowned when they came to a river they had to cross at a rapid and the only canoe capsized, leaving Franklin, Solomon Belanger, and the translator, Pierre St. Ger-main, standing in frigid meltwater up to their waists. St. Germain was able to rescue the boat and ferry Franklin the rest of the way across the river, but Belanger was left in the river waiting for help. It took time and effort to rescue him. When they got him to the riverbank Richardson ordered him to strip and rolled him in a blanket, and two of the men stripped and went to bed with him, but it was hours before he recovered feeling in his body. Franklin, meanwhile, was left on the other shore, by himself, "unprovided either with Gun, Ammunition or even the Means of making Fire, and Seperated from my Companions by this fatal River and Conscious that if the Canoe should be destroyed, or rendered so ineffective as to be unable to cross the Party I never Could rejoin them." This was terror speaking, just barely suppressed. The canoe was not destroyed and the rest of the party joined him soon enough, but Franklin lost one of his journals in the river and his astronomical records, swept away when the canoe capsized. He may have lost his confidence as well.

It snowed some days; other days were mild. One night they boiled up moss for supper, but it was too bitter for most of them to eat. Most often they ate *tripe de roche*, but that was almost as difficult to swallow, and Hood in particular found it inedible. It ran right through him and he was getting steadily weaker. On September 21 John Richardson abandoned the plant specimens he had so laboriously and carefully gathered on the Arctic coast. They were straggling on the march now, some men falling well behind despite all efforts to keep them together. The man carrying the canoe begged Franklin for permission to abandon it as he had the hardest task by far, but Franklin refused. The man abandoned it anyway after falling down and damaging it, as he claimed, beyond repair. The voyageurs had run out of hope, Franklin said. The expedition had run out of canoes, the only means they had to cross rivers. Everyone was eating whatever leather they could find around their person, including their old shoes, the rawhide moccasins the Indian women had made for them. Then on September 25 came a piece of luck—five small caribou killed. They ate for two days and made themselves sick in the process. Then that food was gone.

So was their luck. They had come to that river they had to cross, the Coppermine; the canoes were gone, the river was 120 yards wide, and the water temperature stood at thirty-eight degrees. On the other side lay Fort Enterprise, forty miles away. "Then they deeply lamented their folly & impatience in breaking the canoe," Franklin reported, although there was no evidence that the voyageur carrying it broke it on purpose. He then accused them of stealing food from the officers. He was convinced the officers had suffered more than the men. They were of "less robust habit" because they were "less accustomed to privation." One gets the impression reading him that Franklin believed, once again, that he himself had suffered most of all. "There is little compassion in the human frame," George Back had written in his notebook back on the Coppermine, "when it is in a state of privation."

Obstruction Rapids, they came to call it, this cold, wide, treacherous place they could not walk around because they had no idea how far it would be upriver to a fordable location. The Coppermine was a string of lakes in this part of the territory it drained. It might be thirty, forty miles to a river ford. The nearest wood, they knew, with which they might make a raft, was on Point Lake, downriver and twenty miles away. All they had to work with nearby were some river willows, hardly more than shrubs. The men said they would try to make a raft out of them, tying them together in faggots. If only one man could get across on this craft, with a rope in hand, they could run people back and forth across the river using ropes at either end, so that nobody would have to paddle.

That was the plan this time. Meanwhile they found the carcass of a caribou that had fallen in the cleft of a rock and died. It was putrid, but they ate it anyway, with a kind of grim pleasure. Franklin offered a reward to the man who managed to get the willow raft across the river, and two tried. The willow sticks were green and not buoyant enough to support more than one at a time. They had only one oar; they could not make a pole long enough to reach bottom. A powerful wind from the other side of the river kept blowing the raft back to them.

Then Richardson volunteered to swim the line across. He tied the line around his waist and dove in. He soon lost the use of his arms to the cold, so he turned over and tried to propel himself with his legs. He got almost the whole way over before he sank out of sight. They hauled him back, wrapped him in blankets, and thawed him out, but it was hours before he could speak again. Franklin says that they all stared at his naked body, amazed to see how skeletal he had become. They had all become skeletal; they were all weak. The body eats itself when it is starving, eats muscle, even heart muscle. They were as weak as children now.

They made another, more buoyant raft, but the wind was against them for the next two days. On the second day it snowed heavily again. One of the men brought in the antlers and backbone of a caribou and they dug out the rotting marrow and ate that. Junius, the younger of the two Inuit, had wandered off by himself. He was never seen again and was probably the first to die. Franklin set out to find St. Germain, the interpreter, who was camped by the willows three-quarters of a mile away, trying to fashion a raft. After three hours of walking he could not make it through the fresh snow and gave up. No one had any energy so they did the little they could do in slow motion. "The keen sensation of hunger is no longer felt by any of us," Franklin wrote, "yet it is remarkable that we Scarcely can Converse on any other Subject than the pleasure of eating." This is the common subject of starving people everywhere.

They spent a week in all at the rapids. On October 4 St. Germain finished the canoelike boat he had built out of willow sticks, managed to get a line to the other side of the river, and the entire party got across, one by one. Once again Franklin sent George Back south, taking with him St. Germain, Back's "servant" Gabriel Beauparlant, and the strongest of the voyageurs, Solomon Belanger, Belanger *"le gros,"* to find the Indians and send them back with provisions. On October 5 they all set out for the fort on a meal of *tripe de roche,* wading through snow two feet deep. They ate pieces of leather that they held up to the fire, and again some of their old shoes. The wind blew fiercely. It was hopeless to try to keep them all together. Two of the stragglers were more than a mile behind. Richardson went back to them; when he reached the first one, a man named Registe Vaillant, he found him falling down at every step. He urged him to get up, to keep going. He could not find the other, Matthew Pellonquin. These were the names of the second and third to die.

Plans changed now. Franklin proposed splitting the party in two. He would walk ahead to Fort Enterprise with whichever men were strong enough to go with him, while Hood would stay at the first clump of woods large enough to provide fuel for a fire, and those who could not go on would stay with him. Richardson with his great heart volunteered to stay behind with Hood, and so did Hepburn, the sailor. They found a clump of willows the next day, October 7, and pitched a tent for them. The voyageurs left almost all their burden there, carrying only what they absolutely needed, ammunition, blankets, the other tent, guns, the officers' journals, and two pairs of Franklin's shoes. Then they parted and Franklin, who was "deeply afflicted," took the voyageurs south. The voyageurs Joseph Peltier and Joseph Benoît promised to return with food as soon as they found it, and relieve them. Richardson put little stock in this vow. "Our knowledge . . . of the voyageur character prevented us from confiding in their promises," he wrote. Unless Franklin found Indians they had "no hope whatever of human aid." No one was strong enough to hunt.

Franklin and the voyageurs made less than five miles that day. Two of them barely made it that far. One, Jean-Baptiste Belanger, burst into tears when he caught up with the others; he could not go on. The other, Michel Teroahaute, the Iroquois, was almost as bad. The next morning Franklin let them both return to Richardson's camp. They drank Indian tea, an herb tea, for dinner. There was no other nourishment. The weather was so cold they could not sleep. The next morning two more men dropped out, the Italian Vincenzo Fontana and Ignace Perrault, to return to Richardson's camp. The wind blew at gale force out of the southwest, the air was frigid, the snow deep. Franklin and the men crossed a lake to get out of the snow and the wind blew them down on the smooth ice. They walked another mile or so and camped. Franklin was down to five men: himself, Joseph Peltier, Joseph Benoît, François Samandre, and Jean Baptiste Adam, one of the interpreters to the Copper Indians. Augustus had disappeared by now too; he had gone on ahead.

They marched on, falling on lake ice, slipping on stones hidden under the snow, for three more days, eating *tripe de roche* when they could find it, drinking Indian tea when they could not, finishing off bits of scorched leather they had hid in their clothes for the end. They had no tent now, having saved of it only enough canvas to provide a wind screen. Franklin was not taking temperatures anymore but he repeatedly described the air as bitterly cold.

They reached Fort Enterprise at last, only to find that their ordeal had no limit. Fort Enterprise was empty. The treacherous Akaitcho had cached no provisions for them. Mr. Wentzel had left no note, no explanation. They were dead men.

George Back had, however, left a note. He was heading south, hoping to find the Indians, although he had no idea where they were. If necessary, he would try for Fort Providence, 140 miles to the south. In the meantime, starvation. Franklin could send nothing back to the men he had left behind with Hood, and he was sure now that they would die. He could barely walk himself. It was October 11. The previous winter the caribou had been abundant around the fort on this date, but this year there were none. The only thing they could find to eat were rotting caribou skins that had been discarded at the fort the previous spring. Augustus, who had lost his way again, came in that day.

Franklin kept notes at Fort Enterprise that October from which he later constructed his journal of the days spent waiting there, and while they are in places indecipherable we can catch a glimpse of how they fared. They ate pounded bones, *tripe de roche* when they felt strong enough to go out and look for it or when the weather allowed them to do so, and scraps of discarded skin, including the skins used to hold the mortar when they had built the fort the previous year. One day Solomon Belanger, who had gone ahead with Back, showed up with a note from him saying that he was holed up at a spot where he hoped to find Indians, but none had appeared. Franklin's legs and feet were swollen and inflamed. Jean-Baptiste Adam could not move at all. On the twenty-first Franklin tried to walk south with Augustus and Benoît to look for the Indians himself, but he was too weak to go on and sent the other two men on alone. When a caribou appeared around the fort nobody had the strength to pursue it. On cold days—one day the temperature dropped to twenty below—nobody ventured outside to gather *tripe de roche,* and they ate nothing but the skins and the pounded bones. They prized most of all the skins that contained larvae of the warble fly, which is parasitic on caribou, for the protein in these worms. On October 27 Franklin wrote that his strength was failing daily. "And to this debility is added an indifference to exercise or even moving."

He remembered then that it was the anniversary of the day he had joined the navy. "I have been exposed," he wrote, "to a variety of hardships in my professional . . . , but never placed in such a . . . or afflicting Situation, as at present where even hope seems to be . . . Surely I ought to . . . God for his . . ." The missing words are illegible. Did he think he should curse God or praise him? Did he maintain his Christian faith? In England, later, to those who asked, he would ascribe his salvation entirely to prayer.

On October 29 Richardson and Hepburn made it to the fort to find that of the four there, Franklin, Peltier, Adam, and Samandre, only Peltier was able to bring in firewood. Adam was in bed, unable to move, Samandre could not stir from the fire. They were all shockingly gaunt. "The hollow and sepulchral sound of their voices," Richardson wrote, "produced nearly as great horror in us, as our emaciated appearance did on them." Hepburn still had a little strength. He spent the next day outdoors, hunting caribou, but could not hold the gun steady enough to aim and killed nothing. On November 1 Peltier and Samandre died within a few hours of each other. Hepburn and Richardson were growing weaker by the hour. They were using pieces of Fort Enterprise itself for firewood and spent all day on November 2 trying to dismantle portions of it for the fire, "but the mud between the logs was so hard frozen, that the labour of seperating [*sic*] them exceeded our strength." They had fire for only half a day that day. Hepburn's limbs began to swell. Adam's limbs were so swollen, Richardson had to cut open the skin to release water from his flesh. The soup they made from the old bones was so acid, it burned their mouths.

Then came deliverance. On November 7 three of Akaitcho's hunters arrived with dried meat and fat. St. Germain, the interpreter, had found the Yellow Knives.

Eleven men died in all. Not all of them died of starvation. Four men— Jean-Baptiste Belanger, Michel Teroahaute, the Iroquois, followed shortly after by Fontana and Perrault—had left Franklin's party early in October to struggle the five miles back to the willow grove where Richardson, Hood, and Hepburn were camped. Only Michel arrived. Richardson never wrote up in his journal an actual day-by-day account of what happened after that, but he did prepare an official report to the Admiralty. Those days were spent, he said, hunting for the lichen that poor Hood could not eat and trying to snare partridges. Michel came and went as he wished, keeping himself apart, behaving in a hostile and surly manner. One evening he brought back a piece of what he said was a wolf that a caribou had killed with his antlers, and they ate it, but later Richardson would come to believe that it was a piece of a man he brought back, Belanger or maybe Perrault.

No one knows whether he actually killed these men, or whether they collapsed on the way back to Richardson's camp. It is certain that he killed Hood. By the eighteenth Hood was "so weak as to be scarcely able to sit up at the fire-side, and complained that the least breeze of wind seemed to blow through his frame." He gathered the strength nevertheless to argue with Michel, telling him it was his duty to hunt for them and to bring wood to the fire, which Michel refused to do, while threatening at the same time to leave them and go to the fort by himself. On the twentieth, while Richardson was out of camp looking for *tripe de roche,* he heard a gunshot, and Hepburn yelled to him to return right away. Hood was in their tent, shot through the head. Michel claimed that Hood had shot himself, but that was impossible. He had been shot through the back of the head, with a rifle. "Although I dared not," Richardson explained, "openly to evince any suspicion that I thought

Michel guilty of the deed, yet he repeatedly protested to me that he was incapable of committing such an act, kept constantly on his guard, and carefully avoided leaving Hepburn and me together."

The next day they set out for Fort Enterprise. On the twenty-third, as they were struggling south, Michel began threatening them, told them he hated the white people, by whom he meant the French voyageurs, "some of whom, he said, had killed and eaten his uncle and two of his relations." Michel was well armed. He had besides his gun "two pistols, an Indian bayonet, and a knife." Hepburn and Richardson had no strength left and expected him to turn on them at the first opportunity. When they came to a rock where there was some *tripe de roche*, Michel stayed behind to gather it, and Richardson and Hepburn seized the opportunity, the first they had had, to compare notes. Hepburn offered to do the deed, but Richardson said no, he would do it himself. When Michel came up to them, Richardson put a bullet through his head. Then they looked in his pouch. Michel had in fact gathered no *tripe de roche*.

Hood, then, had been killed, and now Michel, and possibly Jean-Baptiste Belanger and Ignace Perrault as well. Vaillant and Pellonquin had lain down in the snow and died. Fontana had disappeared somewhere in this wilderness. At Fort Enterprise two more, Samandre and Peltier, had died of starvation. Junius had wandered off to his own fate and was almost certainly dead. Ten out of the twenty men who had left the mouth of the Coppermine River to explore the Arctic coast had lost their lives.

There was one more to go. Gabriel Beauparlant, on Back's trek south to find the Indians, died of starvation and exhaustion not long into it. C. Stuart Houston, the doctor and historian who edited Back's journal, raises the question of whether the three men remaining fed on Beauparlant's corpse to survive. In his journal Back attributed their survival to the providential discovery of some frozen caribou heads, which seemed to abound in the area where they camped, because they kept finding more when they needed them. Months later, however, during the winter they spent at Fort Chipewyan recuperating, Back told Willard Wentzel, "To tell the truth, Wentzel, things have taken place which *must* not be known."

CHAPTER EIGHT

A FINE ROMANCE

Franklin was amazed at how tenderly the Indians who brought them food on November 7, when they were all on the point of death, treated them. They cleaned out the room where Franklin and the other survivors were holed up, something the survivors had not had the strength to do, and encouraged them to clean themselves up as well. It was more than a week before they could travel, and then the Indians "gave us their snow-shoes, and walked without themselves, keeping by our sides, that they might lift us when we fell."

They were headed south, toward Akaitcho's encampment, and he was equally tender when they reached it on November 26. Although his band was short of food, he spared nothing to get Franklin and his men back on their feet, and the chief, who never prepared his own food, personally cooked for them. The entire tribe visited them one by one during the day, to show their sympathy for what the survivors had endured.

Later Franklin would learn from Wentzel why no food had been cached for them at Fort Enterprise. One reason was that Akaitcho really had given them up for dead the day he left them at the mouth of the Coppermine. But he might have fulfilled his promise nevertheless if he had had ammunition. Wentzel had applied to Fort Providence for more but there was none to spare. The Indians had been reduced that summer to breaking up old axes to turn them into shot for their weapons. Then three of the tribe's hunters closely related to Akaitcho's family had drowned when their canoe overturned on one of the lakes. This, Wentzel explained, "had the effect of unhinging . . . the minds of all these families." As was their custom, they destroyed belongings in a rage of grief and could hardly be persuaded to hunt for their own survival.

They were still in mourning when Franklin arrived at their camp in late November. One woman, who had lost her only son, wandered around the camp all day calling his name.

On December 1 Akaitcho and the entire tribe decamped with Franklin and the other survivors for Fort Providence. En route Franklin received letters from England, forwarded north from the fort, informing him that he and Richardson and the murdered Hood had been promoted. He was now *Captain* John Franklin. He was also told that the rivalry between the North West Company and the Hudson's Bay Company that had caused them so much grief was over. It was too late to do them any good; nevertheless, the two companies had merged under the name of the latter that very summer. The traders now worked for one organization and were no longer at each other's throats. The news and the letters also came with fresh clothing. Franklin and the others had been wearing the same linens next to their skin that they had been wearing when they left the coast of the Arctic Ocean three months earlier.

They spent the rest of the winter not at Fort Providence but at the HBC facility on Moose Deer Island in Great Slave Lake. Franklin wrote Wentzel that "we pass the time very pleasantly . . . between business, chatting, and an occasional play, the hours are imperceptibly beguiled away and we look to the Sudden appearance of spring & an early departure." They left on May 26 and reached York Factory on July 14. Toward the beginning of September they sailed for England on the *Prince of Wales,* the same ship they had come out on, and by late October Franklin was writing letters datelined from Osborne's Hotel Adelphi in London.

It would be interesting to know what Franklin thought of his experience in the Arctic as it came to an end. Eleven people had died under his command, but when he wrote to John Barrow from Moose Deer Island in April 1822, it was to report on Hood's death. The others, the voyageur deaths, he barely mentioned. Franklin, when he wrote, was not forthcoming about himself. His correspondence tended to the stiff and formal, and he was aware of that fact, confessing to his first wife that he was not adept at putting his feelings into words. He had a positive horror of writing and dreaded the task of writing the account of the expedition he knew faced him on his return. He did some of it in consultation with John Barrow, and Richardson helped too. Needless to add, it was Barrow who reviewed the book for *The Quarterly.* Enthusiastically.

In recent years critics, in particular Canadian critics, have not been so enthusiastic. Richard C. Davis, who published the exhaustively researched edition of Franklin's original journals from this expedition for the Champlain Society, thinks Franklin learned little or nothing from his experience and never achieved any understanding of why the Yellow Knife Indians acted as they did. Franklin's narrative is indeed full of imprecations against what he saw as the unstable and disloyal behavior of the Indians at different times. He seemed equally incapable of understanding why the rival fur companies would not supply him with everything he demanded when he had been assured that they would by the heads of the two companies. Franklin had been in the Royal Navy since he was fourteen years old. He saw the world from a hierarchical perspective. He was a naval officer, on government business, engaged in an enterprise of national importance. That in his mind would have taken precedence over all merely commercial considerations. He had been promised cooperation, furthermore. He clearly looked at his contract with the Indians from the same perspective. He was paying them, if only in goods, and he expected them to do what he told them to do and what they had agreed they would do. He was not one to adapt to local circumstances, which was how the Indians survived in that deadly climate. He lacked the imagination to understand feelings foreign to himself, like the depth of Indian grief.

All this is true, and Davis makes all these points. It seems clear that the fur traders themselves had little respect for Franklin. George Simpson, a trader with the Hudson's Bay Company and the man most responsible for bringing the two companies together, noted of Franklin that he "has not the physical powers required for the labor of moderate voyaging in this country; he must have three meals p diem, Tea is indispensable, and with the utmost exertion he cannot walk above *Eight* miles in one day." Wentzel, who was paid the remarkably large sum of six hundred pounds for his services, wrote in a letter to another official of the NWC that "this much however may be safely said of the officers, that they acted on some occasions imprudently, injudiciously and showed in one particular instance an unpardonable want of conduct." He seemed to be referring to Richardson's peremptory execution of Michel, the Iroquois, after Hood's murder. About fifty years ago a woman named Margaret Macleod discovered a manuscript skit about the Franklin expedition in fur company archives, and Richard Glover, who printed it in *Polar Record*, the journal of the Scott Polar Research Institute in Cambridge, England, notes that the traders believed there was a great deal of dissension among the expedition officers. The skit itself is unremarkable except for its mocking tone. Franklin is portrayed as Mr. Mildmay, an ineffective leader who lacks the decisiveness needed to command.

Some of this characterization is unfair. On the winter trip from Cumberland House to Fort Chipewyan, Franklin walked an average of sixteen miles a day, mostly on snowshoes, and lived, as the voyageurs with him lived, on two meals a day, not three. Much of the impression of dissension between the officers that we see in the fur company records seems to have come from George Back's winter trip of 1820–21 to the trading posts to beg for supplies. Back was young, abrasive, and all too talkative. He had a lively, gossipy mind, and he may have exaggerated minor differences of temperament and opinion into actual dissension. The only real dissension we know about originated in the rivalry between Back and Hood for Greenstockings's affections, which Back had lost.

As for Franklin himself, it would have taken a rare officer to transcend his training, his naval experience, and his instructions from John Barrow and adapt, as circumstances did indeed require, to the weather and the land. The worst thing Franklin did was to go on when he should have turned for home. It is an incredible thing in itself to launch birch-bark canoes on an ice-strewn ocean, yet he might have gotten away with it had he listened to his voyageurs and bolted for the fort when he found himself deep in Bathurst Inlet with his pemmican supply nearly exhausted and winter not quite yet set in.

But risk is the essence of exploration, Barrow had written, and Franklin was a brave man. The voyageurs knew how unpredictable the onset of winter was in the Arctic. They knew what they needed to live on, they knew how hard it was to kill game in open treeless country, and they had found not a single Inuit along the Arctic coast. They were all afraid for their lives. But Franklin would never have listened to them. He regarded them as children, illiterate, excitable, happy only when their stomachs were full. All the officers felt that way. Franklin hardly knew the voyageurs' names, and it is truly striking to see in his published account how much contempt he exhibited toward them, how little interest he took in them. Even while coming back across the barren grounds, he made these men carry heavy weights and burn body tissue they could not replace, exhausting their resources. Yet one of them saved enough food out of his daily allowance to give it to the officers. Franklin was touched by the gesture and took space in his account to commend the man. But a few days later he was full of contempt again when the voyageur carrying the last canoe got blown over by the wind once too often and, as Franklin assumed, deliberately destroyed it. Franklin was carrying only his own personal belongings. Yet Franklin insisted that the officers suffered more. Perhaps he had seen too many dead bodies on the bottom at the Battle of Copenhagen, lost too many shipmates at Trafalgar. Compassion seems to have been drained out of him.

John Barrow wasted no tears on the dead voyageurs, either. "The narrative of Captain Franklin," he wrote in his review of the book (it's worth quoting at length),

> adds another to the many splendid records of the enterprize, zeal, and energy of British seamen—of that cool and intrepid conduct, which never forsakes them on occasions the most trying—that unshaken constancy and perseverance in situations the most arduous, the most distressing, and sometimes the most hopeless that can befal [*sic*] human beings; and it furnishes a beautiful example of the triumph of mental and moral energy over mere brute strength, in the simple fact that, out of fifteen individuals enured from their birth to cold, fatigue, and hunger, no less than ten were so subdued by the aggravation of those evils to which they had been habituated, as to give themselves up to indifference, insubordination, and despair, and, finally, to sink down, and die; whilst, of five English seamen, unaccustomed to the severity of the climate, and the hardships attending it, one only fell, and *he*—by the murderous hand of an assassin.

Here was another instance, in short, of the superiority of the British people. And, he did not have to add, their fitness to rule. No modern spinmeister could have put it better.

Barrow's attitude encapsulated that of the British public. The first accounts of what had happened to the expedition reached Montreal via the four voyageurs in Franklin's employ whom he had sent back to Fort Enterprise from the mouth of the Coppermine River. He dismissed them from service on his way back to York Factory in July and they journeyed to Montreal and told the story, or what they knew of it, to the Montreal papers in August. British publications started running items based on these stories in October, before Franklin returned. The stories are garbled and factually incorrect but one salient fact is true:

> had not the survivors, who, for several days, were driven to the necessity of prolonging a miserable existence by feeding upon the tattered remains of their shoes, and, we fear, upon a more forbidding and unpalatable fare, exerted themselves by a super-human effort to reach the Great Bear Lake, it is probable that they would have all suffered the most exquisite [i.e., intensely painful] and appalling martyrdom.

The *Times* repeated this report and contrasted the "buoyant spirits" of the English seamen during their ordeal with the moral collapse of the voyageurs.

Blaming the victims, clearly, is an old technique. Richardson gave an interview to the *Dumfries Courier*—Richardson had been born in Dumfries—and denied rumors that the voyageurs had been on the point of mutiny. Everything had been quite fair, he insisted, food equally divided, the loads the Canadians were carrying only what they were being paid to carry. The surviving Canadians had told their comrades when they returned about the monsters they had seen and exaggerated all their adventures. The *Times*, reporting on this story, wanted its readers to know that, indeed, everything had been fair, but it was the British seamen who had survived.

And they had done so in part by the extraordinary act of eating their boots. Thanks to the press reports, which were reprinted all over the country, Franklin was already famous when he showed up in London, and he would be known, now and for the rest of his life, as "the man who ate his boots." He had become well known after the attempt with Buchan to penetrate the ice above Spitzbergen, but after this his fame stood at a much higher level. Now he represented the triumph of British grit and spirit even in the face of the greatest hardships, hardships that killed stronger men. He was in demand everywhere. Everybody wanted to know him. When his account of the expedition appeared in a sumptuous quarto edition from John Murray in June 1823, it sold out in no time. A year or two later this first edition was bringing ten guineas a copy in the rare-book market. That was 10 percent of an active-duty lieutenant's annual salary in the Royal Navy. A second edition, completely reset, came out before the end of the year. That was followed by a two-volume octavo edition, which was in turn reprinted. In 1824 a

French translation appeared, preceded by a German in 1823. Franklin's fame was not just national in scope, it was European.

Did he enjoy the attention? Evidently not. Not long after his return he wrote his fiancée, Eleanor Porden, that he likes "a select circle of friends" but not large parties, where "every one feels . . . at liberty to pay some unnecessary compliment to me." Compliments made him uneasy, "from an apprehension that such attention may prompt me to assume individual merit for results which are entirely to be ascribed to the superintending blessing of a Divine Providence." This pious streak in Franklin was deeply felt. He had, after all, been there, on the ground in northern Canada, so weak he could barely stand, near death, unable to care for his companions or himself, and his prayers had sustained him. It may well be that to himself he was no hero at all, only lucky. Men and women who have endured great difficulties often say that it is not they who are the heroes, but the ones left behind who failed to survive. But the public cared nothing for Franklin's demurrals; they wanted only to lionize him. Franklin had become the latest incarnation of British superiority. He had become and would remain a national icon. His fiancée wrote him that he should accept his fame, lie back, as it were, and enjoy it. She compared him to Shakespeare's Coriolanus, who would, she quoted, "rather venture both your limbs for honour / Than one of your ears to hear it."

She was an interesting woman and quite possibly the most unlikely match in London for a man of Franklin's utterly conventional temperament. Her father, William Porden, was a well-connected architect whom the profligate prince regent, later George IV, commissioned to design and build the famous Rotunda at Brighton in the Chinese style. The family friends included distinguished sculptors, artists, men of letters, politicians. The object of Franklin's affections, Eleanor Anne Porden, was herself no slouch. She was her father's darling and received an education totally unlike the usual instruction in the piano and the arts of sewing that middle-class British women had to endure. Accompanying her father, she attended lectures given by major scientists as early as the age of nine and maintained an interest in science throughout her short life. She had her own literary salon, which met Sundays. At sixteen she wrote an epic poem called *The Veils, or the Triumph of Constancy*, which John Murray published. *The Quarterly* reviewed it, and the reviewer was kind. The Institut de France commended it.

It was not *The Veils*, however, but another poem, *The Arctic Expedi-*

tions, that led John Franklin to her. This shorter work had been inspired by a visit to the *Alexander* and *Isabella,* John Ross's ships, in Deptford in the spring of 1818, before they set out for Baffin Bay. Franklin read the poem when it appeared and arranged to meet her, and he renewed the visits while he was preparing for the trip to northern Canada. They wrote each other while he was away, although it was nearly impossible to get mail to and from a place like Fort Enterprise. When no one had heard from Franklin for a year, she wrote that "Mr. Barrow is ready to lay a wager that you and Capt. Parry have met" and told him that the panorama of Spitzbergen had been replaced "and your portrait, which you were so proud of, is swallowed up in Mount Vesuvius." Then finally he was back, and proposing marriage. She seems to have hesitated. But then she relented, and accepted.

Later she thought twice about it and came close to calling it off. She was vivacious, loved company and large parties and dances, and had lots of friends, and she was also deeply committed to her literary career. A few described her as plain, including Jane Griffin, John Franklin's second wife, who became her friend; but in the portrait painted of her by Mary Ann Flaxman she is dressed in a white gown sitting on a chaise, smiling sweetly, pen in hand poised over a blank piece of paper on a table, and she looks, if not quite pretty, then pert and appealing, somebody it would have been interesting to know.

Franklin hated parties, as he had told her, liking only to dine with a select group of friends. Fearful of writing himself, he did not know what to make of her literary ambitions and floated the idea that once they were married she stop. Too late: she was even then publishing a two-volume verse epic about King Richard the Lion-Hearted. She was nothing if not prolific. She would never stop writing poetry, she told him. If he insisted, she would break off the engagement. Franklin came under the influence during this time of Lady Lucy Barry, a Methodist true believer who condemned any sort of activity on Sundays, including, in John Franklin's interpretation, holding a literary salon. Eleanor protested vigorously, and Franklin had to back down, telling her that no, he was not really a disciple of Lady Lucy but a perfectly conventional member in good standing of the Church of England.

All these differences were aired in correspondence because Franklin was so often away in Lincolnshire with his family—hardly where a fiancé should be. In both his behavior and his letters, he came across as lacking passion, as not really being in love. He preferred, says Eleanor

Porden's biographer, the narrow provincial society of his Lincolnshire small town to London, which always, he claimed, made him ill. Eleanor was a Londoner born and bred. Her letters, it should be added, were lively and witty. His were wooden. "As you perceive," he wrote her when she complained about their formality and stuffiness, "my forte does not lie in epistolary composition." He was much better in person, still the man people thought of as charming and nice. The famous Dr. Johann Spurzheim, founder of the "science" of phrenology, did a "phrenological character" of his head that showed him to be "disposed to good humour and cheerfulness, bordering on wit." Perhaps, but the wit is nowhere in evidence in anything he wrote.

They were married on August 6, 1823. Eleanor was already coughing a lot. A trip to Lincolnshire to visit his family was not a success; she no sooner got into the damp climate of the Lincolnshire fens than she found herself persistently short of breath, so much so that Franklin was forced to send her back to London. Characteristically, he sent her alone. He went to Lincolnshire on any excuse, and she wrote him there. In April 1824 the Duke of Sussex, she wrote to him, invited the two of them to dinner and had invited his other guests specifically to meet the celebrated Captain John Franklin. He was with her when their only child, a girl, was born on June 3, 1824, but his own father had recently died, and he felt it incumbent to return to Lincolnshire shortly thereafter to help settle his affairs. By then Eleanor was finding it difficult to climb stairs. The cough persisted and got worse. She was describing herself now as an invalid.

He, meanwhile, was making preparations to return to northern Canada on his second land expedition. When he was home he was always busy, always out and about, at the docks, the Admiralty, consulting with people. A Lieutenant Allen had dropped by to offer to go with Franklin as a midshipman, just to be able to go, she told him in a note. George Back had been by; he did go with Franklin again. She did what she could to help and made her husband a large silk banner of her own design that he promised to plant at the mouth of the Mackenzie River when he reached it. That winter a doctor diagnosed her as having that great killer of Romantic-era poets and other frail young people, tuberculosis. Franklin was scheduled to sail for Canada from Liverpool on February 16, 1825. In an agony of indecision, with plans well advanced, supplies and men sent ahead, his sense of duty lying heavy on his shoulders, his career possibly at stake, he debated with himself what to do.

Finally he chose to stay home with his dying wife. She refused the gesture. No, she told him, you must go. She knew what it meant to him, and she insisted upon it. Five days after he sailed Eleanor died. It was two months before the news reached him.

From this distance it seems like the wrong choice, but we must be careful of making judgments. Marriage then was not what it is now. Passionate romantic feelings, the abandoned style of modern love, had less to do with it then. Neither of these people was what we would call impetuous. It was still common to hear wives call their husbands by their surnames, and vice versa: Captain Franklin; Mrs. Franklin. And in the navy wives and husbands could expect to be separated for long periods of time. A successful career in the navy depended on just such circumstances—on having a command, on going away. It was obvious to others that Eleanor Franklin was dying, but hope, of course, is what dies last. When he left her she was still alive. She may still have hoped to live long enough to see him come home. From this distance and for all his charm, Franklin seems to have had the emotional depth of a puddle. But few mysteries are more difficult to penetrate than other people's marriages.

Lieutenant William Edward Parry

III

AN EDUCATION IN ICE

Miserable they!
Who, here entangled in the gathering Ice,
Take their last Look of the descending Sun;
While, full of Death, and fierce with tenfold Frost,
The long long Night, incumbent o'er their Heads,
Falls horrible.

—James Thomson, *The Seasons*

CHAPTER NINE

FIVE THOUSAND POUNDS

By the time Franklin returned home from his first Canadian expedition in October 1822, William Edward Parry had gone, and come, and gone again in search of the Northwest Passage. He had sailed through John Ross's Croker Mountains and named a bay after Croker on the far side of those fog hills, he had passed the 110th meridian and collected the five thousand pounds the British Parliament had promised in the act of 1818 to the first British expedition to do so, he had indeed sailed halfway to Bering Strait—and been stopped dead by the ice: ice forty feet thick, ice without visible limits and as impenetrable as stone.

Sea ice, to be sure, is not normally forty feet thick. Until global warming the average thickness of the polar ice cap was about ten feet. But sea ice is not a stable material. Even in the dead of winter cracks develop in sea ice that looks from a distance uniform and unmoving. The ice moves with the currents, the tides, and the wind; leads of open water appear, storms come, and huge floes miles across collide and climb thunderously over one another. It is these doubled, tripled, and quadrupled floes that reach such thicknesses, fearsome evidence of the violence of nature. Or else the floes curl up like pieces of paper as they meet, creating ridges that may be fifty feet high and even deeper underwater. When the nuclear submarine *Nautilus* pushed under the ice in 1958, the captain at first dismissed the sonar readings he was seeing of ridges extending down into the water as "ghosts." Then he came to understand that they were real, that what he was seeing was solid ice projecting down on his sonar screen, and it was "dangerous and deadly to our operation."

Sea ice is almost always dangerous and deadly. The English whaling fleet that sailed every year into Baffin Bay to chase bowhead whales lost, on average, one ship out of seventeen a year to the ice. Often the men escaped, grabbing their personal gear if they had time, pitching the gear and themselves onto the ice, then staring at the mighty floes crushing their ship between them. The fleet traveled as a pack, and most ships escaped and were able to pick refugees up, and not many died. But the number of ships lost could be huge. In a pamphlet published twenty years after, William Scoresby described a scene in 1830 when the whaling fleet was in Melville Bay, which lies at the upper reaches of Baffin Bay, and a sudden storm out of the southwest drove the pack ice against the fixed land ice in Melville Bay and caught the fleet between them. Twenty ships went down. The ice ran right through the sides of two ships, forced others onto their sides on the ice, and raised others up, "one ship being reared up by the ice, almost in the position of a rearing horse." Some of the ships were lost when, lying on their sides on the fixed land ice, floes were driven on top of them by the storm and they were crushed. Ice floes even just ten feet thick can weigh thousands of tons. The shell of a wooden ship is nothing to them.

The ice masters on Parry's ships had all been either captains or mates on whaling ships. Few naval officers had much experience with ice, and Parry was no exception. His account of the voyage makes clear that penetrating the ice was a learning experience for him; the account reads in places like a lesson in ice. The book begins with a list of terms defining things like *pack ice, floes, leads, sailing-ice, bay or young ice,* an *ice field.* Parry could have gone on much longer. Stephen Pyne, in his book on Antarctica, *The Ice,* names forty-nine different forms that ice takes in the seas. Icebergs arrive in any number of shapes, depending on their source and their age and degree of dilapidation. Royal Navy officers were often enchanted by their first sight of icebergs in Davis Strait. There on July 3 Parry's two ships came in sight of a chain of "very large icebergs"; a heavy southerly swell, he wrote, "sometimes raised a white spray over the [bergs] to the height of more than one hundred feet." The noise, he said, resembled "the roar of distant thunder," and the whole "presented a scene at once sublime and terrific."

The twin of sublimity is fear. Later Parry and his two crews would watch helplessly as icebergs moved relentlessly toward them through pack ice while they were beset in it, unable to move. Icebergs dance to a different tune from surface ice. A deep current will drive a berg, only one-seventh of which is above the surface, through thick immobile pack ice as if it were nothing more than slush. If you are beset in the pack and happen to be in its way, you are doomed. Ships also come to grief the other way around: a ship is beset, and the ice that surrounds and imprisons it is being driven by currents or wind toward a grounded immobile berg. The result is the same. Whalers sometimes moored to grounded bergs, or even to bergs afloat in Baffin Bay, but it was a risky thing to do. Bergs can split apart, without warning, along unseen fault lines. They flip over without warning. Unseen tongues of ice extend out from them beneath the surface. Sailing in an icy sea was a game of chance, and sometimes no amount of knowledge or skill could save you.

Parry's expedition left the Deptford docks and the cheers of the crowd on May 4, 1819. With the wind against them, the Royal Navy's first steamship towed them downriver to Northfleet, where they took on their last supplies and waited for the wind to change. His two ships were the *Hecla* and the *Griper;* the first, Parry's ship, was a converted "bomb," so called because "bombs" were strengthened inside to withstand the recoil of the heavy mortars used to bombard shoreline fortifications. The much slower, clumsier *Griper* was a converted gun brig. Parry himself was an altogether different sort of man from John Franklin. Whereas Franklin was short and plain, he was tall and good-looking, a better, more fluent writer, not so unnerved by his fame as Franklin was, and higher born. Franklin's father was a grocer and he was born above the store. Parry's father was a prominent Bath physician who reportedly once treated Jane Austen; he was a friend of Joseph Banks, of Edward Jenner, who developed the smallpox vaccine, and of the astronomer William Herschel. In traditional fashion his son, who was always called by his middle name, Edward, joined the navy at twelve under Admiral Cornwallis, who called him a "fine steady lad," and he served in the blockade of France and then on various ships in other parts of the Atlantic, but without seeing serious action. That gave him the time, however, to pen a short treatise, *Nautical Astronomy,* a copy of which he sent to his father, who had it printed. Like so many other young officers, he was eager at the end of the wars to stay employed. In 1817 he heard about the upcoming voyages to the Far North and added a note to a letter he wrote to his father's friend Acheson Maxwell that he would be "ready for hot or cold." Maxwell was connected to John Barrow through their joint involvement in Lord Macartney's embassy to China twenty-odd years earlier. Along with the letter Parry sent Maxwell a copy of

Nautical Astronomy. Maxwell gave both the letter and the treatise to Barrow, and Barrow, pleased by Parry's gung ho attitude and his intellectual ambition, tagged him for the expedition. When Parry turned on John Ross at the end of that first sortie into Baffin Bay, Parry and Barrow became allies. Although Barrow had plenty of reasons to be disappointed thereafter by the results of Parry's efforts in the Arctic, he never had anything but praise for Parry himself.

Parry's first voyage under his own command, the voyage of 1819–20, is considered by many Arctic historians to be the most successful of all Arctic expeditions, largely because Parry's two ships penetrated the ice farther west than any of the expeditions that approached the Arctic through Lancaster Sound in his wake. To a great degree Parry's success was a matter of luck, as the seas in the Canadian archipelago were more open than usual when Parry was there; but Parry deserves credit for his daring when confronted by dangerous pack ice, and for the thoughtful planning he put into the expedition. Once again the Admiralty supplied provisions for two years and reinforced the ships Parry was assigned by adding an extra six inches of planking to the hull and bracing the interior with additional oak beams. The Admiralty quartermasters made sure there was plenty of lemon juice on board to prevent scurvy. This was one of the first expeditions ever to use canned food, which a man named Bryan Donkin had developed in England in 1812. Donkin used tinned iron containers with hand-soldered seams, and the Admiralty was one of his first customers. The method was not always foolproof, but in 1942 a can of Donkin's veal and another of carrots were opened after 114 years and the contents of both were still edible.

But Parry did more. Scurvy was the principal threat to health on long sea voyages, and fresh food, including fresh meat, as well as lemon juice, were known to prevent it. There was little fresh meat available in the high Arctic in the winter, however, and when Parry's lemon juice supply froze in the hold of the ship in the middle of that winter, symptoms of scurvy appeared soon after on both ships. Parry was prepared. He had brought mustard and cress seeds on board. He planted them in flats in his own cabin. They sprouted and grew in the Arctic darkness without turning green, but when he fed them in small salads to those afflicted with scurvy the symptoms disappeared. He was definitely the right man for the job.

Parry also distinguished himself by sailing through what was known as the Middle Ice, the vast ice field that every summer bottled up the central portion of Baffin Bay. Normally, ships sailed up the east coast of Baffin Bay in the channel that formed as the summer warmed up between Greenland and the Middle Ice. At the top of the channel stood the polynya known as the North Water, which was open all year long. Rounding the Middle Ice in that polynya, they then coasted the shores of Ellesmere Island south to Lancaster Sound. That was what Ross had done the year before, and what the whalers always did.

Parry impatiently fought his way across the Middle Ice instead. It was, he claimed, the first time it had ever been done, but it was exceedingly risky. In a heavy fog and perfect calm, surrounded by loose ice floes, a strong current drove the *Hecla* toward a large iceberg. The ship was helpless without wind to give it headway. Parry lowered the boats and towed the ship to the side, clearing the berg just one minute before the surrounding ice floes "came forcibly in contact with it." If the ship had been closely beset by the ice, it could not have been saved. The berg was aground in seven hundred feet of water, which gives some idea of its size. The ship might as well have been driven against a cliff.

Parry had earlier been closely beset by the ice, immured in it like a mosquito in amber. "It is impossible to conceive a more helpless situation," he wrote, "than that of a ship thus beset, when all the power that can be applied will not alter the direction of her head a single degree of the compass." He was learning patience, an essential ingredient in navigating icy seas. When the ships were immobilized, some of his officers would walk about on the sea ice, out of curiosity. Often, he discovered, pack ice dampened the wind. It might be blowing freshly on the open water; a mile away, in the ice, there might be only the slightest of breezes. One day they encountered a stream of ice a mere three-quarters of a mile wide. The wind died inside it, and it took six hours for the ships' boats to tow the ships through. That was often what it was like for the crews: six hours of steady rowing. On a later occasion they warped the two ships, the *Griper* behind the *Hecla*, through narrow leads in the ice. Warping entailed, again, setting ice anchors in the ice forward of the ship, running the lines around the capstan, and then turning the capstan to wind up the lines. After eleven hours of this labor, they had made four miles.

Sometimes they sawed through the ice in their path, using long thin ice saws, which were hung from tripods over the ice. On July 27, when they were closely beset, clear water suddenly appeared to the west and "a narrow neck of ice was all that was now interposed between the ships" and sailing room. Parry sent both ships' companies onto the ice to saw a path through it, when all at once a path opened and the *Griper* slipped through. It sucked a piece of loose ice into the path behind it, however, which filled in the gap. Before they could push it out of the way, the surrounding floes pressed together and wedged this loose piece between them. Their work was undone. It took seven more hours of sawing ice before the *Hecla* was free.

But she was free, they had crossed the Middle Ice, and by August 1, a month earlier than Ross the year before, they reached the entrance to Lancaster Sound. It was free of ice. Detained by winds blowing down the sound, Parry sent one of the assistant surgeons ashore to explore up a small stream. He found footprints beside it "which appeared so fresh, that he at first imagined them to have been recently made by some natives, but which, on examination, were distinctly ascertained to be the marks of our own shoes made eleven months before." On August 3 the winds changed and started to blow them up the sound. The sun was shining twenty-four hours a day. The sound was full of whales; one consequence of this expedition was that the whaling industry expanded its range into Lancaster Sound. The breeze freshened; they put on "a crowd of sail . . . to carry us with all rapidity to the westward." They were approaching the point where Ross had turned around the year before, insisting that mountains closed off the sound.

> It is more easy to imagine than to describe the almost breath-less anxiety which was now visible in every countenance, while, as the breeze increased to a fresh gale, we ran quickly up the sound. The mast-heads were crowded by the officers and men during the whole afternoon.

The mountains had disappeared. Parry began naming headlands, bays, islands. John Wilson Croker, the first secretary, got his bay. By August 4, just a day after the wind picked them up and started to drive them west, they had come so far in these ice-free waters that "we began to flatter ourselves that we had fairly entered the Polar sea, and some of the most sanguine among us had even calculated the bearing and distance of Icy Cape, as a matter of no very difficult or improbable accomplishment." Icy Cape was as far as Captain Cook had sailed above Bering Strait. If they continued on at this rate they would be spending the winter in Hawaii, or possibly Tahiti, while John Franklin was still struggling up the Hayes River, trying to reach Cumberland House before winter set in. They were about to conquer the Northwest Passage.

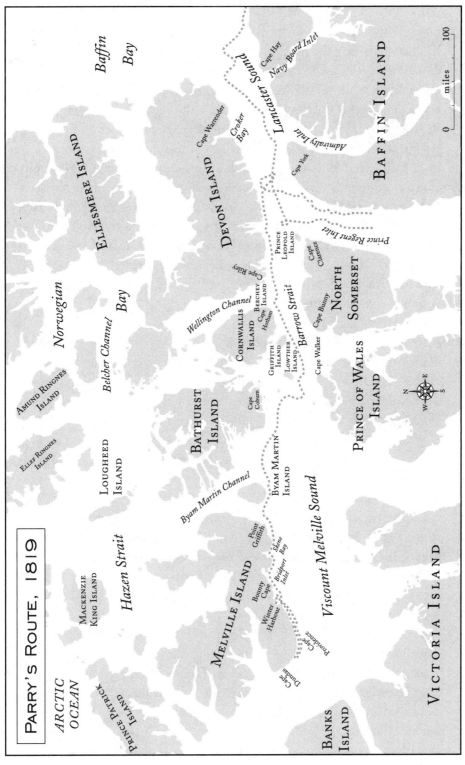

PARRY'S ROUTE, 1819

ARCTIC OCEAN

PRINCE PATRICK ISLAND

MACKENZIE KING ISLAND

Hazen Strait

ELLEF RINGNES ISLAND

AMUND RINGNES ISLAND

LOUGHEED ISLAND

Belcher Channel

Norwegian Bay

ELLESMERE ISLAND

Baffin Bay

DEVON ISLAND

Cape Warrender

Croker Bay

Lancaster Sound

Cape Hay

Navy Board Inlet

Admiralty Inlet

Cape York

BAFFIN ISLAND

Cape Riley

Wellington Channel

BATHURST ISLAND

Byam Martin Channel

Cape Cockburn

CORNWALLIS ISLAND

BEECHEY ISLAND
Cape Hotham

GRIFFITH ISLAND

LOWTHER ISLAND

Barrow Strait

Cape Walker

PRINCE LEOPOLD ISLAND

Cape Clarence

Cape Bunny

NORTH SOMERSET

Prince Regent Inlet

BYAM MARTIN ISLAND

Point Griffith

Skene Bay

Bounty Cape

Bridport Inlet

Winter Harbour

MELVILLE ISLAND

Cape Providence

Cape Dundas

Viscount Melville Sound

PRINCE OF WALES ISLAND

BANKS ISLAND

VICTORIA ISLAND

N W E S

0   miles   100

Late that evening they found the ice, which extended across Lancaster Sound from the north shore to the south without a break. They had been coasting the north shore of the sound; now Parry sailed south down the edge of the ice and soon enough discovered a large inlet, thirty miles across at its mouth. Its western shore was clogged with ice but the east side of it was open, and Parry sailed into it, thinking this might be the way west. He ran into it for a total of 120 miles before he found ice ten feet thick barring his way and had to turn around. He had not found its bottom. He thought, however, that the land on either side probably constituted islands and that the inlet itself would be found someday to communicate with Hudson Bay on the east and the coast of North America on the west. He believed, in short, that it would serve as a more southerly route to the Northwest Passage than Lancaster Sound. But for now it was full of ice. He struggled out of it to the north and was still there on August 12, when he named it Prince Regent Inlet. August 12 was the prince's birthday.

On the fourteenth he was back in Lancaster Sound. Pack ice still barred the way west. Parry probed it for openings and, when he found none, went ashore to look at the land and investigate its geology. On the seventeenth the fog was so thick they could barely see the waters they were sailing in and "the ships were constantly receiving heavy shocks from the loose masses of ice with which the sea was covered." On August 19 it snowed. On the twentieth the weather cleared and they made a little way west in a narrow passage between the ice and the land along the north shore of Lancaster Sound. Then the wind died. They awoke the next day to find the ice had vanished, "the great opening," an astonished Parry wrote, "through which we had hitherto proceeded from Baffin's Bay, being now so perfectly clear of ice, that it was almost impossible to believe it to be the same part of the sea, which, but a day or two before, had been completely covered with floes to the utmost extent of our view." It was another lesson in Arctic ice. They could sail west again.

Parry did continue west, naming islands and capes as he went. One small island at the mouth of another large inlet to the north he named after the officer who investigated it, Lieutenant Frederick William Beechey, who had sailed under Franklin the previous year on the expedition toward the North Pole. Parry named the inlet, which proved to be twenty miles wide, Wellington Channel; it was "open and navigable," and Parry was tempted to sail up it, but the waters to the west were just as open and the west was his destination. The west seemed within reach. "It is impossible," he wrote, "to conceive any thing more animating than the quick and unobstructed run" they were enjoying then. He contrasted it with the difficulty of navigating in ice:

> Most men have, probably, at one time or another, experienced that elevation of spirits which is usually produced by rapid motion of any kind; and it will readily be conceived how much this feeling was heightened in us, in the few instances in which it occurred, by the slow and tedious manner in which the greater part of our navigation had been performed in these seas.

Parry sailed across the bottom of Wellington Channel and named the next island to the west Cornwallis Island, after his original patron, Admiral Cornwallis. Beyond that was what appeared to be another large island; he named it Bathurst Island, after the peer running the Colonial Office. Here the ice reappeared, but it was to the south of them, paralleling the land. Between the ice and the land ran a channel of open water eight or nine miles wide. They sailed on, and the channel progressively narrowed. They reached yet another island, a small one that Parry named after the comptroller of the navy, Sir Thomas Byam Martin. Here the ice arced to the north, to the land, and stopped their progress. He could see a "water sky" to the south, indicating open water there, but he could not find a way to reach it.

On August 29 the ice opened up a little, and they sailed for the opening. Then fog came on, "as thick as before," fog that froze on the ropes and sails. The sailing became exceptionally perilous. They sailed for a time along the edge of a floe,

> along which our course was to be pursued to the westward. As long as we had this guidance, we advanced with great confidence; but as soon as we came to the end of the floe, which then turned off to the southward, the circumstances under which we were sailing were, perhaps, such as have never occurred since the early days of navigation. To the northward was the land; the ice, as we supposed, to the southward; the compasses useless; and the sun completely obscured by a fog, so thick that the Griper could only now and then be seen at a cable's length astern.

The compasses were useless because they were close to the North Magnetic Pole; when the compass cards could be made to move at all, they pointed south, not north. They sailed by the direction of the wind, hoping it remained steady. It was more than a little insane.

On September 1 a breeze picked up, from what direction nobody could tell, and the fog was succeeded by snow and sleet as thick as the fog. But the ice cleared around the ships and they stood to the west again, if it really was west they were sailing. When the weather cleared they found themselves south of yet another island, which Parry named Melville Island after Lord Melville, first lord of the Admiralty. The channel between the pack ice and the land was here about three miles wide, with very large pieces of ice aground here and there between the pack and the land, while the open channel was open only in a relative sense; it was actually full of what is called "sailing ice," loose pieces of ice with colorful names: growlers, ice cakes, brash ice—ice on the cusp between summer and winter. On September 4, at a little after nine in the evening, the ships crossed the 110th meridian. The set of awards for ships searching for the Northwest Passage gave five thousand pounds to the first ships to pass the 110th meridian north of North America. Parry himself would get the lion's share of it. He named the nearest cape Cape Bounty, in honor of the occasion.

Now began the most advanced tests in ice navigation Parry would face in this expedition. The channel between the pack and the land continued to narrow and in places disappeared altogether. A wind out of the north or northwest blew the pack off the land; a southerly wind blew it right up against it. To be caught between the land and the ice, without shelter, was a potential death sentence for the ships. The only shelter they could find was behind large thick floes grounded far enough offshore to allow the ships to hide from the pack behind them. There were patches of such ice all along the coast, but only patches. Arctic winds are as changeable as any other winds. It was all too easy to be caught in the open.

They anchored in a bay on September 5, ice barring their progress to the west, but a northwest wind on the sixth cleared it out and they made a few more miles. From here on out progress was measured in yards. Risk was constant, and there was little time for rest. By the middle of September ice was forming on the sea surface. Every day the situation deteriorated, and by the twentieth he had given up. They had seen small harbors to the east, behind them, and they headed for them, the ships struggling to sail through young ice that now no longer melted during the day after it had formed at night. On the twenty-third they reached the harbors; both were frozen over with ice already four or five inches thick. They had no choice now but to cut a channel into the harbor they chose. Over the next three days, with men and officers working nineteen hours a day, a channel two miles long and just wide enough for the ships took them to safety. To make the work easier, the men set up sails on the pieces of ice as they cut them and sailed them down the channel as it was cut to release them in the open water toward the sea. Young ice formed continually in the channel after it was opened. The temperature was now in the teens. On the third day it rose to a mere nine degrees Fahrenheit. By noon, however, they had reached their berth in what Parry called Winter Harbour. He had already named the strait beyond Lancaster Sound that they had been traveling after the second secretary of the Admiralty: Barrow Strait. All these names remain on the map.

That night the temperature dropped to one degree below zero. The next day, climbing a hill, they could see that the sea was "quite frozen over, as far as the eye could reach." Parry had cut it fearfully close.

This was the first Royal Navy expedition to winter over in the Arctic, and Parry started preparing for it as soon as cables had moored the two ships to the land near their anchorage. He expected to be locked up in Winter Harbour for at least nine months; in fact it would be nearly eleven. He had ninety-three officers and men with him and all of them had to be kept busy, while the ships had to be as warm as possible and the air inside them as dry as possible. Theatrical productions were not unknown on long voyages; the fur trappers in northern Canada amused themselves by staging plays at their forts in the winter. Beechey, who became the manager and scene painter for the expedition's productions, was able to round up editions of some of the better-known dramatists from among the officers. The sun set for ninety-six days on November 4. The next day Parry staged the first play, a farce by David Garrick called *Miss in Her Teens*, in which he himself took the part of a ridiculous character named Fribble, a slang word denoting an effeminate man. Parry was not afraid to make fun of himself.

To keep his crew fit, he sent them ashore every day to walk, and if the temperatures were too low to do that, he had them run around the decks, which he tented over with canvas to keep the worst of the cold out. Edward Sabine was given the editorship of a weekly newspaper named the *North Georgia Gazette and Winter Chronicle*, which the officers filled with poems, jokes, and anecdotes, most written in the style of *The Spectator*, Addison and Steele's journal from a century before, all of them anonymous. The writers used names like "Frosticus" and "Philo-Somnus" and "Richard Roam-About." At one point that winter the editor complained that he was not getting enough contributions. Under the name of David Drowsy, Parry responded that "want of leisure" had prevented him from writing,

> that what with the time necessarily occupied in three regular meals, and two little ones per day, a two-hour's nap after dinner, and another after coffee, with an occasional dose in the forenoon, together with the duties of his profession in these times of constant activity, he most positively deponeth that he hath scarcely been able to snatch his ten-hours' rest at night, much less employ any portion of his time in contributing to the general amusement.

Candles were the main source of light inside the ships, but outside it was seldom entirely black. Around noon every day, after the sun had set for the winter, a kind of twilight filled the southern sky, at least during good weather, and the aurora lit up the land when it came. Moonlight or even just starlight on the white snow and ice provided enough illumination to make it possible to see where one was going on cloudless days. Yet the constant darkness did affect them, as did the bleakness of the landscape. Parry described climbing a hill and gazing out on the scene below "on one of those calm and clear days, which not infrequently occurred during the winter," and feeling the deep melancholy of the place. "Not an object was to be seen on which the eye could long rest with pleasure," he wrote in his journal, and the silence was not at all like the silence of a civilized countryside, punctuated by the cry of an owl or the bark of a dog, but rather "the death-like stillness of the most dreary desolation, and the total absence of animated existence." In such desolation it was imperative that the men keep their spirits up. Sabine, writing in the *North Georgia Gazette*, remarked "that cheerfulness, which is always amiable as a *private* virtue, becomes in *our* case, almost a *public* duty."

Animated existence was not entirely absent from the landscape, to be sure. Animals did survive in this environment: wolves, foxes, musk oxen, hares, ptarmigans. And Parry for his part never seemed to become discouraged. He contrasted the gloom and darkness with "the hopes which the least sanguine among us sometimes entertained, of spending a part of our next winter in the more genial climate of the South-Sea Islands."

There were theatrical entertainments every other week. Parry was an avid amateur violinist and played for his crew. The plays were put on once or twice with the thermometer below zero on the stage. Temperatures below deck where the men slept seldom rose above forty degrees; outside they sank as low as forty-nine below zero. The main source of warmth in the two ships was the cooking stoves, fed by coal. To keep the sleeping quarters bearable, pipes from the stoves were run into and out of these quarters in a makeshift kind of heating system. The worst enemy was damp. Moisture in the air, generated by the men and the steam from cooking, condensed on the beams and on sleeping berths and froze; then it melted during the day and dripped on the bedding, making the berths extremely uncomfortable and dangerous to health. Parry accordingly inspected the sleeping deck every single day for ice and had it chipped away, then had all the wood wiped down with rags. But he never entirely solved this problem. Ice formed regardless.

Other problems cropped up as well. The first case of scurvy showed up on December 1. He was able to deal with that by growing cress and mustard, but frostbite was something else altogether. Feet tended to freeze in the hard leather boots that the navy favored; indeed the boots themselves often froze and might take an hour to thaw in the morning. Parry had boots made of canvas with raw leather soles, had them lined with blanketing, and ordered every man to wear two pairs of socks. This worked. Everyone learned soon enough not to touch metal with bare skin, but in February the hut they had built outside to house the scientific instruments caught on fire, and the man who had started the fire by laying a silk handkerchief on the stove to dry ran out of the cabin with the magnetic dipping needle in his bare hands. He lost seven fingers to frostbite. None of the instruments was damaged, however, and the instrument hut was rebuilt.

The hut was Edward Sabine's domain; he was the expedition's chief scientist. Parry had brought along all the young officers he had befriended on the Ross expedition of the previous year, plus Beechey and James Clark Ross, John Ross's nephew. Young and rosy-cheeked, Ross was a favorite for the women's parts in the theatricals. Among the crew one man died that winter, a seaman named William Scott. The surgeon on the *Hecla* did an autopsy but could not decipher the cause of death. Later in the winter other men showed signs of scurvy, and Parry redoubled his plantings.

Spring does not come rapidly in the Arctic. More snow fell in April than had fallen all the rest of the winter. The ice in Winter Harbour was seven and a half feet thick on average. In the fall when they were frozen in, Parry had kept his ships free of the surrounding ice by having the men chop it out every day, but after a month or so he gave up. The ice immediately around the ships reached a depth of six feet. The winter wore on. Like Franklin in northern Canada, he made attempt after attempt to describe the aurora, but he was never vivid on the subject. The ships' dogs consorted with the wolves that haunted the ships, and one of them ran off and never came back.

Sound carried for great distances in the cold. One day Parry heard a man singing as he walked along the beach more than a mile away; they heard people talking "in a common tone of voice" at the distance of a mile. In March warmer weather made it necessary to scrape the ice that had frozen to the ships' sides from the vapor the crew produced. It amounted to five or six hundred gallons. The sun had returned in February. By April it was shining seventeen hours out of the twenty-four. Yet the sea outside the harbor gave no sign whatsoever of melting, or breaking up, or stirring. He went "to the top of the north-east hill," he wrote, to look at it, and the view was not encouraging. "The sea still presented the same unbroken and continuous surface of solid and impenetrable ice, and this ice could not be less than from six to seven feet in thickness."

In May Parry ordered the ships to be prepared for the sea, which meant sawing them out of the ice. Then he set out with eleven men to trek to the north across Melville Island and do some exploring, using a wheeled cart to carry their belongings. They crossed the island at what turned out to be its narrowest point and discovered that the entire island was a featureless plain. Parry remarked that "it was impossible to conceive any thing more dreary and uninteresting." By the time they got back to the ships they had been cut out of the ice, but it would not be until the beginning of August that the ice in Winter Harbour retreated and they were able once more to sail into Barrow Strait, turn west, and resume the search for the Northwest Passage.

It proved to be a rerun of the previous summer: the ships were trapped against the land when the pack moved in, the only shelter to be found the large berglike pieces of grounded ice they could hide behind, and when the pack moved out, they made a few miles more to the west. One day they saw how ice got to be forty feet thick when a piece of a floe was forced on top of the pack by relentless pressure, doubling the thickness of the ice. Parry sent Lieutenant Beechey over to measure it. It was forty-two feet thick. Hummocks on the ice, which were the eroded remains of ridges, might add twenty-five feet to the thickness.

The ships made it as far as the southwesternmost cape on Melville Island, which he gave the Melville family name: Cape Dundas. From the heights of the cape, land was visible far away to the south. Parry named it Banks Land, after Joseph Banks. It was clear they were going no farther. Ice was everywhere, old thick heavy ice, ice to the most extreme reach of the telescope. Parry was looking at the western entrance to the large basin packed with ice to his south now generally known as Melville Sound. The Beaufort Gyre concentrates the ice that covers the Beaufort Sea into this passage and piles it up in the sound. From there it is driven down into the maze of channels that interlace the Canadian archipelago. The southern shores of Melville Island take the brunt of this pile-up. Parry saw that it would forever be impassable. "It now became evident," he wrote, ". . . that there was something peculiar about the south-west extremity of Melville Island, which made the icy sea there extremely unfavourable to navigation, and which seemed likely to bid defiance to all our efforts to proceed much farther to the westward in this parallel of latitude." After this voyage no other English explorer looked for the Northwest Passage via this route. Any practical route would have to run much farther south.

For the rest of the sailing season he sailed east, then south, skirting the pack, trying to find an opening. There was none. "Our experience, I think, has clearly shown," he wrote, "that the navigation of the Polar Seas can never be performed with any degree of certainty, without a continuity of land. It was only by watching the occasional openings between the ice and the shore, that our late progress to the west was effected." Where the land ended, no more progress could be made. Perhaps they should try next time farther to the south, from inside Hudson Bay, perhaps, into Repulse Bay. "The geography of that part of the world may be considered altogether undetermined," he concluded. He was outlining his next expedition. This one was finished. Parry and his ships reached the Shetlands at the end of October 1820.

It is interesting to compare Parry's reception in England with the reception accorded John Franklin two years later, when he returned from his deadly trek across the barren grounds. The public was eager in both cases to hear what had happened on these expeditions and both men were idolized, but one can sense the press hesitating after Franklin's return about how to deal with the fact of so many men having died— except to blame the voyageurs for not being English enough to tough it out. In the 1820s England did not yet have a press capable of sensationalizing and widely dispersing news of scandalous events. News was expensive then, and illiteracy widespread. The *Times* of London cost 7d, or seven pennies, which is difficult to translate into modern currency but was clearly out of reach for the poor, who mostly couldn't read anyway, at a time when a loaf of bread cost no more than 1d. In pre-Reform England—that is, before 1832—the government deliberately kept newspapers expensive with a heavy stamp duty and was actively opposed to mass literacy. Even after Reform the stamp duty remained in effect. The circulation of the *Times* in 1803 stood at a mere 1,700 copies a day. In 1820 its new editor, the famous Thomas Barnes, increased its circulation to 15,000 by championing the cause of George IV's wife, Queen Caroline, during her trial for adultery. One could never have called it a "popular" newspaper, however, and its reaction to the deaths of the voyageurs was anything but sensationalized. The tabloid press did not yet exist. Faced with Franklin's losses, the press responded in a relatively dignified way. It refrained from asking too much about the details. Men had eaten their boots, and that was certainly interesting. But the main point was that the voyageurs, for all their physical strength, had lacked the spirit, the endurance, of British sailors, and they were the ones who had died.

Parry's expedition, in contrast, was clean. There was only the one death to report, and it appeared to have been caused by a preexisting condition. It had been the first Royal Navy expedition to winter in the Arctic in modern times; it had won the five-thousand-pound reward for crossing the 110th meridian. A handsome man, Parry *looked* heroic. *Blackwood's Edinburgh Magazine* rushed into print with an account of the trip gathered from conversations with the officers when storms forced the *Hecla* to take refuge in Leith Roads, Edinburgh's harbor. A science magazine, *The Edinburgh Philosophical Journal,* published a long article in the January 1821 issue. "The wish of the public for some account," wrote its author, "however imperfect, of the discoveries made by Captain Parry, is, we find, so pressing, that we have been induced to collect from various sources, many of the particulars." In February *The European Magazine and London Review* chimed in with a profile of

Parry that included an engraving drawn from a portrait by Samuel Drummond, a well-known marine artist. By February, in other words, Parry had had his portrait done. The article was suitably adoring. England had another hero.

He was promoted to commander as soon as he arrived in London, and visits from friends and acquaintances, as well as a spate of correspondence, soon became overwhelming. "Even strangers in the coffee room," he wrote his father, "introduce themselves, and beg to shake hands with me." At home in Bath he was given the keys to the city, presented to him in an oak box fashioned from one of the *Hecla's* timbers. Bath did not stop there; the citizens voted him a silver platter engraved with his name. The Bath and West of England Society for the Encouragement of Arts presented him with its "Belfordean gold medal." Unanimously, without a dissenting voice, the Royal Society made him a member.

And when his account of the expedition was published—his father helped him write it—John Barrow put the official government stamp of approval on it. Parry's account came out in the spring of 1821 in what would become the style for these books, a large quarto edition filled with illustrations and maps, far too expensive for anyone but the wealthy to buy; it would be followed later by a cheaper edition in octavo. Murray was again the publisher, and he was irritated when Alexander Fisher, the surgeon on one of the ships, once again beat him to the punch with his own inexpensive book about the expedition and it enjoyed an extensive sale. Eleanor Porden, John Franklin's future wife, read Parry's book in quarto but found it not as interesting as she had expected, since much of the information had already "filtered into conversation."

But Barrow was triumphant. He began his review with Ross's spectacular failure to sail on in Lancaster Sound, claiming that "no extraordinary degree of skepticism was necessary to deny the existence of mountains gratuitously asserted, or of continuous ice on the surface of a sea a thousand fathoms deep," thereby both taking his shot at Ross and repeating his belief that ice could not form on deep waters. He went on to take credit for the entire enterprise: "we may, perhaps, be pardoned if, on this occasion, we take some little merit to ourselves for having revived the subject of a North-West Passage," citing the number of *The Quarterly* in which he had done so. He took further credit "for having kept alive the public attention to it by collecting and examining such reports and facts as appeared to bear on the question, and to be

favourable to its existence and practicability," citing another of his
Quarterly articles, "as well as for having first suggested (. . . by way of
higher encouragement) a graduated scale of rewards." By now everyone
in the government and many outside it must have known that Barrow
was the author of these pieces. We will see later that John Ross knew.
"On all these grounds," Barrow went on, "we certainly do feel some little exultation."

One would think from Barrow's remarks that Parry had actually
found the Northwest Passage. He moved on to the book then, noting
that few books "since the commencement of our labours, have afforded
us more to praise or less to censure." He clearly thought the world of
Parry; if there is a Passage, "Captain Parry," he wrote, "is the officer most
likely to accomplish it. Should he fail, we sincerely believe that it will be
useless hereafter for any other to attempt it; and we are quite sure, that,
whether he succeeds or not, his exertions will be honourable to himself
and satisfactory to his employers." By the time this appeared, Parry was
already launched on his next trip to the Arctic.

What is most interesting about the review is Barrow's utter failure to
deduce from Parry's experience with the massive pack abutting Melville
Island that perhaps he was wrong about sea ice. Based on Parry's map of
his findings, Barrow's guess that there is a polar basin was correct; it is
more or less circular and surrounded by North America, Asia, and
Greenland, with no continental land above 70 degrees north latitude.
But as to ice, he simply could not give up his pet theory. Parry had
described the hummocks common on sea ice; Barrow believed that
"these hummocks could be formed only by an open and agitated sea
tossing one mass of ice upon another, and drifting them down by the
prevailing northerly winds till wedged in by the peculiar situation of
islands." From this deduction he inferred that while "ice may occasionally be formed on the surface of such an ocean, it never arrives at any
very considerable thickness, but is broken up and dispersed by every
gust of wind, and the sea left open and navigable as in all the deep parts
of Baffin's Bay, Sir James Lancaster's Sound and Wellington Channel."
It was an astonishing statement. Not only was Baffin Bay full of ice even
in the summer months; not only had Parry himself been stopped by ice
at the western end of Barrow Strait; but Parry had decided not to sail up
Wellington Channel and therefore had no idea what he would have
found. He had sailed down Prince Regent Inlet, which also looked clear
of ice, only to be hemmed in by pack ice stretching from one side to the

other within a hundred miles. William Scoresby had seen sea ice form, and thicken, and thicken some more. All of human experience in the Arctic to that date, including the experience of his own explorers, testified to the abundance and permanence of ice in the high Arctic.

A stubborn man, his acquaintances called Barrow. At some point being stubborn shades into being stupid. He was approaching that point. He agreed with Parry now that the best chance of finding the Passage was not to return to Lancaster Sound, although Parry for all his success had learned very little about the maze of channels that surround it, but to try Hudson Bay, taking the ships into Repulse Bay and Foxe Basin (where previous explorers had always been blocked by ice), and see if the currents that seemed to proceed out of them came from a strait. This is where Parry had suggested the search should continue. Lord Melville acquiesced to the idea, and this is where Parry was going. The high expectations of the nation were going with him.

CHAPTER TEN

FOREVER FROZEN

L ord Melville not only acquiesced to the idea of finding the Passage in Hudson Bay, a dream now as old, as derelict, as Henry Hudson's scattered bones; he took Parry and two of his officers to meet the king before he left. Parry was surprised to find His Highness—no longer merely the prince regent, now George IV—friendly and easy to approach. The king was known in the realm as Great Britain's very own party animal, interested mostly in lavish dinners and balls, but Parry found him as eager to hear about Arctic exploration as the rest of the nation. Melville also brought along a new member of the Parry team, George F. Lyon, "about to accompany Captain Parry [as commander of the second ship]. 'Yes,' said his Majesty, 'and to share in his honors!'"

It was precisely the expectation of honors that most worried Parry about this voyage. What if he should fail? He wrote letters to influential friends, telling them to pass the word around: don't expect too much. Once again thousands of people came to see them off, the gentry and the well connected among them sending their calling cards down to the cabins of the two captains. He warned anyone who would listen that there might be no passage in upper Hudson Bay. Parry was familiar with the history of exploration there; he knew that Luke Foxe, two centuries before, had been driven back by the ice. "Foxe's farthest" was not very far into whatever body of water or land lay above Southampton Island. Ice was unpredictable. Anything might happen.

Parry's doubts did not, of course, prevent his "team" (what Clements R. Markham later came to call the "Parry school") from joining him. They were a group of young officers, most of them under thirty, who knew a good thing when they saw one—employment, for one, at a time when employment in the Royal Navy and the consequent hope of advancement were scarce; a chance to see an unknown part of the world; the reflected glory an officer would acquire at having been with Parry; and of course a share in that twenty-thousand-pound reward should they actually find the Northwest Passage and reach Bering Strait. The seamen went for the same reasons, and more. They could learn to read and write in the winter schools Parry set up. They could watch the officers perform plays, almost all of them farces, and make fools of themselves.

And they could do it in relative comfort. With his typical thoroughness Parry had taken the business of heating the interior of the ship this time even beyond what he had done before, working with the stove maker, a man named Sylvester, to improve dramatically the jury-rigged ad hoc arrangement of the previous voyage. In the voyage into Lancaster Sound the stove had heated the ship fairly well but had not solved the problem of condensation. This time Sylvester designed a more sophisticated arrangement of pipes, lined the sleeping and living quarters with cork insulation, and covered the pipes themselves with a kind of woolen material called fearnought to insulate them; it would keep the ships not only warm but also dry. They managed this feat, furthermore, on a mere five pecks of coal a day—a bushel and a quarter. This system, using the same source of heat and without using any additional fuel, also served to melt ice and snow for water. When it was a few degrees above zero outside, Parry reported, the temperature in his cabin stood at seventy degrees. Even at twenty-seven degrees below outside, it was still comfortable inside the ship. Between them, in other words, Mr. Sylvester and Captain Parry had invented a remarkably efficient form of central heating. It's a shame the system was not applied to British housing, which remained heated entirely by coal fireplaces into quite recent times.

Parry set up the same heating system in both ships. He had demanded that the Admiralty retire the slower, smaller, harder-to-sail *Griper*, and they had given him what he wanted, another "bomb" like the *Hecla*, reinforced to handle the mortars fired from their decks, then reinforced again to withstand the ice. It was named the *Fury*, and Parry made it his own, giving the *Hecla* to Lyon, another Barrow protégé. Lyon had recently returned from one of Barrow's three-man expeditions across the Sahara to try to be the first white men into fabled Timbuktu and discover the course of the Niger. He had lived and traveled with Bedouin, eaten mud worms at an oasis, taken an Arab mistress, and learned Arabic. He was up for anything.

He had no experience with ice, however, and this voyage was, like the previous one, an ice school. The two ships first encountered it at the very beginning of their explorations, in Hudson Strait, in early July. Great masses of ice moved back and forth in the strait, east and west, with the tides. Parry was beset almost from the moment he entered the strait on July 4. A naval officer is bred to be unflappable; it's his role to underplay dangerous situations. But this first part of the voyage proved to be as harrowing as anything he had faced in Barrow Strait. They moored the ships regularly to the larger floes in the hopes of finding shelter, only to be swept into the tidal currents by ice moving past or the floe breaking apart or by a brisk wind. The hawsers that moored them, ropes five or six inches thick, were snapped like cotton thread. Massive pieces of ice broke bower anchors that weighed over a ton. More than once they were caught between floes, their sterns lifted five or six feet out of the water, the ships' beams groaning, doors starting under the strain. Nothing they could do availed. Luck determined the outcome.

This went on for weeks. Yet they managed to creep west a little at a time, relatively undamaged, toward their goal, the strait north of Southampton Island that Christopher Middleton had named Frozen Strait; from there to Repulse Bay, still not thoroughly explored; then north up the coast of Hudson Bay to wherever it came to an end. If their luck held, the land would come to an end, a point rounding to the west; they would have found the northeastern corner of North America and from there it would be an easy sail to the Pacific. North America had to have a northeastern corner somewhere—that much was certain. By the end of July they had made real progress west. The ice had freed them.

Halfway up Hudson Strait they were met by the local Inuit, who were used to trading with the ships of the Hudson's Bay Company. Kayaks and umiaks, the larger women's boats, came out to greet them where they were moored to a floe, bringing with them narwhal horns, bags of sealskin filled with oil, seal and whale blubber, bear skins, fox skins, spears, whalebone. They wanted saws and steel-tipped harpoons; Parry could not spare any and was hard put to acquire a total of two barrels of oil "in exchange for several knives, large nails, and pieces of iron hoop." Parry had seen Inuit before, on his voyage as second to John Ross, when they had discovered the Arctic Highlanders, so trading with them was not new to him. But he did not like these particular Inuit, who tried to steal anything they could get their hands on and were not embarrassed by being caught. As for their eating habits, "it is impossible to describe the horribly disgusting manner in which they sat down, as soon as they felt hungry, to eat their raw blubber," Parry wrote in his account of the voyage, "and to suck the oil remaining on the skins we had just emptied, the very smell of which, as well as the appearance, was to us almost insufferable." They also offered their wives in trade for knives and other goods. Parry, just as pious as John Franklin, was clearly shocked.

Lyon gives a much fuller, richer account and is far less squeamish. When the sailors offered one old man rum, he notes, "he spat it out with signs of great disgust." Both children and adult Inuit refused sugar. When the ships' musician took his fiddle onto the ice and started to play, both the sailors and the Inuit began to dance; ultimately even the officers joined in. When it was all over and the men retired to the ships, the Inuit returned to their boats "to take their supper, which consisted of lumps of raw flesh and blubber of seals, birds, entrails, &c.; licking their fingers with great zest, and with knives or fingers scraping the blood and grease which ran down their chins into their mouths." They were amused by one of the ships' dogs, a Newfoundland retriever, but would have nothing to do with Lyon's black cat. Not one of them would touch it.

This was a voyage particularly marked by fraternization with the Inuit. The ships and their crews would spend two winters in Inuit neighborhoods, seeing them almost every day, feeding them when they were starving, treating their sick, and learning their ways, and we are fortunate to have had Lyon with them. He had an anthropologist's eye for behavior, and he liked them even when they did steal. "A few instances of dishonesty occurred," he wrote about the Inuit of Hudson Strait, "where iron lay neglected in view; but it is scarcely to be wondered that such a temptation should prove irresistible: had small golden bars been thrown in the streets of London, how would they have fared?" Lyon, like so many other naval officers, was an excellent illustrator. It is his drawings that illuminate Captain Parry's expedition account. During the first winter he submitted to being tattooed by an Inuit woman in a traditional Inuit tattoo design. He looked, he took notes, and, for the most part, he did not judge.

Repulse Bay, when they reached it, proved free of ice, and Parry took pains to trace the coast and map it. He was all too aware of what had happened in the past to any explorer who, for whatever reason, did not go far enough, did not explore to its limit any inlet, however unlikely that it opened onto a passage, however obvious it was that it was a dead end. Christopher Middleton in the 1740s had judged Repulse Bay to be a dead end but had not made sure, which allowed Arthur Dobbs to berate him endlessly when he returned to London. Middleton was much on Parry's mind and he explored Repulse Bay to its limits. They spent what passed for the summer moving slowly up the coast from Repulse Bay, sending the boats through a little strait they named Hurd Channel, taking soundings to make sure the ships could get through it, then exploring little Gore Bay: again, making sure. No Europeans had ever seen this land, so it was naming day in America once again, and friends, officers, patrons, and the lords of the Admiralty were granted the honor of having a piece of land, or a cape, or a bay named after them.

Just above Gore Bay a long, twisting inlet bites into the landscape, and Parry spent most of September exploring it. Conditions as always were difficult. The weather was intermittently bad. At its entrance, and for perhaps twenty miles inland, the inlet is navigable for sailing ships; then an arm of it shoots off to the north, while another turns west, turns north itself, then circles around a headland to end in a small bay. Parry called it Ross Bay, after James Clark Ross, who was still with him, a definite member of his "school." A month wasted, then, but he had no choice, he could leave no openings unexamined. He named this piece of frustration after George Lyon: Lyon Inlet.

By October 1 the two ships were dodging the new ice in Lyon Inlet, the young ice that formed every night, then melted during the day. "It is indeed scarcely possible," Parry wrote, an uncharacteristically bitter note in his voice,

> to conceive the degree of hinderance occasioned by this impediment, trifling as it always appears before it is encountered. When the sheet has acquired a thickness of about half an inch, and is of considerable extent, a ship is liable to be stopped by it unless favoured by a strong and free wind; and even when still retaining her way through the water, at the rate of a mile an hour, her course is not always under the control of the helmsman, though assisted by the nicest attention to the action of the sails, but depends on some accidental increase or decrease in the thickness of the sheet of ice.

The boats could not tow the ships, as they might on a windless day, because the process of breaking through the ice was even more difficult for oarsmen. "A ship in this helpless state," he went on, "her sails in vain expanded to a favourable breeze, her ordinary resources failing, . . . has often reminded me of Gulliver tied down by the feeble hands of Lilliputians."

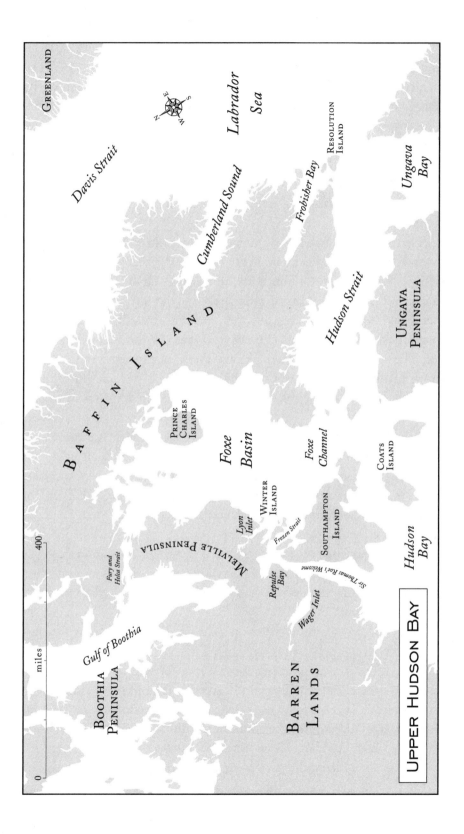

GREENLAND

Davis Strait

*Labrador
Sea*

RESOLUTION
ISLAND

Frobisher Bay

Cumberland Sound

*Ungava
Bay*

Hudson Strait

UNGAVA
PENINSULA

B A F F I N   I S L A N D

PRINCE
CHARLES
ISLAND

*Foxe
Basin*

*Foxe
Channel*

COATS
ISLAND

WINTER
ISLAND

LYON
INLET

MELVILLE PENINSULA

Frozen Strait

SOUTHAMPTON
ISLAND

*Hudson
Bay*

*Fury and
Hecla Strait*

REPULSE
BAY

Sir Thomas Roe's Welcome

Gulf of Boothia

WAGER INLET

BOOTHIA
PENINSULA

B A R R E N
L A N D S

miles

0   400

UPPER HUDSON BAY

It was time, clearly, to find winter quarters. Off the mouth of Lyon Inlet lay an island that provided some shelter from northern gales. They named it Winter Island and moored the ships in a little cove on its southern shore. Parry claimed to be satisfied with his progress to date, "however trifling . . . progress might appear on the chart." They had in fact not gone very far, but he had been thorough. "I derived the most sincere satisfaction," he concluded his account of the summer's exploration, "from a conviction of having left no part of the coast from Repulse Bay eastward in a state of doubt as to its connexion with the continent."

The winter was like Parry's previous winter in the Arctic. They grew cress and mustard greens in boxes; they put on shows; they taught school. Parry had his violin with him again and there was chamber music in his cabin and Lyon's alternately. He did not suggest a newspaper this time, so there was no *North Hudson Gazette*. The men slept in hammocks instead of bunks, in order to improve the circulation of the air. There were magic lantern shows. The moisture in the air outside froze in tiny spicules, and it thereby snowed, the spicules glittering in the light, on perfectly clear, very cold days, and this went on all winter. They caught eighty to ninety foxes in traps over the course of the winter; some of the officers tried to tame one or two of them but most were eaten. The lowest temperature was a mere minus forty degrees, but Parry's cabin, exposed in the rear over the stern, proved to be the coldest room in the ship, and he admitted to occasional discomfort. He did not admit to boredom, however; Parry was adept at keeping his men busy and at entertaining them. On the first voyage two marines had gotten drunk and Parry had ordered them thirty-six lashes apiece; on this voyage there was no hint of disciplinary problems of that kind. But more men got sick this trip, and five died of disease. One man died when he fell from a masthead.

Halfway through the winter, on February 1, a party of twenty-five Inuit were seen approaching the ship. They were living, it turned out, just two miles away in a set of igloos nobody on board had noticed, and they were there for the winter. These were a different tribe and a different sort from the Hudson Bay people they had encountered earlier, who had perhaps dealt a few times too often with the ships and men of the Hudson's Bay Company. They were scrupulously honest for one, running after the officers and men to return possessions they carelessly left behind when they visited their igloos. They were cheerful even when suffering from hunger, as was often the case. And they were fascinating. Parry never quite got over their eating habits, but Lyon reports them with a kind of barely suppressed glee. "The first specimen we had of the indifference of the Eskimaux, as to what they put into their mouths," he writes,

> was in consequence of Captain Parry's purchasing a lamp at the time it was burning. The woman who sold it instantly extinguished the light, and vigorously commenced cleaning the lamp, which contained as much soot as oil, by scraping it with her fingers, which, with their load of sweets, she conveyed rapidly to her mouth. The tongue finished the operation; the lamp was licked perfectly clean, while in return it covered her face with soot, and caused us all a laugh at her uncouth figure, in which she joined most heartily.

In another "hut," as they called the igloos, a woman gave Lyon a piece of caribou fat; he ate it, he said, "and found it sweet and good."

The igloos themselves never ceased to amaze them. Parry and Lyon both spent a night in one. Most of them had wings, to accommodate more than one family, and most of them were high enough that a man could stand up in them, although the long entrance passages had to be crawled through. They took only two or three hours to build, even one with wings. To let in light from outside, they had skylights, pieces of solid clear ice set into the blocks of snow; they saved these pieces of ice when they abandoned an igloo for a new site.

From the beginning six men from each ship were allowed to visit the Inuit village each day, and the Inuit themselves were daily visitors to the ships, so over time the ships' crews got to know them extremely well. Lyon made drawings of them hunting, waiting for seals at a seal hole, creeping toward seals lying on the ice, and the interiors of igloos. One woman in particular, a woman named Iligliuk, impressed Parry with a quick understanding. Showing her their chart of the coastline, she understood right away what it was. When asked what lay to the north, she knew what they wanted to know.

It had already occurred to Parry to send a party to explore north up the coastline on foot before the ice broke up. If they knew beforehand how the coast trended and what would be worthwhile to explore in more detail, and what not, they could save a lot of time. On March 15, a warm day, Lyon set out with a small group of men dragging a sledge loaded with provisions for twenty days and a tent, whereupon the thermometer instantly began to fall, the wind to pick up out of the north, and a small blizzard set in. They were gone one night. The sledge proved to be overloaded and could barely be dragged through soft snow "in which we waded knee deep." The tent proved useless; the temperature inside it stood at one below zero. They dug a snow cave and huddled into it while the temperature outside dropped to fifteen below, the wind howling around them, then to twenty-five below. After a mostly sleepless night, halfway through the next morning they decided to return but were unable to find their way, so thick was the snow and drift blowing around them. Nobody measured the windchill factor then, but it must have been murderous. Confused, cold, anxious, they were soon, Lyon writes, "completely bewildered. Several of our party began to exhibit symptoms of that horrid kind of insensibility which is the prelude to sleep." Many of them were suffering from frostbite but could not make the effort to rub their skin to restore circulation. Lyon had them build a snow wall to protect them from the wind, "for standing still must have proved fatal to men in our circumstances." They knew the ships were nearby, but where? They could see nothing; they could hardly see each other. The whole side of one man's face was frozen "as hard as a mask, the eye-lids were stiff, and one corner of the upper lip so drawn up as to expose the teeth and gums." Deceived by the whiteout conditions, the men ran to every dark stone, thinking it might be the ships. Finally somebody came across a fresh track, and they decided to follow it no matter where it led. Ten minutes later they were on board the ships and safe. Lyon waited until May before he tried this excursion again.

In the meantime Parry asked Iligliuk and other Inuit as well to make charts of what they knew of the country to the north. It was hers that held their rapt attention. The officers set her up in Parry's cabin at a long table and watched her draw Repulse Bay with considerable accuracy, then Lyon Inlet, and then other indentations in the coast, along with the island where, she informed them, she had been born. And beyond that? "It would have amused an unconcerned looker-on," Parry wrote, "to have observed the anxiety and suspense depicted on the countenances of *our* part of the group till this was accomplished, for never were the tracings of a pencil watched with more eager solicitude." And there it was. Just above her birthplace the land bent to the west and continued west to open on a vast expanse of water where "no land to the westward [is] seen from the hills." Land to the north, yes, but not to the west. This was a strait. If her chart was accurate, this could be what they were looking for. "Our business was to see and not to speculate," Parry observes in his expedition account, but Iligliuk's chart elated him.

The ice freed the two ships on July 2. The Inuit had already left toward the north themselves, and Parry had grown tired of them. He had fed them when they were starving, he had enjoyed their company, he had traded with them and indulged them, but in the end what he called their ingratitude put him off. The British had taken sick Inuit on board and nursed them, and the Inuit had left when they were better without saying thank you. The Inuit had gotten used to the largesse of the British, both officers and seamen, who had fed them whenever their hunts failed, despite the fact that the Inuit themselves made no provision for the future but ate everything they caught at once, as fast as they could, stuffing their faces with nine or ten pounds of meat at a sitting, sometimes more. Parry used the example of Iligliuk to express his disappointment. Just before they were to leave Lyon had asked her to make some pieces in miniature of Inuit clothing, and she had agreed to do so. Parry finding her at leisure one day put some skins before her and suggested she begin. She said she had no caribou thread. Parry rounded some up. She said she had no needle. Parry found her one. He found "scissors, pattern-clothes, and all the other requisites." She made other excuses and refused to do the work. But when they later threw her some beads "she eagerly employed herself for half-an-hour in stringing them that not one might be lost." She was willing to work for herself. Said Parry, "This anecdote shews in a strong light that deep-rooted selfishness which . . . , notwithstanding the superiority of Iligliuk's understanding, detracted from the amiability of her disposition." Her head had been turned, he went on, by the attention she had received precisely because of the superiority of her understanding. They had spoiled her, in short, and perhaps the entire tribe with her.

Sailing north through July, the ships danced with the ice just as they had the summer earlier, dodging huge floes bearing down on them, hiding behind the points of shallow bays, mooring to shore ice, making progress as they could. By the end of the month they had reached the place where, if the strait existed, it would have lain. There were Inuit there, a separate group, but with some few individuals they were familiar with; and there was ice. Parry wrote that

> it is impossible to describe our disappointment and mortification in perceiving an unbroken sheet of ice extending com-

pletely across the supposed passage from one land to the other. It is important to notice that our chief disappointment arose, not from the mere presence of ice blocking up the desired passage, to which our most anxious hopes had long by anticipation been directed, but from the *nature* of the ice . . . This consisted of a floe so level and continuous, that a single glance was sufficient to assure us of the disagreeable fact, that it was the ice formed in its present situation during the winter, and still firmly attached to the land on every side.

Nature, he went on, "seemed scarcely yet to have commenced" the business of thaw. They had sawn their way out of the ice at Winter Island a few weeks before. There was no sawing this ice. Miles and miles of it projected from the shoreline. There was nothing to do but to wait for it to melt.

They spent the time actively; Parry had no trouble thinking of things for them to do. They mapped the area thoroughly and explored the coastline of the land to the north, on the other side of the strait, and called it Cockburn Island. In fact it was the western end of Baffin Island. Some of the officers and men learned to kayak. They made excursions by sledge to the south, checking Inuit reports of inlets, seeing nothing because of persistent fog. They killed a whale. Yet more islands and islets were given names. They visited the Inuit. "The men shewed me some curious puzzles with knots on their fingers," Parry reports, "and I did what I could in return. The little girls were very expert in a singular but rather disgusting amusement, which consisted in drawing a piece of sinew up their nostrils, and producing the end out of their mouths."

That was all very well, but disgusting amusements were not what they were after. The ice got more and more rotten every day, but it broke up slowly, all too slowly, drifting off in small pieces. And it was August. They were stopped at the "very threshold of the North-West Passage, for nearly four weeks," he wrote, "without advancing twice as many miles to the westward." He decided to check it out on foot and left on August 14 with another officer and two men from each ship, working their way over bad ice to an island in the approaches to the strait, or what they hoped was the strait, and then west and north. On the eighteenth they reached a peninsula that pointed north, climbed the hills that composed it, and found themselves finally looking down on a passage two miles wide between the end of the peninsula and an island. To the west lay another island, but beyond it they could see that the shores widened to "a distance of several leagues, and for more than three points of the compass in that direction no land could be seen to the utmost limits of a clear horizon." Parry had no doubt that they had found the Polar Sea, "and loaded as it was with ice, we already felt as if we were on the point of forcing our way through it along the northern shores of America." If the ice would only break up in the strait itself.

Parry named it the Strait of the Fury and Hecla, and it bears that name today. It is dotted with islands in its eastern half, but a current runs through it under the ice perpetually to the east, just as John Barrow was sure it would. They were all sure—Parry and his officers, Barrow, John Franklin, the whole crew of northern explorers—that once you rounded that corner, which it looked like Parry had just discovered, the shores of America ran in a fairly straight line west and east at about seventy degrees northern latitude, and it would be open sailing to Icy Cape in Alaska, then Bering Strait, then victory. How maddening to be stopped by the ice!

The ice in the eastern portion of the strait did finally break up, and Parry and Lyon were able to get the two ships past the strait's narrowest point and just into its western half. But the western half stayed frozen solid. Nothing budged. The ice was fast to the land, and impenetrable. As far as they could see to the west, furthermore, the sea itself was frozen solid. Parry tried everything, ran his ship into the ice blocking the way, dropped weights over the bow in an attempt to break it up. Nothing worked.

> And thus after a vexatious delay of six weeks at the eastern entrance of the Strait, and at a time when we had every reason to hope that nature, though hitherto tardy in her annual disruption of the ice, had at length made an effort to complete it, did we find our progress once more opposed by a barrier of the same continuous, impenetrable, and hopeless nature as at first!

Stopped cold again, Parry sent out still more exploring parties on foot. They confirmed the existence of the strait. The ice piled up in the strait to the west was hummocky, adding confirmation that it was sea ice. By the middle of September it was imperative that Parry get out of the strait to find a place to winter. His plan now was to send the *Hecla* back to England next summer and go on himself with some of the other ship's supplies, somehow force his way through the strait, and sail west.

They spent the winter, once again, among the Inuit, and developed a more serious interest in their way of life. It baffled the officers that the Inuit gorged themselves when there was food and, in Parry's words, "never bestow a thought on to-morrow"; they did not, in other words, put any aside for the future, did not store it, which they could easily have done, since deep-freezing was right outside their door. They decided to run an experiment on how much an Inuit man would eat in a single day if he were freely supplied with food. The answer? Four pounds and four ounces of frozen walrus flesh, four pounds and four ounces of boiled walrus flesh, and nearly two pounds of bread. The young man they ran this experiment on also consumed more than a pint of "rich gravy soup" and more than a gallon of water. "Certain it is," notes Parry, "that on a particular occasion of great plenty, one or two individuals were seen lying in the huts [i.e., the igloos] so distended by the quantity of meat they had eaten, that they were unable to move, and were suffering considerable pain arising solely from this cause." Parry thought the alternation of feast and famine was unhealthy, not to mention shortsighted, and the cause of the many deaths they saw that winter among the Inuit. It did not occur to him that the presence of Europeans and European diseases, to which the Inuit had developed no immunity, might have been a factor; but he would have had to be far ahead of his time to have understood this. Gorging after famine is a common practice among hunter-gatherer cultures around the world. Parry could not have known.

The officers learned more of the Inuit language that winter and tried to explain to them who they themselves were, where Great Britain was, what it was like. The Inuit had "extreme difficulty" understanding differences of rank; they had none of their own. They thought the ships belonged to the captains and called them, respectively, *Lyon-oomiak* and *Paree-oomiak; oomiak* or *umiak* is the name the Inuit gave large boats. The smaller items on board the *Fury* and the *Hecla*, however, they believed to belong to other members of the crew. No, no, Parry tried to explain, everything belonged "to a much richer and more powerful person, to whom we all paid respect and obedience, and at whose command we had come to visit and enrich the *Innuees*," using their own name for themselves rather than the term *Eskimo*, which is not an Inuit word. He drew a rough chart of the Atlantic for them, did what he could to convey the distances involved, and told them how to pronounce *King George*. It pleased him when some of them were able to master the sounds.

Lyon was a more dispassionate observer. He devoted a long chapter in his own journal of the voyage (which would be published at John Barrow's request precisely for its ethnographic interest) to a full description of Inuit dress, hunting methods, kayaks and other equipment, customs, and character. The ingratitude that Parry complained about in the person of Iligliuk was a universal trait, Lyon says; he found the sense of gratitude to be "not only rare, but absolutely unknown amongst them." This fault, if fault it was, was tempered, however, by their genial good humor, which nothing seemed to disturb. They did not quarrel much among themselves and murder was unknown. And they were brave. "There is an independent fearless expression in the countenance and person of an Eskimaux," he writes, "which is highly striking." These were people who dared to take on a polar bear "in single combat, with only the assistance of their dogs." But they did lie, they were envious of each other's possessions, and they all begged for things from the Europeans.

But even Lyon had trouble accommodating to the casual infidelity that prevailed among both men and women. Men willingly offered their wives to friends or visitors, the women often suggesting the trade themselves. "A woman details her intrigues to her husband with the most perfect unconcern, and will also answer to any charge of the kind made before a numerous assemblage of people. Husbands prostitute wives, brothers sisters, and parents daughters, without showing the least signs of shame." He does not say whether any of the British, officers or men, took advantage of this situation. What amazed him was that their behavior otherwise was so decorous. "In general conversation not an immodest word or gesture can be detected. . . . In dancing or singing parties, the females have a seat apart, the conduct of both sexes being extremely decorous."

What did it add up to? Lyon does not answer this question. Their mission, as Parry had put it, was to see, not speculate, and his report is just that, a report, full of interesting detail, and not a judgment on this culture and the methods it had developed of adapting to its environment. But judgment is implicit. Both Lyon and Parry, although they never saw an instance of savagery among them, called the Inuit "savages" throughout their books. It never occurred to Parry or Lyon in their accounts that they had anything to learn about themselves from the Inuit or the way they adapted to this environment. They were curious about how the Inuit built their igloos but did not think to build them themselves and abandon the use of their heavy, hopelessly inefficient tents. Despite numerous cases of generosity and hospitality on the part of the Inuit, the two officers saw themselves exclusively as benefactors, superior people who treated diseases, fed the Inuit when they were starving, and introduced them to the wonders of cold sharp steel and wool clothing. Neither of them was sensitive enough to see, or at least report, any evidence that the Inuit didn't buy it. On the contrary, the Inuit were delighted, Lyon wrote, with woolen clothing, wore it over their own much warmer furs, and were amazed at how hot it made them; and the advantages of steel over stone are obvious to all human beings. But otherwise no revolutions of thought took place; there were no sudden insights; there was none of the kind of learning that leads to changes in behavior. Neither group was moved to adopt any of the lifeways of the other.

By the summer of 1823 it became clear to Parry that his plan to send the *Hecla* home and go on alone would not work. Supplies had already been transferred from the *Hecla* to the *Fury*, but two Arctic winters had taken their toll on his crews. Men were beginning to sicken now from their own European diseases, and despite the lemon juice, the fresh seal and walrus meat they purchased from the Inuit, the mustard and cress salads, evidence of scurvy was appearing not just in the crew but in the officers as well. They were all exhausted, not just from the winters but from the constant battle with the ice. Fury and Hecla Strait showed no signs of opening up any earlier than it had the previous summer, if it opened at all.

The decision to leave was wiser than Parry could have known. A glance at a map of the Arctic shows that Fury and Hecla Strait opens up not on the Arctic Ocean but on Prince Regent Inlet. The shores of the North American continent do not run in a straight line west from the strait; they run up and around the inlet. If he could have sailed through he would have been forced to turn north and would have emerged in Lancaster Sound, in the same area he had explored in the previous voyage. What a bitter salad that would have been.

As it was, they had a wild ride down Foxe Basin to the south. They sawed their way out of the shallow bay that had sheltered them over the winter and emerged into open water on August 8. The strait was still frozen solid. One of Parry's crew was down with scurvy by then. He died of it before they got back to London. Soon after escaping from the ice the two ships found themselves beset in drifting ice again, unable to escape; it took them wherever the currents ran, but generally south. At one point it drove Parry's ship up Lyon Inlet and threatened to beach him there. It was continuously dangerous and once again their fate was a matter of luck. Not until September 17 did they find open water in Hudson Strait and cut themselves free.

> We thus finally made our escape from the ice after having been almost immoveably beset in it for twenty-four days out of the last twenty-six, in the course of which time the ships had been taken over no less than one hundred and forty leagues of ground, generally very close to the shore, and always unable to do any thing towards effecting their escape from danger.

One hundred and forty leagues is 420 miles. Parry called it "one of the most providential escapes it has ever been our lot to experience." They were back in Great Britain a month later.

What now? When Parry returned, John Franklin had been home for a year and his findings had been published, and they confirmed what Barrow and the Admiralty had suspected—that the northern shores of America were more or less free of ice during the summer. But Barrow and the Admiralty also believed that this shoreline extended all the way to the other side of Fury and Hecla Strait. They believed, again, that Prince Regent Inlet was actually a channel between an island to the west and the land that lay to the north of Fury and Hecla Strait. At its bottom the channel would open up and there it would lie, the coast of America and the run west to glory.

Here was religion without revelation. They had no evidence, no authority for this geographical speculation, only their own wishful thinking. Franklin had reached only Point Turnagain, and that was 450 miles from Parry's new strait. That's longer than Pennsylvania. Parry imagined himself sailing south out of Prince Regent Inlet into a sea that may or may not have been full of ice, and reaching that imaginary coast. It simply never occurred to him that another body of land might intervene. He and Barrow were of one mind on the subject, and that therefore was where Parry would go next, to Lancaster Sound once more, then south into Prince Regent Inlet, this time making it, he hoped, through the ice he knew waited for him, just as he had eased, sawn, and dragged his way through or around other immense bodies of ice. He would, he was sure, make it. "I never felt more sanguine of ultimate success . . . than at the present moment," he wrote in the winter of 1823–24; "and I cannot but entertain a confident hope that England may yet be destined to succeed in an attempt which has for centuries past engaged her attention, and interested the whole civilized world."

CHAPTER ELEVEN

FURY BEACH

P arry reached England only to find that his father had died a year and a half earlier, and that his younger sister had married. From Scotland he rode to London to report to the Admiralty and promptly fell ill; his newly married sister, who saw him the day after his return, said that he could "neither eat nor speak," and the next day he was delirious with fever. But he was well enough toward the end of October to reply to John Franklin's congratulatory letter on his voyage in a manner that indicates Franklin's current standing in the kingdom: "To place you, in the rank of travelers, above Park, and Hearne, and others," Parry wrote him, "would in my estimation, be nothing in comparison of your merits." He went on to refer to the fact that the English sailors survived on Franklin's expedition, while the voyageurs did not, although he ascribed it not to English superiority of spirit but to Christian belief: "But, in you, and your party, my dear friend, we see so sublime an instance of Christian confidence in the Almighty, of the superiority of moral and religious energy over mere brute strength of body, that it is impossible to contemplate your sufferings, and preservation, without a sensation of reverential awe!" The letter Franklin had written him, he said, he had "cried over . . . like a child." It would be hard to say which of them was more religiously inclined. The two men had not known each other well before their respective expeditions. They now became fast friends. The record contains no trace of competition between them.

They were both between expeditions in the winter of 1823–24, but Parry would go back to the Arctic before Franklin would. Franklin had proposed an attempt at the North Pole to the Admiralty, using small boats on runners to travel over the ice, the boats to be towed not by dogs but by tame reindeer from Norway. The Admiralty wanted him instead to return to the northern coast of Canada, this time to the mouth of the Mackenzie River, where he would make a left instead of a right and survey the unknown coastline between the Mackenzie delta and Icy Cape in Alaska. The Admiralty would at the same time send Lieutenant Beechey to Icy Cape to wait for him there. Franklin took a full year to plan this second trip.

For Parry there were honors to be awarded again, as the king had said there would be. He had been promoted to post captain while he was spending the winter at Winter Island in 1822. The city of Winchester, like the city of Bath after the previous voyage, gave him the freedom of the city. Lord Melville invited him into his office and surprised him by offering him the post of official hydrographer of the Royal Navy, the person, that is, in charge of the navy's charting of the world's oceans. The offer took Parry aback; he thought it would mean giving up his Arctic explorations. Not at all, Melville assured him. According to Ann Parry, a direct descendant and his modern biographer, Melville "did not consider the two incompatible." The job, in other words, would still be there when he returned from what would be his third Arctic expedition, or his fourth, or however many more there were.

Despite the disappointing outcome of the expedition, Parry remained a popular, heroic figure in the press. While he had been spending winters in the ice, notices had appeared at Christmastime in the papers reminding revelers that brave British sailors were enduring, alone, the brutal temperatures of the frozen north while they were sitting comfortably by their firesides enjoying themselves with friends and family. When it became clear that Parry had returned without finding the Northwest Passage, the press zeroed in on reports of their life with the Inuit, which it regarded as the most interesting part of the expedition, and repeated the stories at length. About the geographical findings, however, real disappointment did prevail. *The New Monthly Magazine* wrote, "The expedition has in fact neither added much to geography, nor been able to explore farther than was done by Middleton and preceding navigators," which was not true. "The last year seems to have been so unproductive, that the ships might as well have returned home in the autumn of 1822." The author of this piece also took wry note of the naming of geographical features, Parry having "immortalized all his friends, relatives, and patrons, by bestowing their names upon capes, creeks, straits, bays, points, inlets, and islands," and suggested that any-one who wanted lasting fame might secure it by "making interest with the Captain." The magazine itself requested that Parry bestow the name "Point New Monthly" on an Arctic cape in his next trip. No publication before had taken this cheeky tone with Parry.

Parry had warned his public in advance not to expect too much from this voyage. But he had been gone more than two years, with not a word of his whereabouts reaching home, no sightings by whalers, nothing. The public had expected him to reappear not from the north but from the south, rounding Cape Horn, cruising north from the South Atlantic, and sailing triumphantly up the English Channel to drop anchor in the Thames. So had John Barrow. When Parry published his account of the expedition, a spectacular quarto nearly five hundred closely printed pages of narrative long, Barrow began his review in *The Quarterly* by making it clear that he shared in the disappointment. "To effect, on our part, any exemption from this general feeling, would be absurd in the extreme," he wrote. He was, after all, the main proponent "of the existence of a navigable passage from the northern Atlantic to the Pacific." How could he not be upset at the outcome of Parry's voy-age? But he recovered quickly, for what did Parry's account do, he said, if not strengthen the presumption that such a passage existed; and Parry's findings showed the route where it could not be found fixed "on that by which it *can,* and in all probability *will,* ultimately be effected. Our dis-appointment, therefore, is confined solely to the delay of accomplishing what we have very little doubt will, ere long, be done."

Barrow went on to describe Parry's findings and his relations with the Inuit—in short, to summarize the book—then ended with a ringing appeal to British patriotic feeling. "Is then any further attempt," he wrote, "to be abandoned as hopeless?

> We are glad to find that the government think otherwise, and that a pursuit which has already added so many brilliant names to the pages of our naval history; which has already extended the physical and moral knowledge of the globe; and which for two centuries and a half has been the favourite object of the highest persons in the realm in station and char-acter, will not hastily be abandoned, but, we trust, continue to be persevered in until it is accomplished or proved to be impracticable.

He attacked those critics who were pointing out that even if the Northwest Passage existed, it would be commercially useless. "Knowledge endureth forever," he added, "and the names of Cook, Parry, Franklin, and a host of others who have contributed so amply to enlarge the sphere of knowledge, will shed a lustre on our naval history, and stimulate the youth of ages yet to come, to imitate their bright example."

But the British did have a practical side; there were men who wondered what was the point of all these winters spent in the ice, and the disappointment in the press over Parry's failure reflected this fact. In 1824, the year Parry left on his third voyage, a skeptic writing under the name "Scrutator" and describing himself as an experienced sailor published a book called *The Impracticability of a North-West Passage for Ships, Impartially Considered*, in which he attacked Barrow's earlier suppositions about currents and ice conditions in the Arctic (he calls Barrow "the Reviewer"), then went on to point out obviously discouraging facts drawn from Parry's and Franklin's books, the most telling, perhaps, being that the ice floes at the western end of Melville Island, blocking Parry's progress on his first voyage, were forty feet thick. A navy captain named John Dundas Cochrane argued in *The New Monthly Magazine* that the outcomes of the three expeditions to date "afford no ground of reasonable hope that any maritime expedition will ever succeed from the Eastward." Cochrane thought the Admiralty should send ships through Bering Strait and try to navigate the passage from the back end, taking advantage of the current that was presumed to run from west to east along the north coast of the continent. Cochrane had walked alone into "the remotest parts of Asia," and he recommended that Franklin's forthcoming expedition to Canada should travel light, just as he had. "The more numerous . . . the party composing it, the more likely to fail," he wrote. Six to eight people were plenty. Send only the toughest men. Cochrane was prescient. He had ample experience with dogs and thought them the best way to travel anywhere in the Arctic. He believed as well that the best time to attempt to reach the North Pole over the ice was in winter. Odd as that sounds, it's true. In winter the ice remains hard and firm and is much easier to travel on. The Admiralty sent Parry toward the North Pole over the ice in the middle of summer in 1827. Meltwater was everywhere on the ice, and traveling on it was torture.

Barrow did not respond to these criticisms, but it is noteworthy that they were beginning to appear. They would become bolder when Parry returned from his next voyage, to Prince Regent Inlet. This voyage was conceived in Barrow's usual way as just one prong of a broad attack on the problem of the Passage, four attempts all leaving within a year of each other. Franklin would be going back to Canada the following year, 1825; Beechey was bound to Icy Cape; and George Lyon had been given his own command as well. Lyon was to sail back to Repulse Bay and cross Melville Peninsula, the name Parry had given to the body of land south of Fury and Hecla Strait, to the sea. It was a mere three-day trek, the Inuit had told them; then he would explore all the way to Franklin's Point Turnagain. Barrow was determined to fill in all the blanks on the map, determined to prove his point at last.

Before Barrow's men left on their separate voyages they were much in demand, Parry in particular. He told his brother Charles, "I dined on Monday at Lord Bexley's and went to the Blackheath Ball, to which I have been often before invited. Nothing can exceed the attention I everywhere meet with." Various dukes had asked him to dine. He was asked to give speeches, which he disliked doing, so his brother wrote them for him. In April 1824 he attended a dinner party at the Franklins' that has become semilegendary in Arctic circles for putting together on one occasion not only Parry and Franklin but also George Lyon, Beechey, and John Barrow, who sat at the head of the table. Jane Griffin was there and said of Parry that he was a "tall large, fine looking man, of commanding appearance, but possessing nothing of the fine gentle-man." He was too rough and blunt. That would only have made him a naval man, but she also found him "far from lighthearted & exhibits traces of heartfelt & recent suffering, in spite of which he occasionally bursts into hearty laughs, & seems to enjoy a joke." The suffering may have arisen more from embarrassment than anything else. He had come home the previous fall to find out that an "understanding" with a Miss Browne, who was Sabine's niece, had dissolved. He was blamed for it, and his relationship with Sabine had cooled as a result. But it turned out to be Miss Browne's fault. She had become engaged to someone else while he was gone.

He met his future wife shortly thereafter, however, on board the *Hecla* before he left for Prince Regent Inlet. Once again hordes of visitors swept into Deptford to see the ships. Among them were a group that included old friends of Parry's, plus Lord Sheffield, Sheffield's half sister Lady Maria Stanley, and her daughter Isabella. It was Isabella he would marry two years later, after returning from the Arctic for the fourth time.

Parry left from Deptford amid the usual hoopla. Whether a similar level of excitement attended the departure of George Lyon's expedition to Repulse Bay, the record does not show. Parry took the *Hecla* this time, giving the *Fury* to his old friend Lieutenant, now Commander, Henry Hoppner, who had been with him from the beginning, having served with him on the *Alexander* in the 1818 expedition, then on the two following. Hoppner was a charter member of the "Parry School." Parry and Sylvester had made still more improvements to the heating arrangements; the stove was now placed in the bottom of the ship, in the hold, and the ships were even warmer as a result, the mean temperature in Parry's cabin now standing at sixty-three degrees, December through April. On John Franklin's advice he took some pemmican with him to use on land expeditions during the winter months. James Clark Ross, John Ross's nephew, was also aboard. He too had been on every one of Parry's Arctic voyages, as had most of the sailors.

It was a disastrous voyage and makes a brief story. The last time Parry had been in these parts, he had boldly crossed Baffin Bay directly through the pack ice, instead of sailing up and around it, and had arrived in Lancaster Sound at the end of July instead of the end of August. This time the ice took its revenge. From July 17 on, "the obstructions from the quantity, magnitude, and closeness of the ice, were such as to keep our people almost constantly employed in heaving, warping, or sawing through it," he wrote, "and yet with so little success, that, at the close of the month of July, we had only penetrated seventy miles to the westward." On August 1 a hard gale from the southeast turned the pack into turmoil, with "mass overlaying mass for hours together," and the pressure caught the *Hecla* in a nip that came close to destroying her, one floe driving beneath the ship from one side while on the other a separate floe climbed the ship's side, flipping it half over and sandwiching it between the floes. If the floes had been thicker, he wrote, they would have crushed the ship. Only her reinforced beams saved her—that, says Parry, and the fact that she was as closely packed as an apple in its skin, crammed with supplies and equipment to the sides. Parry is quite cool about this incident, not bothering to explain how the ship came upright. He leaves it to us to imagine what it must have been like aboard, men scrambling to find footing or clinging to the rigging, knowing that at any moment the ice floe climbing the side could break over the deck, smash the masts, smash the ship's boats, strip off the rudder, and leave them helpless, if it did not instantly kill them all.

Through all of August the two ships remained locked in the ice, unable to escape, and in that time there was only one day in which rain, snow, sleet, or fog was absent. Some of the floes stood 20 feet at their edges *above* the surface of the sea, meaning that they measured 120 feet *below* the surface. On September 9, the sailing season now mostly gone, the ice at last released them. On September 11 they reached Lancaster Sound and two days later they found it covered with young ice. They spent a good part of September in a maneuver called "sallying," in which the crew runs from one side of the ship to the other, en masse, so that it rocks back and forth, breaking the ice's incipient hold on it. Not until September 26 did they reach Prince Regent Inlet. They took shelter for the winter in a small harbor they called Port Bowen on the east side of the inlet only twenty miles inside its mouth.

In the inevitable expedition account, Parry spares us the details of the long months there waiting for warmth, waiting for the ice to let go. Since so many of the men and the officers were the same as those on his previous voyages, they decided to forgo the plays and take up masquerades instead. They were a great success. The schools continued; by now the men could read well enough that the officers were teaching them some of the finer points of Christian theology. Parry was moved once again to note the melancholy the landscape inspired in him: "here," he wrote feelingly,

> when once the earth is covered, all is dreary monotonous whiteness—not merely for days and weeks, but for more than half a year together. Whichever way the eye is turned, it meets a picture calculated to impress upon the mind an idea of inanimate stillness, of that motionless torpor with which our feelings have nothing congenial; of anything, in short, but life. In the very silence there is a deadness with which a human spectator seems *out of keeping*.

The emphasis is his. Although only in his thirties, he was beginning to suffer from rheumatism. The Arctic was beginning to get to him.

They sawed their way out of Port Bowen on July 20, 1825. For a few days they dodged back and forth across the inlet, looking for an opening that would let them sail south. At last a channel opened up on the western shore, one to two miles wide, between the ice and the land. Parry took the same kinds of chances he had taken on the coast of Melville Island, pushing south down this channel, hoping the wind would hold the ice off the land. On July 30 the wind shifted and the ice closed with the land, forcing the *Fury* ashore. It came off without much damage, but two days later, on August 1, both the *Fury* and the *Hecla* were driven aground again by the ice. Shortly afterward Hoppner sent Parry a note to the effect that the *Fury* was leaking badly, four inches an hour; she was still heavily pressed; the ice had forced her not only aground but up onto the fixed land ice; the rudder was "very awkwardly situated"; and a ship's boat was badly damaged. In Hoppner's own words, the ship had "trembled violently, whilst the beams and timbers cracked, and a crash like the report of a musket was heard under the larboard quarter." Both ships again got free, but the *Fury* was leaking faster than her four pumps could be worked. The sternpost was broken; so was the forefoot. The main keel had been "much torn." She could go no farther without repairs. Repairing her, as they all knew, meant heaving her down— emptying the ship, in other words, of all her supplies, unshipping the masts, and positioning the *Hecla* beside her as an anchor for the ropes that would have to be used to turn her on her side and expose the bottom to the carpenters. It was a huge job, and time-consuming. They all knew that too.

The two crews did everything they could to save the *Fury*. A harbor was needed, first of all, to protect the ships from the streams of thick ice that swept constantly by, first north, then south, with the winds and tides. No harbor was available, so they had to create one by rowing the heavy bower anchors to the shore, securing them there, then tightening the huge hawsers running between the anchors and the ships so that they would deflect, like the ropes of a boxing ring, the ice floes that approached them. They took shelter among small icebergs that formed a kind of cove and anchored the icebergs, too, so that they would not be swept away. Only then could they unload the *Fury*, an arduous task that meant transferring the supplies to the shore in ship's boats, tun by tun, package by package, bucket of coal by bucket of coal. It took weeks of constant labor to do these things. All the while the icebergs to which they had quite literally tied their fate got smaller and smaller as they melted.

In the end it was hopeless. The *Fury* was too badly damaged. The icebergs disappeared one day, and there was no more shelter. It is a serious thing in any navy to lose a ship, but this ship was clearly lost. The *Fury* would have to be abandoned, her stores left onshore in Prince Regent Inlet at a place that is still known as Fury Beach. Parry was seeing open water to his south but he could not go on alone, overloaded with two crews and without the backup of a second ship if something should happen to the *Hecla*. He had little choice but to sail for home, with no new ground gained, no new knowledge, to face John Barrow and Lord Melville, having failed for the third time to discover the Northwest Passage, having lost three battles with the ice.

It is a measure of the man that he was quite philosophical about the whole thing. No one who had any acquaintance "with the true nature of this precarious navigation," he told his devoted public, would be surprised by what happened. It should be plain that such an accident "was at all times rather to be expected than otherwise, and that the only real cause for wonder has been our long exemption from such a catastrophe." He pointed out that to make progress in the Arctic, a commander must seize every opportunity of open water he finds, even if it puts ships into the danger of being pinned against the shore by the ice. He could, he said, have let the ships, beset in the ice, drift in comparative safety wherever the ice took them, but that would have denied him the chance of moving forward in the inshore channels that did open up. It wasn't about the ships, he noted. "The mere safety of the ships has never been more than a secondary object in the conduct of the expeditions under my command." The primary object was to make progress, whatever it took. If that involved "constant and unavoidable risk," so be it.

He made these remarks, he added, because there had been "a very general, but erroneous notion, that our ships were proof against any pressure to which they might be subject." Even some of his own crew thought so. But Parry knew better. "In truth, a ship, like any other work of man, sinks, and must ever sink, into insignificance, when viewed in comparison with the stupendous scale on which Nature's works are framed, and her operations performed." Yet he did not allow this thought to discourage him about the Northwest Passage. The next attempt, he thought, should be in this very place, Prince Regent Inlet, and he had no doubt there should be a next attempt. Finding the Passage would be accomplished, he was sure, "one day or other," and he only hoped it would be England that took the honor of it. As for him, he was ready to try again should the Admiralty decide that he was still their man.

. . .

Barrow sent him to the North Pole instead—or rather, toward it. Barrow of course remained convinced even after all this time, with all the accumulating contrary evidence from his own explorers, that the Polar Sea was open. He still believed that one needed only to penetrate a rim of ice before the Arctic Ocean would reveal itself in all its blue-gray splendor. It was his hobbyhorse, his idée fixe, and it is fascinating to watch Edward Parry try to break through the ice in the worst season for traveling on the ice, with the worst possible equipment, and the worst luck.

Parry sailed north in the spring of 1827 on the *Hecla*, taking most of his familiar entourage with him, and headed for the northern shore of Spitzbergen. The plan was to find a safe harbor for the ship somewhere on the north coast of Spitzbergen itself or else among the small islands to its northeast, then set out over the ice in two boats, two officers and ten men to each boat, and row, or sail, or drag the boats over the ice, whatever the situation demanded, the six hundred miles remaining to the Pole. Known as "troop boats," each boat was twenty feet long, seven feet wide, and flat-bottomed. They were mounted on steel-shod runners and weighed some 1,500 pounds empty. The gear, food, and supplies for ninety days that they were loaded with more than doubled this weight to a total of 3,755 pounds, or 268 pounds per man. Parry was hoping, however, that the men would not have to pull the boats over the ice. The *Hecla* stopped in Lapland and picked up eight tamed and trained reindeer to pull the boats. He also picked up the hundreds of pounds of dried mosses and grasses needed to feed them.

They sailed on into the pack, which they reached in the middle of May, southern gales driving them into it just as Buchan and Franklin had been driven into it in 1818. Parry had wanted to begin his ice march in June and be back by September. By May 21 they found themselves so closely beset by the ice that they had to cut a hole in it in order to drop the lead and determine the depth of the water. He was so closely beset that he could not escape. For three weeks the *Hecla* drifted with the ice in and around the shores of Spitzbergen. Not until June 8 did he work his way to the edge of it, and then—for the ice remained in the area— he was forced to play hide-and-seek with it, looking for a harbor, first on this island, then that. Most available harbors were blocked with ice. Perhaps, he thought, he should just leave, let the other officers find a harbor while he and his party set out for the Pole. After a night he thought better of that idea. How would he know where to find the

Hecla when he returned? What if she were driven far away? The fractured nature of the ice he would have to travel over this far south made the idea unattractive at any rate. Barrow had sent him out thinking that the pack above Spitzbergen was a vast sheet of ice, flat and unbroken. So Constantine Phipps had described it in 1773 in his attempt at the Pole; so Scoresby had once described it. Parry found no such easygoing prairie. The ice he could see from the ship was broken up into small floes, it was rough and irregular, and it was covered with pools of meltwater.

Parry found a harbor for his ship on June 20. On the twenty-first he left for the North, leaving the reindeer behind; he would have had to crowd them into the boats with all their feed, for he had to row north now to find the pack. Twenty-four straight hours of rowing brought them to the edge of it. Then the ordeal truly began. They worked at "night" in the twenty-four-hour daylight, when the glare on the ice was somewhat reduced. That way it was a little warmer when they were resting, and the snow was harder at "night" when the sun was lower in the sky. Parry's own words serve best to give a sense of what they went through.

> Setting out again at half past nine in the evening, we found our way to lie over nothing but small loose rugged masses of ice, separated by little pools of water, obliging us constantly to launch and haul up the boats, each of which operations required them to be unloaded, and occupied nearly a quarter of an hour. It came on to rain very hard on the morning of the 26th; and finding we were making very little progress, (having advanced not more than half a mile in four hours,) and that our clothes would be soon wet through, we halted at half past one, and took shelter under the awnings.

The ice they were hauling the boats over was like the half-melted river ice that Franklin had found on the Coppermine,

> composed, on its upper surface, of numberless irregular needle-like crystals, placed vertically, and nearly close together . . . At this early part of the season, this kind of ice afforded pretty firm footing, but as the summer advanced, the needles became more loose and moveable, rendering it extremely fatiguing to walk over them, besides cutting our

boots and feet, on which account the men called them
"penknives."

Franklin's men, too, had left blood in their tracks.

Day after day it was like that: "We halted at midnight, having waded
three-quarters of a mile through water from two to five inches deep
upon the ice." Fog settled in and they could not see ahead.

> We came to a floc covered with high and rugged hum-
> mocks . . . , occurring in two or three successive tiers, so that
> we had no sooner crossed one than another presented itself.
> Over one of these we hauled the boats with extreme diffi-
> culty, by a "standing pull," and the weather being then so
> thick that we could see no pass across the next tier, we were
> obliged to stop at nine, A.M.

When Scoresby had proposed in 1818 that it might be possible to
reach the Pole, he had suggested that the best way to do it would be on
light sledges, Inuit style, and in late winter, when the ice would be
frozen solid. In the Arctic summer, as Parry was discovering, the ice was
broken up, patchy, covered with water. Most modern attempts on the
Pole depart in February. "After six hours' severe toil, and much risk to
the men and boats, we had only accomplished about a mile and a quarter in a N.N.E. direction," Parry wrote. He had planned on making thirteen miles a day. On good days he actually might make six. The
hummocks were as high as twenty-five feet above the level of the floes
they stood on. Once they had to cut through a hummock with axes.
Parry speaks of the "dense and dismal fogs which so generally prevailed." The men dragged some of the supplies on light sledges they had
constructed out of snowshoes; then they went back for the boats. The
loads were clearly much too heavy, the labor exhausting, the food insufficient. Each man got ten ounces of ship's biscuits a day, nine ounces of
pemmican, one ounce of cocoa powder, and one gill of rum. It had taken
a pound and a half of pemmican a day to feed Franklin's men. Parry's
men floundered through soft snow up to their knees and meltwater
ponds hundreds of yards across. The glare blinded them. It is painful to
read about. They sank to their knees, sometimes their waists, crossing
ponds of snow and meltwater that might be a quarter of a mile across. It
took two hours once to travel a hundred yards.

The farther they went, the more the ice was broken. Where was the vast, level-smooth pack Scoresby and Phipps had seen? A Dutch whaling captain had one year seen "one continued plain of smooth, unbroken ice, bounded only by the horizon." Where was it? Did it even exist? They were baffled, too, by the fact that every time they made a latitude reading, their position was farther south than the distance they had traveled over the ice would seem to indicate. They were discovering one of the signal facts of the Arctic Ocean, that on this meridian, running north from Spitzbergen, the current runs south, taking the ice with it. For every laborious mile a person might make north over the ice, the current will take him perhaps half a mile in the other direction. On July 20 their instruments gave them a latitude reading of 82 degrees, 36 minutes, and 52 seconds north, "less than *five* miles to the northward of our place at noon on the 17th, since which time we had certainly traveled *twelve* in that direction." On July 26 they lost thirteen miles in a northerly gale. The southerly drift, Parry calculated, amounted to four miles a day. Parry called a halt. This road was obviously closed.

And what of George F. Lyon and his voyage to Repulse Bay? Perhaps because it was so expensive to launch four expeditions at more or less the same time, the Admiralty had given Lyon the *Griper,* the ship Parry had refused to take back to the Arctic, and Lyon was going alone. He had a supply ship, but it would turn back when they reached Hudson Strait. The *Griper* was small, difficult to maneuver, and the bow lay a foot lower in the water than the stern. So sluggish was it that the supply ship had to tow it across the Atlantic Ocean every second or third day, and when that ship left the *Griper* to its lonely fate the latter was so piled with supplies, which lay all over the deck, that the men had trouble moving about; it was indeed so crowded, Lyon reports, that "we were obliged to place casks and other stores, in every part but that allotted to the ship's company's mess tables; and even my cabin had a quantity of things stored in it." The Admiralty expected Lyon to be gone two years, perhaps longer, one season to get there and set up camp, another to go trekking and mapping across Melville Peninsula, and then the return walk back to Repulse Bay and the voyage home.

"It must indeed be owned," Barrow wrote many years later, "that there was more than usual want of prudence in sending such a small and sluggish ship alone, through a navigation which had been proved and

condemned as one of the most difficult and dangerous of the many difficult ones that occur in this part of the Arctic Seas." This was one of the
few times Barrow admitted to making a mistake. In the event it nearly
cost everyone aboard his life. From the mouth of Hudson Strait things
went bad. The ship struck a rock and almost capsized. Ice choked the
strait almost as thickly as the ice choking Baffin Bay that Parry was
encountering at the same time. Lyon decided to go south of Southampton Island and up Sir Thomas Roe's Welcome to Repulse Bay. It was an
unlucky choice, although the other, through Frozen Strait, might have
been just as unlucky. Ice held him up, and foul weather, and halfway
up the Welcome a tremendous gale, accompanied by a thick fog, left
the ship nearly helpless. Lyon could not keep her prow headed into the
wind and waves, the sea was breaking over the decks, and thanks to
the fog he had no idea how close he was to land. He only knew the
water was becoming shallower and shallower. In the trough of one wave
the ship struck bottom, hard. He tried to hold the ship with its anchors,
but they were slipping. Thinking they were doomed, he ordered supplies, arms, and ammunition into the longboat and four other smaller
ship's boats, but everyone knew that only the longboat and the two
larger of the boats could survive such a sea. The officers and men drew
lots for which boat they would leave the ship in. "Every officer and
man," Lyon reports, "drew his lot with the greatest composure, although
two of the boats would have been swamped the instant they were lowered." Then, exhausted, they gathered to pray. Lyon had not slept for
three nights. Shortly after prayers the gale subsided. Lyon called the
place of their deliverance the Bay of God's Mercy.

But the Ice Queen was hardly done with them. Less than two weeks
later the weather turned sour again, wind and snow and high waves
thick with ice buffeting the ship. Staying on deck was like riding a rodeo
bull and they stretched ropes across the deck so the men could hold on.
Seas broke over them again and again and again. Anyone swept overboard would have been lost. Because the ship could not maintain steer-
age in this weather, Lyon anchored it once more. The "best bower
anchor" did not last the night. Lyon had no reason to believe the others
would hold, either, and at six in the morning the cables duly snapped.
They were now adrift, all their anchors gone. A foot of snow and ice
covered the decks. The crew was wet through and through, and the tide
and a gale were sweeping them helplessly south. The ship was so
unmanageable that it "could not beat off a lee-shore even in *moderate*

weather." Lyon gave up. The *Griper* headed for the mouth of Hudson Strait, for England, for safety. They struggled home, arriving in November, and sent three men straight from the ship to the hospital. George Lyon was unjustly blamed for the outcome of this voyage. He never returned to the Arctic. Nor, thankfully, did the *Griper*.

CHAPTER TWELVE

FOG

Four times William Edward Parry had beaten his fists against the ice, first through the wide inviting portal of Lancaster Sound, sailing through the Croker Mountains all the way to Melville Island and Melville Sound to the frozen lip of the Arctic Ocean; then two years later to the forever frozen Fury and Hecla Strait; then to try his luck in Prince Regent Inlet; and finally, in 1827, he had tried to reach the Pole. Including the 1818 voyage with John Ross he had devoted nine years to this project, won a five-thousand-pound prize, risen from lieutenant to captain, and become the Royal Navy's chief hydrographer and a national hero. Little Emily Brontë, making up stories and games with her two sisters, Charlotte and Anne, in their remote parsonage in Yorkshire, gave her toy soldier—each of the Brontë children had one—the name Parry in his honor. Later in life she would use his name as a pseudonym.

But on every voyage he had failed. The ice had defeated him as it had defeated all comers before him. Ice stretched to the horizon, built up on the coastlines, moved with the currents, broke and piled up floe on floe, held ships tight in its embrace, and crushed them at will. It clogged the inlets and straits of the Canadian archipelago so thoroughly that the Admiralty still did not know that Prince Regent Inlet was a dead end, or how many islands there were in the archipelago, or where they lay. The "Parry school" of Clement Markham's book was a school in ice, in young ice and brash ice, floes, packs, bergs, hummocks, leads, slush, in ice spicules that materialized on very cold days out of a clear sky, in fast ice, ice ridges, ice brine, pancake ice, ice crystals. It was also a school in fear. Time and time again they had barely escaped a nip or had nearly been driven ashore; they had lost anchors, seen ice shelters vanish, icebergs flip, been carried helplessly this way and that wherever the ice that enclosed them had it in mind to go. Survival, they had learned, was largely a matter of luck.

By 1826 the public was growing tired of it, and so was the Admiralty. Poor George Lyon had come back the previous year without even reaching Repulse Bay and minus all his anchors and had had to take the blame, even though it was obvious the *Griper* was a disaster waiting to happen. Parry came back from Prince Regent Inlet having gone so far as to lose a ship. The navy required a court-martial in all cases where ships were lost, and the court quickly exonerated his old friend and companion, Lieutenant Hoppner, commander of the *Fury*. Nobody blamed Parry or Hoppner for what had happened. Parry, after all, was a hero, and practically untouchable. The Admiralty sent Parry to scout out the North Pole. But it was a last gasp, and all concerned, even John Barrow, knew it.

And the press was increasingly unkind. Parry's voyage to Prince Regent Inlet had produced no new information; he might as well have stayed home. Why had the Admiralty sent him there in the first place, when Parry's great success had been to reach Melville Island to the north? If the polar sea was indeed open, why not pursue that route? Why not try there again? The press did not often venture to instruct the Admiralty. A certain fed-up tone is evident in the press accounts. Nobody blamed Parry, but enough was enough.

The person who enjoyed these failures the most was John Ross. Ross had kept silent for years, but in 1826 he published a pamphlet under the pen name "Alman" with the provocative title *A Letter to John Barrow, Esq., F.R.S. on the Late Extraordinary and Unexpected Hyperborean Discoveries.* He began by congratulating Barrow on his role in restarting the search for the Northwest Passage and commiserating with him at the same time for having been said to be the author of all those review articles in *The Quarterly* on the subject, a fact he found hard to believe, "for the honour of the *True Blue,*" the Royal Navy blue. "For although, properly speaking, Sir," Ross wrote, "you are not one of the cloth, yet being officially connected with it, it is a pity you should be made answerable for the absurdities of blundering critics" like this author, whom he hereafter called the "Reviewer." And then he went on to outline the absurdities.

Ross knew perfectly well that Barrow was indeed the Reviewer. Probably everyone in the navy with any interest in the Arctic knew it. But few had studied Barrow the Reviewer as closely as Ross. He found contradictions in Barrow's pieces from one to the next. He contrasted Barrow's insistence that a powerful current runs from west to east across the top of North America with Parry's observations in Lancaster Sound that there seemed to be no such current. Barrow was far too smart to have indulged, he went on, in so many contradictory statements about where the Northwest Passage could be found. He took note of the scorn Barrow had originally leveled at Scoresby for suggesting that the North Pole might be reached on sledges; four years later Barrow proposed that the North Pole be reached on sledges.

If Ross had been a better writer, this could have been great fun; but he went on too long, lapsing into a technical discussion of ocean currents, and when he wrote toward the end that "a volume might be filled with the absurdities, inconsistencies, and self-contradictions of the Reviewer," one can only think, yes, here it is, and it's a bore. But at least Ross was having his revenge. Parry, who had usurped what Ross must have believed was his rightful place as a hero of British exploration, had come to grief again and again in the ice. Barrow had been wrong about currents, about geography, about Parry. Ross was generous enough at the end of his pamphlet to agree that the whole project was worth undertaking. The Northwest Passage ought to be found. But there's no mistaking the schadenfreude.

Barrow did not answer Ross's attack. To get into a pissing match with a discredited officer would have been beneath his dignity. Besides, he was not quite ready to abandon ship. In his review in *The Quarterly* of Parry's account of the disastrous voyage to Prince Regent Inlet, which is less a book review than a plea for the continuance of his Arctic project, he acknowledged that Parry had added nothing to knowledge of the Arctic or the route but quickly jumped to the details of the voyage, commending Parry for the improvements to the stove, for the school for seamen, and for various new scientific experiments. Barrow was, like Parry, philosophical about the loss of the *Fury*, agreeing with Parry that "it is quite certain that no combination of wood and iron, however skillfully disposed, can withstand the continued pressure between unyielding ground on one side, and an enormous moving body of ice on the other." But this led him to contradict Parry on the best method of making progress in an icy sea. It might be better, he suggested, not to follow "the narrow channels formed between the land and the main body of the ice, but to let the ships drift with the ice." "It is true," he added, that, on running the ships into the midst of a field of ice, there is no knowing whither they might be drifted, or when disentangled, but in other respects we are apt to think such is the safest way to navigate frozen seas; and when we are told by Captain Parry that, during the time the Fury and the Hecla were made fast on the coast of Prince Regent's Inlet, the ice was setting to the southward, and sometimes at a rapid rate, . . . we cannot help expressing a wish that both vessels had been shut up in the midst of it.

This would be the tactic chosen, whether purposefully or not nobody knows, on John Franklin's last voyage in 1845.

Barrow went on in his review to minimize the dangers of Arctic exploration, observing that only two men had died on this voyage, "one drowned in a pool of water, the other after a fall." The Irish seas, he claimed, were rougher and deadlier; disease in tropical waters killed far more. Parry continued to believe in a Northwest Passage, he pointed out, continued to think that Prince Regent Inlet was the place it might be found. The land party Parry had sent south in the winter had discovered "favourable appearances of a navigable sea near the south-western extremity of Prince Regent's Inlet," which in fact that party had not come close to reaching. In short, said Barrow, "we see nothing whatever to object to the continuance of these Polar voyages—so long as there is anything to discover," for they "do honor to the country even when they fail," and, he concluded, quoting Parry himself, "'the page of future history will undoubtedly record them, as every way worthy of a powerful, a virtuous, and an enlightened nation.'" At the time he wrote this John Franklin was in northern Canada exploring the coast of the Arctic Ocean west of the Mackenzie River. Barrow hoped that the search for the Northwest Passage by sea "has only been suspended till the issue of Captain Franklin's expedition shall be known."

In similar words, perhaps, he was trying to persuade the Admiralty. He had already persuaded the Admiralty lords to send Parry toward the North Pole, and he was still beating the drum of national pride, national honor. What if the Americans should take an interest in the Northwest Passage and be the ones to discover it? How shameful would that be? These projects belonged to Great Britain. It was Great Britain's task to explore the world, the noblesse oblige attached to empire. "*Her* flag should be the first to wave over the most remote and hitherto inaccessible portions of the globe, from the Equator to either Pole."

And speaking of the Pole, he could not help but add, he was sure that "Captain Parry will find an uninterrupted navigation for his boats to the North Pole, provided no land intervenes between that and Spitzbergen." Because, of course, the deep ocean does not freeze. "Though the fact of the great deep sea not freezing may not be strictly and universally correct," he insisted, "we may safely affirm that it never remains *frozen over*."

Barrow never explained what difference he thought Franklin's findings in the Canadian North would make to the Admiralty, or how he would use those findings to persuade the Admiralty not to give up the enterprise. Franklin had already disappointed him by not leaving for the Arctic when Parry left for Prince Regent Inlet, Lyon for Repulse Bay, and Beechey for Bering Strait and the protected sound north of it that the Russian-German explorer Otto von Kotzebue had discovered. Barrow had planned a four-pronged assault on the Arctic. Lyon would map from Repulse Bay west while Parry fought his way south down Prince Regent Inlet and across the top of North America to meet Beechey at Kotzebue Sound for resupply and perhaps, in Barrow's imaginary navigable Arctic, pick up Franklin on the way.

Part of the impulse for the ambition of the enterprise came from rumors reaching Barrow that Kotzebue was heading back to the Arctic to extend the Russian fur trade and its dominion farther east across the top of North America. (Kotzebue was actually heading to Kamchatka to resupply Russian posts there.) Franklin's job was not only to map the Arctic coast but to plant the British flag and the British fur trade all the way into Alaska at Icy Cape. He and his party would descend the Mackenzie to its mouth, then sail westward in small boats to hook up, like Parry, with Beechey, who by this time would have sailed around Cape Horn and set up shop on Chamiso Island in Kotzebue Sound, stocked it with supplies, and be waiting for Franklin and Parry to appear out of the fog. This rendezvous was supposed to occur in the early fall of 1825. That meant that Franklin would have had to leave for Canada in 1824.

Franklin, wisely, would not be rushed. He was not going to depend this time on the supplies that tribes of untrustworthy Indians might or might not furnish him, according to whether they were mourning dead relatives or not. He was not going into the Arctic Ocean with birchbark canoes and nervous French-Canadian voyageurs sporting massive appetites. Franklin wanted English seamen for his crew. He wanted caches of supplies in front of him and behind. He wanted large quantities of pemmican prepared for him before he even got there. He wanted a fort ready and waiting for him. Knowing that it took mail six months or longer to reach its destination in upper Canada, he started writing letters to the relevant Hudson's Bay Company factors in 1823, expecting to depart from England in 1825. Franklin had learned the lessons of the North. He was going to be ready for every eventuality. In the event, this meant that Beechey would have to wait at Kotzebue Sound twice—over two Septembers. For him it was going to be a long trip.

Less so for Franklin. By starting to plan early, he could leave later and go farther. In fact he reached the mouth of the Mackenzie on a reconnaissance trip within seven months of leaving England, which, given the distance traveled and the kind of terrain covered, is downright remarkable. The planning began as early as July 1823, when Franklin and Barrow discussed what would be required for a trip down the Mackenzie. The Hudson's Bay Company had already signed on and had agreed to build a fort for whoever commanded the expedition wherever on the Mackenzie he might wish, and stock it, and provide its own personnel to go with him, if that was what the commander might want. It was in its interest to do so. The HBC wanted to forestall the Russians and increase the range of its trade. Franklin's longtime companion John Richardson was ready to go again.

Everything had to wait for Parry to return from the northern reaches of Hudson Bay—there were rumors that his ships had been seen in Valparaiso, on the west coast of South America, in August—before decisions could be made. It would have changed the situation dramatically if Parry had actually succeeded. But he had not. In November, after Parry returned from iced-up Fury and Hecla Strait and suggested to Barrow that Prince Regent Inlet might be the best chance to find the Passage, Franklin presented a formal proposal for his trip to Barrow and outlined what he wanted: provisions ready for him at every post on the route, and a fort at the western extremity of Great Bear Lake, which lies near the Mackenzie and feeds into it. He would be sending his own boats ahead, not canoes but solid wooden boats, the same sort of boats Parry had dragged over the ice so laboriously toward the Pole, designed for river and coastal travel and built to Franklin's specifications. Most of his supplies, in fact, would be sent ahead. He would bring his own hand-picked crews. He wanted strong British seamen and marines, good marksmen, men with carpentry skills. It might be a good idea to send a party eastward from the mouth of the Mackenzie as well, he added, to map the coastline between the Mackenzie and the Coppermine, thus filling in that blank on the map. He thought John Richardson should command it.

Barrow approved the plans by late December, and so did the colonial secretary, Lord Bathurst, who would have to arrange things with the HBC. Franklin consulted Richardson at once about what other officers should go with them. Neither man wanted George Back, now a lieutenant, as a companion, for reasons they never explicitly stated, and the Admiralty fixed on Lieutenant Bushnan, who had been with Parry on his last voyage and had served well. Then Bushnan died. Franklin tried to get Back promoted to captain so he could not go; it would never do to send two captains on such a journey. The Admiralty refused to promote Back, and in the end he got the job. Franklin asked that Augustus be sent as an interpreter to the Inuit again, and so it happened. Augustus had had a difficult time in the interval between the two expeditions. During the first he had lent his wife to the brother of Junius, the Inuit who vanished on that expedition; Junius's brother had died, and his tribe thought Augustus had conjured his death from afar. He had to go back among his people fully armed to defend himself against the accusation. Thereafter the traders at York Factory had set him to work fishing, which he hated to do.

By the end of January 1824, a full year before he intended to embark himself, Franklin was sending requests for supplies to Canada, and after that it all went according to plan. He hired Peter Dease, one of the HBC's chief factors, to build and equip the fort on Great Bear Lake, and to run it after Franklin left for the coast. A decade later Dease would be exploring the coast of Canada himself. Franklin had a light portable boat that could be taken apart and put back together again designed and built in case he needed such a boat to cross rivers and lakes; he tested it on the Thames, taking a few delighted ladies across the river. It was for lack of such a boat on the return trip in 1821 that so many men had died. He was busy all the time, too busy, he told a correspondent, to follow the news, and of course his wife was pregnant and needed what attention he could spare. It was the spring of 1824, his departure was less than a year away, and he wanted to be thoroughly prepared.

He took a break in the summer, shortly after his wife had given birth to their daughter, and spent a little time with his new family in Tunbridge Wells, a town and spa still popular today with the British upper middle class. To his surprise he found Barrow there, also on vacation, and they discussed whether Back should go. Franklin once again urged Back's promotion to captain, "but of course received no other answer than a Smile to this point," he wrote Richardson. "I could not without entirely injuring his professional prospects mention my reasons for declining his Service, and it might be retorted on me why did you permit these to be dormant So long? An explanation on this point would only lead further into the mire." We never do get an explanation. An officer whom Franklin did not know offered to go without pay, even to waive his rank. Sorry, said Franklin. He needed a man who could draw and knew surveying. He made arrangements with John Murray to publish his account of the expedition when he returned. He wanted better terms this time. When he left for the first expedition he had been a comparative unknown, he pointed out to Murray. Now, he said, things were different. Now, Murray admitted, he was "a public character."

When the party left in late February 1825, they sailed to New York, not to Hudson Bay; it was longer but they could move faster and more comfortably to the north and west of Canada from there than from York Factory. New York was effusive in its reception of the Arctic hero; "invitations from the Gentlemen to dine and the Ladies to Evening parties crowded on us." The British consul gave them a breakfast and invited "the principal men of the city"; Columbia College gave them a tour of its scientific collections. They took a steamer to Albany and dined with the governor, De Witt Clinton, then rode west to Niagara Falls in coaches. The falls, by then a major tourist attraction, Franklin thought "the grandest feature in Nature." The only thing he had ever seen that compared to it was an iceberg in Spitzbergen, "1¼ mile long, 300 feet above the water—but that was a still scene," while "the first view of Niagaras mighty rush of Waters instantly absorbs all former impressions and wraps the mind of the spectator with awe, admiration and silent reverence." They spent two days there looking at the falls from every possible point of view before moving on.

They were in Canada now and made haste to the west, crossing Lake Ontario to the city of York (now Toronto), traveling by canoe along the northern shores of Lakes Huron and Superior, up rivers to Lake Winnipeg, on to Cumberland House. At a major jumping-off point for the fur traders, a place called Penetanguishene on Lake Huron, which they reached on April 25, Franklin found out his wife had died. From Cumberland House the route was familiar, the rivers high, the mosquitoes "troublesome." From Lake Winnipeg John Richardson wrote his wife a description of their mode of travel:

> At two oclock or half past two if the morning is dark Capt Franklin or myself call the guide, who . . . awakens the men. They are on their legs in an instant, and every man marches to the beach with his blanket under his arm. Part of them put the canoe into the water and load her, while others take down our tent, & roll up the bedding in which operation we assist. In 10 minutes or at the longest half an hour we are all embarked, and the men after their morning dram . . . strike up a cheerful song and paddle away vigorously at the rate of about 4 miles an hour. Every half hour they lay in their paddles for about two minutes to rest a little and light their pipez, hence these pauses are termed by them pipez. At 9 oclock we put ashore to breakfast. My occupation is to strike a light and I therefore jump ashore at once with my fire bag in my hand. Capt Franklin brings a handful of dry twigs or grass or a piece of birch bark. Two of the men bring dry wood, a fire is speedily kindled, our servant who in the mean time has been filling the kettle, hangs it to the troi pied or tripod, three sticks which another of the men has by this time tied together and set up.

Breakfast takes three quarters of an hour at the most, he says, and then it's back to the canoes until three in the afternoon, when the men take a longer break than usual and eat a little pemmican. At eight they put ashore for the night, and dinner is prepared with equal dispatch; it consists of "tea, cold meat, eggs, cheese, butter &c according to the state of our larder," and then they sleep. "We consider it a good days journey when we travel 60 miles, but two days ago we traveled about 80 having paddled all night. . . . When this letter reaches you . . . we shall be quietly seated at our winter quarters at Fort Reliance."

That was Franklin's choice of a name for the fort they were building for him at Great Bear Lake. He would arrive to find that it had been named Fort Franklin in his honor. By early August they had reached the mouth of Great Bear River, which empties into the Mackenzie, and the fort was nearly complete. So swiftly had they come that Franklin now had time to do what he had wanted to do when he had come to Winter

Lake on the previous expedition—keep on going. He did just that, sending Richardson up the Great Bear River to the fort while he took a crew down the Mackenzie to its broad delta and its mouth. There, standing on a hill on a small island, gazing on the Arctic Ocean, which was "entirely free from ice, and without any visible obstruction to its navigation," he planted the flag his wife had made him the previous fall. "I will not attempt to describe my emotions," he wrote, "as it expanded to the breeze." Whatever they were, he suppressed them in front of the men. Besides, the sea was free of ice, and "seals, and black and white whales were sporting on its waves; and the whole scene," he adds, "was calculated to excite in our minds the most flattering expectations as to our own success, and that of our friends in the Hecla and the Fury." These friends were at that moment desperately trying to save the *Fury* from being crushed between the ice and the shores of Prince Regent Inlet.

It was a quiet winter for Franklin and his men. Among the fifty residents of the fort were five officers—Franklin, Richardson, George Back, Peter Dease (not exactly an officer but in charge of the voyageurs and Indian families), and an Admiralty mate named E. N. Kendall who was a good mapmaker—and nineteen British seamen, marines, and HBC personnel, many of them Scots in origin. Besides these there were nine Canadian voyageurs, Augustus and another Inuit he had brought along as a companion, four Dogrib hunters, and Beaulieu the interpreter, the same man who had been with Franklin on the first expedition. There were also three Dogrib women, who were the hunters' wives, six children, and one "Indian boy." A few sick Indians stayed at the fort as well, under Richardson's care. Because they were in Dogrib country, Akaitcho and his Yellow Knives were not in evidence. A good number of them had been killed the year before in a Dogrib raid.

Franklin too established schools for the men, most of whom were illiterate. When the men were not busy hunting or fishing or gathering wood for the fires or learning how to read, there were games in the hall, in which the officers took part. Their location on Great Bear Lake was chosen because the fishing was good there and they lived mostly on fish. With their nets, and with fishing posts set up at intervals along the lake, they were taking in four to five hundred fish daily. Peter Dease, who was in charge of the stores, allowed them seven "herring salmon" per man per day. They froze the surplus. They were seldom hungry. The day after Christmas they played a game called "snapdragon" in which brandy was heated in a shallow bowl, raisins were thrown in, and the whole was set aflame. The idea was to snatch the raisins out of the flame and pop them in your mouth while they were still afire. "The party consisted," reported Franklin, "of Englishmen, Highlanders, (who mostly conversed with each other in Gaelic,) Canadians, Esquimaux, Chipewyans, Dog-Ribs, Hare Indians, Cree women and children, mingled together in perfect harmony." A peaceable kingdom. "The amusements were varied by English, Gaelic, and French songs." The temperature outside on January 1 stood at forty-nine degrees below zero.

In January mail arrived, including copies of *The Quarterly*. They spent the spring building a new boat so there would be two for Franklin's party and two for Richardson's. In March they heard rumors that a party of white men had been seen on one of the rivers leading into Bathurst Inlet. White men! This could only have been Parry, wintering over in the inlet. He sent letters to the Hudson's Bay Company asking it to investigate. Despite the scarcity of people in northern Canada rumors spread like the wind. Then May came, the new boat had been completed, it was close to the time to go. To make sure that in case they had to come back food would await them, Franklin ordered Dease to stay put at the fort and stock it all summer long for the winter ahead. In case they didn't reach Icy Cape and Kotzebue Sound, which Franklin was confident they would. Just in case. Memories of starving at Fort Enterprise after crossing the Barren Lands were no doubt vivid in his mind.

They left the fort in late June when the ice broke up. By July 3 they had reached the point on the Mackenzie where its delta begins and the river splits into branches. Richardson was going east, and Franklin west, and they left each other here at a place they called Point Separation. Franklin, who had two more men with him than Richardson, took thirty-two bags of pemmican, Richardson twenty-six, enough food for eighty days, or one hundred days in an emergency. "It was impossible not to be struck," said Franklin, "with the difference between our present complete state of equipment and that on which we had embarked on our former disastrous voyage." His meticulous planning had paid off. The boats were strong and sound, the food plentiful. He was traveling with British sailors, not Canadian voyageurs.

He had even planned for Inuit contact: he had trade goods for presents, and he had Augustus to speak to them and explain who they were and what they were doing there. But he had not planned for hundreds of them gathered in one place. Franklin's party first encountered them on July 7 at the western mouth of the Mackenzie, where they occupied an island. As soon as he saw them, and he was the first to see them, Franklin instructed his men to keep the boats afloat and their weapons on the ready, "but on no account to fire until he was convinced that our safety could be secured in no other way." The "our" here is Franklin and Augustus. Only they would go ashore with the Inuit after they had made contact. The plan came to nothing; within moments of speaking with the first arrivals—three old men, the village elders—they were surrounded by hundreds of kayaks, as many as three hundred persons, Franklin guessed, "and they all became anxious to share in the lucrative trade which they saw established, and pressed eagerly upon us, offering for sale their bows, arrows, and spears, which they had hitherto kept concealed within their canoes." It took little time for them to become "more and more importunate and troublesome," and Franklin soon found himself trapped in their midst. The tide was going out. Shallow as the draft of their boats was, the bay proved to be even shallower. They were aground, unable to move, and there were sixteen of them all told, Scotsmen, a couple of Canadians, an English sailor or two, Franklin, Back, and Augustus. Accidentally one of the English oarsmen flipped over a kayak and the Inuit inside got his head stuck in the mud. They extricated him and brought him into the boat while they emptied the water out of his kayak. Inside the boat he saw for the first time what these strangers had with them. Goods galore. Whole bales of goods, things they had never imagined could exist in the world, a surfeit of knives, hatchets, ice chisels, cloth and clothing, bags of pemmican, and who knew what else. This Inuit wanted everything, and he shouted out to his friends what "inexhaustible riches" were to be had.

Then it got ugly. Inuit were jumping into the stranded boats; others tried to drag them toward shore. The water was not even knee deep now. At Franklin's instruction, Augustus tried to persuade two of the chiefs to take their men to shore so that Franklin could go to a large ship he expected to meet nearby and come back with a still greater abundance of goods, and that worked briefly, but only long enough for the Inuit to plan another attack, coming back in force and dragging the boats ashore in earnest now, where they started hauling goods out and handing them to the women. Franklin's men tried to resist, snatching things back from the hands of the Inuit. One man grabbed the knife from one of the Canadians and cut the buttons off his coat. The men in Franklin's boat were trying to beat the Inuit off with the butts of their muskets.

Augustus stepped ashore at this moment and "our bold and active lit-tle interpreter rushed among the crowd on shore, and harangued them on their treacherous conduct, until he was actually hoarse." This had lit-tle effect. The Inuit surrounded Franklin's boat brandishing knives, grabbing at anything and everything. "Many attempts," says Franklin, were made to steal the box with the astronomical instruments in it, until a sailor named William Duncan, "after thrice rescuing it from their hands, made it fast to his leg with a cord, determined that they should drag him away also if they took it." The Inuit were trying not only for the box but for the arms the sailors had about their persons. Back lost a pistol. Three men tried to disarm Franklin. The Inuit were stabbing at some of the men, who had been ordered not to fire. Back was able to get his boat afloat, however, and as soon as he did he ordered his men not to fire, but to level their muskets at the Inuit. They must have had experi-ence of firearms, because this finally drove them off, and Franklin's boat floated soon after. One hundred and fifty yards off the coast they ran aground again. Unable to move, they tied the boats together and waited for five hours for the tide to come in. They had not, it turned out, lost all that much to the natives, nothing of real importance, no oars, no firearms—Back had been able to retrieve his pistol—and none of the scientific instruments or the food. But they had no idea what to expect next.

Augustus went ashore at this point at the request of the natives to parley. He told them how disgusted he was with their conduct, how his own tribe had been like theirs before the white men came to Hudson Bay, "but at present they are supplied with every thing they need, and you see that I am well clothed." He went on to tell them they could never expect to see white people again unless they gave back what they had stolen. According to Augustus—and Franklin had no reason to think he would have lied—they were full of contrition at this speech and said they had never seen white people before; the things they carried were so new to them, and so desirable; they would never do anything like this again. At Franklin's suggestion, Augustus told them that if they meant it, they were to bring back a large kettle they had stolen, and one of the tents. They did, along with some shoes they had taken. Augustus then went ashore again and joined them in a dance, until finally, as the night advanced, the Inuit all retired.

By that time the tide was returning, and at one in the morning Franklin and his men were able to drag the boats to a point where they floated. They rowed six miles up the coast and went ashore to rest. The next morning the Inuit returned in full force. Quickly Franklin and Back loaded the boats and they fled to sea. Within hailing distance the Inuit called out and said they were only bringing back the rest of what they had stolen. He told Augustus to tell them to go back. He was not going to risk his party for the few things they had succeeded in taking. When that failed to stop them, "I fired a ball ahead of the leading canoe, which had the desired effect—the whole party veering round, except four, who followed us for a little way, and then went back to join their companions." He discovered later that the Inuit plan, until he fired his weapon, was to surround them with their kayaks, kill them all, including Augustus, and pillage the boats.

That day they sailed west until eleven in the evening, and the next day, July 9, they made another twelve miles until they ran into ice "adhering to the shore, and stretching beyond the limits of our view to seaward." When they found a place to land, they climbed the bank

> to look around, and from thence had the mortification to perceive that we had just arrived in time to witness the first rupture of the ice. The only lane of water in the direction of our course was that from which we had been forced to retreat: in every other part the sea appeared as firmly frozen as in winter; and even close to our encampment the masses of ice were piled up to the height of thirty feet.

The polar sea was not open after all. They would not be going anywhere until the ice broke up.

So began yet another minuet with the ice. It retreated from the shore when the wind was off the shore, came back when the wind blew off the ocean. But the coast was shallow, and grounded ice held fast to the shore even when the wind did blow from the south. The coast was so shallow, in fact, that it was frequently difficult to bring the boats ashore; it was rocky, too, hard on the bottoms of the boats when they ran aground. And they constantly ran aground. Days went by when they couldn't move at all, and the mosquitoes were so bad they could endure them only by sitting in their tents and filling the tents with smoke. After weeks of this Franklin reported their frustration:

> More tedious hours than those passed by us in the present situation, cannot well be imagined. After the astronomical observations had been obtained and worked, the survey

brought up, a sketch made of the encampment, and specimens of the plants and stones in the vicinity collected, there
was, literally, nothing to do. The anxiety which was inseparable from such an enterprise as ours . . . left but little disposition to read . . . and still less composure to invent amusement.
Even had the musquitoes been less tormenting, the swampi-
ness of the ground, in which we sank ancle deep at every step,
deprived us of the pleasure of walking.

From time to time they had good days and made progress, but on many
days conditions forced them to stop and wait. There were no natural
harbors for large ships anywhere along the route. This was not promising. Worse, the season was advancing fast, as summer does in the high
Arctic. Franklin could see his time dwindling away.

After August 1 they had a free run for a few days; then on the seventh
more ice, unbroken from shore to horizon, stopped them again. Past an
island Franklin named after his late wife's artist friends John and his sister Mary Anne Flaxman, the flats extended so far offshore that it took
two hours of dragging the boats through the mud, wading through
water that stood at about forty degrees, to reach water deep enough for
the boats. And there was always the fog. It rose off the swamps on the
land side, off the ice at sea; fog was like fate, inescapable. "Fog is,"
Franklin wrote, "of all others, the most hazardous state of the atmosphere for navigation in an icy sea, especially when it is accompanied by
strong breezes, but particularly so for boats where the shore is unapproachable." They got as far as Prudhoe Bay before it began to be clear
to Franklin that he could not make it. When they reached a campsite he
called, aptly, Foggy Island, the fog held them up for a week. On August
18 they came to yet another of the huge flats that extended out into the
ocean and made it so hard to reach shore. He called it Return Reef, and
there he turned back. To his west, 160 miles away, a barge from F. W.
Beechey's ship, the *Blossom*, had doubled Icy Cape. "Could I have
known," Franklin noted in his expedition account, which of course he
wrote after he did know, ". . . that a party from the Blossom had been at
[that] distance, . . . no difficulties, dangers, or discouraging circumstances, should have prevailed on me to return." It was just as well he did
not know. The barge had doubled Icy Cape, but its commander was
about to turn around and struggle under similar circumstances to
Franklin's to get back to his ship. Franklin could never have caught up.

Winter would have overtaken him somewhere on the north coast of Alaska. All of them would have died.

Franklin chose another route up the Mackenzie and was back to his fort by September 21. On the way back along the coast they ran into small groups of Inuit, part of the main group that had attacked them in early July. In small groups they were much friendlier, and it was they who told Franklin about the massacre the Inuit had planned for them. They also said that a tribe of mountain Indians had been told of the abundance of things available on the boats and were laying an ambush. Franklin and his party hurried to leave them behind. The Indians never caught up to them and they dodged the main body of Inuit, returning to the fort without losing a man.

Richardson had had a similar run-in with Inuit on his descent of the eastern branch of the Mackenzie, but the number of Inuit involved was much lower, Richardson was never aground, and he never let them drag his boats to shore, although they tried. Instead he traded for their bows and arrows, thereby disarming them, and kept on going. His run along the coast was much more successful than Franklin's. The shoreline was what seamen call bold—that is, the ocean was deep almost to the coast and the coast itself was defined by bluffs, many of which were on fire. He explains in his account that they were composed of bituminous shale, which was full of sulfur, in a powdery form that readily attracted oxygen and caught fire spontaneously. He encountered serious ice only when he got close to the Coppermine, in the narrow strait between the coast and what is now known as Victoria Island, which he named Dolphin and Union Strait, after the names of his boats. It still bears the name, as does Barrow, Alaska, which Beechey's men named; as do all the Melvilles, islands and peninsulas and sounds; as do the Franklin Mountains, the range that runs down the west side of the Mackenzie River at the same latitude as Great Bear Lake. They may not have found the Northwest Passage, but these first Arctic explorers certainly left their mark on the landscape.

Franklin left Fort Franklin on February 20, 1827, almost two years to the day after he had embarked at Liverpool, and spent a comfortable winter at Fort Chipewyan before returning through Montreal and New York. He was back in Liverpool on September 1. Richardson had pursued his own travels that winter, gathering plants and natural history specimens farther south in Canada, but Franklin caught up with him at

Cumberland House and they went home together. Back brought up the rear, taking the men out through York Factory. Two of them died en route, one of them of tuberculosis, one of drowning. Franklin did not let it bother him. "It is pleasing to reflect," he wrote at the end of his expedition account, ". . . that the loss of life which has occurred in the prosecution of these discoveries does not exceed the average number of deaths in the same population at home under circumstances the most favourable."

That would change before he was finished.

Another failed expedition, then. It had not been the disaster of Franklin's first raid on the Canadian coastline, but it was certainly disappointing. The ice did not leave the coast, there were no harbors for ships, navigation was difficult in the shallow waters, and the Inuit were murderous. To the west of Franklin's farthest, 160 miles of coastline remained unknown. The coastline between Repulse Bay and Point Turnagain was still unexplored. The maze of inlets, channels, and ice-choked straits winding among the barren islands of the Canadian archipelago had baffled all attempts to penetrate them. Franklin came back thinking that it might be wiser next time, if there were to be a next time, to attack the maze from the west, sailing through Bering Strait, wintering in Bathurst Inlet, then having a full summer season to pick a way through the maze. He was convinced there was a way through. Everyone was still persuaded that the Northwest Passage existed. But where? Ice had defeated them all.

It had defeated Barrow too, and he knew it. Franklin came home to a changed government and a changed Admiralty, and to a discontented public that was weary of hearing about one brave failure after another and bored by the long, uneventful winters in the ice. The public had other things on its mind, most notably reform, Reform with a capital R. For decades the pressure for Reform had been building as the nation industrialized and population shifted and Parliament grew increasingly unrepresentative of the real economic forces at work in Great Britain. The great landed families still ran the country while mill owners remained grotesquely underrepresented. The poor could express themselves only in riots.

That this situation could not last indefinitely was obvious even to the most conservative of the ruling class, and the growing pressure toward Reform would culminate in 1832 with the passage of the Reform Bill, which went a long way to getting rid of so-called rotten boroughs in the gift and under the thumb of a single peer, and giving greater representation to the industrial Midlands and to towns and cities generally. The bill also lowered the property qualifications that divided those who could vote from those who could not. Only a few radicals envisioned a future of universal suffrage or what we would call democracy, but the bill did, to some extent, democratize the country. It came to pass in a Whig administration, the first in two generations. The Whigs were just as aristocratic as the Tories, a combination of great landed families allied with the newly wealthy merchants and industrialists who were turning Great Britain into the world's first industrial power. But whereas the Tories looked back to the glorious past, the Whigs looked forward. They were sympathetic to change, and more realistic than the Tories about the need for reform. They first took control in 1830. That meant a new government, made up of Whig ministers. The first lord of the Admiralty was a cabinet-level minister. Lord Melville was gone. With him went the government's support for Arctic exploration.

Actually the change had come earlier, in 1827, even before Franklin returned from Canada, when the prime minister, Lord Liverpool, died, and the charismatic Tory politician George Canning took the job. Canning supported Catholic Emancipation, a movement to allow Catholics to serve in Parliament and hold government office, and when he took power, half of Liverpool's cabinet, including the first lord of the Admiralty, resigned in protest over this issue. What followed had an element of comic opera about it, another of the ridiculous sons of the late George III making a fool of himself. To gain support for his program from the royal family, Canning decided not to appoint another first lord but to revive an ancient office that had not been occupied since the reign of Queen Anne more than a hundred years before, Lord High Admiral. Then he appointed the king's brother to it, the old navy hand the Duke of Clarence (later William IV). Some politicians thought the move was brilliant; others thought Canning was an idiot. The idea was that the duke would serve as a figurehead while the Admiralty lords would actually run the navy. But nobody seems to have told the duke about this, and he was not known as the most responsible of the royals in any case. He had fathered innumerable children with his mistress, the actress Mrs. Jordan; his manner was bluff, unrestrained, and thoughtless of consequences; he drank too much; and he spent money as if he had invented it. His brother the king, George IV, had no confidence in him.

What he loved to do most of all was to give dinner parties, and when he found out his office required him to entertain he was thrilled. On the positive side he did try to bring reform to the navy, to do away with flogging, improve gunnery, and the like. On the negative he took ships to sea without telling the Admiralty where he was going and became obsessed with changing the navy's uniforms, down to the smallest detail. He despised John Wilson Croker and told him as soon as he took office that, once he became king, he would throw Croker out, a promise he fulfilled when George IV died in 1830 and he did become king. But he took a strong liking to John Barrow and had him tag along on visits to the fleets and tours of the naval ports. Barrow liked him too and said of him in his autobiography that he "never met with a more kind-hearted man, more benevolent, or more desirous of relieving distress, than William, Duke of Clarence." In 1835 William IV knighted John Barrow.

The duke's big mistake was to take his office seriously and think that it gave him powers he did not have. Those powers belonged to the Admiralty Board, which he studiously ignored. By September 1828 the government had run out of patience and the king informed his brother that he would have to retire. Before he left he gave Barrow a silver inkstand with his own and Barrow's initials intertwined. The Duke of Wellington, prime minister after Canning, reappointed Lord Melville to the job of first lord. Too late. The government had clearly made up its mind about Arctic exploration: there would be no more. In June 1828, while the Duke of Clarence was still in office, Franklin had approached him about another project, a third expedition to northern Canada to complete the job of exploring the coastline. The duke asked him to write a proposal. The reply from the Admiralty Board came within twenty-four hours of Franklin's submitting it. The duke, said the note from a clerk, "does not intend to recommend any more Northern expeditions to His Majesty's Government." The board, clearly, had already put a lid on the Duke of Clarence. When Melville returned to office he lacked the will or the energy to revive this enterprise of the North. The press was tired of it. The people were no longer enthusiastic about it; they thought only, pro and con, of Reform. Then the Whigs came to power in 1830, and Melville was gone once more.

Barrow continued to wave the flag, but in subdued despair. He opened his review of Franklin's account of the expedition down the Mackenzie River and along the coast by invoking Alexander Pope's poem *The Temple of Fame*, arguing that no poet, nor historian, nor biographer of the present day, would think of excluding from their due share of fame such names as those of Cook, and Parry, and Franklin . . . Captain Franklin must be considered, beyond all dispute, as one whose name has a right to be enrolled, eminently conspicuous, and in durable characters, in that sacred temple to which we have alluded.

He was sure still that the Northwest Passage existed and that it was navigable, but he thought the practice of following leads along the coast a mistake. Explorers should keep to the open sea, allow themselves to be beset in the ice, and take their chances with it. "In such a situation they seldom remain long . . . But besides this, there is every reason to believe that at all times a very large portion of the Polar Sea is entirely free of ice."

The man was nothing if not stubborn. He added that he did not know whether the government planned to continue exploring in the Arctic, or anywhere, but that, he said, with brazen disingenuousness, "is no business of ours; we have taken every opportunity to express our own humble approbation of [its] value in a scientific point of view." He went on to thank by name "those in power who have given countenance to these expeditions of discovery," Viscount Melville and the Earl of Bathurst. And then, in a moment that arouses a certain sympathy for the man, with the Passage still elusive and his dreams having come to nothing, he said good-bye to all that: "We now take leave of the subject—perhaps for ever."

Jane Griffin at twenty-four
(Scott Polar Research Institute)

IV

Prologue to Tragedy

I sayled not without great feare unto this Ice, and I observed, that this Ice was violently cast against the Rockes by force of the winds, and so made a mournfull sound afarre off, as if miserable howlings were heard there. Hereupon the Islanders thinke the soules of the damned are tormented in this Ice.

—Dithmar Blefkins

CHAPTER THIRTEEN

WARMER WATERS

The Whig government that came into office in November 1830 was led by Lord Grey, who named a rising young MP named Sir James Graham to be first lord of the Admiralty. Graham was well known as an orator, a Reformer, and a man totally devoted to cutting costs. He knew little about the navy but was an expert on finances, management, and budgets. While a liberal in politics, he was not a Whig but an independent; he had a sharp tongue, though not as sharp as Croker's, and like so many people with sharp tongues, he took offense at the slightest provocation. He belonged to one of the oldest, most prominent families of the Borderlands, the counties abutting the Scottish border; he was, in fact, one of the country's largest landowners. Despite his wealth, which made most of his kind as conservative as bankers, he believed in reform, not just of Parliament but of the ways of government *in toto*. He lasted less than four years at the Admiralty, but in that time he lopped some 20 percent off the naval budget; abolished the Navy Board and all its subsidiary boards, the Victualling Board, the Transport Board, the Naval Pay office, and so on; brought them all under the control of the Admiralty Board, making individual Admiralty lords responsible for running them; and fired a significant percentage of staff. He also stopped supplying beer for seamen who were home in port, saving three shillings a day per man.

"The bureaucrats in the various branches of the service," writes Arvel B. Erickson, one of his biographers, "feeling as if a bomb had been dropped in their midst, were completely dismayed at Graham's demands for accuracy, economy, and efficiency." So was Croker, out of office but still an MP, who complained that Graham was discarding a system "which had stood the test of a century and a half." Croker was disgusted. Not so John Barrow. Barrow wrote the reform plan for the Admiralty that Parliament ultimately adopted, and he claimed as his the idea to make individual members of the Admiralty Board responsible for the different departments. The Duke of Clarence, now William IV, had personally intervened in Barrow's future, insisting that he be kept on despite the change of government. When Graham introduced himself to Barrow, Barrow told him that he himself was apolitical: "I am neither rich nor reckless enough to become a party man." The net effect of all this change, indeed, was to increase Barrow's power. The man who replaced Croker as first secretary, the Honorable George Elliot, an inactive navy captain, was not an MP, thus could not defend the Admiralty in Parliament, and also had no administrative experience. Thereafter no first secretary during Barrow's tenure as what was now known as permanent secretary had anything like the influence Croker had had. That influence now belonged to Barrow.

He did not have enough influence, however, to restart the search for the Northwest Passage. The government had little interest in exploration in other parts of the world either. Under the long-standing regime of Lord Melville, Croker, and Barrow, the Northwest Passage in particular had become an Admiralty hobbyhorse. A reform government had no money or time for such useless extravagance. It was all business. To be sure, reform went only so far; nepotism, for example, was still common. But Graham was too upright to countenance nepotism at the Admiralty. He made his own appointments on merit alone. If that meant appointing Tory officers to important posts, so be it. His first major appointment, to the command of the Mediterranean fleet, went to Admiral Codrington, who had protested loudly against Graham's economies. Graham may have had no interest in the Arctic, but he knew how to run a government ministry properly.

Barrow came to admire Graham's honesty and ability. He had lost the project he had spent so much passion promoting, but he had gained power, and his position at the Admiralty had been made even more secure. As long as the king was alive Barrow had his job. And he had other interests besides the Arctic. In the yearlong intervals between waiting for Franklin and Parry in Bering Strait, F. W. Beechey had sailed all over the Pacific Ocean, visiting ports in China, on the East Coast of Siberia, San Francisco, the Hawaiian Islands, and various smaller islands, one of them the dot on the map known as Pitcairn

Island. It was here that Lieutenant Christian and the other mutineers had fled after they set William Bligh adrift in the South Pacific during the mutiny on the *Bounty*. Beechey found the last survivor of the famous mutiny there, a man named John Adams, and interviewed him shortly before he died. It made a fascinating chapter in Beechey's book, incidentally one of the best travel narratives of the nineteenth century, but the book did not appear until 1832. In the meantime, inspired perhaps by Beechey's interview, which of course he had had access to, Barrow had written his own book: *The Eventful History of the Mutiny and Piratical Seizure of H.M.S. Bounty: Its Cause and Consequences*. John Murray brought it out anonymously in 1831, in the middle of the Admiralty reform Barrow was so much involved in, and one can't help but wonder where on earth he found the time to write it. But he had all the primary sources available to him, not only Beechey's report but ships' logs, correspondence, manuscript journals, published journals, Bligh's own book about the mutiny, and the minutes of the court-martial of the mutineers. He also had known Captain Bligh personally. By virtue of his position at the Admiralty, Barrow could not have had much sympathy for the mutineers, but he is not uncritical of Bligh, recognizing the martinet in the man, and the book is more balanced than one would expect. It was good enough, in fact, to remain continuously in print for more than one hundred years. Oxford University Press brought out a new edition of it in 1989 to mark the bicentennial of the mutiny.

Barrow also found time in 1830 and the years immediately following to become the principal founder and first chairman of the Geographical Society of London, later the Royal Geographical Society, established "to collect, digest and print . . . new interesting facts and discoveries . . . , to accumulate a library of the best books on geography, and a complete collection of maps and charts from the earlier period to the present time . . . , to correspond with similar Societies in different parts of the world," and so on; but most of all "to render pecuniary assistance to such travellers as may require it": that is, to sponsor expeditions. Not surprisingly, the first expedition the society sponsored was to the Arctic. The society had grown out of the Raleigh Travellers' Club, an eating club founded in 1827 where, once every two weeks, the forty members would gather to eat a meal presented by one of the members and prepared from food acquired where he had been traveling. (Parry was not a member, but he sent Barrow a haunch of reindeer from Lapland when he returned from his attempt to reach the North Pole.) Barrow was a founder of this club too. Perhaps it evolved from a conversation he had had once with Sir Joseph Banks, who claimed to have eaten "every fish and animal in existence and was none the worse for it." Ah, said Barrow, had he ever tasted the meat of a hippopotamus? Alas, no. Barrow told him that it tasted something like pork.

The Arctic expedition the society sponsored was George Back's expedition in relief of John Ross's second, privately financed expedition to discover the Northwest Passage (see the next chapter), but the organization never became the substitute sponsor for expeditions to the Far North that Barrow may have dreamed of when it was founded. By the time it became involved in the search for Franklin in 1848, Barrow was dead. In the meantime the society had sent men to Antarctica, British Guiana, South Africa, Australia, Kurdistan, and in 1842, Ethiopia; but not to the Arctic. Barrow was a founder of the society, but he did not dominate its agenda the way he did that of the Admiralty in the 1820s. The society had too many other distinguished, cranky, influential members whose interests ranged worldwide for that to happen. For John Barrow the Arctic remained a field half plowed, a book half read. Not until near the very end of his career would circumstances change.

For Edward Parry the Arctic was over forever. He returned from the North Pole attempt in 1827 a family man. He had married before he left; now his wife, Isabella, was close to delivering their first child, a boy they named Stanley after her family name. Despite the failure of the expedition to get anywhere near the Pole, he received the usual acclaim for his efforts. Prince Leopold, another of George IV's brothers and notable primarily for having fathered the Princess Victoria, who would become queen after William IV died, asked him to dinner. The princess told him "she had read all his books." With Franklin and Richardson he went to a dinner given by the head of the Hudson's Bay Company. Like Franklin, the Parrys were in demand in London. Everyone wanted to know them. It was the same in Europe. On a brief vacation he took there in the summer of 1828, the Duke of Orléans, who became Louis-Philippe, king of France, in the Revolution of 1830, made much of him.

But international fame did not make much of a difference at the Admiralty to Parry's career. The Hydrography Office, the sinecure Lord Melville had given him, was still his, but it was hardly worth having. Established in 1795, its mission was to "take charge of such plans and charts as are now or may hereafter be deposited" and to assemble useful navigational information, such as the location of reefs or hazards, the site of likely harbors, and so on. These duties grew over time, and when Parry came into office he was supposed to oversee as well the preparation of charts for the engraver so they could be printed. But the office had never been properly staffed, and Croker disliked the whole idea of it and did his best to starve it to death. Parry had so little help that he wound up writing his own letters, at times even the copies of his letters that went into the letter book. That was a clerk's job. The office was years behind getting charts engraved. When the Duke of Clarence was in power at the Admiralty, he took an interest in the office, and Parry came back from the North to find six more draftsmen there bringing charts up to date to prepare them for engraving, and more clerks. But as soon as the duke was out, Croker was back in, and the six draftsmen were fired. Parry was fed up. He was also going broke. Ann Parry prints a portion of a letter that Parry wrote to his brother about his financial difficulties: "I am losing both health and money (about £200 pr annum) in my present situation. This will not do." To say the least: Parry might be an Arctic hero to the public, but at the Admiralty he was only one of hundreds of captains hoping for promotion to flag rank.

While Parry's career was stagnating, his personal life was hit by shock after shock. His little boy, Stanley, died in a fit that developed while he was teething. Shortly after that blow, Isabella Parry gave birth prematurely to a daughter who lived a week. Parry was already a religious man, but the loss of two children in such short order and the illness of his wife that followed turned him harder in the direction of Christian piety. He thought the death of their little boy was God's punishment for loving and doting on him too much. He quarreled with his wife's mother, Lady Stanley, to whom religious enthusiasm was distasteful. As Ann Parry remarks, the quarrel between them represented "the skeptical eighteenth-century encountering the evangelical nineteenth." England was indeed changing. Victorian religiosity and morality had begun to establish themselves in the English psyche well before Prince Leopold's daughter came to the throne in 1837. The Society for the Suppression of Vice was not a Victorian invention but pre-Victorian. Movements to ensure the strictest possible observance of the Sabbath belong to this period, and there were other movements to restrain and reform the boisterous behavior of the poor. Parry and Franklin were very much men of their time, and both of them retained this pious cast to their thinking for the rest of their lives.

Parry took an extended leave of absence from the Royal Navy in the summer of 1829 when he was offered a job Franklin had already turned down, to become the resident manager of the Australian Agricultural Company. The company had been given a grant of a million acres; it was trying to raise cattle and had yet to turn a profit. There were problems with the staff, with the governor of Australia, and with the land itself. The directors wanted a man of Parry's stature and ability to put things right. The job paid a comfortable salary of two thousand pounds a year, and Parry and his wife sailed away from England on the last day of July 1829. Before they left, Parry and Franklin were awarded honorary degrees at Oxford, and before that, in April, they were both knighted by the king. They were now Sir John Franklin, Sir William Edward Parry.

Parry's replacement at the Hydrography Office was Francis Beaufort, the inventor of the Beaufort wind scale and one of the greatest mapmakers of the nineteenth century. But even he struggled with insufficient funds and staff until Croker was gone in 1830. And in other fields the Admiralty had begun a long period of decline. Without a credible military threat to Great Britain appearing anywhere in the world, the navy did not have much to do. The Hydrography Office became the navy's most active, with dozens of survey ships spreading out to map coastlines, harbors, reefs, and rocks around the globe; but without a war, warships hardly seemed necessary. By 1844 the Mediterranean "fleet," once numbering in the hundreds, had dwindled to one ship. Sending additional ships to the Mediterranean meant leaving the British Isles themselves unprotected. And the great period of Royal Navy exploration that began with Captain Cook in 1776 had come to an end. As time went on, notes N. A. M. Rodger, "the Admiralty became a curiously parochial organization, increasingly bound up with routine administration." The Cabinet, he adds, ignored it. So did the country. Until George Nares made yet another ill-conceived and spectacularly unsuccessful attempt at the North Pole in 1875–76, Parry and Franklin were the last of its explorer heroes.

Unlike Parry, however, Franklin obtained a command. He had to wait nearly three years after coming back from northern Canada for it, until August 1830, but he was at last assigned to a twenty-six-gun frigate named the *Rainbow*, and in November he sailed to the eastern Mediterranean to back up ongoing British and French diplomatic efforts to bring the newly independent Greeks out of chaos and into some semblance of governmental order and control.

But a much more significant event had already occurred in Franklin's career. Two years before, on November 5, 1828, at Stanmore Church in a pretty village of the same name near London, Franklin remarried, taking Jane Griffin, by all accounts still handsome at thirty-six, as his wife. He had become interested in her even before he left on his second trip across northern Canada in 1825, giving her his arm when they strolled to the dinner table at dinner parties at the Franklin house, then seating her at his right. Jane Griffin had made a point of befriending Eleanor, Franklin's tubercular wife, coming to visit on a regular basis, sometimes taking her for jaunts in her carriage. Eleanor was obviously fading away, but it would stretch the evidence to suggest that something was already going on between Franklin and the woman who would be his second wife. Franklin was about to leave for the Arctic, women tended to crowd around him at any social occasion, and Franklin when he left still entertained hopes that Eleanor would survive. But he liked Jane Griffin, that much is certain, and he must have thought a lot about her when he was in Canada. Struggling west from the mouth of the Mackenzie in the late summer of 1826, he named a point of land Griffin Point. The day after he reached London in September 1827, he called at the Griffin house. The Griffins were traveling in Scandinavia; they were often abroad. He called again in October, when he knew they would have returned, and found Jane's father, John Griffin, at home. He asked after Jane "so assiduously," writes Ken McGoogan, Jane Griffin's most recent biographer, ". . . that her father realized what was afoot: the captain was seeking permission to court his middle daughter."

One wonders whether the captain knew Jane Griffin's courtship history. She kept track of it in a long series of manuscript journals running to millions of words and covering in detail much of her life over its lengthy course. According to Frances J. Woodward, whose 1951 *Portrait of Jane* consists largely of extracts from the journals, there were two hundred of them, plus two thousand letters. The Web site of the Scott Polar Research Institute in Cambridge, England, where they are now on deposit, lists 151 journals, six volumes of correspondence, and six of papers. Whichever listing is correct, her output was prodigious. She kept minutely detailed accounts of her travels, and she was one of the best-traveled women in Great Britain; she wrote witty, sometimes catty impressions of dinner parties, of people, of events; and she kept a remarkably revealing record of her emotional life and her endless vacillations about accepting or rejecting—until Franklin, always rejecting—the many proposals of marriage she received.

She was certainly marriage material. Only one portrait of her as a young woman survives. Done by an artist named Amélie Romilly at a sitting in Geneva when Jane was twenty-four, it shows a pretty young woman with a smiling face, a peignoir pulled back off her shoulders, a simple white gown underneath. Her face was broad and she was short, about five feet two. Even when she was in her late thirties, somebody described her as one of the most beautiful women she had ever seen. Her allure was as much intellectual as it was physical, and her wealth was also a factor. John Griffin, her father, was a silk merchant and a member as well of the Worshipful Company of Goldsmiths, meaning not that he was a jewelry maker but rather a merchant involved in the international gold trade. He adored his three girls and made sure they received the best education possible for women of their position. Jane Griffin, like Eleanor Porden, attended Royal Institute lectures on a regular basis. She learned French as a matter of course, read the famous work on logic of the early eighteenth-century theologian Isaac Watts, and her uncle taught her to play chess, a rare accomplishment for a young woman. She had what her uncle called a "furieuse curiosité." She liked to climb mountains and on a trip to northern Wales made it to the top of Mount Snowdon, Wales' highest mountain. In the Alps she and her uncle climbed the Montanvert, then scrambled down to the Mer de Glace, the great glacier that spreads over Mont Blanc. She proved to have a feeling for ice. "Treading upon the frozen waves," she wrote in her journal of the trip,

> imprisoned in a desert of frozen mountains, looking up & beneath & around me upon nothing but dead masses of congealed & rock-bound waters, I felt amazed & confounded— it was wonder, admiration, awe, more than fearful caution that retarded my advancing steps. . . . It was curious & beautiful to look down the glassy walls, which hidden from the sun were of a transparent blue colour, to hear their caverned waters flowing in some places at a depth unseen by the eye, in others rushing over ledges & forming cascades which whitened & foamed in narrow abysses of ice.

She sounds a bit here like Byron's *Manfred*, bitten by the sublime.

She had no doubt read Byron. On a trip to Cornwall she spent an hour with Sir Humphry Davy, the great chemist, who talked about "earths and grasses and electricity." She sometimes felt what she called "a most unfeminine degree of interest on the subject of politics." Her avidity for learning and travel and political news did not, however, make her unfeminine. Her father made sure that she learned how to dress in the latest fashions, and she herself disliked women who made a fetish of being intellectual. Given a choice of books, she would opt for something like Dr. Johnson's *Journey to the Western Islands of Scotland* rather than the latest romance novel. But she was constantly thinking about men and the chance that she might have her own romance. Despite her toughness and her intellectuality, she was a sensitive person, easily moved to tears. In her journals she endlessly questioned her own motives, resolving to do better, to study more, to improve.

There were numerous suitors and Jane considered them all, came close to accepting one every once in a while, then backed off. For the men it must have been maddening. Jane wanted to marry, and she felt an obligation to her father to accept *somebody*. But the sharp eye she turned on the men who approached her was unlikely to find anyone up to her intelligence, the range of her interests, and her adventurous, ambitious nature. Most of her suitors seem to have embarrassed her. John Franklin, on the other hand, was a keeper. Unfortunately we know very little about their courtship. Someone, perhaps Jane herself, destroyed the journal or journals in which it would have been recorded.

We do know the circumstances of their marriage, however. In September 1828 Jane went with her father, her sister Fanny, and two other women for a visit to Russia. Franklin, unemployed, would have gone with them, but Jane thought it improper, although they were engaged by then, so he traveled to St. Petersburg by himself and met them there when they had finished touring the countryside. An invitation to dine from the Empress Mother of Russia quickly followed. The two of them met Kotzebue, the Russian explorer who had lent his name to the bay in Alaska where Beechey waited for Franklin and Parry, and various other dignitaries as well. Then Franklin accompanied the Griffin party back to England. A few days after they returned they were wed. As the wife of a baronet Jane Griffin was now Jane, Lady Franklin. (Later on, when she was famous all over Great Britain, it would be just Lady Jane.) The couple spent a week at Ascot, the manor house of one of Jane's cousins. The marriage made Franklin well-to-do. Her father settled £3,000 on her, and on her own she had a fortune of £7,000. In the United Kingdom a wife's property automatically devolved on her husband once they married unless they made other arrangements. Franklin offered to let her keep her money. She adamantly refused. If she was going to be married, she was going to be *married.*

They traveled to Paris soon after the wedding and there met the same kind of reception Parry had received. Louis-Philippe invited Franklin to dinner and let him and Jane use his box at the opera. He was introduced to French scientific notables, they went to the theater, they made a splash. Then they settled into their London life, which was equally social. In the almost two years that elapsed between their marriage and Franklin's next command, Jane later wrote him that she felt a certain "shame and remorse" at "our career of vanity, and trifling, and idleness." Franklin became heavy during this time. He was a short man, five feet six inches tall, and came to weigh more than two hundred pounds. He was waiting for a ship. He waited and waited. Here were Britain's two great Arctic heroes, Parry and Franklin, world famous, sought out, applauded wherever they went, and the Admiralty could find nothing for them to do.

When the assignment did come, it was not uninteresting. The captains of Royal Navy ships often played a quasi-diplomatic role in the countries whose waters they patrolled. In the eastern Mediterranean, in 1830, the hot spot was Greece, which had achieved its independence from the Ottoman Empire, not formally but in effect, at the Battle of Navarino in 1827, when the combined naval forces of England and France completely destroyed the Egyptian navy and forced the Egyptian army to return to Egypt (an ally of the Ottoman Empire)—in French ships. But if the battle was conclusive, making it plain to the sultan that he would have to give up sovereignty in Greece, it by no means settled the question of who would rule Greece or what kind of government it would have. Greece was a bottle stuffed with scorpions, each determined to seize power and the money it generated. *Condottieri* were the norm. Russia, France, and Great Britain, which had formed a temporary alliance in 1827 to support Greek independence, all agreed that Greece needed a king to stabilize its politics.

Franklin sailed into this delicate, confused situation in November 1830, while the search for a king was getting under way. Like most Europeans with even a modicum of education, he came expecting to find the same noble, civilized people he had read about in Homer and Plato and Thucydides. But Greece had only just emerged from centuries of Islamic rule, and the ancient self-governing people depicted in the orations of Demosthenes no longer existed; they had long since been reduced to poverty and powerlessness. Franklin's role in the eastern Mediterranean was to represent the empire, to be a presence on the scene, ready to protect British interests and citizens if needed. He had plenty of time to observe the Greek people, and he was not impressed. A year after Franklin arrived, assassins killed the Greek president outside his church. The leading Greeks, he wrote his wife, "instead of uniting and doing their utmost to restore the agricultural and other useful occupations of the country, seem to be squabbling for power and places of trust." Officials and would-be officials strutted the streets of the capital, "occupied only by dress and parade."

But Franklin had to deal with these people. He spent most of 1831 in Corfu, twiddling his thumbs. He had occasion to visit Athens and found it in ruins from the war; he climbed the Acropolis to gaze at the remains of the Parthenon and to deplore Lord Elgin's "wanton rapacity" in stripping the temple of so much of its best sculpture. In 1832 he was ordered to take on a more active role. The British admiral in charge in the area, Sir Henry Hotham, sent Franklin and the *Rainbow* to Patras (in Greek, Patrai), a major port controlling the Gulf of Corinth, to serve, along with French and Russian forces in the area, as a mediator between the two main Greek political factions and to protect the interests of British subjects, most of them Ionian merchants; the Ionian islands were, at the time, part of the British Empire. He was also there to keep an eye on the Russian ship captain. Although the British, French, and Russians were nominally allies, the Russians had taken sides in the internecine fighting for power among the Greeks and were perfectly capable of delivering Patras, and thus the Gulf of Corinth, into the hands of the side they favored. Franklin's orders included the admonition not to use force unless it was absolutely necessary.

He turned out to be unusually adept at his job. He had to deal, among other things, with the illegal levying of "contributions" from Ionian merchants by the governor of Patras, the invasion of the city by a Greek warlord, and the spying and obfuscations of the Russian captain. He did so with what one of his biographers calls "dogged British pertinacity," persuading the governor to give up his forced contributions from the merchants and getting the warlord to withdraw from Patras, all without firing a weapon. As for the Russian sea captain, Franklin rebuked him for his behavior to a supposed ally and reminded him that only four years before the Empress Mother of Russia had introduced him to her eldest son "and all the younger branches of Her Majesty's family." Abashed, the Russian apologized. He had been under orders, he said. He had the utmost respect for Franklin personally.

The allies found a king for Greece late in 1832 and he arrived with his advisers and entourage in 1833, and Franklin's work in the Gulf of Corinth was finished. The *Rainbow* returned to routine patrolling of the Mediterranean. Franklin had done an excellent job and he was rewarded for it. When he returned to England, the government made him a Knight Commander of the Guelphic Order of Hanover, which entitled him to wear the star-shaped medallion of the order on his chest on ceremonial occasions. The new Greek king sent him something similar, the cross of the Order of the Redeemer, which he, in the manner of newly minted kings, had just established. The Guelph medallion was among Franklin's personal effects recovered from the Inuit in the Arctic during the search for him and his crew twenty years later.

And Lady Franklin? She was her own woman, and during this period of separation she did what she always did: she traveled, to the Mediterranean, to be with her husband as much as possible. They spent the winter of 1831–32 on Corfu together. But she also traveled on her own, up the Nile, to Jerusalem, to Athens, Malta, the Gulf of Corinth, where she hoped to reach Patras and see Sir John. "On her own," to be sure, is a stretch. She usually found parties of other travelers to go with. But this was not travel as it is understood in our time. They put up with unbelievably bad accommodations. She was sometimes sick, and travelers to Egypt and the Levant often died of the illnesses they contracted. Sick or not, nevertheless, she did things that no other woman of her time would have dared, and she wrote brilliant letters to her sister Mary and to her husband describing what she encountered.

She could not leave London until 1831. Little Eleanor, Franklin's daughter, was ill, and it would not have been proper for Jane to leave her. The country was in turmoil besides. The Reform Bill had not yet passed, the streets were threatening to explode, and people of property, Jane's sister Mary included, were hedging their bets, investing in foreign real estate in case revolution came and they were forced to leave the country. But late in 1831 she set out, traveling with her father to Gibraltar, where he turned back, and then into Morocco as far as Tetouan, a town south of Ceuta on the coast, "doing," says Frances Woodward, "what no European lady had done within living memory at least."

White women simply did not travel into the interiors of Arab countries. She arrived at Malta to find Franklin there, but unable to spend time with her thanks to strict quarantine regulations. She was allowed only to converse with him on a wooden platform in front of her lazaretto at enough of a distance that they had to shout to each other to talk at all, a situation made worse by Franklin's deaf ear. The next day they talked again, this time on a rock, guarded again to make sure they did not come near each other. They talked for two hours this way.

At Corfu they could be together; they lived in a crumbly old house on the esplanade facing the sea "having wretched stained and cracked walls" with the plaster falling off in patches "and dirty open bookcases crammed with books which cannot always be drawn forth from their homes without bringing a variety of novel-looking and flourishing insects along with them." When Franklin was posted to Patras, she made arrangements immediately to set out again, this time to Egypt and Palestine. An American corvette, the *Concord,* took her and a couple from Boston named the Kirklands to Alexandria. Its commander was Matthew C. Perry, who in 1852 would open Japan to commerce with the West. She found him to be a gentleman, and quite charming.

From Alexandria she sailed with Mrs. Kirkland for Syria, then being invaded, and came "within the sight & sound of actual war." From Jericho she described the experience to her sister Mary, herding "under a filthy shed, with our horses and Bedouins, obliged to cling close under the dwarf walls of the most wretched of villages, in order to be safe from robbers, devoured by mosquitoes, so entirely lame in one inflamed leg in consequence, that I was obliged to be carried whenever I moved or got up." She had with her a servant acquired in Egypt, five Turkish Janissaries, twelve Bedouins, her longtime female servant Owen, and a guide. She was better in the morning, she reported, writing, "You should have seen our mounted guard, as we crossed the desert plain of Jericho toward the Jordan . . . exciting one another by wild screams; letting off their muskets and pistols, balancing and thrusting their lances at full gallop, wheeling, pursuing, receding, sweeping across our path, yet always with the nicest care avoiding being actually in our way." When they reached the Jordan she bathed in it, "becomingly dressed, and with our guard keeping a respectful distance." She sipped the salty waters of the Dead Sea and preserved samples of its waters for friends. She took branches from the Mount of Olives "picked by my own hand." She was having a wonderful time.

From the Holy Land she sailed north toward Constantinople, taking a ship that stopped in Cyprus, then in Rhodes. She traveled to the plains of Troy; she went to Ephesus to see the ruins; she made a tour of the seven ancient Christian churches in the region mentioned in the Book of Revelation. The plague showed up at the same time she did back in Constantinople, but it was clear by this time that she was close to fearless.

Franklin did not seem to mind her doing any of these things. He admired her. "What a most fortunate person I must be to have gained such an enviable prize," he wrote her at one point. She scolded him for not accepting an invitation, close to an order, from the British high commissioner for the area to sail back to Corfu and meet the newly arrived king. Franklin felt his duty—*duty* was the most important word in Franklin's vocabulary—lay in Patras, doing what Admiral Hotham had told him to do, protecting the commerce of the gulf. Lady Jane told him he should inform the admiral he would like to accept a second invitation. She was thinking harder about his career than he was himself.

She was still in the eastern Mediterranean when, his job done, Franklin sailed for England late in 1833. She went on traveling, back to Alexandria, where she somehow gained permission to visit a harem, then up the Nile as far as Aswan in company with a Protestant missionary named Lieder who spoke Arabic, dressed in Arab dress, and sang religious songs to her on his guitar. Lieder shepherded her back to Greece and they visited Damascus on the way. This in itself was extraordinary, pushing the bounds of propriety far beyond the norm. Her latest biographer, Ken McGoogan, believes that she fell in love with Lieder. Perhaps so, although he suggests as well that their relationship was not physical. In any case, not until October 1834 did she arrive back in England, nine months after her husband.

What are we to make of it? She was often sick; indeed, when she returned, she was sick for months, suffering from headaches, fever, and general debility in a time when doctors hardly knew more than to recommend a change of scene and fresh air for such vague maladies. But it is the lingering in the Mediterranean that's odd. Few married women then, or even now, were this independent, this loath to be with their husbands. If she had followed him promptly home she might have worked on his career. He himself was working on it. From Greece he had written John Barrow twice asking after the possibility of another trip to the Arctic. Back in England he had put in an application for another ship. He had seen the king, the first lord of the Admiralty, and the president of the Royal Society and discussed the situation in Greece with them. He wrote that he was "disconsolate" without her and that he had done all this "because I knew you would have wished me to do so."

Yet she did not return for months. Perhaps it was the Reverend Lieder. Or it may have been that Jane Franklin discovered herself in the Mediterranean, found out, as all the trips with her father would not have revealed to her, that she was not like other Englishwomen; that she could manage in the most exotic places, under the most difficult circumstances. Real freedom is heady. After you have enjoyed it, life can never be the same. She had done things that no other woman of her acquaintance could have imagined doing. Her husband had almost starved to death. He had saved himself and his men from hostile Inuit bent on murdering them and stealing their goods. At Trafalgar he had lost half his hearing. He had eaten his boots. But she was more than a match for him. For all the illness, the professions of shyness, the fragile state of her nerves, she was just as tough, and at least as interesting.

CHAPTER FOURTEEN

BOOTHIA

John Franklin returned to England about the same time that John Ross returned from his second voyage in search of the Northwest Passage. While Franklin had been dealing with Greek *condottieri* and trying to keep track of his wandering wife, Ross, the scarred veteran, now in his fifties but still robust despite his wounds, still hoping to salvage his damaged reputation, had finally sailed through the Croker Mountains for himself, down Prince Regent Inlet past Fury Beach, past Parry's farthest, hunting for the strait Parry and John Barrow and so many others believed lay waiting at the inlet's bottom—the on-ramp to the Pacific, and for Ross the only hope for redemption.

Ross's voyage was not evidence of a change of heart at the Admiralty toward either the Northwest Passage or Ross. Ross had suggested the voyage in 1828 to the Lord High Admiral, the Duke of Clarence, with whom he seems to have been on good terms, but whatever the king's brother might have thought of the plan, the Admiralty had no intention of funding it or Ross and dismissed the proposal out of hand. Ross's idea was to use a steamship to plow through the ice. He had been studying steam technology since he had retreated to his home in Scotland in 1819 and gone on half-pay. He possessed enough of a fortune, perhaps from prize money, to build himself and his wife a substantial home on Loch Ryan at Stranraer that he called North West Castle, and pursue his interests. They were extensive. He joined the craze for phrenology that was sweeping England, particularly Scotland, at the time. Phrenologists claimed to be able to read the character of human beings from the configuration of their skulls. Ross thought the British military should take up the study of phrenology and use it to assign men to their tasks. The

Admiralty ignored the suggestion, but James Clark Ross, John Ross's nephew, would lighten the long Arctic evenings from time to time by reading the skulls of crew members in the mess.

Ross also tinkered with the construction of the sextant, adding a range finder to it, and the Admiralty did take this suggestion seriously enough to study Ross's invention; but once again nothing came of it. It is hard not to feel for Ross. He must have known that John Barrow's unforgiving spite would prevent his ever getting another command, yet he kept on trying to interest the Admiralty in his schemes. He was not stupid; nor was he as vindictive as Barrow was. When Parry returned from his first voyage through Lancaster Sound, the voyage that established the nonexistence of the Croker Mountains, Ross wrote him a friendly congratulatory letter. After the contretemps with Sabine about who deserved credit for the geomagnetic work on the 1818 voyage, in which his nephew James Clark Ross took Sabine's side, Ross tried to make up with the younger Ross. James Clark Ross was close to Parry and was with him on every voyage he took to the Arctic, but his uncle seemed not to hold it against him. He could be charming in a rough-hewn sort of way, enterprising, and with respect to steam navigation he was far ahead of his time—too far. The advantages of steam power in ships were obvious, to be sure. Ships would no longer be dependent on the wind for their motive power. Under steam they could move in any direction, while the direction of the wind dictated what direction a sailing ship could take. Steamships, it was clear, were going to cut travel time significantly.

But the technology was young. The screw propeller was not developed until the 1840s. Paddlewheels propelled steam-powered ships instead; they were mounted on the sides and were inherently inefficient. The early engines and everything that went with them—the boilers, the furnace or furnaces, the drive shafts—were bulky, taking up nearly half the hold of a ship, thus reducing the amount of material she could carry. They were also prone to breaking down. The Admiralty was an old-fashioned institution and loyal to wind. It did experiment with steamships a little, building its first one in 1821. She was designed primarily to tow ships up and down the Thames when the wind was insufficient to power them. Two more followed in 1823. The Greek rebels deployed a steamship during their war of independence and used it effectively. Franklin may have seen it in operation during his tour of duty in Greece. It should have been obvious that steamships were not going to go away, that they were the future. But the navy was content to crawl ahead, not run.

And it was right in one respect—it was definitely too soon to take a steamship to the Arctic. The first crossing of the Atlantic in a steamship had not been performed until 1821. Steam engine technology was a young technology. But Ross was always sure of himself and his opinions. His study of steam power had been thorough, he was persuaded steam would give him an edge in the ice, and that was that. He wrote a book, *A Treatise on Navigation by Steam,* in which he rehearsed the history of steam engines and pushed for the adoption of steam power by the navy. In an article that appeared anonymously in *Blackwood's* he chided the navy for its backwardness, for the sentimental attachment of its admirals to the beautiful but out-of-date ships of the line that flew their personal flags. Then, insultingly, Ross named the pride of the navy, the *Regent,* the *Britannia,* the *Vincent,* and others, each of 120 guns, all built since the war, none of them ever at sea. "It is a lamentable truth," he wrote, "but it is *indeed too true,*" that all they would be good for in a war would be to "*carry coals* for the steam-vessels" that would wage the war. The article so incensed the Admiralty, not to mention the admirals, that it was said they would have struck its author—designated only as a Captain, R.N.—from the lists if they had known who wrote it. Ross's book came out in 1828. By that time he was looking for private financing for his second voyage to Lancaster Sound and his hoped-for revenge on John Barrow.

He got the money from an old friend, Felix Booth, who at first turned Ross down; Booth did not want the public to think that he was after the twenty-thousand-pound reward that was still in force for the first British subject to make it through the Northwest Passage. Ross tried to find other financing, without success. Then Parliament removed the obstacle in 1828 by abolishing the Board of Longitude, under which the rewards would have been administered, and with it the rewards themselves. The government no longer had any interest in encouraging British subjects to pursue the old dream of a Northwest Passage. Booth, who manufactured Booth's Gin and was well known and well regarded as a philanthropist, now felt free to help Ross, secretly, if possible. Booth wanted none of the honors for himself.

For reasons known only to himself, Ross wanted the whole project kept secret. That was impossible, but he did his best. He made no announcements, searching the quays for a steam vessel he could buy at a decent price and have adapted, telling those who asked that he wanted it for experimental purposes. He told the manufacturers he hired to refit the engine that this was to be an experimental vessel as well and that he wanted the source of power to be below the water line, so that a cannonball penetrating the sides would not hit the engine and disable the ship, thereby giving them the mistaken impression that they were preparing a warship. He did not make it clear to the manufacturer that he was going to the Arctic until he made a general announcement to that effect in February 1829.

The manufacturer was a man named Braithwaite, who had just made the brilliant young Swedish engineer John Ericsson his partner. It was Ericsson who put together the mechanical insides of the ship, which was named the *Victory*. It was, said Braithwaite, "a very complicated contrivance," with innovations in the boilers, the furnace, the condensers, the paddlewheels, and just about everything else. The engine had to drive not only the ship, which had paddlewheels on both sides, but a large bellows and a water pump.

In the event the cylinders proved too small. The furnace was also too small. The engine did not generate enough power. The boilers leaked. New boilers generally leaked at first in the early days of steam, and the engineers who ran steam equipment used a mix of dung and potatoes to stop them up from the inside. This time it failed. The whole setup was too new and too complicated; it was born to fail. Ross began to realize this fact before he even put to sea, but too late. He was stuck with it.

Other things went wrong. Because the steam equipment took so much space in the hold Ross had hired a whaling ship and its crew to follow him to Prince Regent Inlet to carry extra supplies. He left London late, delayed by repairs to the steam machinery. On the voyage up the Irish Sea to Loch Ryan to pick up the whaler, one of his men caught his arm in the machinery; it was past fixing, the muscles mangled, the bones splintered to the elbow. Ross had no surgeon on board yet, so he had to amputate the man's arm himself, relying for guidance on nothing more than the amputations he had seen during the war. At Loch Ryan the whaling crew mutinied and refused to go. The season was too late, they said; Ross was cutting it too close. They would be trapped in the ice. The whalers tried to entice Ross's own crew off the *Victory*. A small drunken riot ensued. Ross took what supplies he could fit into his small ship from the whaler's stores. He made yet more repairs to his machinery. On June 13 he finally set sail for Davis Strait and Lancaster Sound.

The whaling fleet had left months earlier; all previous Arctic expeditions had left London in April. A day after he set sail a sudden wind-
storm took Ross's foretop mast. When it was working, and it did work
sometimes, the steam engine could generate no greater speed than
about two miles an hour. A man can row that fast.

But once they were under sail, they made decent time. They were able to
repair the foremast at Disco Island, just off Greenland, by taking a spar
from an abandoned whaling ship; Baffin Bay was largely free of ice, and
by August 6 the *Victory* had reached the entrance to Lancaster Sound.
Very shortly thereafter the ship was cruising south in Prince Regent
Inlet. By August 12 they had reached Fury Beach. No sign of the
wrecked ship was there—the tents Parry had left behind had been
shredded by bears and foxes—but the *Fury*'s stores were almost entirely
intact. Ross had counted on this when the crew of the whaling ship he
had engaged opted not to go. Nothing in the cans was spoiled. The contents were not frozen; "nor did the taste of the several articles appear to
have been in the least degree altered." Their success in the Arctic, nay
their very existence, Ross went on, had depended on these supplies.
Now they had enough: "wine, spirits, sugar, bread, flour, and cocoa,"
lime juice, pickles. The *Fury*'s sails were "not only dry, but seemed as if
they had never been wetted." The beach was lined with coal; they put
ten tons of it aboard the *Victory*. It was like finding a supermarket in the
middle of a desert. They took all they wanted and thought they would
need, yet it "seemed scarcely to diminish the piles of canisters." And it
was free.

But that was the end of *Victory*'s luck. By August 21 they were beset in
the ice, fog obscured their view, and the engine lacked the power to bull
the ship out of the pack. When they climbed nearby hills, they could see
open water to the south, but could not reach it. The tide was irregular
and unpredictable, unlike the tides to be found everywhere else in the
world. Northerly gales drove water south into this cul-de-sac, southerly
gales pushed it out, all on their own willful schedule. Conditions
became increasingly dangerous. Caught in a rip in a narrow channel
between an island and the mainland, they were almost wrecked themselves, only to escape at the last minute. Ross despaired of telling his
readers what it was like to be trapped in such a situation:

> Let them remember that ice is stone; a floating rock in the
> stream, a promontory or an island when aground, not less

solid than if it were a land of granite. Then let them imagine, if they can, these mountains of crystal hurled through a narrow strait by a rapid tide; meeting, as mountains in motion would meet, with the noise of thunder, breaking from each other's precipices huge fragments, or rending each other asunder, till, losing their former equilibrium, they fall over headlong, lifting the sea around in breakers, and whirling it in eddies; while the flatter fields of ice, forced against these masses, or against the rocks, by the wind and the stream, rise out of the sea till they fall back on themselves, adding to the indescribable commotion and noise which attend these occurrences.

Commanding a ship trapped in this chaos, what does one feel? "Utter helplessness."

They spent most of September working their way down the west coast of the inlet through constantly shifting ice to a point where the ice ahead consisted of "hundreds of icebergs wedged together into a solid mass." That was as far as they were going to go. The land tended westward here, as if they might have reached the mouth of a strait, but they had not; they had actually reached the isthmus of the peninsula Ross came to call Boothia, after his patron, a place where it is only seventeen miles across to the "western sea," the Arctic Ocean. Below this isthmus lay a gulf, which Ross named the Gulf of Boothia, and North America. Here, then, in a place Ross named Felix Harbor, after Booth's first name, they would spend the winter.

And three miles farther north, the next. And a few miles north of that, the next. Not until the summer of 1832 would they leave this little pocket of paradise, and then only to spend the winter of 1832–33 at Fury Beach, crowded into a makeshift canvas tent the size of a small ranch house that they covered in ice and snow for insulation. Four years—it added up to one of the worst ordeals in Arctic history, topping Parry, Franklin, all of them in terms of sheer longevity. When it was finally over and Ross came to write about it in his expedition account, he tried to tell his readers what was for him its most punishing aspect. That first year when he looked toward the water he could see, hc says, "nothing but one dazzling and monotonous, dull and wearisome extent of snow." When he looked toward the land, he adds,

> this land, the land of ice and snow, has ever been, and ever will be a dull, dreary, heart-sinking, monotonous, waste,

under the influence of which the very mind is paralyzed, ceasing to care or think, as it ceases to feel what might, did it occur but once, or last but one day, stimulate us by its novelty; for it is but the view of uniformity and silence and death. Even a poetical imagination would be troubled to extract matter of description from that which offers no variety; where nothing moves and nothing changes, but all is for ever the same, cheerless, cold, and still.

He never mentions the Arctic's splendors, the lovely inner blues of the ancient ice of icebergs, the constantly rippling curtains of color in the auroras, the extraordinary plenitude of stars illuminating the black Arctic nights. None of this seems to have touched him. Yet Ross survived the ordeal without damage. Perhaps the Arctic is made for people like him, people who can be matter-of-fact about things and trim their hopes and expectations to their circumstances. Parry described the Arctic winterscape in similar terms, but he fought off its radical bleakness by keeping himself and his men as busy and purposeful as possible. Ross simply rode it out.

There were twenty-three of them all told, including Ross, James Clark Ross, and William Thom the purser, who were all officers of the Royal Navy; a first mate named Thomas Blanky, who had some experience with Arctic voyages, having sailed with Lyon on his disastrous voyage to Repulse Bay and with Parry on his equally disastrous try for the North Pole; a surgeon; and eighteen others, some of them also with Arctic experience. The first thing they did when they reached their winter harbor was to scrap the useless steam engine, taking it apart and leaving it on shore. Pieces of it remain there to this day. They set up the usual walls of snow and ice around the ship to protect it from the wind, took down the masts and rigging, draped a canvas roof over the deck, and drew moisture out of the living space between the decks by placing iron containers upside down over the hatches. The moisture from inside the ship condensed on the cold metal and instantly froze, and the system worked. The temperature inside hovered between forty and fifty degrees, but because it was dry, it was relatively comfortable. Ross did not produce plays, but he did set up a school, although the reading matter on board consisted mostly of religious tracts. He also persuaded the men to give up their daily ration of alcohol—a remarkable feat, and an odd turn for an expedition sponsored by a gin manufacturer.

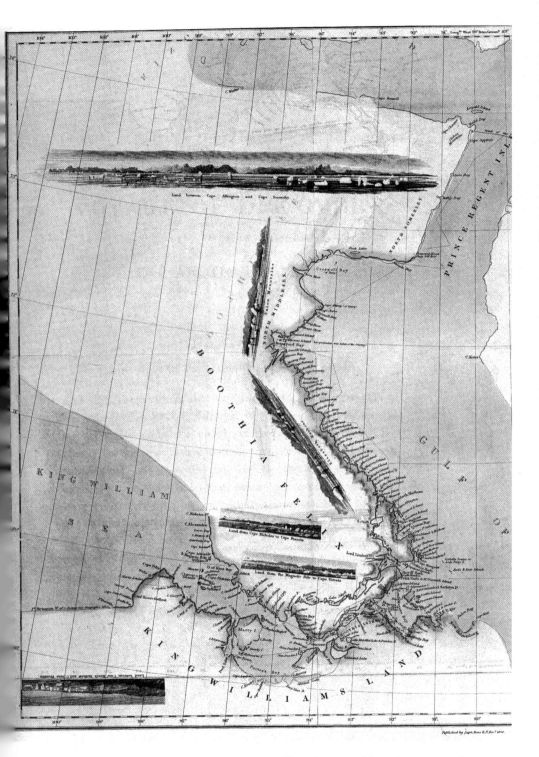

The principal portion of John Ross's map of Boothia, 1833. Note the presumed connection between King Williams Land and the Lower Boothia Peninsula.

(Source: John Ross, *Narrative of a Second Voyage in Search of a North-West Passage*, 1835.)

Ross's account of the expedition runs to 740 pages in its original quarto form, which is a wonder, considering how little actually happened. The first winter a whole village of Inuit showed up, and the crew throve on the fresh food the Inuit provided, and their exotic company. Thanks to his extensive service with Parry, James Clark Ross understood the Inuit language to a limited degree and could communicate with them. One man was lacking a leg from the knee down, and the crew endeared themselves to the tribe by making him a wooden leg and fitting it to his stump. Within three days he was walking again.

The Inuit knew their surroundings intimately and an Inuit woman drew a map of the coastline that made it plain that there was no strait to the south of their position, thus no exit from Prince Regent Inlet. The Northwest Passage was elsewhere. James Clark Ross nevertheless spent much of the following spring, and the spring after that, exploring the region on foot, using Inuit as guides and Inuit dogs to drag the sledges. Inuit survival skills were, as always, impressive. Lacking wood or animal bones, as the case might be, they could make a sledge entirely out of frozen salmon. If necessary, they could make one out of nothing but ice. Igloos went up generally in less than an hour. An igloo is a remarkably warm, snug protection against the elements, but building them was an art English explorers never bothered to master, even though they watched Inuit erect them countless times.

The younger Ross's exploring expeditions on foot and dogsled were the highlight of the voyage and produced the most useful information. He was able to determine that the isthmus abutting their harbor was only fifteen miles across, ten miles of which were occupied by a lake. West of the isthmus, on his longest trek, Ross gazed upon what he assumed was the longed-for western sea, with no land on the horizon to stop anyone from sailing to the Pacific. "It was the ocean that we had pursued, the object of our hopes and exertions," he wrote; "the free space which, as we had once hoped, was to have carried us round the American continent, which ought to have given us the triumph for which we and all our predecessors had laboured so long and so hard." The western ocean: he could see it, he could stand on its shores. But the *Victory* was on the other side of a piece of land fifteen miles wide and hundreds of miles long. He tried to take it as philosophically as he could; he bowed to the will of heaven and traveled on, following the coastline that ran beside this empty sea, first to the northwest, then, turning at a cape he called Cape Felix, to the southwest. He named the land he was skirting

King William Land. He was pretty sure that he was following the north coast of North America. It was only some two hundred miles to John Franklin's Cape Turnagain. He did not have enough provisions to go that far, however, and had to turn back. At his farthest point he named a cape he could see in the middle distance Cape Jane Franklin. A second small cape at the limit of his vision he named simply Cape Franklin, after Jane Franklin's esteemed husband, John.

It was a strangely prophetic act. Ross was not in fact following the North American coast but the northern coast of what would become known as King William Island, and that was where Franklin's final expedition would come to rest. Ross's mistake in identifying the island as part of the mainland was understandable. He remarked at the time how difficult it was when everything was covered with ice, sea and land both, to determine which was which. A frozen sea could be as rough in appearance as snow-covered land; the land might be as flat and level as water; and most difficult of all, everything was indistinguishably, dazzlingly white.

He also noticed the tremendous amount of ice that was piled up on the coast he was following. It consisted of "the heaviest masses that I had ever seen in such a situation," and some of the lighter floes had been driven "as much as half a mile beyond the limits of the highest tidemark." The younger Ross was the first white man to see with what immense force the Beaufort Gyre drives the ice of the then-unknown, unnamed Beaufort Sea down the inlets and channels of the Canadian archipelago. It was like seeing a glacier in reverse, sea ice piling up on the land to depths of forty feet or more, pushing its way half a mile inland. *Half a mile.* Even a tsunami will not often penetrate that far. What mere ship would stand a chance, locked into ice this implacable?

Yet the younger Ross concluded that this was the route to pursue if and when another expedition went out, sailing down the west side of the Boothia Peninsula during some warmer summer than usual toward this terrible ice-walled coast. And this was the route John Franklin and his expedition would pursue sixteen years later when the Admiralty decided to try, one final, climactic time, to risk the clotted waters of the archipelago and claim the Northwest Passage at last.

That first summer, the summer of 1830, the men rerigged and repaired the *Victory*, dug it out of the ice, and prepared to depart. They had plenty of supplies, and if they had been able to leave, Ross would probably have sailed out of Prince Regent Inlet and turned west, to get around the top of Boothia Peninsula, then turned south to do precisely what the younger Ross suggested, sail down its west coast toward King William Island and then west again along the coast of North America. But a real thaw never came. They waited in vain for the ice to break up in the inlet. At the end of August Ross noted that they had spent

> eleven months fixed to one spot. Whatever value voyages of discovery may have in these countries, they are certainly purchased at a high price in time . . . We might have circumnavigated the globe in the same period: and I imagine no one was very sanguine about future north-west passages, even should we contrive to make one ourselves.

It was a time of "daily and hourly anxiety," Ross went on, "of hopes and fears, promise, and non-performance." Not until September 17, an early winter already setting in, did they find a lane of open water and actually set sail. They made three miles before the ice stopped them. Three days later new ice was forming around the ship. Within a few days more it was clear they were going nowhere. By the end of September they were busy cutting their way through the new ice toward a safe harbor for their second winter. This new ice was already sixteen inches thick. By the middle of October it was, in spots where it froze around pieces of the previous year's ice, sixteen *feet* thick. The entire month was spent cutting their way a total of 850 feet toward a more sheltered spot near the coast. "I believe," wrote Ross about this laborious month, "that some of us could not help calculating the number of centuries it would require to make a single north-west passage, at this rate."

That winter the Inuit, who generally sought out places where the hunting was best, did not come back.

Ross is not especially revealing about how the men fared during these stagnant winters. He lost three men all told, one to tuberculosis, another to debilities associated with the man's epilepsy, and the third to scurvy and the exhaustion and poor health that befell them all during the fourth winter. When so few men are confined together for so long, there are bound to be problems. In his expedition account Ross sometimes philosophizes about the adaptability of mankind, using the example of the Inuit, perfectly content in their murderous environment, but his own men were clearly suffering. On December 15 of that second winter he notes that "a strong breeze, with snow, formed a sort of variety just now; but it imprisoned the men, and that was an evil. No one is much the better for thinking: those who had nothing very cheering to think of, were always the worse." And what was there cheering to think about for any of them? The officers, he notes, had their fame to look forward to, even if the expedition had only minor successes. Ross recognized clearly enough that the rest of the crew had nothing to look forward to but their return to England, and their meager pay. Plus another year in this terrible dead white corner of the earth.

Ross tells us from time to time that they all got along pretty well, but we have reason to doubt this was so. The steward, a man named William Light, sold his story to a writer named Robert Huish when he returned, who wrote a book almost as long as Ross's about the expedition using the materials Light gave him and information, he said, from other members of the crew as well. Huish mocks Ross at every opportunity. On Ross's interest in phrenology, for example, he writes that Ross's mastery of this arcane subject has enabled him to determine "by certain prominences on his own head . . . that he possesses in an eminent degree all the virtues which are necessary for the discovery of the North West Passage. It is rumoured . . . that it is owing to the extraordinary size of the organ or bump of conceitedness that Capt. Ross was induced to undertake his last voyage." That would be the voyage of 1818. Huish goes on to describe Ross removing a head from a dead Inuit, whom the tribe had abandoned, so that he could "read" the skull, then hanging the head in the water under the ice for the ever-present shrimp to clean. The men would not eat the shrimp after that.

According to Huish, the crew disliked Ross from the beginning and took their orders largely from James Clark Ross. The younger Ross did nothing to dispel this claim. Shortly after their rescue and return to England a parliamentary committee looked into the voyage, taking testimony from Ross, his nephew, Felix Booth, Francis Beaufort (now thoroughly in charge of the Hydrography Office), and Admiral Desaumarez, whom Ross had served under in the Baltic. The committee was trying to determine whether the government should reimburse Ross for the losses he had sustained on the expedition, losses he estimated at three thousand pounds. The younger Ross was asked about the command structure on the ship. Was he, James Clark Ross, second in command?

"Not precisely," he replied, ". . . but in a great measure sharing with him [John Ross] the chief command; that is to say, I had the entire direction of the navigation of the ship, without being under Captain Ross's command." It was, he went on, "quite understood that having been so long employed on former similar voyages, I best understood the nature of the navigation of those seas." Felix Booth had made it clear to him, he added, that he would not finance the expedition unless he, James Clark Ross, led it in this de facto way. "I never received an order of any kind from any person on that expedition," he concluded. When he was recalled the older Ross denied this was true, and Felix Booth said he never told the younger Ross such a thing, but the genie was out of the bottle. Ross also assured the committee indignantly that he had not, "certainly not," undertaken the expedition to recover his reputation. The Admiralty had promoted him, after all, when he returned in 1818 from Lancaster Sound and the Croker Mountains. Lord Melville had told him at the time not to worry about anonymous notices in the press. Why then should that have been on his mind?

Not only was the younger Ross, in effect, sharing command, he was also responsible for the expedition's one major success, the discovery of the North Magnetic Pole. He was, he explained to the committee, "the only person who at all understood the nature of those subjects"—that is, geology, botany, and natural history—on the expedition, and geomagnetism had become a special interest of his. It was a special interest to scientists all over Europe, who had already come to understand that the magnetic poles moved over time from place to place; and several scientists, using readings from John Franklin's work in northern Canada and Parry's readings in Prince Regent Inlet, had figured out approximately where it was. It was simple enough to run vectors from magnetic directional readings in different places in the Far North. Where they intersected was where the pole was likely to be.

So it proved. Commander Ross—this was not a naval expedition, but the younger Ross had by then achieved that rank, just below the rank of captain that his uncle held—had been taking readings of his own wherever he had trekked the previous year. This year, the spring of 1831, he set out with a small party of men and closed in on it. On June 1 he arrived at a spot on the west coast of the Boothia Peninsula marked only by some abandoned Inuit stone huts where the dipping needle, the vertically mounted magnetic needle designed to point down rather than in any horizontal direction, reached 89 degrees and 59 minutes—one minute off the vertical. The ordinary horizontal magnetic needles, hung in the most delicate possible fashion from strands of flax, did not swing at all from any position in which they were placed, indicating that the source of attraction could only be below. So this was it: the North Magnetic Pole. Ross's one regret was "that there was not a mountain to indicate a spot to which so much of interest must ever be attached," or even something so "romantic and absurd" as "the fabled mountain of Sinbad, . . . or a magnet as large as Mont Blanc. But Nature had here erected no monument to denote the spot which she had chosen as the centre of one of her great and dark powers." Ross did what he could to supply the want, claiming the place in the name of the king, ordering as large a cairn of stones to be erected over it as they had time to build, and placing a British flag on top. He was clearly excited. "I must," he says,

> leave it to others to imagine the elation of mind with which we found ourselves now at length arrived at this great object of our ambition: it almost seemed as if we had accomplished everything that we had come so far to see and to do; as if our voyage and all its labours were at an end, and that nothing now remained for us but to return home and be happy for the rest of our days.

It was his uncle, not Commander Ross himself, who, in an act of genuine absurdity that was quickly mocked in England, named the site after William IV. John Barrow was one of several to point out that the pole was migratory, and that there was nothing to prevent a Frenchman, say, from finding the pole the next season, or the season after that, and naming this new spot after King Louis-Philippe—and so on ad infinitum as the pole moved, the names of kings and presidents dotting the Arctic map. William IV himself, however, had no objection to the idea when John Ross asked his permission to put his name on the magnetic pole. Nor did the elder Ross stop there. His nephew had discovered three low islands in the seas to the west of Boothia Peninsula and named them after Francis Beaufort. The elder Ross, when he drew up his map, changed the number of islands to nine, scratched out Beaufort's name, called the group the Clarence Islands, and named each of the nine after a member of William IV's immediate family. It was the Croker Mountains all over again.

With the pole discovered and the inlet a dead end, Commander Ross was right—there was nothing to do now but go home and be happy. For the second summer in a row, however, the ice held. A genuine summer failed to appear. Not until mid-August did they escape from their winter harbor. By the end of August they had sailed four miles and a new winter was beginning. By the beginning of October all hope of escape was gone.

They determined that fall that in the spring they would abandon the ship and move north on foot, dragging the ship's boats on sledges, taking as much of the ship's supplies as they could, to Fury Beach. There they would recoup their strength and, at the first sign of open water, take to the boats and try to reach Barrow Strait and Lancaster Sound, and hope for the best. Ross has little to say about their third winter. The men were getting weak, not so much from lack of food as from the sameness, the absence of anything to do but wait, and the despair. Snow blindness affected a few. One man lost half his foot to frostbite; he could hobble but not walk, and walking was their way out. In the end he had to be carried out. In April 1832 they started ferrying supplies northward along the coast, loading the boats, which happened to be the same boats Franklin had used on his second journey to northern Canada; the Admiralty had given them to Ross. The plan was to take the boats as far north as they could, along with a stock of provisions, and leave the boats there as a fallback. Then they would go on to Fury Beach, renew their supplies, and use the *Fury*'s boats to get out. This work was extremely hard. The loads were too heavy to take at once, so multiple trips were necessary on every stretch of distance. It might take five hours to make a mile. They slept in what they called snow huts, caves they dug in the snow and covered with canvas, seven men in a cave. The temperature reached fifteen below zero in these caves at times, thirty below outside. Low on supplies, they had to do this tremendous work on half-rations. There was no shelter from the weather. Ross calculated at one point that they had gained 18 miles on this first leg but walked 110. It was 180 miles to Fury Beach all told, 300 if they followed the shoreline closely, which the ice forced them to do. This ordeal, which lasted until the first of July, made heroes of them all.

At Fury Beach they checked the remaining stores, feasted on them and rested, and found the *Fury*'s boats scattered up the beach, but intact. They built themselves a house of sorts, using the *Fury*'s spars as posts and beams, and covered it with canvas to protect themselves from rain and snow. In August and September they worked their way north. They camped under sheer cliffs where the thaw was melting the ice and raining stones down on them. By the end of August they had reached Barrow Strait in the boats. It was frozen solid. They waited through most of

September. When they climbed the hills to look out over the water, all of it—Prince Regent Inlet, Barrow Strait, Lancaster Sound, as far as the eye could see—was ice. In late September they gave up. They would have to make their way back to Fury Beach and their canvas structure. They were lucky to reach it, such was the condition of the ice.

The carpenter died that winter. The wounds Ross had suffered in the Napoleonic Wars started to bleed. The men built up snow and ice around the outside of their canvas house to protect themselves from the wind, and thus spent the winter, in effect, inside an iceberg. Their clothing was inadequate; it took decades for the British, showing their characteristic inability to learn from the natives, to figure out that wool uniforms are no match for subzero temperatures and far inferior to fur. Scurvy made its appearance, and the lime juice no longer seemed to work its magic. The "least active of mind," Ross writes, "dozed away their time in . . . waking stupefaction . . . ; they were the most fortunate of the party. Those among us, who had the enviable talent of sleeping at all times, whether they were anxious or not, fared the best."

But none of them fared well. They all knew, furthermore, that yet another winter in Prince Regent Inlet would finish them off. Early in July they started the journey north up the inlet toward the strait, moving everything in stages, the sick coming last, who could not walk and had to be dragged in sledges. At a place called Batty Bay they waited for several weeks for the ice to break up, or at least for open leads to develop. On August 15, 1833, four years and two months after they had left Loch Ryan, the ice did open, and they set sail in their three small boats for Lancaster Sound and the whaling fleet they hoped was there. After crossing the top of Prince Regent Inlet, they coasted the southern shoreline of Lancaster Sound, along Baffin Island. When the wind failed to blow they rowed, once for nearly twenty hours straight. Gales sometimes drove them ashore. On August 26, the eleventh day, one of the lookouts thought he saw a sail. They took off after it, but it had not seen them and sailed away. Then they saw another, and it too sailed off, and then the wind died and they were able to row close. Then the ship saw them and put down a boat, which rowed toward them.

"She was soon alongside," wrote Ross,

> when the mate in command addressed us, by presuming that we had met with some misfortune and lost our ship. This being answered in the affirmative, I requested to know the

> name of his vessel. . . . I was answered that it was "the
> Isabella of Hull, once commanded by Captain Ross;" on
> which I stated that I was the identical man in question, and
> my people the crew of the Victory. That the mate, who com-
> manded this boat, was as much astonished at this informa-
> tion as he appeared to be, I do not doubt; while, with the
> usual blunderheadedness of men on such occasions, he
> assured me that I had been dead two years.

Not quite—but they looked it.

> Unshaven since I know not when, dirty, dressed in the rags of
> wild beasts instead of the tatters of civilization, and starved to
> the very bones, our gaunt and grim looks, when contrasted
> with those of the well-dressed and well-fed men around us,
> made us all feel, I believe for the first time, what we really
> were.

However foolishly John Ross may have behaved in other ways, he
deserves a world of credit for bringing home so many of the men he led
down Prince Regent Inlet into that world of cold.

Their rescue was a sensation in Great Britain. They had indeed been
given up for dead. A year before the rescue, in a July 1832 article on Ross
in *The Athenaeum,* evidently written by someone who knew him, the
author abandoned "all hope of his safety. . . . What destroyed these
brave men, or how their ship was set fast or crushed, we shall never
know." He went on to quote Ross's last words, from a letter sent back
from the west coast of Greenland in 1829. Thanks to the mast they had
retrieved from the abandoned whaling ship there, "we are," Ross wrote,
"in a more complete state than when we left England; and if ever the
north-west passage be made, it should be this year."

Now it was enough that they had survived. *The Gentleman's Magazine*
caught the nation's mood, announcing that Ross's safe return "has dif-
fused one universal feeling of joy throughout the empire." The day after
his return Ross and his nephew were received at court, where Ross laid
the flag flown over the North Magnetic Pole at the king's feet. The public wrote Ross more than four thousand letters, notes his latest biographer, congratulating him on his rescue. The king knighted him and
Felix Booth too; they were now Sir John Ross, Sir Felix Booth. Honors

flowed in from the crowned heads of Europe. In Leicester Square, home of the panorama, Ross got one of his own, based on the many drawings he had made at Boothia. The public gardens at Vauxhall, an early British version of an amusement park, opened in late May 1834 with an exhibition devoted to a representation of the Boothia landscape, erected under Ross's own supervision. Viewers could look at icebergs, frozen seas, polar bears, an Inuit village, and of course the North Magnetic Pole, with the British flag flying over it. The whole thing covered sixty thousand square feet of ground. In the evenings there were fireworks.

The Admiralty was sufficiently moved by Ross's return to cough up, at his urgent request, nearly five thousand pounds to pay the crew. This was a decision Sir James Graham, still first lord, took himself, without waiting to consult the Admiralty Board. The crew, of course, had come home penniless. All of them had lost everything they owned. The *Victory* and its stores were irrecoverable. Ross had lost all his instruments, his books, his clothing; so had his nephew; the crew had nothing left but the rags they wore when the *Isabella* picked them up. Paying the crew was an uncharacteristic act of mercy on the government's part. This had been a private expedition; the government was not liable. Not only did it pay them, the Admiralty found comfortable positions on Ross's recommendation for those who had been in the Royal Navy previously. But Ross would do nothing for William Light, the source for Robert Huish's nasty book. Toward Light and his accusations, Ross would struggle to maintain a dignified silence.

All was triumph for Ross, then, but he was the kind of man who could stain his own success, and he did. It was not enough that his crew be paid off. He had lost scientific instruments and other possessions whose value he estimated at three thousand pounds and he petitioned the Admiralty for help. When it came to Ross himself, however, the Admiralty saw no reason to come to his financial rescue. He had organized the expedition, found financing for it, and led it into the Arctic. Just as the glory would be his, and his alone, so must the risks. Besides, he had been on half-pay the four years he was gone. The Admiralty refused his petition.

Ross went behind its back, finding friends in Parliament to propose that the kingdom reimburse him for his losses, to the tune now of five thousand pounds. He asked the mayor of Liverpool to organize a petition on his behalf. He had already persuaded the people of Hull to back him. Even friends of his in the navy found this distasteful. "He has no right," wrote Admiral Sir Byam Martin, one of the navy's grand old men, "to bring discredit on the service, which he does, as a naval officer, by canvassing members for their votes. . . . I would vote to reimburse his expenses, but no reward. What claim has he beyond those distinguished officers who so ably conducted other voyages?" The admiral was also skeptical of the value Ross placed on his scientific instruments, which, he claimed, was "higher than those supplied to all the other expeditions put together, though they had what they pleased!"

Parliament seemed favorably disposed to Ross, but named a committee to look into the question nevertheless. The committee consisted of some of the most distinguished names in British politics, including the up-and-coming young William Gladstone and Sir Robert Peel. It was at the committee's hearings that the question of who was actually in command of the expedition emerged, John Ross or James Clark Ross, and was not answered. The committee also looked into the question of why Commander Ross, whose losses of instruments and personal belongings amounted to five hundred pounds, not as large as his uncle's but still considerable, was not asking for compensation in the same fashion as his uncle, and if he wasn't, why the elder Ross had no plans to share the parliamentary loot with his nephew. The elder Ross's answers on this issue were equivocal. When it was his turn to testify, the committee asked the younger Ross whether he had been offered money to write his own account of the expedition. Yes, he said, by two publishers, one offering £1,200, the other £1,500. For a man whose losses had amounted to £500 and who was also on half pay for four years, this was a lot of money. Why had he not accepted? Because he did not want to interfere with the success of his uncle's book, he explained. The younger Ross came out of the hearings with his honor intact. His uncle looked greedy and considerably less than magnanimous.

Even more embarrassing were some of John Ross's scientific claims. The level of the sea on the west side of Boothia Peninsula was thirteen feet higher than on the east side, he told the committee. The claim was ridiculous on the face of it, and not a fact they could have measured in any case by any means they had. When the younger Ross was asked about it, he said that this was the first he had heard of it. The elder Ross claimed that light affected compass needles. He noticed this, he said, when the compass needle suspended over the North Magnetic Pole moved with the sun. John Ross was never within forty miles of the North Magnetic Pole, and light has no effect on compass needles.

In the end, Ross got his money. The committee reported that "a great public service has been performed," namely the discovery of the magnetic pole. It had also ruled out at last (or so it thought at the time) Prince Regent Inlet as a route to the Northwest Passage. Furthermore, it noted, "Your Committee cannot overlook the public service which is rendered to a maritime country, especially in time of peace, by deeds of daring, enterprise and patient endurance of hardship, which excite the public sympathy and enlist the general feeling in favour of maritime adventure."

Ross then went on to sour still further the taste in his brother officers' mouths when his book came out. He turned down Murray's offer to publish it and decided to do it himself, by subscription, opening an office in London where buyers could sign up and sending subscription agents around the country, even abroad, to solicit sales. Applying to Parliament for reimbursement was one thing, but peddling one's own book was well below the dignity of a naval officer of any rank. Naval officers were gentlemen. They did not hawk things for a living; they served the country. John Franklin, after being pursued by one of Ross's agents, refused to be listed as a subscriber to the book. And the book itself struck off-notes all through its exceedingly lengthy text. The younger Ross specifically asked his uncle to make it plain that he, James Clark Ross, was exclusively responsible for finding the North Magnetic Pole. His uncle promised to do so but then did not. The book makes it seem as if its author were intimately involved in that particular quest and deserved credit just for being the commander of the expedition. "It must," the elder Ross wrote, "be hereafter remembered in history, and will be so recorded, that it was the ship *Victory,* under the command of Captain John Ross, which assigned the north-west Magnetic Pole in the year 1831, and that this vessel was fitted out by him whom I can now call Sir Felix Booth." The pomposity, and the attempt to steal credit for himself, grate even now.

Whenever Ross got the chance in the book, furthermore, he took aim at Parry, conveniently forgetting that he had tried to be friendly to Parry after Parry's successful voyage of 1819–20. He claimed for one that Parry had actually agreed with him in 1818, when he sailed out of Lancaster Sound, that this was not the doorway to the Northwest Passage. For if he hadn't agreed, he would have spoken up, as it was his duty to do; and since he didn't speak up, he must have agreed. This blatant piece of casuistry ignored the fact that he had soundly squelched Parry when, just a week or two earlier, he had questioned Ross on his decision not to investigate Smith Sound. Ross had made it plain to Parry and the other officers that he would not stand for anybody questioning his decisions. Ross also ignored the fact that when he did decide to quit Lancaster Sound so precipitously, he sailed past Parry's ship on the way out of the sound at top speed and without signaling any message to him of any kind. If Parry had wanted to consult with Ross he would not have been able to.

Nor was this all that was wrong with Ross's book. His text is filled with Inuit place names, but the map he drew of the Boothia Peninsula contains none of them, making it impossible to trace on the map where the junior Ross had gone on his explorations. Instead Ross filled in the coastline, every little cape, harbor, bay, and island, with the names of friends, relatives, and people who subscribed to his book, making the map almost useless. He filled in unknown coastlines with purely speculative dotted lines. This was especially damaging at King William Land. The younger Ross had been uncertain whether or not it was an island. When he looked down the east side of it he found the horizon so hazy he could not be sure he was looking at a coastline. The elder Ross simply drew one in, thereby reinforcing the idea that King William Land was part of the continent. He was so caustic about the steam engine they had left behind them on the Boothia shores that yet a second pamphlet war broke out, this one between Ross and Braithwaite, the manufacturer. Things nearly came to a duel when John Ericsson, the Swedish inventor, accused Ross of lying.

When it was over, John Ross had rubbed the shine from his reputation that his amazing survival had restored. The Irish journalist and wit William Maginn, founder of *Fraser's Magazine,* had begun a series of one-page satirical profiles at the back of the book titled "The Gallery of Illustrious Literary Characters," with drawings of the subjects by the artist Daniel Maclise. The persons were indeed illustrious. Scott, Croker, Wordsworth, Leigh Hunt, Coleridge, Bulwer-Lytton, Lamb, and Disraeli had all been bitten by the Maginn snake. Now it was John Ross's turn. Maclise drew him sitting in a chair in his cabin, his feet propped on the wall over his little cabin stove, smoking one of those long clay pipes used at the time and sipping a brandy and water. "As the season is yet young," Maginn wrote,

> any animal will do for a lion; and the animal now dressed in the skin is Captain Ross, who is playing the part at the various *soirees* and *conversazioni,* such as they are, which are now giving. . . . If the captain has seen the magnetic pole, to use

the language of a Scottish newspaper, which evidently considered it to be somewhat like a barber's pole stuck up in the way of a finger-post for the lodestone, he has seen nothing else. His discoveries, as far as we can learn, have been precisely nothing.

But in the end it was Barrow who as usual had the last word. His review of Ross's book is nothing short of savage. Using the parliamentary committee's findings, he mocks Ross's scientific ineptitude, confutes Ross's claim that he most certainly did not undertake the voyage to salvage his reputation, cannot forgive Ross's foolish map, excoriates him for seeking the parliamentary reward only for himself and nothing for his nephew, suggests that Ross had hired a ghostwriter to help him with the book, and finds the text full of vulgar absurdities and coarse jokes. "On the whole," he concludes, "Sir John Ross, C.B., K.S.A., K.C.S., &c. &c., is utterly incompetent to conduct an arduous naval enterprise for discovery to a successful termination."

Whatever hope Ross might have had of recovering his naval career, much less his reputation, was sunk. He had managed to pull the plug on it himself. Back in Stranraer, Ross added a large room to his beloved North West Castle that reproduced his private quarters on the *Victory*. It had a window that folded down so that Ross could point his telescope out of it and watch the comings and goings of ships on Loch Ryan. The room was designed, clearly, as a monument to his Arctic adventures. M. J. Ross writes that the room

> was lit from the roof. Embrasures round the walls contained relief maps of the polar regions and could be filled with water so that, with model boats, he could illustrate the course of his voyages. At one end of the room, he had a panorama on moveable screens painted from his own sketches and the dinner table was decorated with glass, mirrors, and lights that he could manipulate to entertain his guests on the properties of ice.

The room still exists. In 1960 North West Castle was sold to a hotel chain and completely rebuilt, but the chain kept the room intact. It serves now as the hotel's bar.

Ross had this to comfort him: Even though his voyage had failed, and his claims were false, his map an embarrassment, he had shown that public interest in the Arctic was not dead. It could be revived with a stirring tale of derring-do and survival under extreme circumstances. To Barrow and many of his fellow officers, he was incompetent and somewhat dishonorable, which is close to the worst thing you can say about a military man. But to the public he was a hero.

CHAPTER FIFTEEN

THE QUESTION OF BOOTHIA

Despite his contempt for Ross, John Barrow at some level must have welcomed the attention Ross's voyage engendered in the public. If the public could become enthusiastic again about exploring in the Arctic, even if the object of attention was John Ross, Barrow might still entertain hopes of reviving his Arctic project. According to William Desborough Cooley, writing in *The Edinburgh Review* in 1836, public sympathy for Ross's project had been strong from the beginning. "There was," he wrote, "in Captain Ross's adventure something so personal in its origin, so generous in its equipment, and so like self-immolation in its risks, that he was followed to the scene of peril by a national anxiety never before extended to any scientific expedition." When three years had gone by and nothing had been heard of them, the "thrill of fear" extended to all classes, he went on—even, presumably, the unlettered— and the "general anxiety" was further roused by rumors of their death.

Out of this public worry a mission to rescue Ross evolved more or less spontaneously early in 1832. The immediate catalyst was John Richardson, who proposed a rescue operation not to the Admiralty but to the Royal Geographical Society—of which Lord Goderich, the colonial secretary, was then president—traveling from Point Turnagain to Fury and Hecla Strait, a route that would (not, of course, by accident) have filled a major gap in the chart of the Arctic coast. When that suggestion fell flat, George Ross, John Ross's brother and James Clark Ross's father, took up the flag and wrote a petition to the king. William IV and John Ross, if not exactly friends—did kings have friends?—were certainly well acquainted with each other, and the king sent the petition to Lord Goderich with his approval. That changed the landscape entirely. Lord

Goderich pledged two thousand pounds of government money to the mission, under the condition that the rest of the project's cost be raised privately.

Who would command it? George Ross had his man—George Back. Like most of the official navy list, Back was on half-pay, living in Sicily at the time, studying art, having risky affairs with the wives of Sicilian gentlemen, and hoping for a command that would bring him once more into the Admiralty's eye. He had left Italy on his own prompting when he had heard about Ross's long absence. If a rescue mission were to be mounted, he wanted to be on the spot to offer his services. He did, gratis. George Ross was delighted to have him.

In November 1832 a public meeting was held at the Horticultural Society in London to solicit support. It filled to capacity. Such was the eloquence of Sir George Cockburn, an Admiralty lord and one of the navy's most prominent men, that eight hundred pounds were raised on the spot. Another three thousand had already been raised from John Ross's friends. The organizers then named a governing committee, mostly naval officers, to manage the expedition. It called itself the Arctic Committee. One of its members was John Barrow. He may have hated Ross, but he didn't necessarily want him dead, and of course a rescue mission would serve to move explorers back into the Arctic. Barrow persuaded the newly formed Royal Geographical Society, of which he was then president, to sponsor the expedition as well. "It was an early example," writes Canadian historian Hugh Wallace, "of the paradoxical fact that in arctic discovery the humanitarian aim to find a lost expedition might be a much stronger incentive to explore than was exploration itself." The search for Franklin would be a later instance of this same fact.

Back left for northern Canada in mid-February 1833, traveling by way of New York and Montreal, just as Franklin had done on his second expedition to the shores of the Arctic Ocean, and along the usual Hudson's Bay Company routes into northern Canada. The enthusiasm for the mission was international; in New York Back was given free passage up the Hudson to Albany, and one thousand people came to see him off at the dock. The plan was to take two small boats, much like those Franklin had used on the Mackenzie, from Great Slave Lake (where Franklin had wintered on his second land expedition) and up into the unknown lands to the northeast. The Yellow Knives had told trappers of a river that arose in the highlands there and emptied into the northern

ocean. The Indian name for it, Thlew-ee-choh in Back's spelling, translated as the Great Fish River. They described it as powerful and dangerous. None of them had ever followed it for its entire route because it led
into Inuit lands, and they would not go there. But that was what Back
proposed to do in his wooden boats. From the mouth of this rumored
river, assuming that it emerged on the Arctic Ocean, it should be just a
few hundred miles to Fury Beach. The reasoning was that if Ross and
his men were still alive, they would have retreated there, to live on
Parry's abandoned supplies.

The reasoning was sound, but even so the mission could not fail to
seem quixotic. Absent for three years, Ross and his party might have
been anywhere. The distances were enormous, the map blank, and the
climate deadly. In the "Zoological Remarks" he appended to Back's
book on the expedition, John Richardson noted that "Captain Back's
journey from New York to the Gulf of Boothia may be likened to that of
a traveler who should embark in a canoe at Naples, and proceed up or
down various rivers, and across portages, until he reach Arkhangel and
the entrance of the White Sea." That would have been a journey
through inhabited lands. Not so in northern Canada. If Ross and his
men were not at Fury Beach, hopes of finding them in that vast barren
nothingness were next to zero.

Back took only three men with him to Canada, two of them ship-
wrights to build the boats he would need to descend the Great Fish
River. The third was a surgeon named Richard King, young, smart, and
as prickly an explorer as the Arctic ever saw, always ready to disagree
with Back, always sure he was right, opinionated, proud, and abrasive. It
would be King's fate to be right on numerous issues, but to ensure,
thanks to his character, that nobody would ever listen to him.

Back intended to hire the rest of his crew in Canada, mostly from
Hudson's Bay Company employees. The HBC was eager to cooperate
with him. The HBC, under its governor, George Simpson, whom
Franklin had met a decade before when Simpson first took control of
the company on the ground in Canada, had changed its attitude toward
exploration. As fur stocks declined in known areas, it was looking to
expand into the unknown; within a few years it would be sending out its
own explorers to fill in the map. At Great Slave Lake, Back had been
given the services of George McLeod, an HBC manager who built, to
Back's specifications, a fort—Fort Reliance—for him and his party and
gathered a stock of provisions, including 120 bags of pemmican. Back

arrived at Great Slave Lake in the late summer of 1833, made his way to its eastern end, where the fort would be built, and, leaving McLeod in charge, left at once with a small party of men toward the northeast, to find the river he would descend the following summer. He had with him an Indian guide, an old man who remembered seeing its headwaters when he was a child, and thought he knew where it was. He was soon lost.

But they did find it, fighting their way from Great Slave Lake in a bark canoe up a river system full of falls, rapids, and lakes so large that, once they were well into them, no land could be seen on any horizon. Finally they reached a height of land where they crossed a portage a quarter of a mile long and two feet in elevation above the respective river systems and found the Great Fish River. They descended it as far as they could safely go, then returned to the fort, which McLeod had finished, to wait out the cold.

That winter was particularly severe. Temperatures dropped to seventy below zero at one point, or one hundred degrees below the freezing point of water. The game retreated to its comfort zone and the Indians who hung about the fort were starving. Some of them did starve to death. Back tells affecting stories about children begging for scraps from their table, Indians sinking into despair and abandoning the old and weak, and an Indian who killed and ate his own wife and all his children but one. Back and his men would themselves sometimes go for days without food, trying to preserve as much of the pemmican as they could for the summer's journey. Not until spring did the famine ease.

Akaitcho was living in the area, and the remnants of Akaitcho's tribe. They had been decimated by the Dogrib Indians in revenge for years of harassment, theft of their women and children, and theft of their goods at the hands of the Yellow Knives. When Back moved north that spring, he found Greenstockings in a crowd of Indians. When he called her name, she laughed and told him "she was an old woman now." Old or not, she was pleased when Back asked her to sit for her portrait.

Back seemed at home in this place in a way Franklin never had. He could be as condescending as any Englishman about the ways of native life, but his accounts of Indian suffering had a human sympathy that was missing from Franklin, who never trusted the natives. Back seemed to have two distinct sides to his character. In Europe he was a bit of a dandy and loved to splash about in society, to make romantic conquests and treat his inferiors with a hauteur born of an oversupply of vanity. In wilderness he was someone else. He could be abrasive and difficult, but he could also inspire loyalty. When Augustus, the Inuit who had been with Franklin and Back on both the earlier land expeditions, heard that Back was in Canada, he set off to find him and go with him to Inuit lands as an interpreter again, only to lose his way in the forests west of Hudson Bay and starve to death. The HBC man, McLeod, was indefatigable in his desire to help. Back's ready willingness to endure the same hardships as the rest of his men, together with his physical toughness, was one reason he gained people's respect. People remembered that Back had traveled more than a thousand miles on foot in the winter of 1820–21 to bring what supplies he could cadge from the two warring fur companies back to Franklin's party.

Now he was going to run an unknown number of miles down an unknown river to an unknown destination to rescue the survivors of an expedition that was already safely home in England. He got the news on April 25, 1834, when a packet arrived with letters, newspapers, and an excited messenger announcing, "He is returned, sir!" The "he" was John Ross.

No matter—Back's instructions were, in case Ross did turn up, to proceed down the Great Fish River anyway and fill in that still-elusive stretch of coastline from Point Turnagain to Fury and Hecla Strait. The Arctic Committee, displaying the usual overconfidence of officials in London about the success of Arctic expeditions, was sure he could accomplish this in a single season. Despite Parry's failures, and Franklin's, and Lyon's, despite the accounts of long ferocious winters, ice-choked seas, the nipping and ultimate destruction of ships, starvation, frostbite, scurvy, and weather fit only for polar bears, they maintained their touchingly simple faith in quick, easy Arctic expeditions to the end. Why they did so remains one of the enduring mysteries in the history of exploration.

Not having to rescue anyone, Back at once reduced his boats from two to one and his crew to ten: five HBC men experienced at running rivers; three strong soldier volunteers from the Royal Artillery stationed in Montreal; himself; and Richard King. The boat he chose, of the two that his boatwrights had built for them over the winter, was thirty feet long, pointed at both ends, and, fully loaded, weighed 3,360 pounds. Even unloaded it was impossible to carry. But it did prove to be tough, which was fortunate, because the river was formidable. "After a violent and tortuous course of five hundred and thirty geographical miles,"

Back wrote of it at the end, "running through an iron-ribbed country without a single tree on the whole line of its banks, expanding into fine large lakes with clear horizons, most embarrassing to the navigator, and broken into falls, cascades, and rapids, to the number of no less than eighty-three in the whole," the Great Fish River finally reached the Arctic Ocean. To be precise, it was an inlet of the Arctic Ocean, much like Bathurst Inlet to the west, but smaller. Back named it Chantrey Inlet, after Francis Chantrey, Esq., a name he does not otherwise explain.

Five hundred and thirty miles, eighty-three falls, cascades, and rapids—it makes a terrific adventure story, and Back tells it well. He is a vivid writer with a genuine talent for making things real. No one was more descriptive than he of what it is like to endure the tiny sand flies that appear in the accounts of nearly every Arctic expedition. "How can I possibly give an idea," he asked his readers,

> of the torment we endured from the sand-flies? As we dived into the confined and suffocating chasms, or waded through the close swamps, they rose in clouds, actually darkening the air: to see or to speak was equally difficult, for they rushed at every undefended part, and fixed their poisonous fangs in an instant. Our faces streamed with blood, as if leeches had been applied; and there was a burning and irritating pain, followed by immediate inflammation, and producing giddiness, which almost drove us mad.

He spoke of men throwing themselves on their faces and moaning "in pain and agony." Even the Indians did this. Then he remembered John Franklin's reaction to them, how "it was the custom of Sir John Franklin never to kill a fly; and, though teased by them beyond expression, especially when engaged in taking observations, he would quietly desist from his work, and patiently blow the half-gorged intruders from his hands—'the world was wide enough for both.'"

He brings to life as well the tortuous route the river took and the anxiety this caused them all. The lakes that punctuated its course were vast enough to dissipate the main current of the river and often, out of sight of land, it was impossible to know where the outlet was, and therefore which direction to pursue. Back worried constantly about where the river was taking him. Too often for his taste it led east, toward Hudson Bay; sometimes it veered south. By the end of July it spat them out in Chantrey Inlet and they spent the first two weeks of August jockeying to get into open seas. The inlet was chock full of ice. Back's instructions were to proceed west from the mouth of the Great Fish River to Point Turnagain, then double back and map the coastline as far east as he could go.

But he could not even reach the mouth of the inlet. They met an Inuit tribe, but Back understood Inuit speech poorly, and when he asked one of them to outline the surrounding region for him, he had trouble following what the man was trying to tell him. He had thought of leaving the boat and four men in the inlet and walking to Point Turnagain, but the ground was so soggy that the men sank in to the middle of their calves when they walked across it, and he abandoned the idea. The weather was abominable. It rained nearly every day. He climbed hills, trying to make out the outline of both the inlet and the coast beyond. Rain, fog, and haze made it hard to see far. When they reached the westernmost end of the inlet they saw land to the north, and ice to the west. The land was actually King William Island; the ice covered what would become known as Simpson Strait. The ice barred their way. There was no way to know whether the land to the north joined the mainland farther west.

Toward the middle of August the ice cleared out to the east, and he could have worked past the mouth of the inlet, explored the coastline toward the Boothia Peninsula, found the western coastline of the lower Boothia Peninsula, and put an end to the idea that the Gulf of Boothia had an exit in the south. But that course of action did not fit his plans. Now that Ross had been rescued, Back's instructions were to proceed to Point Turnagain and map the intervening coastline. And in that direction lay solid ice. So Back missed his opportunity; he failed to discover the crucial fact that the land James Clark Ross had named King William Land was in fact an island, divided from the peninsula by a strait, and add that highly significant bit of information to the map of the Arctic. He gave up instead, turned around, and went back the way he had come. He spent another winter in northern Canada but left for home in February and reached Liverpool on September 8, 1835. He had mapped the Great Fish River, which the Royal Geographical Society eventually named after him; and he had himself named any number of points of land after various sponsors and friends. But he had not gone that extra mile and figured out the complicated geography at the southwest corner of Boothia. As for the great question—where is the Northwest Passage?—Back had made no advance on it at all.

He hardly bears any blame for it, given the difficulties he encountered, and when the news of his safe return came out nobody did blame him except Richard King. Back had climbed a height of land he called Mount Barrow and had seen no land bearing away from the eastern end of Chantrey Inlet to the northeast, but only an island in the distance, rising mountainous out of the sea; but King believed he had seen a faint blue ribbon of land between the eastern end of Chantrey Inlet and this mountain island. King was correct, for the land is indeed there. They had disagreed about it, and Back, looking for a second opinion, sent three men back to the same height with his telescope to check the view. Two of them agreed with Richard King. King urged Back to make the attempt. The water was open in that direction. It would have taken only a few days of sailing to find out. But Back was worried about his men, who were worn out and dispirited. One man was weak, bloated, and clearly ill. The season was getting late, and they had five hundred miles and more of river to navigate, upstream.

It is always this way in the Arctic. One can go too far. Even a day can make the difference between living and dying, and Back had seen precisely that happen with Franklin a decade before. Back had reached his farthest at the same season, on practically the same day of the year, that Franklin—too late—decided to turn around. Richard King had nothing like Back's experience, and he was a much younger man. King was sure that he was right and was already planning to come back and prove it. Before they left for home King cached supplies at the mouth of the Great Fish River. He would need them, he believed, for his own expedition.

Back returned to England to universal acclaim. He had written to the Royal Geographical Society the winter before, describing the extreme cold, and his letters got into the papers; they were, of course, intended for publication. He had washed his hair, he told his readers, three feet from a roaring fire consuming twelve full-size logs, and his hair had frozen before he could apply a towel to it. "My guitar is cracked, and jars abominably; but you will not be surprised at this when I add that I have been obliged to grease my hands daily to prevent their cracking also, for such is the dryness of the atmosphere that nothing can stand it." Writing to John Franklin about the famine in the area, he reported that "my own men, thank God, are, generally speaking, well, though they have frequently been three, and even four, days without food of any kind. My companion, Mr. King, and myself, have, for a long time, been living on half a pound of parmesan, and a little flour each a day."

This is the kind of experience that makes heroes, and the public followed it eagerly. With news of his safe return came letters describing the journey down the Great Fish River. It was exciting stuff. Back had had a great adventure. Some of the publications, furthermore, understood the nature of the geographical issue surrounding the Boothia Peninsula—whether it in fact was a peninsula—quite well. The editor of *The Athenaeum* must have known Back personally, for shortly after his return he was able to see the sketches and drawings Back had made. He was impressed. He hoped that Back would publish as many as he could in his book. Then he congratulated the public for its role in sponsoring the expedition. "It was a noble thing," the anonymous author writes,

> for the country, torn as it was, in 1832, with political dissension [over the Reform Bill], still to think of its absent wanderers [the Ross expedition], and raise so large a subscription . . . to go in search of them. It was a noble thing, also, in Captain Back to volunteer, as he did, to conduct the search . . . ; and so absolutely disinterested, that besides serving entirely without pay, he even defrayed, himself, the expense of his personal outfit.

Noble indeed, although Back certainly understood that leading such an expedition could hardly hurt his career.

George Back had become a national hero, then, leading an expedition that *The Athenaeum* described as "more than usual a national enterprise," and this was clearly the moment to strike, to build on the national pride in his achievement and send another expedition back to the Arctic to finish the job. The national mood was such that the public could be counted on to support a new voyage. Late in 1835 the Royal Geographical Society published a set of proposals for further exploration to find the Northwest Passage and map the coast of North America. They came from well-known establishment sources: John Franklin, John Richardson, Francis Beaufort, John Barrow, and even John Ross, every one a knight of the realm. Barrow's was the most ambitious, another great expedition under Admiralty auspices to penetrate the ice beyond Barrow Strait and sail triumphantly around the world. The others were more modest coastal expeditions to fill gaps in the coastal charts and answer the vexing question of whether Boothia was an island.

Richard King had also proposed an expedition to the RGS, but the society ignored it. King is only a footnote in Arctic history, a man destined to be ignored because of his own cocky, abrasive personality; yet he did understand what the HBC also understood, that in the high Arctic the best way to travel was light, with just a few men, living, as much as possible, off the land. King wanted to go back with a few men and a light canoe and travel mostly by land, using dogsleds, the canoe when sleds were no longer feasible, and winter as close to the route to be traveled as possible, just below the tree line. When the RGS refused to listen to him, he went to the public, calling public meetings, just as the Arctic Committee had done to raise the money to rescue John Ross. He wrote a pamphlet outlining his proposal and claimed that he could finish the job, fill in the gaps in the chart of the Arctic coastline, for a mere one thousand pounds. He wrote his own account of the Back expedition, appending his proposal to it as the final chapter. It was published six months after Back's popular book hit the market. It too was ignored. The review in *The Athenaeum,* one of the only reviews it got, summed up public opinion. "The salient features of this book," the reviewer wrote, "are implied condemnation of the opinions and plans acted upon, and wrought out by former discoverers, and an insinuated complaint of personal neglect shown to the writer. Mr. King has gathered together his journals, seasoned them with some vexation of spirit, and here laid them before the public."

But what if the public—or the RGS—*had* listened to him? He might well have pulled it off. The Hudson's Bay Company already knew how to travel in the latitudes below the Arctic Circle, and it traveled light. Mackenzie had gone to the Pacific in 1793 in a light birchbark canoe. In the 1840s Dr. John Rae, an HBC employee, would explore northward in the high Arctic, living with and like the native Inuit, traveling by dogsled or kayak and sleeping in igloos. The English never abandoned their heavy canvas tents. Richard King never got the chance to open the cache he had left behind in Chantrey Inlet.

But if King failed, Barrow succeeded. The renewed public enthusiasm for the Arctic, plus the collective weight of the Royal Geographic Society's most famous Arctic names, proved to be enough to change the Admiralty's mind, for the first time since 1827, about Arctic exploration. No doubt Barrow was the prime mover, though the Admiralty chose to finance not the major expedition Barrow wanted but one of the much smaller efforts the RGS had proposed, a replay of George Lyon's abortive mission to Repulse Bay ten years before. John Franklin had suggested the plan, but Franklin was on his way to Tasmania and would not lead it. The man of the hour would lead it: George Back.

The assignment, once more, partook of that cockeyed optimism about what was possible in the Arctic that could only have come from the second secretary. Back was given one ship, the *Terror*, a crew of sixty, and provisions for eighteen months. He was to sail to Repulse Bay, take two parties overland to Prince Regent Inlet, each party dragging sledges and a boat, send one party north to Fury and Hecla Strait and the other west all the way to Point Turnagain, and return to Repulse Bay via the roundabout route of the North Magnetic Pole—all in one season. They were to leave in June 1836 and be back home by late fall of the same year.

Leaving as late as June all by itself made the assignment impossible. The terrain they had to travel was unknown, but it was certain that it was barren, and if it were like the rest of the barren lands, it was guaranteed to be littered with boulders and half-frozen lakes, and treeless. The chances that straits or even shorelines would be free of ice were no better than fifty-fifty. Bad weather, it was by now obvious, could shut an exploring party down for a week. Nevertheless "this Arctic Expedition," the instructions read, "may be distinguished from all others by the promptitude of its execution, and by escaping from the gloomy and unprofitable waste of eight months detention."

Held up by contrary winds, the *Terror* had to be towed all the way to the Orkney Islands by steamship. The decks were crowded with small boats and the pens for twenty sheep and ten pigs, plus ducks and chickens. Winds from the west made progress across the Atlantic slow. Not until August 1 did they reach Hudson Strait, which was full of ice. Two weeks later they reached Salisbury Island, where Back had to make a choice—sail north of Southampton Island up Frozen Strait to Repulse Bay, which was the shortest route; or take the longer to the south of Southampton Island, round it, then sail north to Repulse Bay up Sir Thomas Roe's Welcome. Back chose the former. Who knows whether it was right or wrong? The Welcome might have been just as clogged with ice. The weather might have been just as bad. Somewhere near the mouth of Frozen Strait, at the end of August, after struggling through ice, "the heaviest drift ice I had ever beheld," the *Terror* was nipped, then beset, then locked into the ice; the ship was forced over on her starboard side from the pressure. By August 31 "the rigour of a precocious winter was thrust upon us." After that Back had no control over the ship. It remained locked into the same huge floe, the safest, happily for the crew, in a sea of floes, until the following July.

The *Terror* was another of the navy's "bombs," a warship designed to handle the weight and the recoil of heavy mortars, then doubly reinforced inside and out for the stress of sailing through ice. Its ten months in the ice would prove to be a test of just how strong these ships were, and also of Barrow's idea that the best way to make progress in the Arctic was to allow a ship to be frozen in and then drift with the pack, trusting the pack to take you where you wanted to go. The pack in this case drifted back and forth with the winds and the tides in and out of Frozen Strait, past a point on Southampton Island named, with an irony not lost on George Back, Cape Comfort; then it slowly moved east as the season wore on toward the eastern end of Southampton Island and eventually into the western end of Hudson Strait.

But *drift* is an inappropriate word. Pack ice, as we have seen, is not stable, and there is no safe harbor within it. One day in late September, "shortly after 9 A.M. a floe piece split in two, and the extreme violence of the pressure curled and crumbled the windward ice up in an awful manner, forcing it against the beam fully eighteen feet high," Back wrote.

> The ship creaked as it were in agony, and, strong as she was, must have been stove and crushed, had not some of the smaller masses been forced under her bottom, and diminished the strain, by actually lifting her bow nearly two feet out of the water. In this perilous crisis steps were taken to have everything in readiness for hoisting out the barge.

Through the fall and winter crisis succeeded crisis, all of the same type. The ice was moving. Tremendous pressures were being brought into play. "What, of human construction, could withstand the impact of an icy continent, driven onward by a furious storm?" Back asked. What indeed? Time and again the ship creaked and groaned; time and again only a sudden slacking off of the pressure or the dying of the wind saved them. Doors started and could not be closed; oak beams eighteen inches square bent or were raised off their shelves. They shored the ship from the inside and added planking and heavy stanchions, reinforcing the ship even more. "The concussion was absolutely appalling," Back wrote on a bad day in February, "rending the lining and bulkheads in every part, loosening some shores and stanchions, . . . and compressing others with such force as to make the turpentine ooze out of their extremities. One fir plank placed horizontally between the beams and the shores, actually glittered with globules."

Bolts started; nails were forced out of wood. Seldom was the ice quiet. Rushing noises were heard under the ship, and the ice ground constantly. Even the ice master, an experienced whaler, had never heard the rushing noise and did not know what it was, but it usually preceded another attack from the ice, another heaving and cracking of beams. Ice forced under the ship by pressure from behind froze to the ship, to a depth of twenty-four feet; other ice would then strike against this ice, tilting the ship up, listing it to port or starboard, while the ship itself groaned with pain.

Sometimes in major storms the ice would hold firm, the ship safe and quiet in its ice cradle. At other times there would be no wind at all, yet the ice around the ship would begin to stir, to break up, drive on the ship. "Such," Back wrote, "are the strange caprices of Polar navigation, and such the revolutions of feeling to which the adventurer is continually subject." But in truth anxiety was constant. Moments of peace did come; the men exercised outside the ship, made men and women out of snow. The officers put on a show once. The crew countered with its own show. Social conditions in England had improved to the point where only two or three of the crew were unable to write. All could read. But by January the symptoms of scurvy had appeared. Three men ultimately died of it. Back doubled the lime juice allowance, but it helped only a little. Lime juice is not nearly as strong an antiscorbutic as lemon juice, but England was growing lime trees in its West Indian colonies, so lime juice it was. Men complained of a stiffness in the legs that would not go away, no matter what the surgeons tried. Worse, perhaps, was the moisture. The heating apparatus, an experimental design never before tried in a ship, failed miserably, and the water vapor in the lower decks where the men lived and slept condensed on the beams, ran down the sides and dripped on their heads. The groaning of the ice, the unpredictability of its movements, the sounds of the ship in pain—anxiety was a constant for all of them, the inescapable drone of their daily lives. That they did not all go mad is a wonder.

By March 7 the *Terror* had been wedged up by the ice four feet eight inches above her flotation line. A week later the pressure broke her stern post and the rate of leaking in the ship increased to three feet of water an hour. Then the leaks closed up from counterpressure in another direction. Not until July 14 did the ice finally let them go, and even then the ship nearly capsized as half of the huge block of ice that was frozen to the bottom relaxed its grip and the other half of the block rose toward the surface, tilting the ship so sharply on its side that the surface of the water was within inches of flooding and sinking it. This ice had to be sawn off the bottom. Then they were free at last, but the ship was broken. The pumps would have to be manned twenty-four hours a day. The keel was damaged, the stern post smashed. It was the unanimous opinion of all on board that they should go home. The crew could not keep up with the pumping; the ship listed to starboard; it was so heavy in the water that it could move no more than two or three knots an hour. They barely made it to Ireland, where Back ran the ship aground on the first available beach to save it from sinking. The *Terror* had passed its test; it had survived, just. But Barrow's idea—that it was safe to let a ship be frozen into the pack—had proved to be wrong.

That did not mean, to be sure, that he was ready to change his mind.

Back was knighted for his efforts, but with his return the bubble of interest the Admiralty had shown in a revived program of Arctic exploration popped. The Royal Geographical Society gave Back its Founders Medal, other honors came from other sources, but the Admiralty had strict budgets to meet. The Admiralty was sending ships all over the world to map its oceans; it was riding shotgun on trade with India, with South America, with Africa. Russia and France were both building up their navies, no one was sure to what end. It was the policy of the Royal Navy to match the size of its fleet with those of its two biggest rivals put together, and the Admiralty was hard pressed, indeed it failed, to keep up the rate of shipbuilding this required. Back's expedition had been utterly profitless, even scientifically. The scientific aspects of exploratory work were becoming more important, but James Clark Ross's discovery of the North Magnetic Pole had capped scientific interest in the Arctic. A few scraps of coastline remained undiscovered, and public interest was still strong, up to a point. That point had been reached when Richard King asked the public for a mere thousand pounds to go back to Chantrey Inlet. He came up six hundred pounds short.

Yet exploration in the Far North did go on. The Hudson's Bay Company, that old, dusty, parsimonious organization of complacent London businessmen combing their splendid livings from the skins of beaver, caribou, fox, buffalo, and the occasional wolverine, and the labors of Indian hunters, had become tired of supporting Royal Navy expeditions and watching the credit go exclusively to Royal Navy personnel. The company also faced a problem. As the Canadian historian Kenneth Coates explained in a 1988 paper, the HBC's charter was coming up for renewal in 1841. Royal charters with huge land grants and monopoly trading rights had stopped being the way to do business a century or two before. "Chartered enterprise," wrote Coates, "once the engine of the Empire, no longer found favour with the British public, and in the eyes of many politicians and government officials, the Hudson's Bay Company was becoming increasingly anachronistic." The event called for a public relations effort on the HBC's part to show the government that the HBC was more than just a fur trade monopoly. "The Board of Trade and the Colonial Office, it was hoped," Coates went on, "could not help but take note of the Company's unselfish commitment to scientific adventure."

In 1836, accordingly, the HBC organized a small party of traders and their voyageur employees, now mostly transplanted Scotsmen, to take up residence on Great Bear Lake that winter, the same severe winter George Back spent listening to his ship crack and groan in Frozen Strait. The following spring they would descend the Mackenzie, follow Franklin's route west along the coast, and make it all the way to Point Barrow this time, tracing at last the two-hundred-mile stretch of coastline that Franklin had not been able to cover. Then, as circumstances permitted, it would descend the Coppermine to the coast during the following summer, 1838, head east, make it to Franklin's Point Turnagain, go on from there to Chantrey Inlet and beyond, and solve what was now the great question of Boothia's status, raised by Back's failure to sail northeast out of Chantrey Inlet and find out whether Boothia was an island or a peninsula. They would travel much the same way Franklin had traveled on his second expedition, in two small wooden boats, with a few men in each boat. They would hire Indian hunters to hunt for them along the way, living as much as possible off the land. Those were their instructions, and that was what they did.

Peter Warren Dease, who had held down the fort and cached food for Franklin on Great Bear Lake when Franklin descended the Mackenzie ten years earlier, was named as one of the two leaders. The other was Thomas Simpson, a young man with only limited experience in the wilderness but a great deal of energy; he was the nephew of George Simpson, the HBC's resident governor. The younger Simpson came with a chip on his shoulder. He resented the Royal Navy explorers, most especially George Back. He was ambitious and craved fame. In private letters to friends he took credit for the expedition's successes, both as it was going on and after it was over, and blamed Dease for its failures. Simpson was also a bigot, hating the half-breeds who made up so much of the population of northern Canada and such a large percentage of the employees of the HBC. This poisonous attitude, as we shall shortly see, would bring to a temporary conclusion the HBC's interest in any further search for the Northwest Passage and an end to Simpson's life.

The first excursion was all successes. Dease and Simpson and a party of eighteen HBC men wintered in 1836–37 at Fort Chipewyan on Lake Athabasca, where they built their two boats, *Castor* and *Pollux,* gathered pemmican and the other necessary supplies, and waited out the winter. Simpson amused himself by reading George Back's account of his trip down the Great Fish River; "it contains, indeed, little thought," he wrote his uncle, "with no small portion of French sentimentality and self-admiration." They left for the Mackenzie on June 1. A month later they reached the mouth of Great Bear River, which empties Great Bear Lake into the Mackenzie. On June 30 George Simpson wrote to remind his nephew, in case he needed reminding, that failure might lead to the end of the HBC's charter. In other words: succeed or else.

At Great Bear River four of the eighteen men were detached and sent up to the far eastern end of Great Bear Lake to build a fort, Fort Confidence, for their winter residence. The rest, Simpson, Dease, and twelve others, continued down the Mackenzie to its mouth and arrived July 9. They ran into small groups of Inuit, not the threatening crowd Franklin encountered, and found them all friendly and eager to trade. They moved west along the coastline, running into the same ice, shoals, persistent fog, the same hardships that Franklin had faced; but they were a little luckier than Franklin. They reached Return Reef and passed it on July 23, the season still young. Franklin had been stuck there for a week. Six days later, however, they ran into ice "so packed & Close in Shore that we were obliged to land, & from the highest spots we Could find no open Water to be seen." By July 31 they had been able to move only a mile or two farther. They were fifty-two miles in a straight line from Point Barrow. Simpson took five men with him and walked it. On August 6 they returned, triumphant, singing a boat song. They were in an Inuit umiak they had borrowed from a group farther west to cross the mouth of a river. They had reached Point Barrow and filled in one of the two remaining unknowns in the map of the Arctic coastline, and they had made it look easy.

They wintered at Fort Confidence, and the Indians starved once again as game fled the area and the fisheries were fished out. The trappers did what they could to feed them. This winter Simpson read

"Plutarch, Hume, Robertson, Gibbon, Shakespeare, Smollett, and dear Sir Walter"—Sir Walter Scott. He also read Richard King's account of the Back expedition down the Great Fish River. It was, he said, "the most venomous thing I have read for a long time." Simpson saw himself as in competition with Back and mentions him again and again in his letters, wondering whether he would encounter him somewhere on the coast that coming summer. He could not know that Back had returned from his disastrous voyage by this time. Simpson spent much of the winter hunting with Dogrib and Hare Indians and living with them, hardening himself, learning Indian methods for surviving in the wild and the intense cold.

On June 6 Simpson, Dease, and their party left Fort Confidence and had reached the Bloody Falls of the Coppermine by July 1. Seventeen years earlier the Inuit had vanished at Franklin's approach; now another family of Inuit ran away at theirs, leaving their dogs and possessions behind. The sea beyond was rock solid. They were going east, over Franklin's route again, but it was two weeks before they could go anywhere, and this time things were not so easy. In the letter they wrote to the governor and the board in London, they described their movement along the coast as "one incessant, we may say desperate, struggle with the same cold obdurate foe [i.e., ice], in which the boats sustained serious damage, several planks being more than half cut through." On August 20, about the time John Franklin had turned back, yet more ice stopped Simpson and Dease on the shores of Kent Peninsula just a few miles from Point Turnagain, Franklin's farthest. Once again Simpson offered to walk on, taking a few men with him down the shore of the peninsula for a hundred miles. The sea opened up there into a gulf, now named Queen Maud Gulf, and the ice was gone, and he hoped on his return to find Dease following him in the boats. But the boats were still frozen in. They could go nowhere but home. They left the shore of Kent Peninsula, struggled through ice for a day—and then, suddenly, the ice was simply gone. They were at the mouth of the Coppermine in four days, under full sail, with little ice in sight. Five days after that they had returned to Great Bear Lake. They had discovered a gulf to the east of Kent Peninsula, and a strait they named Dease Strait between Kent Peninsula and a body of land to the north that they named after the new queen, Victoria. But they hadn't gotten close to Boothia, or even Chantrey Inlet. They had hardly gone farther than Franklin.

In accordance with his nature, Simpson blamed Dease. Once the ice went out he would have soldiered on, he told his friends in private letters. Dease was too cautious, too old, too unadventurous. Simpson still did not understand that forethought and caution are how people survive in the Arctic. He was, however, beginning to understand that their exploits were gathering increasing attention in England and that honors, or at least a measure of fame, might be in store for them. The journal of the Royal Geographical Society had published their account of the expedition to Point Barrow, and that had stirred up the press. Simpson played to this interest, emphasizing the adventurous aspects in his accounts. His letter to a friend in Scotland, written shortly after their return, was designed for the press and appeared in *The Inverness Courier* when it reached Scotland. "On the 30th we reached the Copper Mine," he wrote,

> and found it still fast! It gave way a few days afterwards, and we descended all its terrific rapids, then swollen to their utmost height, along with the driving ice; grand but perilous running I assure you. Often we had to pull for life or death, to avoid the suction of the precipitous cliffs, along whose base the waters raged with overwhelming fury.

If it appeared in one British paper, it would soon appear in others. Even *The Times* reprinted articles from the provincial press. Nowhere in the piece does the name *Dease* appear. Simpson closes by remarking that he has "three tamed white wolves, too, of my own taking." One wonders what Peter Dease thought about all this.

Next summer their luck returned, and they headed east again, reaching Point Turnagain and then Queen Maud Gulf a month earlier than they had the previous year. What ice there was was broken and navigable, and they made their way along the coast to Adelaide Peninsula, naming features of the landscape as they went, including Simpson Strait, which separates the peninsula from King William Island. They crossed to the island's south shore. By mid-August they were at Chantrey Inlet. On August 16 they found the cache Richard King had left behind on Montreal Island in the inlet. The two bags of pemmican were "alive with maggots," and the cocoa was spoiled, so they took the fish hooks and the gunpowder as "a memento of our voyage having succeeded," wrote Dease, "in Joining what was unknown between Point Turnagain & the discoveries of Captn. Sr. Geo Back." That day they polled the men: should they go on and find out "whether or not the Sea we are now on is connected by Straits or otherwise with the Gulph of Boothia or whether what is named by Sr. John Ross Boothia Land is a part of, or separated from, the Continent of America"? The sea was free of ice, the weather still good. They voted to go on. Near the head of the inlet, however, the wind picked up to a gale and they were forced to shore.

The wind held for four days. They made some progress up the coast-line, climbed hills to search out the landscape, and tried to determine what lay to the east, which looked so much like an open sea, but by the twentieth they had changed their minds about continuing. It was simply too risky. They were convinced, nevertheless, as George Back had been, that Boothia was separated from the continent by a strait. They took that conviction home with them. There they found a letter from George Simpson granting them leave for a year from life at the ends of the earth in Fort Confidence. They could winter in the much more comfortable quarters at Great Slave Lake. They left for it at once.

Simpson would claim that he—and characteristically, he alone—had discovered the Northwest Passage, but evidently he meant by that the passage to the Northwest (that is, the stretch between Return Reef and Point Barrow), while he referred to the coastline to the east of Chantrey Inlet as the Northeast Passage. He hoped to open that to geography as well and had planned another trip to the area, following Back's route down the Great Fish River, then east. Dease spent their year off getting married to his common-law wife—they were grandparents—then sailing for Great Britain, where he had never been. Simpson spent his time making his plans. He wrote to his uncle in Montreal, and to the gover-nor of the HBC, Sir Henry Pelly, in London, and waited for an answer. That last stretch of coastline, the strait that he, and nearly everyone else, now believed connected the Gulf of Boothia with the Arctic Ocean, had to be mapped; it was all that was left, the last stone in the arch. He offered his life savings, five hundred pounds, to the HBC to use if money were an issue. "Fame I will have," he wrote his uncle yet again, "but it must be *alone.*"

When no answer was forthcoming, he decided to take passage for London himself and confront the HBC face to face. He left the north country for the Red River settlement, en route to Europe through the United States. On the same day, June 3, that the governor and commit-tee in London were writing to approve Simpson's plan, Simpson left Red River for Minnesota with two half-breeds, John Bird and Antoine

Legros. Simpson hated half-breeds, hated what he thought of as their moral laxity, but that by itself does not explain what happened. On June 14, now accompanied by two others as well, Simpson shot Bird and Legros, for reasons nobody knows. The two other men fled. When they returned the next day with reinforcements, someone shot at them. They could hear the bullet whistling past their heads. Who shot at them remains unclear, for they then found Simpson dead in his bedroll. The top of his head was blown off. The testimony, writes historian William Barr, "clearly pointed to suicide," but the jury has never come in on this event and some historians believe that the arrogant Simpson, accompanied by nobody except half-breeds on an empty trail in the middle of the Minnesota wilderness, let his hatred get the better of him, and paid the price.

It was a pity. The queen had already honored Simpson and Dease with a lifetime pension of a hundred pounds a year for their achievements in the Arctic. Dease retired on it, and on the money George Simpson had invested for him in, among others, railroad stocks. He was feted in London at a meeting of the Royal Geographical Society where he met, among others, John Barrow. He lived to be seventy-five. The real honors, it is worth noting, went to Thomas's uncle, George Simpson, whom the queen knighted, and to Sir Henry Pelly, boosted to a baronetcy. Thomas Simpson himself got a plaque in a Scottish church claiming that he had discovered the Northwest Passage, but he was a suicide and the congregation insisted it be removed.

And what of the Northwest Passage? If there had in fact been a strait connecting the Gulf of Boothia with the Arctic Ocean, Simpson might have gone on to claim the discovery of the whole length of such a passage, from the mouth of Lancaster Sound down Prince Regent Inlet to this mythical strait, then out through the passages—Simpson Strait, Dease Strait, Dolphin and Union Strait—separating the big islands of the Canadian archipelago from the mainland of North America. With Simpson's death, the HBC shut down exploration in the North for a time, and the question remained unsettled, but that did not prevent men from drawing conclusions. The spirit of speculative geography was not dead. John Barrow, certainly, was convinced that Back and Simpson were right, that the Gulf of Boothia emptied into the Arctic Ocean. At a meeting of the Royal Geographical Society held in 1845, Barrow stood up, according to Richard King, who wrote a letter to *The Athenaeum* describing the event, and said that the Northwest Passage had been discovered. It was a sensational claim, if true. Richard King was sure it was not true. He had seen the faint blue line of land that Back had missed to the east of Chantrey Inlet.

And Barrow should have known better. In the next-to-last paragraph of the book he wrote in 1845 summarizing the Arctic voyages he had been promoting so persistently since 1818, he discussed the existence or nonexistence of the strait in question, noting that "it must be admitted that conjectural geography is never safe: the direction of a coast-line, or the course of a river, can only be known, and then imperfectly, to the distance of the farthest point of sight; to arrive at correctness, they must be traced."

In the last paragraph, however, he neglects to take his own counsel. Sir John Ross's claim that the strait in question did not exist, he insists, "has since been proved to be wholly incorrect." He never stopped trying to score off John Ross's failures, and he never gave up any of his ideas. The depth of Barrow's stubbornness was truly remarkable.

CHAPTER SIXTEEN

IN EXILE FROM THE LAND OF SNOWS

With Thomas Simpson's death, the enthusiasm for further exploration in the Arctic faded away. The Simpson-Dease expeditions had answered enough questions about northern Canadian geography for Sir John Barrow to declare in that meeting of the RGS that the Northwest Passage had been found, even if it had not been navigated.

Barrow was in his late seventies in 1840, when Simpson was killed. His son, John Barrow, Jr., was an Admiralty clerk himself, known for having discovered in the attics of the Admiralty "a mass of archives lying all over the place, gnawed by rats, mouldering with damp, stuffed into miles of shelving, or lying loose on the floor." Although he had worked in the building for forty years, the senior Barrow had never visited the attic. His son brought order to the archives, found a place to house them, and thereby preserved the sources for the history of the Royal Navy. He too was a prolific author, writing four or five books of travel, then a biography of Francis Drake, after that a miscellany called *Memoirs of the Naval Worthies of Queen Elizabeth's Reign,* followed by more books of travel. His father kept busy after George Back's last voyage writing biographies of the Royal Navy figures Richard, Earl Howe, and George, Lord Anson.

His age seems not to have suggested to Barrow that he should retire. Knowing the time was not ripe for the Arctic, he had given up his quest for the Northwest Passage for the time being, but he was still capable of lobbying for support from the scientific societies in which he was a major figure—the Royal Society, the Royal Geographical Society—for expeditions to various parts of the world to solve various scientific problems. With the notable exception of Africa, where an imperial scramble for territory among the major European powers was in its initial stages, exploration was becoming more scientific, and James Clark Ross's discovery of the North Magnetic Pole had galvanized those scientists interested in the earth's magnetic field.

The magnetic crusade, one of the largest international scientific operations in the history of science, was one consequence of the younger Ross's achievement. In an 1840 article in *The Quarterly* the astronomer John Herschel, son of the much more famous astronomer William Herschel, explained what the crusade was about. The science of terrestrial magnetism was a science of observation, not experiment, he wrote, and it required the taking of magnetic measurements "in every region of the globe and extending over long periods of time." Unlike other physical facts about the globe—prevailing winds; tides and currents; geographical configuration, all of them relatively stable—"the magnetic state of our globe is one of swift and ceaseless change." Keeping track of this change was of obvious utilitarian value for navigation, but it might also contribute to solving the problem of what caused the earth to generate a magnetic field in the first place, and why it fluctuated so constantly.

All of Europe was interested in terrestrial magnetism, and theories about what caused it and how it worked circulated through scientific societies in France, Germany, and the United States as well as the Scandinavian countries and Great Britain. The theories were mostly wrong. One British scientist thought the earth's magnetism was a result of "ferruginous" matter in the atmosphere—iron filings, presumably, floating in the sky. A Dane argued that there were four magnetic poles, not two. The idea behind the magnetic crusade was to add facts to these speculations, establish magnetic stations all over the globe, map isogonic lines—which are lines of equal compass variation—globally, and coordinate all the observations by having the people who manned the stations make them on fixed days of the year, simultaneously throughout the day. Stations in Europe had already been set up. Scientists now wanted to extend them to more remote regions. Alexander von Humboldt, the German geologist and naturalist, wrote the Royal Society in April 1836, arguing that no nation was so well placed as Great Britain to undertake the setting up of stations in far-flung areas.

Edward Sabine, one of John Barrow's protégés, was deeply interested in the earth's magnetism and had become a powerful figure in the Royal Society. He adopted the crusade as his own; eventually he would become the repository and interpreter of the vast amount of data it generated. In 1838 the recently formed British Association for the Advancement of Science voted a set of resolutions supporting the crusade. One of them called for a naval expedition to sail into the high southern latitudes, establish magnetic stations on remote southern islands and discover, if possible, the South Magnetic Pole. Herschel was a member of the committee that was appointed to approach the government and sell this proposal. The Royal Society threw its whole weight behind the idea. The East India Company would cooperate. The Royal Navy said yes. So did the Whig government under Lord Melbourne. It would be a naval expedition. James Clark Ross would lead it, and it sailed in 1839.

Ross was the ideal, practically the only, candidate for the job. He was by now thoroughly familiar with the hazards of polar navigation. In 1836, when a portion of the whaling fleet got trapped in the ice in Davis Strait, the Admiralty had chosen Ross to lead the rescue mission. Most of the whalers, as it happened, saved themselves, but Ross had had the chance to test himself with a command of his own and he could give himself high marks. A whaling captain who watched him work called him "the finest officer I have met with, the most persevering indefatigable man you can imagine. He is perfectly idolized by everyone." Not only was he capable, he was well versed in the science of terrestrial magnetism, having spent nearly two years on a magnetic survey of the British Isles and having served on a committee that developed an improved shipboard compass that became standard for the Royal Navy.

This is not the place to tell in any detail the story of Ross's four-year voyage into the Antarctic region. On the first of his three attempts to penetrate the pack ice that surrounds Antarctica, he broke through into the great body of water now known as the Ross Sea and found land: a mountain range ten thousand feet high and, farther south, two volcanoes, one of them active, which he named Mount Erebus, after his own ship. The other was dormant, and he named it Mount Terror, after the second ship, the *Terror,* the same ship that George Back had beached in Ireland after his disastrous attempt to reach Repulse Bay. The Admiralty had recovered and rebuilt it.

Ross was also the first to see the astonishing barrier known now as the Ross Ice Shelf, whose western end abuts the two volcanoes; it is a layer of ice a thousand feet thick, two to three hundred of it above water, and extending to the east for hundreds of miles. The Ross Shelf is the largest of the great ice shelves that are now beginning to disappear from the Antarctic shore with global warming, and the source of many of the tabular icebergs that characterize the waters that surround the continent of Antarctica.

Ross's two other attempts to penetrate the pack were not as successful, but he did establish his magnetic observatories, staying at some islands for months to make the instrument readings called for and generating thousands of pages of data in the process. He did not return to England until 1843, four years and five months after he left. A knighthood awaited him (although he hesitated to accept it because he did not want to be confused with his uncle), as did medals from the Royal Geographical Society and its French equivalent, and marriage to the fiancée he had left behind. The public, however, was much less interested in Antarctica than in the Arctic. Ross was not lionized as Franklin and Parry had been. He was worn out, in fact; he had gone on every one of Parry's voyages; he had commanded the other small boat that the two of them and their crews had tried to drag over the ice to the North Pole; he had spent four years with his uncle in Prince Regent Inlet, and now four years in the ice-riddled seas of Antarctica. That was enough ice and cold for any man. He promised his young wife he would never again lead an expedition to the ends of the earth. It took him four years to write his book on the expedition; Murray, knowing that interest in it had died, printed only fifteen hundred copies. Ross never finished the descriptive work on oceanic invertebrates he had taken on as his own scientific task.

What, then, did the world learn from this last voyage? The evidence Ross gathered indicated that in the south, at least, only one magnetic pole existed, exploding the theory that there were four. Otherwise the trip turned out not to be that useful in geomagnetic terms. The magnetic crusade as a whole was declared a success in 1849 and most of the magnetic stations Ross had set up were abandoned. But the data were so voluminous it took Sabine another twenty years to analyze and publish it, and it led to no new theories about the origins and nature of the earth's magnetic field.

The crusade did, however, highlight a problem with British science that was troubling many scientists and that affected the Admiralty. Geomagnetism was, as Herschel had pointed out, a science of observation, the collection of data on a grand scale. So was much other science of the early Victorian period. It lacked theoretical rigor, or theory of any kind in some cases. It was inductive, dependent on the collection of large amounts of data or large numbers of specimens, like the young

Charles Darwin's prodigious collection of English beetles. That could take science only so far. Science, men like Herschel argued, ought properly to begin with theories, which scientists could then devise experiments to test.

Furthermore it was led by amateurs. The Royal Society membership and its governing board were dominated by dilettantish aristocrats with no scientific training who might like to collect rock samples or chase butterflies but could not have come up with an *idea* about biological diversity or geological strata to save their estates. Worse, scientific expeditions to the far corners of the earth were conducted primarily by military officers doubling as scientists. One thinks immediately of all those Arctic expeditions in which Franklin and Ross and Parry spent so much time trying to describe auroras, which are the most ephemeral of phenomena, or heroically measuring magnetic dip, variation, and intensity in weather that constantly threatened frostbite and the loss of toes or fingers. Nearly every account written by the commanding officers of Arctic expeditions sports a scientific appendix (some published as separate volumes) containing daily, weekly, or monthly weather reports, magnetic readings, and descriptions of newly discovered species of animals and plants.

Data like this were useful, but they were not enough. Herschel and his allies wanted to professionalize science, to theorize it, to create an awards system that would inspire young men entering the sciences to seek fame and fortune by providing fundamental explanations— theories—of natural phenomena. The gold medals of the scientific societies now went to people like James Clark Ross and George Back— heroic men, perhaps, but not professional scientists.

In 1859 Charles Darwin did theorize British natural history with the theory of evolution, but the Admiralty stuck by its old methods of sending its officers for scientific training, when the need arose, to instrument makers, or to people like Sabine, who taught them how to collect, label, and preserve specimens; how to use the dipping needle or the pendulum that measured gravitational intensity; what kinds of questions to ask the natives in whatever part of the world they might wind up; and how to compile vocabularies of their native languages. In 1849 the Admiralty published the *Admiralty Manual,* which put these instructions into writing. John Herschel prepared it. Despite Herschel's interest in theory, it deals only with the hows of data collection.

In a sense the *Admiralty Manual* is a noble document, codifying for its nonscientist officers what their responsibilities were in the collection of data for scientific use, not only for British scientists but for scientists worldwide. But the Admiralty's own scientific interests remained primarily geographical, its principal scientific, or quasi-scientific, mission the making of coastal charts and maps. After Croker's departure in 1830 the Hydrography Office under Francis Beaufort flourished. Not only were more surveys undertaken of more coastlines, islands, shoals, and other features of the seas, but Beaufort exacted a level of precision from his surveyors that was new. Everyone remembers the voyage of the *Beagle* because Charles Darwin was the ship's naturalist, and the ultimate result was the theory of evolution, but few remember that the *Beagle* was a survey ship, sent to South America and thence around the world to map the Straits of Magellan, the southwest coast of South America, and various Pacific islands, and that Robert FitzRoy, the ship's captain, produced definitive charts of these areas, charts Beaufort's biographer calls "a monumental achievement." Many of the charts prepared under Beaufort's direction were in use well into the twentieth century. Beaufort also expected his surveyors to keep track of weather, tides, and magnetic variation. He was aware that the work was descriptive, not theoretical, but it was still worth doing. Weather readings, for example, must be collected "with a view of assisting to provide authentic data collected from all parts of the world, and ready for the use of future labourers whenever some accidental discovery, or the direction of some powerful mind should happily rescue that science [meteorology] from its present neglected state." Beaufort was banking scientific data for the future.

Beaufort believed, by the way, that Herschel was right and that English science was not only untheoretical but not rigorous enough even in the amassing of data, and he was one of the leaders in a fight to reform the Royal Society in 1827 that failed to limit the power of the aristocratic amateurs who saw it as a kind of club. Afterward he refused to rejoin the society's council, and Sir John Franklin was substituted in his stead. In 1830 a second attempt at reform also failed, which prompted the founding of the British Association for the Advancement of Science, an organization limited to genuine scientists.

But mapping was always the most important scientific, or semiscientific, activity to Beaufort, and to the Admiralty, and it is interesting in that respect to look at John Barrow's second map of the Arctic, published in 1845 in his *Voyages of Discovery and Research within the Arctic Regions, from the Year 1818 to the Present Time.* What had been gained?

How much had all these costly, dangerous expeditions learned? For twenty-seven years the British had been sawing their way into and out of frozen-up harbors, pulling their surveying equipment on sledges over the ice, eating hardtack and salt meat, waiting out endless silent lightless winters. Was it worth it?

What is immediately noticeable about the map is how scattered the results were, and how much remained to be learned. The east coast of Greenland, for example, was still nothing but a dotted line, a conjecture. The Spitzbergen archipelago, often surrounded by open water in the summer, was only partly mapped. No one with surveying skills had sailed into Frobisher Strait, apparently, since Frobisher, and where it reached an end no one knew. Fury and Hecla Strait, connecting the upper reaches of Hudson Bay with Prince Regent Inlet, was delineated, but everything to the east of it was conjectural, including Cockburn Island, which was in fact not a separate island but part of Baffin Island. Wellington Channel, running north out of Barrow Strait, was a route to who knew what. Most of the surrounding islands of the Canadian archipelago were unknown as to their extent and existed simply as truncated lines on the map where Parry, or Simpson and Dease, or Franklin had seen a portion of their coastlines. Other islands in the archipelago were completely unknown.

Names, however, were everywhere, confusing the picture. At the Hydrography Office Beaufort tried to persuade his captains to use native names when naming landmarks, but in vain. Few, says Alfred Friendly, "were completely indifferent to what a little judicious flattery might accomplish for their future careers." Thus some eighteen features of the earth's landscape are named for the two Lords Melville, father and son. There are nearly as many Barrows—capes, straits, islands, hills. Beaufort himself for that matter appears "a dozen or so" times, most notably on the Beaufort Sea, and he let the designations stand.

But the coast of North America from Point Barrow on the west to Chantrey Inlet and a little beyond in the east appears as a continuous line on the map, and this was a genuine achievement, even if, in Franklin's case, it came at the cost of eleven lives. In a sense Barrow was right. The Northwest Passage had in fact been discovered, assuming it was possible to get a ship to that coastline and follow it west to Bering Strait. That is the route Amundsen took when he sailed it for the first time in 1903–06. How to get to the coast, however, remained a major issue. Barrow was now thoroughly convinced that from Lancaster

Sound it would be possible to get there via Prince Regent Inlet, because Simpson and Dease had supposedly shown that there was a strait at the bottom of the inlet. Parry, Franklin, even Beaufort seemed to agree. Barrow's unwillingness to believe anything John Ross said was one reason for this belief. Ross, relying on Inuit testimony, had not investigated the Gulf of Boothia. The Inuit had said it was closed, there was no outlet, and had drawn a map of what the gulf looked like. Even the younger Ross did not think it worth investigating under the circumstances. Here Barrow, who had relied on native guides as a young man when he surveyed the interior of South Africa, proved to be too much the imperialist. Trust a native? How typically foolish of John Ross. It was a shame. Inuit knowledge of Inuit territory is generally what one would expect—thorough and precise. In 1909 the American explorer Robert Flaherty asked an Inuit named Wetalltok to draw by hand a map of the Belcher Islands. According to Clifford Ando, writing in *TLS*, Wetalltok's map, compared to a satellite image of the islands, is "an image of stupendous accuracy."

In the end it hardly mattered. Barrow no longer believed in a coastal route for the Northwest Passage. He thought the best, the only road to victory was the road Parry had taken on his first expedition—sail west through Lancaster Sound and Barrow Strait to Melville Island, then into the pack, and let the pack take it from there. The ice would most likely liberate the hardy voyager who trusted to this route at the edge of the open polar sea, and it was easy sailing from there to the Pacific. Barrow's certainties had only hardened with age. Now in his early eighties, under the receptive Tory government of Robert Peel, Barrow was planning the crown of his career, his final expedition to the Arctic. The *Erebus* and the *Terror* were back from Antarctica, waiting to do what they had been designed to do: withstand the pressures of the pack. And this time there would be no flirting with coastlines. The fate of the *Fury* was not to be repeated. The pack would not force *Erebus* ashore somewhere near, say, Kent Peninsula, because *Erebus* and *Terror* would be in the ice or, more likely, free of it, out of the pack, sailing rapidly, blissfully across what Barrow was still dead sure tossed out there in the vast uncharted emptiness—an open polar sea.

The only question was, who would lead this expedition? He wanted James Clark Ross. Everyone wanted James Clark Ross. He was the obvious choice. But Ross had promised his wife he would not go back into the ice. He kept his promise and turned the assignment down. Barrow's second choice was an eager young officer named James Fitzjames, who had not yet reached captain's rank. Fitzjames, for all his eagerness, had no experience in the Arctic, and the Admiralty thought he was too young for such an important command. Parry was fifty-five years old, busy managing both the navy's packet service and its steam department; by 1845 about a quarter of the navy's ships were powered by steam engines. Parry was not well besides. Who then among the Arctic veterans was available? Back? Beechey?

John Franklin was the one who wanted the assignment the most. He had been badly bloodied in Tasmania, fired from his job as governor of the island in a way that reflected on his honor. Franklin had something to prove. At an age when most men of his stature in Great Britain, indeed in the world, would have been looking toward a comfortable job, a comfortable retirement, Franklin wanted nothing more than to tackle the ice yet again.

Poor Franklin. It's the only way to describe his bad luck in being assigned to the governorship of a prison colony, this one in particular. During Franklin's tenure as governor, London abolished the transportation of prisoners to Australia, and Tasmania became the British Empire's only prison colony, the dumping ground for the empire's jails, forced to accept whatever their honorable lordships sent its way. By 1837, when Franklin arrived, the island had a population of some 42,000 people, 17,000 of whom were convicts, the rest free. Of the latter, some were settlers who had come to Tasmania in search of opportunity. The others were "ticket of leave" freedmen and -women, convicts who had completed their terms. When the first colonists arrived, the island was occupied by indigenous people, perhaps three to five thousand of them. In 1837 only fifty remained. Franklin did what he could to protect them. The last one is supposed to have died in 1868, but in fact aboriginal bloodlines still exist in Tasmania, all, however, of mixed race.

Franklin's official title was Lieutenant Governor, but the "Lieutenant" was merely a holdover from the time when the government of the island had been run from Australia. Franklin did not have to answer to anybody but the secretary for the colonies in London, Lord Glenelg in 1837. It was Glenelg who had named him to the post. On his return from Greece in 1834 Franklin had hung about the Admiralty with other unemployed naval officers, hoping for an assignment and seizing, rather pathetically, on marks of favor. Sir James Graham, still first lord at the time, had shown him "a marked attention," Franklin wrote Lady Jane, "by leaving his wife's side to come forward and shake me by the hand, which I did not observe him to do to any other captain, though there were others around me." Marks of favor or not, in 1836 Back was picked, not Franklin, to lead the expedition to Repulse Bay. Lady Jane suggested that he try to obtain service with a foreign government. Franklin would have none of that; foreign service was a career killer in the Royal Navy. For the time being, the Admiralty had no use for him.

The government was not unmindful of Franklin's eagerness for a post, and the Colonial Office eventually offered him the governorship of Antigua. Lady Franklin advised him to turn it down. This post was a lieutenant governorship in fact as well as name, the salary was commensurately low, and, as Franklin explained to Glenelg, he had been accustomed to command. To be taking orders would affect his reputation. Glenelg agreed that the post would be beneath his dignity. Not long before, the governorship of Tasmania had come open. Would that be acceptable? The salary was twice as high as at Antigua, the post much more important. The Franklins said yes.

Franklin Square stands in the heart of Hobart, the capital of Tasmania, and in the heart of the square stands a statue of Franklin himself. A river in the west of the island is named after him, as is a township in the interior. But it was no wonder he was so eager to go back to the Arctic when it was all over. Poor Franklin indeed. He was not prepared for a life in politics. He ran harmonious ships, but he was a commander, used to being obeyed, not to negotiating with subordinates, and in Tasmania he inherited a set of subordinates who were deeply attached to the previous governor—two of them had, indeed, married the governor's daughters—and were determined to run things the way they had always been run. He tried to bring a modicum of culture to a colony interested almost exclusively in making money. His attempts to establish a school were a dispiriting failure. He asked his wife's opinions on governmental matters and was attacked for practicing petticoat government. He also had to contend with a virulent and vicious opposition press that mocked and opposed him at every opportunity and was only slightly less obnoxious to Lady Jane. "Ignorance animated by self-interest and disguised by typography: such was the prevailing note of Tasmanian journalism in this period," says Franklin biographer H. D. Traill. Most of the policies Franklin had to administer were made in London. Whether he agreed with them or not, and they were often themselves ignorant and animated by self-interest, he had no choice but to administer them. In the early 1840s the market for Tasmanian land collapsed along with demand for Tasmanian farm products, and Franklin had to preside over a major economic downturn and was of course blamed for it.

Lady Jane traveled, as she always did, sailing to New Zealand to visit the governor of that colony and to the new settlement at present-day Melbourne in Australia, traveling overland from there to Sydney with a police escort through what was then mostly wilderness. She was gone nine months. She was the first woman to make the trip through that part of the Australian bush. Lady Jane and Sir John traveled together across the western Tasmanian wilderness and were briefly happy while this adventure lasted. James Clark Ross spent the southern winter with them after his discovery of the Ross Sea; his second in command, Francis R. M. Crozier, fell in love with Sophy Cracroft, one of Franklin's nieces and Lady Jane's lifelong traveling companion; but she turned him down when he proposed marriage. Ross was a welcome break from Tasmanian politics.

Franklin was recalled in 1842. Much too late in the game he had fired the most troublesome of his subordinates, a man named John Montagu, who at once took his grievances to London and complained to the new colonial secretary, the famously haughty and intractable Lord Stanley. Stanley ignored Franklin's written explanation of events, interviewed Montagu in person, and sided with the latter, issuing a report that reflected not only on Franklin's abilities but on his sense of honor. Franklin's tenure in Tasmania was over, and he and his family sailed for London.

His departure, at least, was more satisfying than his dismissal. The people, as opposed to the press, liked Franklin, lined the streets when he left, doffed their caps, cheered him, and waved handkerchiefs. It was not unlike the send-offs given to expeditions on their way to the Arctic, and he was still, after all, Sir John Franklin, Arctic hero, the man who ate his boots. And he had done his best and stayed honest in difficult circumstances. As a politician, however, his best was nowhere good enough. Lady Jane wrote home that Tasmania was "a country where people should have hearts of stone and frames of iron," and she knew her husband was no such person. He could not calculate his responses. If he saw his duty, he did it, no matter what the damage to his own interests. He could not read people, took them at face value. He was badly hurt when they betrayed him. "Sir John's sensitiveness," she wrote, "is beyond conception."

Back in London Franklin went to Lord Stanley and tried to get some sort of satisfaction from him, some acknowledgment at least that he had been treated very badly by the Colonial Office. He did not mind being recalled; it was the deeply embarrassing way it was handled he objected to. Stanley, who seemed incapable of making an apology, conceded that perhaps here and there Franklin had a point, but his concessions were so grudging, so mean, that Franklin could not feel that his honor had been vindicated. He wrote a short book in his own defense, not for publication but for distribution to his friends. He finished it only a week or two before he left for the Arctic for the final time and never saw a copy of it. It tries to present the facts as drily as possible and to avoid any hint of self-righteousness. It does not entirely succeed, but it is, generally, a dignified account. Lady Jane helped him write it. Preparations for the voyage were occupying most of his time and attention in any case. He was back in his element now, on deck, a sea captain again. If his little book would not redeem him, discovering the Northwest Passage certainly would.

Sir John Franklin just before his departure, 1845
(*Illustrated London News*)

TOWARD NO EARTHLY POLE

For now the strong snows in some iron place
Have covered them; their end shall not be said
Till all the hidden parts of time be plain
And all the writing of all years be read.

—Algernon Charles Swinburne,
"The Death of Sir John Franklin"

CHAPTER SEVENTEEN

The Glorious Departure

It was not without hesitation that the Admiralty chose John Franklin to lead the climactic final expedition in search of the Northwest Passage. Franklin had not had command of a ship since he sailed the *Rainbow* home from Greece in the spring of 1834, and he had not sailed a full-size ship into the ice since 1818, when he took the *Trent* to Spitzbergen with Buchan. Most of his experience in the Arctic had been on land, or in small boats coasting the land. Barrow had doubts about him, chiefly owing to his age. James Fitzjames, Barrow's first choice, was a lively, droll man of thirty-three, very charming, very appealing. Franklin was fifty-eight years old; he would be fifty-nine when the expedition left. Heavy to begin with, he had grown heavier as he grew older. A formal portrait, taken by the daguerreotype process on board the *Erebus* not long before the ships left, shows him trussed up in full dress uniform with his medals pinned to his chest and looking something like a stuffed bear.

But he was determined to go. He *had* to go, *had* to wipe out the memory of Tasmanian politics and his own political ineptitude. The Far North was his comfort zone. His Arctic brethren could see how desperate he was. George Back, Franklin came to believe, conspired against his appointment, perhaps wanting the glory for himself, but the Admiralty was unlikely to choose a man who had done as badly in the ice as Back had done in 1836. And the rest of Franklin's friends were in his corner. Franklin was "a fitter man to go than any I know," Parry told the first lord, then Lord Haddington, "and if you don't let him go, the man will die of disappointment." From his old friend John Richardson, who was a doctor, Franklin secured a note that stated, "I believe your constitution to be perfectly sound, and your bodily strength sufficient for all the calls that can be made upon it in conducting a squadron even through an icy sea." The council of the Royal Society, of which Franklin was a member, recommended him to the Admiralty, which sent the recommendation to Peel, the prime minister. Beaufort, enormously influential in the Admiralty, thought he was the right man and said so. The first lord summoned Franklin to his office for an interview. He raised the issue of his age, his fitness, the wear and tear of time on the human body. "I know time has made great inroads on my constitution," said Hadding-ton. Franklin replied that if it were a walking expedition, "he should not have undertaken it, being a much stouter man than he was . . . In a ship it was different." In a ship one had only to walk the deck.

Two days later the Admiralty appointed Franklin to the command. He was old, yes, but he was also a national hero, a man whose name everybody knew. He was forthright, honorable, old school, and this was definitely an old-school kind of project, a project dating deep into the nation's past, a road still to be carved out to the frontiers of national pride. Edward Sabine lobbied for the expedition for its value to science, particularly to the magnetic crusade, but in truth practical considera-tions hardly entered into it. The prime minister wanted to know all about the expedition, but he raised no objections to it. Nobody objected to it except Richard King, and he did not so much object as try once again, an obsessed man, to get the Admiralty to sponsor his own pet project back to the Great Fish River, where he could serve as a backup, a rescue operation, should Franklin find himself trapped in the ice nearby. King took his arguments to the weekly magazine *The Athenaeum,* but the Admiralty ignored him, just as the Admiralty had always ignored him. King wrote Barrow to tell him that the whole expedition was a dreadful mistake. He was sending Franklin to become "the nucleus of an iceberg."

Barrow did not reply. King's objections were easily brushed off. The Admiralty's feelings about this final expedition were positive, matching the positive mood of the nation generally. Even men like Parry, with long and hard experience trapped in the ice, seemed optimistic about Franklin's chances. As for the nation, it was 1845, the nation had enjoyed thirty years of peace, and it was feeling good about itself. Just fifteen years earlier Parliament had passed the first act to open a passenger rail-way in Great Britain, a line that ran between Liverpool and Manchester. By 1851 there would be six thousand miles of railway in the British Isles, with trains traveling up to forty or fifty miles an hour. In 1811 the first passenger steamship, nothing more than a ferry, opened service on the Clyde. By 1848 there would be 1,253 steam vessels in the Isles. Mail service in London was so efficient that in some sections mail was delivered ten times a day. Great Britain as a nation was unstoppable, a juggernaut of industrial growth and social change creating new kinds of jobs and new aristocracies of wealth. Its population had doubled in fifty years. London had grown from a city of one million to a city of two million. In 1846 the Corn Laws were repealed, free trade in agricultural products became a reality, and the work of reform seemed finally done. Literacy rates were soaring and new magazines, new newspapers appeared to satisfy the demand of readers for information. Gas lighting had replaced the old oil streetlamps in London and the city positively glittered at night. Huge sewers were being built in the city to drain it of its appalling smells.

In such a context, surrounded by success, by improvement, by an empire already the most extensive in history, what could go wrong? The new screw propellers had transformed the use of steam power in ships and both the *Erebus* and the *Terror* were fitted with railway steam engines and screw propellers. How could the ice stop them now? Nature was bowing to the power of engineering. What was pack ice but another mechanical problem to be solved?

Franklin did not have much time. He won the assignment in February and the Admiralty scheduled his departure for May. Everything had to be rushed—manning the ships, fitting steam engines into the holds and propellers into the sterns, stocking them with food. Barrow, with his usual unshakable confidence, thought the whole voyage could be pulled off in a single season, but the ships were stocked with enough food to last three years. Franklin chose Francis R. M. Crozier, the same man who had been second in command to James Ross in Antarctica and who had wanted to marry his niece Sophy Cracroft, to command the *Terror*. On his own ship, the *Erebus*, James Fitzjames was second to Franklin and responsible for the day-to-day running of the ship. Fitzjames also picked most of the junior officers for the expedition, young men like himself. Large numbers were clamoring to go and would-be explorers crowded into Franklin's house to plead their case in person.

Both ships, as usual, had ice masters who were whaling captains with years of experience in the ice. The ships themselves were strengthened even beyond the strengthening they had been given for Ross's voyage to Antarctica, and encased with iron plates from the bow to twenty feet back of the bow. The smaller ship, the *Terror,* had an engine of twenty horsepower, the larger an engine of twenty-five, and each carried ninety tons of coal. To keep the men happy should they have to spend a winter in the ice, each ship was provided with a large library, twelve hundred books in the case of the *Terror;* there were educational equipment, slates, pens, ink, paper. The Admiralty provided Franklin with a daguerreotype camera. The public subscribed money for a mechanical hand organ for each ship capable of playing fifty different tunes. Ten of them were hymns. Franklin also took his own personal sterling flatware, decorated with his crest.

Whether twenty-five horsepower was enough to force a ship through pack ice was a question yet to be answered. But so far only one naval expedition ship, the *Fury,* had failed to return from the Arctic, and her crew had been saved. Even George Back in the *Terror,* and George Lyon in the miserable *Griper,* had managed to limp home. Sir John Ross had been forced to abandon his ship, the *Victory,* but that was Ross, and Ross's had been a private, not a naval, expedition. Francis Crozier, furthermore, was an expert on steam. He had taken paddlewheel steamers up the Euphrates River, an extraordinary feat in itself. Everyone's spirits were up, positive, even blithe.

The one discordant note was merely superstitious. Lady Jane made a flag for Sir John, just as his first wife had done, and was sitting beside him one day shortly before the expedition left when he fell asleep on the couch and she threw the flag over his feet to protect him from the chill air. "The touch of it startled him into half-wakefulness," Frances Woodward writes. "'Why, there's a flag thrown over me,' he exclaimed. 'Don't you know that they lay the Union Jack over a corpse.'"

Thoughts like that were no doubt far from his heart when he waved a handkerchief at his wife, his daughter, and his niece as the ships left their pier. Eleanor, his daughter, reported that a dove had alit on one of the masts and stayed "for some time. Every one was pleased with the good omen." She added that "Papa has been looking so much better since he left off snuff." Nowhere does it say whether the crowds were as huge as those that came to say good-bye to the earlier Arctic expeditions, but surely there was a crowd. In its issue of May 24 *The Illustrated London News* ran an engraving of the two ships moving downriver; a portrait of Franklin, copied from the daguerreotype of him in his uniform; a picture of his comfortable cabin; and, next to it on the page, another of the little cabin occupied by Fitzjames. The reporter had toured the *Erebus* with an artist. What seemed to impress him most were the steam engine, which had once powered trains on the Greenwich Line, and the mechanism that raised the propeller out of the water so it would not be damaged by ice. Lady Jane had given the officers a monkey as a pet to take with them. Fitzjames mentioned it when he wrote from Disco; they had dressed it in trousers and a frock.

They stopped at the Orkneys, took on water and live sheep and cattle, then left for Greenland. On board "everyone's cry was, 'Now we are off at last!'" wrote Fitzjames to a friend. "No lingering look was cast behind. We drank Lady Franklin's health at the old gentleman's table, and, it being his daughter's birthday, hers too."

Fitzjames went on to characterize his shipmates. He was quite happy with the officers he shared the mess with, and they were all, he said, "very fond of Sir John Franklin, who improves very much as we come to know more of him. He is anything but nervous or fidgety; in fact, I should say remarkable for energetic decision in sudden emergencies; but I should think he might be easily persuaded where he has not already formed a strong opinion." Franklin had already given them "a pleasant account of his expectations of being able to get through the ice on the coast of America, and his disbelief in the idea that there is an open sea to the northward." So much for John Barrow's hobbyhorse.

Respectful toward Franklin, Fitzjames was livelier in his descriptions of some of the others. He found Mr. Goodsir, for example,

> long and straight, and walks upright on his toes, with his hands tucked up in each jacket pocket. He is perfectly good humoured, very well informed on general points, on natural history learned, was Curator of the Edinburgh Museum, appears to be about twenty-eight years of age, laughs delightfully, cannot be in a passion, is enthusiastic about all 'ologies, draws the insides of microscopic animals with an imaginary pointed pencil, catches phenomena in a bucket, looks at the thermometer and every other meter, is a pleasant companion, and an acquaintance to the mess. So much for Mr. Goodsir.

Mr. Reid was "the most original character of all—rough, intelligent, unpolished, with a broad north-country accent, but not vulgar, good-humoured, and honest-hearted." The purser, Osmar, had been with

Beechey in the *Blossom* when it waited in vain in Kotzebue Bay for Franklin and Parry to appear out of the fog in 1827. "I was at first inclined to think he was a stupid old man," wrote Fitzjames, "because he had a chin and took snuff," but no, he beat Fitzjames at chess and he was "always good humoured, always laughing."

Clearly it was a merry bunch, charming, delightful fellows, full of life and spirit, Fitzjames himself most of all. He wrote his journal at the little table in his cabin shown in *The Illustrated London News* and sent it back by the supply ship. He advised his correspondent, "Should you hear nothing till next June, send a letter, *via Petersburg, to Petro Paulowski,* in *Kamschatka.*" Their next stop, that is, would be Bering Strait. When he was with the *Blossom,* Osmar had received letters from England addressed to him in Kamchatka in just three months. Fitzjames, who had never been in the ice before, thought they would be in Kamchatka that summer and wrote his friend the younger John Barrow to that effect.

They sent three sailors and one marine back with the supply ship from Disco, invalided out. Another had been sent back from off the coast of England as unfit. They had started out with 134 men, including Franklin and all the officers. Now they were 129. On July 12 the *Erebus* and *Terror* left the Disco area and sailed north. Ice held them up in the northern part of Baffin Bay. While they waited for an opening, they came upon two whaling ships, and the captain of one of them, Captain Martin, spoke briefly with them and asked Franklin about his provisions. Franklin said he had "enough food for five years, and that it could be made to last for seven." It was not until 1851, however, that Captain Martin reported Franklin's remark to the Admiralty, and doubt remains whether he misheard what was said. They had food for three. Even on half-rations five years would have been a stretch, for almost certainly the bulk of their food would have been consumed before it became clear that they would have to go on half-rations. These whalers in any case were the last to see the *Erebus* and the *Terror* before they entered Lancaster Sound and disappeared.

Now there was nothing to do but wait. To distract herself, Lady Jane went traveling, taking Eleanor to see France; then she came back to England before proceeding to Madeira, where her name "procured me instant attention & civility." From Madeira she sailed to the West Indies and thence to the United States. She toured "hospitals, schools, factories, and deaf-and-dumb and blind institutions," discussed Dickens and July Fourth patriotic speeches with the mayor of Boston, and climbed the highest mountain she could find, Mount Washington in New Hampshire. She returned home in the summer of 1846.

If it took mail only three months to reach London from Kamchatka and they had made it to Bering Strait the previous summer, Jane would certainly have heard from her husband by the summer of 1846. It passed without news of any kind. The fall of 1846 came and the whaling fleet returned from Davis Strait and Lancaster Sound, but they had seen nothing. Franklin had been ordered to fill out forms, printed in six languages, that listed his latitude and longitude, put them in watertight copper cylinders, and throw them overboard; there were instructions on the forms to forward them to the Admiralty. It was standard practice, the idea being to compare the latitude and longitude of the places the cylinders were found to the latitude and longitude where they had been dropped into the ocean, to determine the direction of ocean currents. But the whalers had found no copper cylinders. They had seen no wreckage floating on the sea, no cairns along the shoreline of Lancaster Sound. A year and a half had gone by. Franklin was now sixty years old.

Lady Jane took what comfort she could from her experienced Arctic friends—Edward Parry, John Richardson, James Clark Ross, the knights of the North. They assured her that he had plenty of food, the ships were strong, they had Sylvester stoves, and the officers and crew were handpicked, the finest men in the Royal Navy. It was premature to worry. What could go wrong?

But more people than Jane Franklin were starting to worry. The first to voice alarm was Sir John Ross, who had promised Franklin that he would come for him if he should get into trouble. According to Ross, he had approached Franklin before he left and asked him, "Has anyone volunteered to follow you?" Franklin said no. "Then," Ross replied, "I shall volunteer to look for you if you are not heard of in February 1847; but pray put a notice in the cairn where you winter, *if you do proceed,* which one of the routes you take." Ross refused full retirement in September 1846 because it would have precluded him commanding a rescue expedition should the Admiralty decide to mount one. In January 1847 he wrote the Admiralty that Franklin clearly had not reached Bering Strait and in February that he had probably taken the ice "at the western end of Cornwallis or Melville Island"—the latter was Parry's farthest, where he had spent the winter of 1819–20—"and, if not totally lost, must have been carried by the ice that is known to drift to the southward, on land seen at a great distance in that direction, and from which the accumulation of ice behind them will, as in my own case, for ever prevent the return of the ships."

Ross was reasoning from what he knew were Franklin's intentions and his instructions: to proceed through Barrow Strait past Cape Walker, then run to the southwest toward the distant Banks Land, then to the Canadian coast and west. Ross proposed to sail to a harbor on the south side of Barrow Strait and use it as a base to deposit provisions at Melville Island and elsewhere in the area. The Admiralty replied to Ross's second letter the day he delivered it. No cause for alarm. The board had "already consulted and taken the opinions of Sir John Barrow, Sir Edward Parry, Sir James C. Ross, Colonel Sabine, Doctor Richardson and others, who were unanimously of the opinion that it was quite unnecessary to send out an expedition of relief in that year." It is hard to see why Ross in particular should have expected any other reaction. He was about as welcome at the Admiralty as Richard King. Ross then talked to the Marquis of Northampton, president of the Royal Society, trying to elicit his support. The marquis replied, "You will go and get frozen in like Franklin, and we shall have to send after you and then perhaps for them that went to look for you." Ross claimed to have tried to see Lady Jane, but she too was not interested in his plans. Not yet.

Ross was the first, but he was not alone. One hundred and twenty-nine men were on the two ships, they had left in high spirits, they had expected an easy sail to the Pacific—where were they? The anxious families of crew members in the expedition were beginning to talk to local papers around the country. On April 17 *The Athenaeum* reported in its gossip column that "a statement was some time ago promulgated in some of the local papers, that great fears were entertained as to the fate of Captain Sir John Franklin and the officers and crews of the *Erebus* and *Terror* steam vessels," because nothing had been heard from them. *The Athenaeum* took the official line: There's no need to worry. "Franklin had told his crew to tell their friends there was no reason to expect them before October 1847." It was only April.

Only April, but two years had passed now, and still, out of the Arctic, only silence. The Arctic was populated; surely the fur traders ought to have heard rumors, *something*, about ships or white men from the Yellow Knives or the Inuit. The Admiralty had already decided by April that perhaps, after all, it should give the matter some thought. What, the

Admiralty Board had quietly asked the Arctic knights, would you advise us to do in case a search for Franklin does become necessary? Officially nobody was worried, but two weeks after *The Athenaeum* reassured the public that October was the earliest to start worrying, it was reporting that Sir John Richardson was fitting out an overland expedition to the shores of Canada under Admiralty auspices. In fact, it was quick to explain, Richardson was only sending out a party of volunteers from the army with supplies to be cached along one of the routes Franklin might have taken out of the ice if the ships had been damaged, or frozen inescapably in. Richardson himself would not join them until after January 1848 and then only if necessary. Only if Franklin had not arrived home or been heard from—which, officially, still seemed highly unlikely. It was just a precaution. There was nothing to fear. He was definitely going to show up soon. In mid-June 1847 Richardson's volunteers left for Canada.

Too late, in Richard King's opinion. In the same issue of *The Athenaeum,* the issue of May 1, that this announcement appeared, King published a copy of his own letter on the matter to Earl Grey, the current colonial secretary. "My Lord," it begins, "one hundred and twenty-six men are at this moment in imminent danger of perishing from famine."

Imminent? They had a year's worth of rations left. If they were stuck in the ice somewhere, they would already be cutting down consumption, saving food for a long haul out. King was, of course, once more proposing that a relief expedition be sent out, that he lead it, and that it proceed down the Great Fish River. Why there? He argued that from what he knew of Franklin's orders, he must have been beset or even wrecked somewhere west of the upper Boothia Peninsula. Depending on which was closer, he would be heading either back to Barrow Strait to look for whalers, or toward the HBC posts in northern Canada. If the latter, the HBC should be stocking their posts with extra supplies and setting out caches right now, and he, Richard King, should be on the spot to lead survivors to the caches and help. But either way the most important thing was to act at once. It took half a year or longer to get word to the remote posts in northern Canada, indeed to get a rescue mission going of any kind.

The Colonial Office, on Parry's advice, ignored King just as the Admiralty had, and a friend of Franklin's named C. R. Weld replied in *The Athenaeum.* The Admiralty had consulted the Arctic veterans; they had plenty of food: "There are no grounds whatever for the assertion 'that one hundred and twenty-six men are at this moment in imminent danger of perishing from famine.'" King's figure of 126 is an odd one, by the way. When Franklin left Greenland in 1845 he had, including himself, 129 aboard. Perhaps King was clairvoyant. By the time he wrote his letter, three men had died. That left 126.

King gave up in July; no more letters came from his pen until the following November, by which time it had become increasingly clear that something had indeed gone wrong. Do not expect us before October, Franklin had told his friends; now it was November and the Arctic was still keeping its secrets. Wherever the expedition was, whatever had happened to it, it was facing another winter in the unbearable cold. Unable to contain himself any longer, King wrote Earl Grey again, his voice even more sepulchral on the page: "The last ray of hope has now faded that Sir John Franklin by his own exertions can save himself and his one hundred and twenty-five followers from the death of starvation." He offered to lead "the boldest journey which has ever been proposed" down the Great Fish River to save the survivors. Two weeks later he wrote the earl again, predicting that everyone on the two ships would have died by the summer of 1848. The prediction was more than a little melodramatic, but it was clear the public was becoming alarmed. *The Athenaeum* was by then taking a totally different line:

> the time has unhappily arrived when no tenderness for the feelings of others and no concession to the exigencies of official reserve can justify us in further hesitating to call attention to the doubt that hangs over the fate of Sir John Franklin and his party. Dr. Rae brings not a hint of their existence from his Arctic Expedition,—and one by one the whalers are dropping in and "giving no sign."

The writer urged the Admiralty to share what it knew about the situation with the public, then added, "Whatever has been the course of the party, if they be alive and *free* [i.e., of the ice] we should have heard of them this autumn. If alive and not free, the question of their delivery by life or death may depend on instant action."

The Dr. Rae whom the writer mentions was Dr. John Rac of the Hudson's Bay Company. The HBC had sent its own exploring party north under Rae in 1846 to decide once and for all the question of whether a strait connected the bottom of the Gulf of Boothia with the

Arctic Ocean west of the Boothia Peninsula—whether, that is, Boothia was indeed a peninsula, as Sir John Ross said it was, or an island, as nearly everybody else except Richard King said it was. Rae was a remarkable man, born in the Orkneys and raised hunting, fishing, and sailing; he had trained in medicine at Edinburgh; and he was the first Arctic explorer in all of Great Britain's history in the Arctic to learn how to live like an Inuit, off the land, building snow shelters as he needed them and traveling light and fast. He could walk fifty miles a day *on snowshoes.* He did not stop, he explained once, "to take lunch and dinner . . . A mouthful of pemmican carried in the pocket or placed conveniently on the sledges served to keep away hunger sufficiently until supper time." His traveling kit consisted of Inuit snow goggles, his gun, a few instruments—a watch, chronometer, telescope, octant—and a sewing kit to repair his clothing. He also carried the tools necessary to build an igloo and, to occupy his mind, two books: the works of Shakespeare in one volume and a book of religious poetry.

Rae left on his expedition in July 1846, taking a dozen men to Repulse Bay, where they established a base and spent what remained of the summer probing up both coasts of the Gulf of Boothia. That winter they lived largely off the land, hunting caribou, hare, ptarmigan, seal, trading with the Inuit for salmon and char. In the spring they extended their explorations. Rae did not determine definitively that Boothia was a peninsula. He could not quite close the gap between the bottom of the gulf and Sir John Ross's farthest south. But he was sure in his own mind that it was. He found no sign of a strait—no currents, no tides that would suggest one.

And he found no sign of Franklin. He heard nothing from the Inuit about large ships or large numbers of white men being in the area, and gossip like that would have traveled fast. Rae was back in Churchill in August 1847 and sailed from there to England to report his geographical findings directly to the HBC board. Rae's lack of news was another toll of the bell for Franklin. If he had reached the Canadian coast anywhere near the Boothia landmass the Inuit would have known.

The Admiralty still held back from committing to rescue operations beyond what it had already done by sending the provisions to northern Canada for a possible search in 1848 under Richardson. It was still, officially, early in the game. For their part the Arctic heroes remained optimistic. Sir James Ross told the Admiralty that he did not think "there is the smallest reason of apprehension or anxiety for the safety or success" of the Franklin expedition. They had food on half-rations for four years. "They cannot want from that cause until after the middle of July 1849; it therefore does not appear to me desirable to send after them until the spring of next year." Sir John Ross had survived in Prince Regent Inlet for four years, after all, and James Ross had been with him. Starvation was definitely not "imminent." They would wait a little longer.

That remained the official word, but the Admiralty was already making plans, not just for Richardson's search expedition along the Canadian coast but for two others. It could have been ten others. Franklin could have gone, or been swept away by the ice, anywhere. The Arctic was still mostly unknown. Along the Canadian coast there were straits and channels and open sea extending all the way from Boothia to Bering Strait, that at least was certain. But to the north? Islands of unknown size, straits between them of unknown direction and length, ice of unknown thickness and extent. Since Parry's first voyage of 1819–20 no one had been farther west than the top of Prince Regent Inlet. There were capes on the map, Cape Walker, for instance, a high point seen from scores of miles away, lying to the west of the top of Boothia Peninsula, and Banks Land loomed in the far distance from Melville Island. What was behind these cliffs rising out of the ice? What was up the wide channel Parry had named Wellington Channel? The vastness to the west of Melville Island was completely unknown.

It is possible even a century and a half later to feel sympathetic toward Richardson and Parry and Beechey and Back as they stared at the map, wondering where the searching expeditions should go. Since the coast of Canada was the one solidly known quantity in the emptiness, it made sense to send somebody there, and Richardson's party of army volunteers was already on the way, holed up for the winter somewhere in one of the HBC's posts. Richardson left in January to join them. He was within a year of Franklin's age and this was a noble act, evidence of the devotion Richardson felt for Franklin. John Rae was in London at the time. He was asked to go with Richardson and agreed. The plan was to descend the Mackenzie to its mouth and search the coast to the east of it in small boats, a reprise of the journey Richardson made in 1826 while Franklin was fighting fog along the coast to the west. It had been part of Franklin's instructions in 1845 to make the coast if he could and sail west along the coastline to Bering Strait. If he were stuck along this section of coast, they would find him.

But perhaps he was stuck farther west, wrecked even, or beset in the ice, along the same shallow coast that extends from the Mackenzie to Point Barrow that Franklin had explored so many years before. Shouldn't that be searched as well? Accordingly a second expedition under Thomas Moore, commanding a bark called the *Plover*, left for Bering Strait. Small boats would explore eastward from Bering Strait toward the mouth of the Mackenzie. But the best chance of finding Franklin, everyone seemed to agree, was the third expedition, which the Admiralty sent to follow his route into Lancaster Sound and through Barrow Strait. And the man leading it was the Admiralty's most experienced Arctic man: Sir James Clark Ross. Ross had agreed to the proposal despite his promise to his wife and his wife's family that he would go on no more voyages into the ice.

In a way Ross's voyage was the only one that actually offered genuine hope in case Franklin's ships were indeed wrecked or inextricably beset. If more than a hundred men were huddled in some barren spot along the Canadian coastline, Richardson, or the Bering Strait expedition under Moore, might find them, but what then? In a letter written to *The Athenaeum* in response to Richard King, an old HBC hand named A. K. Isbister pointed out the obvious. Isbister agreed that Franklin might very well be where King thought he was, somewhere along the meridian of longitude that ran through the mouth of the Great Fish River. An approach via the Coppermine or Great Fish River thus did offer the best hope of finding them. But the whole area of northern Canada was suffering from a prolonged famine. "Only three years ago one half of the Hare tribe perished around Fort Good Hope, after having killed and eaten two of the Hudson's Bay Company's people who imprudently ventured beyond the gates." How could anyone think, Isbister asked, that he could bring 126 men to safety up such difficult rivers as these, when only small boats could navigate them? The Great Fish River had eighty-three sets of falls and rapids. And what would have happened when they arrived in the barren grounds? "Could it be accomplished," he wrote, "that wintering ground would be their grave." Everyone remembered what had happened to Franklin in the barren grounds.

Should Richardson's expedition find them, he went on, the four boats they were using could not possibly carry enough provisions for both the rescuers and the rescued in any case. Only large ships could do that. He calculated the weight of the pemmican necessary for not only the original 126 men—the number King was using—but the thirty members of the rescue party as well. It was impossible. Any way you cut the numbers, there would not be enough food. "What relief 126 famishing men can look for from such a source," he said, "I leave the candid reader to judge." Richard King, usually ready for any argument, made no reply.

Sir John Richardson—that Richardson be knighted had been one of Sir John Barrow's last requests on leaving office—and John Rae left for Canada in February 1848 and thereby began what was almost certainly the largest, most expensive, and lengthiest search-and-rescue operation in the nineteenth century. Before it was over, it became international in scope. The Russians sent ships north of Siberia to search for Franklin. French naval officers crossed the channel and volunteered to help. The Americans sent ships too; in fact, the Franklin search marks the beginning of American interest in the Arctic and the American effort to reach the North Pole, and it created an American national hero in the person of Elisha Kent Kane. It is hard to come up with a precise number because expedition faded into expedition—Rae's second expedition along the coast, for example, was a continuation of Richardson's first, although it had its own orders from the Admiralty—but nearly thirty separate expeditions went looking for Franklin, some of them privately financed, and the search lasted until 1859—longer, if the efforts of the American explorer Charles Francis Hall are included. The interest was international and the press coverage was extraordinary. Alan Day's indispensable bibliography on the Northwest Passage has more than fifteen hundred entries under the search for Franklin.

The first three search expeditions gave an indication of what the search was going to be like throughout—difficult, confused, and time-consuming. The westernmost search, small boats coasting the shoreline between Point Barrow and the Mackenzie, has become known as the Pullen Expedition, after the name of the young lieutenant, William J. S. Pullen, who took the small boats east along that coast. Pullen came from a navy family and was just returning from a survey voyage mapping the Bay of Fundy when Beaufort asked him if he would sail with Commander Moore on the *Plover*, which was to leave for Bering Strait four days later. He said yes when Beaufort offered to let him catch up with her in Panama. By then mail steamers were crossing the Atlantic on a regular basis. In May Pullen took one to Panama and arrived in mid-June, then crossed the isthmus. The *Plover* never showed up. The voyage had been "greatly protracted by calm and contrary winds, and the very indifferent sailing qualities of our vessel." Pullen waited a month, then joined another ship, the *Asia*, and served on her until the spring of 1849.

Meanwhile a third ship, the *Herald*, under Captain Henry Kellett, had been ordered to round up supplies and meet the *Plover* in Kotzebue Sound, north of Bering Strait, and serve as its store ship. The *Herald* picked up stores in Panama in May and sailed for Kamchatka, then Kotzebue Sound, arriving in September 1848. It waited there two weeks. Again, the *Plover* did not show up. On September 29 the *Herald* left to return to its normal surveying duties. The *Plover* was on its way at the time but unable to reach Kotzebue Sound. She was a poor sailer, the winds were against her, and winter was coming on fast. In mid-October Commander Moore took the ship into harbor in eastern Siberia and she spent the winter among a tribe of Inuit there. Lieutenant Pullen was, of course, still serving on the *Asia*. Not until May 1849 did he connect with the *Herald* in Honolulu, and not until July 15 did the *Herald* and the *Plover* finally come together in Kotzebue Sound. A full year had been lost, thanks to the poor sailing qualities of the *Plover*. Richardson had been to the coast of North America, followed it from the Mackenzie to the Coppermine, and was back in England. Absolutely nothing had been accomplished to the west of the Mackenzie. In a situation calling for the maximum of haste, everything seems to have conspired against it.

Pullen, who had met Lady Franklin in South Australia some years before, did take two whaleboats and an umiak they bought from natives at Point Barrow east from Point Barrow to the Mackenzie that summer, easing his way between the pack ice on the north and the shoals, reefs, islands, and Inuit to the south. They were fourteen officers and men. They encountered Inuit at Return Reef who were intent on obtaining powder from them. One Inuit was brandishing a musket that had been left behind on the second Franklin expedition, the one that ended at Return Reef. He had no ammunition but wanted the powder anyway, and it got ticklish. These people would not take no for an answer, and they were a crowd—Pullen counted eighty of them. Ultimately they attacked, shooting at Pullen's party with bows and arrows. The English fired back with guns. No one was hurt, and that ended it.

Along the way they buried caches of pemmican for the Franklin party, should it pass that way. They battled the same ice, the same shoals, the same fogs that Franklin had battled more than twenty years before. Pullen reached the Mackenzie without seeing any evidence that Franklin or his men had passed that way, not a scrap of clothing, not a cairn, nothing. He still had 750 miles to go to reach Fort Simpson up the Mackenzie, where he had been ordered to spend the winter. His crew, unaccustomed to the kind of labor that Arctic travel entails, were exhausted. He left most of them behind at a nearby HBC fort on the Peel River, a tributary of the Mackenzie located near its mouth, where they could recover their strength. He went on to Fort Simpson. He left for home after the rest of the men joined him in the late spring and the ice broke up.

On June 25, 1850, as Pullen and his men were nearing Great Slave Lake on their way south, a canoe party moving north intercepted them with a letter from the Admiralty ordering Pullen to do it again. He was to take a party of men down the Mackenzie, then head east to Cape Bathurst and across the waters to Banks Land to look there for the Franklin expedition. His men all promptly volunteered to go with him.

The year before John Rae had received pretty much the same orders. Rae and Richardson left Liverpool on a steam packet on March 28, 1848, and arrived in New York April 10. They were in Montreal by the fifteenth and at Sault Ste. Marie on the twenty-ninth, covering fifteen hundred miles in fifteen days, almost all in paddlewheel river and lake steamships. They covered the next two thousand in express canoes in the remarkable time of fifty-five days. At Methy Portage, which separates the waters flowing into Hudson Bay from those flowing into the Arctic Ocean, they caught up to the men Richardson had sent out the summer before. Then they raced for the Arctic Ocean, dividing into two parties on the way, one to head to Great Bear Lake and construct winter quarters, the other to look for the Franklin party along the coast. They reached the Mackenzie delta on August 3, 1848.

There they were met by Inuit, 150 of them in kayaks and umiaks, and again it took musket fire to drive them off. After that they moved east along the coast easily enough until they reached Dolphin and Union Strait, where the ice was "more closely packed," in Rae's words, "and a strong gale of wind from the N. W. brought it close upon the shore on the 22nd. From this time on our advance was very slow, but by much exertion and making frequent portages over the ice and rocks, and by moving aside small floes and chopping off projecting points of large ones we generally advanced a few miles each day." They cached supplies for the Franklin party at Cape Krusenstern, but by September 3, with new ice knitting the old into an impenetrable mass, they knew it was time to retreat. They abandoned their three wooden boats, which had been damaged by the ice, taking only the Halkett boat, an inflatable India rubber boat recently invented by a navy lieutenant named P. A. Halkett, son of one of the directors of the Hudson's Bay Company, and walked to the mouth of the Coppermine. They crossed the streams they met on the way in the Halkett boat, Rae using tin plates for paddles. It was snowing heavily by then and they were wearing snowshoes, each man carrying about seventy pounds on his back. On September 15 they reached Fort Confidence on Great Bear Lake, where Simpson and Dease had wintered.

They found no trace of the Franklin expedition.

That meant they would have to go out again the following summer. But not with these men. Richardson, now sixty-one, was just too old for this work, and Rae wrote Sir George Simpson, governor of the HBC, that his "excellent superior officer was not of much use." It was the soldiers and sailors who had volunteered in England for this work who disgusted him, however.

> I may now mention that they were the most awkward, lazy, and careless set I ever had any thing to do with. I believe they would have been disobedient to me had they dared, one of them tried it once but did not venture to be so a second time. The only things they were good at, were eating, sleeping and smoking, and also taking care of themselves.

Rae was used to company men, who were inured to the Arctic. They spent the winter at Fort Confidence, and Richardson, before he left for England, wrote him new orders. Rae was to examine if he could the shores of Wollaston Land and Victoria Land, which he believed to be two separate islands, to see if Franklin might have become locked into the ice in the strait between them. Richardson knew that Sir James Ross was heading in the same direction from the north and planning to send sledging parties there. If Ross hadn't made it that far, or his sledging parties needed help, Rae was to provide it.

If, if—*ifs* dominate travel in the Arctic. The first *if* was, could Rae get across Dolphin and Union Strait to Wollaston Land and Victoria Land—which are all one, by the way, with no strait between them—in the first place? As events proved he could not. He left with five men and one boat on June 9, 1849, but the summer was late in coming, the ice on the rivers broke up late, Rae's boat had to be dragged over it for thirty miles just to get to the Coppermine, and it was a month before he reached the Bloody Falls. He learned from an Inuit man he found there that none of their people who were living on Wollaston Land "had ever seen white people or large vessels." They made their way to the most convenient point Rae could find to cross the waters to Wollaston Land, only to find the waters frozen, the ice rough and impassable. Not until August 19 was there even a chance to cross it. They

> pushed out among the driving floes, and when a mile from shore were able to use our oars. We now made rapid progress towards Douglas Island and had gone nearly 8 miles when a close packet stream of ice impeded our way or through which we found it impracticable to pass. The current, too, was now driving us faster past the Island than we could have advanced in the direction of it, even had the ice been sufficiently smooth to allow us [to] launch the boat on it.

Rae turned around. They had been on the water ten hours, "during which our craft was more than once nearly squeezed among the driving masses." The next two days a northeast gale jammed "our cold and persevering opponent in large heaps along the shore. Some open water now appeared to the South and S. E. but all in the direction we wished to go was as impervious as the solid rock." On August 23 Rae gave up.

That was it, in this section of the Arctic, along Franklin's possible route, for 1849. Pullen, meanwhile, was making his way east from Point Barrow and would soon reach the Mackenzie. It was he, not Rae, whom the Admiralty would send back to the coast to try to reach Wollaston and Victoria Lands. The HBC made John Rae the chief factor for the Mackenzie area while Pullen spent the summer of 1850 in a York boat named the *Try Again*, with a Halkett boat as a backup. They struggled east toward Cape Bathurst, their assignment to cross over to Banks Land, west of Victoria and Wollaston Lands. Short of Cape Bathurst the ice closed in and forced them to land. Pullen climbed the highest point of land he could find to look for a way through the ice. "Whichever way we turned," he wrote the Admiralty, "to seaward, presented an unbroken field of ice, excepting the narrow belt of shoal water between it and the shore." This water was so shoal they could barely cross it even in a small boat. On July 27 the wind shifted to the north and picked up strength, turning the sea into a churning mass of white; thick fog came in at the same time. To venture out into such dangerous waters would have been suicidal. On August 1 they woke up to find the water in their kettles, left there overnight, frozen solid. Liverpool Bay, a huge bay on the mainland, was full of heavy ice. "I have now seen more than 22 years of a sailor's life," Pullen told the Admiralty, "and can safely say have never been engaged in such laborious and disheartening work as we have gone this day and since the 27th." The ice was everywhere. The temperatures hovered at or just below freezing. He wrote that on August 2. On the fourth he wrote, "From appearances there are yet more delays to be met with, and I begin to fear our expectations so frequently indulged in previous to entering the Arctic regions were too sanguine and doomed to be disappointed." He might have said that about the entire Arctic enterprise from 1818 onward.

On August 15 Pullen turned around and started the journey back to the Mackenzie delta, where he got lost for a week among its confusing channels. No more orders awaited him that year, and he returned home, arriving in the fall of 1851. He had seen no sign of Franklin on his latest journey. Neither he nor John Richardson nor Rae had made it across the water to the big islands opposite the coastline. Two of the Admiralty's three initial expeditions to rescue the Franklin party had come to nothing. No new coastline had been explored, nothing of significance was added to the map, and no trace of Franklin was discovered to give hope to Lady Jane and to an increasingly anxious nation.

Sir James Ross, in the meantime, had also come back with nothing. He had taken two ships to Lancaster Sound, the *Enterprise* and the *Investigator,* which the Admiralty reinforced in the usual way, adding the Sylvester stove for heating, and supplied with three years' provisions, plus another six months' worth of food for Franklin and his men should they find them. Ross carried the public's, and the Admiralty's, highest hopes. His expedition to Antarctica had been one of the most successful exploring expeditions in the Admiralty's history. He had the know-how and expertise to do the job. He had spent years in the Arctic with Parry. He had as much experience with ice as any man alive. He picked his own officers, almost all of them Arctic or Antarctic veterans. If anyone were going to find Franklin, it would most likely be Ross.

Ross planned to spend his first summer, if he arrived soon enough—if, if, if—cruising the north shore of Barrow Strait as far as Melville Island, looking for signs of Franklin's expedition. Then he would sail across to the south shore and do the same. He hoped to establish winter quarters at or near Parry's Winter Harbour and send the *Investigator* to winter at Cape Rennell, which capped the north shore of North Somerset. In the spring sledge parties would cross the ice from the *Enterprise* to Banks Land, one to trace its west coast and the other its east. The one on the east was to join Sir John Richardson and return with him to England. The other was to head for the HBC posts on the Mackenzie. The *Investigator* for its part would send sledge parties down both sides of the Boothia Peninsula.

Nothing went according to plan. The ice in Baffin Bay refused to break up that summer and it was late August before Ross got into open water, August 22 before he got to Lancaster Sound. Prince Regent Inlet was clogged with ice. So was Wellington Channel to the north. Heavy ice blocked Barrow Strait. They got nowhere, found nothing. New ice was forming. At the opening of Prince Regent Inlet, at the northeast corner of North Somerset, lay a harbor Ross was familiar with called Port Leopold. Both ships wintered there. They occupied themselves that winter by trapping Arctic foxes, fitting them with copper collars that had been engraved with their own latitude and longitude and the positions of food caches, and letting them loose. Someone in the Franklin party might find one. But foxes are as territorial as most other animals; they did not wander far from the two ships. The collars were useless and the winter was dreadful. Thirty years before Ross had been with Parry at Winter Harbour on Melville Island and, eighteen at the time, rosy-cheeked and slender, had taken the women's parts in Parry's theatricals. At forty-eight he had no stomach for theatricals, and there were none. The ship was badly ventilated and one mess dripped water constantly from the condensation on the beams. "For the men," reports Sir Clements Markham, who many years later interviewed the few remaining crewmen for his biography of Francis McClintock, who was a junior officer on this voyage and would become famous for his sledging work in the Arctic over the next decade, "the winter was a time of dullness and discomfort. Two actually died of despondency."

That spring four sledging parties left the two ships to look in four different directions for traces of Franklin. This became the standard pattern for all the search expeditions: voyages in ships to wherever the ice allowed them to sail, then spring sledge expeditions to the most likely coastlines in the immediate environs. Ross's sledge party, on which Francis McClintock would first learn how they were performed, followed the top of North Somerset west to a place called Cape Bunny, where the coast abruptly turned south. To the north Barrow Strait was solid ice. When he turned south Ross was discovering an entirely new body of water, Peel Sound, named after the prime minister; across it he could detect high land here and there, thirty miles away, which as it happened was all part of a large island which became known as Prince of Wales Island. Ross could only chart the high land as capes; he had no idea whether they belonged to an island or not. Nor could he be sure he was discovering a strait or a sound. At the time it was full of ice, rough, thick, dangerous, and too difficult to cross. Ross and McClintock decided it would be disastrous for ships to attempt it. When, as it was later discovered, John Franklin sailed down Peel Sound in 1846, clearly it had been open.

Had Ross gone on he would have found not only that he was on the shores of a strait, but that the Boothia Peninsula came to an end at another strait, hitherto unknown, a narrow channel connecting Prince Regent Inlet and Peel Sound. Had he gone on from there, back to the location of the North Magnetic Pole he had discovered in 1830, he might have come upon the last survivors of the Franklin expedition, making their way to the Great Fish River in search of food. That was the position he was hoping to reach when he set out. But things did not go well. Ross had not brought enough food. He had not brought dogs, and the sledges were man-hauled. They walked at night, to reduce glare, and slept during the day. At five in the afternoon they were woken up; breakfast was chocolate melted in a tin kettle warmed by a spirit lamp. Lunch came at midnight and consisted of nothing more, wrote Markham, than "a mouthful of biscuit and frozen meat, some snow water, and half a gill of rum." Supper was a pound of meat, a pound of biscuit. They left on May 15, returned on June 23. "All of the men had to be put on the sick list," wrote Markham, and Ross himself took to his bed. They were all suffering from scurvy. John Rae averaged more than twenty miles a day on his sledge journeys. Ross had averaged about twelve.

One of the other sledging parties explored the east coast of the Boothia Peninsula all the way to Fury Beach, finding the stores there still in fine shape. Another crossed Barrow Strait on the ice, trying to reach the mouth of Wellington Channel. Unhappily, it failed to do so. Franklin, a later expedition would find, had spent his first winter at the mouth of Wellington Channel, on Beechey Island.

That summer they sawed their way out of Port Leopold and regained the open seas of Lancaster Sound on August 28. Ross hoped to repeat, successfully this time, his attempt to reach Wellington Channel and

Melville Island; but within two days pack ice moved east from Barrow Strait, grabbed the ships in a giant bear hug, and would not let go. Three and a half weeks later the ice let them go—well out in Baffin Bay. Now it was late in September, the start of another winter. The whole project was clearly hopeless.

Ross turned tail for home and was back in London by early November 1849. Jane Franklin was in the Orkneys at the time, where she thought Franklin would land first if he were still alive. So much anxiety had attended the search that the Admiralty had sent out another ship, the *North Star*, to find Ross, resupply him, and ask him to stay out another year; but alas, Ross was back, and the *North Star* was wintering in Greenland. The public was dealing with a report from an Inuit interviewed by a whaling captain that he had seen four ships frozen into the ice in Prince Regent Inlet and had provided a rough, very rough map, and that was in the news. A. K. Isbister wrote *The Athenaeum* that the way he read the map, the Inuit meant two of the ships were in Prince Regent Inlet, and the other two *west* of Boothia. *The Illustrated London News* caught the sense of the country. In its issue of October 13, 1849, the editors wrote that "the several expeditions for the discovery of the northwest passage are looked upon by the people of this country, and by the world in general, with the greatest interest and anxiety. The failure of one expedition is but the incentive to fit out another." By this time Jane Franklin had offered a thousand pounds to any whaler who sailed in search of her husband and found him. (The government would soon up the ante to twenty thousand pounds.) "The connubial anxieties of Lady Franklin," the piece continued, ". . . [have] touched a strong chord in the national heart." The national heart was all for finding the lost expedition at all costs. The Northwest Passage, after all, was a historic mission, an emblem, the magazine went on, "of the indomitable energy, the daring love of adventure, and the enthusiasm for discovery which so predominantly distinguish the Anglo-Saxon race." It was unthinkable that Franklin would not be found.

W. Francis Ainsworth, cousin of the novelist W. Harrison Ainsworth, had a different take on the subject. Writing in the January 1850 issue of *The New Monthly Magazine*, Ainsworth could only look upon the entire enterprise with a kind of bemused awe. "It is easy," he said, "to understand the spirit of adventure and love of enterprise that carries one or more individuals across pathless forests, or over arid deserts, into mountain fastnesses or savage lands; but it is difficult to imagine a government or a nation seized with the same impulse, or communicating it to the crews of so many doomed ships." He called the search for the Northwest Passage "a miracle of misdirected energy and enterprise."

Yet he was interested enough in the search for Franklin that he devoted nine more articles to the subject over the course of the next three years. The search was now too big to be stopped, too important to abandon. Franklin had melted away in the fastnesses of the Arctic. The nation *must* find him. It went beyond humanitarian concerns. The search for Franklin, wrapped up as it was in the ancient quest for the Northwest Passage, was becoming by this point a test of the nation's identity.

CHAPTER EIGHTEEN

ARCTIC MAZE

Ross's failure was a blow to Lady Jane. She, like everyone else, had put a great deal of faith in Ross and his abilities, and Ross was a friend besides. To have him come home after only a year and a half, after a store ship had been sent out with fresh supplies, was extremely discouraging. Racked with anxiety, she could lead a life that was only superficially normal. In 1847 she took Eleanor to Italy for a few months. She was at a dinner party in the spring of 1848 where Thomas Carlyle was also a guest when news came that Louis-Philippe had been overthrown. Europe was wrapped in turmoil, while in London the Chartists, a lower-class movement demanding economic reform, had called a meeting for April 10 that many in the middle and upper classes believed would lead to a revolution in the streets. The meeting came and went, but the streets remained quiet and orderly. Europe would suffer the revolutions of 1848; Great Britain would not. The nation congratulated itself.

When the searching expeditions went out, each one carried letters from Lady Jane to her husband full of this kind of news. She said nothing about her fears, nothing about the growing anxiety in the nation over their disappearance. At the beginning of 1849 sixty churches scattered throughout the kingdom where members of the Franklin expedition had worshiped held public prayer sessions for their safety. The press kept track of every new expedition, every little piece of Arctic news. Over the next few years, wherever she traveled, hotels refused to bill Jane Franklin, railroads gave her free passes, and restaurants fed her gratis. She had upped the ante; now she was offering £3,000 to any ship that came to Franklin's rescue. The reward was aimed at the whaling fleet, and it was enough of an embarrassment to the British government that Parliament voted to top it with its own rewards: £10,000 to whoever came back with news of the expedition's fate, £20,000 to whoever found survivors. In April 1849 she wrote the president of the United States, Zachary Taylor, calling for help from the United States in the search. This, and a follow-up letter in December, written after Ross came back empty-handed, had their effect. Both letters were published and Henry Grinnell, a New York shipping magnate so successful he was able to retire in his forties, offered two of his own ships to the government and paid for refitting them for Arctic service. The U.S. Navy staffed them, and among the other search expeditions that left for the Arctic in 1850 was the Grinnell expedition. The expedition's doctor, Elisha Kent Kane, wrote in his account that he

> could not help being struck with the universal sympathy displayed toward our expedition. From the ladies who busied themselves in sealing up air-tight packages of fruit-cakes, to the managers of the Astor House, who insisted that their hotel should be the free head-quarters of our party, it was one continued round of proferred services.

The New York press was already regularly covering the many rescue attempts. Kane's book on the expedition became a best seller in the United States.

The craze for phrenology that had been so prevalent in Great Britain in the 1820s had been replaced in the 1830s and 1840s with a craze first for mesmerism, then for clairvoyants and mediums. In May 1849 Lady Jane made her first visit to the clairvoyant Ellen Dawson, who was popular with the upper classes. She took Sophy Cracroft with her and it was Sophy whom Ms. Dawson chose as her interlocutor. After retreating into a trance, she reported that she "had been a long way, . . . on the sea and into the ice, and she saw a ship in the ice, and several people on it, all gentlemen; one of them was rather old, and rather short, and stout, rather dark, with such a nice face." When Sophy asked whether he was well Ms. Dawson replied, "Oh no! he is quite well, and looks happy and comfortable," although "rather anxious." Sophy's next questions—which way was the ship heading, and when would it be home—went unanswered. "There was a cloud before her," said Ms. Dawson. Other questions elicited similar clouds, but she did see Franklin's cabin clearly. In it hung portraits of two women, and this happened to be true: Lady Jane's and the queen's.

Lady Jane returned to Grosvenor Square to see Ellen Dawson again in November. That September a friend of hers had consulted Emma, the Bolton Clairvoyant, as she was known, who "described bodies underneath the snow, a leaping animal with black and white stripes, some tangled forests, wild cattle and wild men." She did not attempt to explain what the leaping animal might be, or where the tangled forests came into it. Franklin was well above the tree line. In February 1850 Lady Jane made a visit to the thirteen-year-old son of a Lieutenant Morrison who had a crystal ball; he saw Franklin on his way home with "sledges and ice boats."

A little girl provided the most fascinating of these experiments with the paranormal. Louisa Coppin, called "Weasy" by her family, had died in 1849 at the age of three. Not long after her death she began to appear to her siblings—her older sister Anne in particular, who was ten—with news from the other world. Her father, William Coppin, was a down-to-earth former sea captain turned shipbuilder. Weasy, dead but not gone, established her credibility by telling Anne on one occasion that a certain banker was dead. He was found later that morning lifeless in his bed.

At some point one of the children thought to ask Weasy about Sir John Franklin. At once "the room they were in appeared to be filled with ice, some channels and a ship in one narrow creek or harbour between two mountains of snow and ice in a sort of dilapidated state, with another in the distance and in a distinct channel of water." When asked where the ships were the scene vanished, and on one of the room's walls the letters *BS* and then *P.RI-NF* appeared. *BS* might be Barrow Strait. *P.RI* was clearly Prince Regent Inlet.

Captain Coppin wrote Lady Jane in the spring of 1850 telling her what had occurred, and she met him in Liverpool. An account of this meeting did not reach print until 1889, however, and the writing on the wall in response to questions about Franklin's whereabouts did not correspond to the above. What appeared instead in this 1889 account were the words "EREBUS AND TERROR, SIR JOHN FRANKLIN, LANCASTER SOUND, PRINCE REGENT'S INLET, POINT VICTORY, VICTORIA CHANNEL." Presented with these words, Lady Jane reportedly exclaimed, "It is all true! It is all true! Your children are right. Three months before Sir John set sail, we were sitting by the fire when he said: 'Jane, recollect if I find any difficulty I shall seek to return by the American continent, and if I fail in that I shall go up by the Great Fish River and so get to the Hudson Bay territory.'" Of course, the route of the *Erebus* and *Terror* had been determined years before 1889, and the fact that survivors had tried to reach the Great Fish River was well known. In 1850 Victoria Channel—more precisely, Victoria Strait—had not been discovered and therefore did not have a name.

Nevertheless Lady Jane could read a map, she could see where the search expeditions were planning to search, and almost from the beginning she had believed that the area west of the Boothia Peninsula, which is where Victoria Strait is, was being neglected and ought to be searched. George Back, among others, strongly disagreed. Franklin would never make for the Great Fish River, he said. He knew all too much about the barren grounds, the difficulty of finding food there, the distance to the HBC forts. The old food stores abandoned at Fury Beach—and still edible, as it turned out—were much closer than any source of food in northern Canada.

Jane was no longer living at the Griffin family home in Bedford Place by 1849. Taking the ever-faithful Sophy Cracroft with her, she had moved to an apartment in Spring Gardens, across the street from the Admiralty. The letter to the President of the United States was just one of her many efforts to apply pressure on the powers that be. She became friendly with Baillie Hamilton, who served as the second secretary of the Admiralty from 1847 to 1855. During his tenure in the post he came to know as much as anyone about the Franklin search and was deeply sympathetic to Lady Jane. His opinions sometimes quietly echoed hers, and he did what he could for her with the Admiralty lords, going so far as to interview Captain Coppin about his dead daughter's revelations himself, then suggesting to the lords, without telling them what his sources were, that they direct at least one search where Weasy had said Franklin was. They did not take his advice. The area in question remained untouched.

The Lords were generally slow to act, but Jane did have one advantage: she had the considerable power of public sympathy behind her. The press accounts often referred to her, though sometimes, out of an exaggerated sense of delicacy, not by name. It didn't matter. Everyone knew who was meant. She was England's Penelope, patient and enduring. In one of the many letters sent to Franklin via the search expeditions, Sophy Cracroft told Franklin that Jane was "honoured and respected and sympathy for her has been expressed and conveyed to herself by all ranks, from the Queen down to the lowest of her subjects." It was common knowledge that she was spending her private fortune offering rewards and financing expeditions. This was another kind of pressure to put on the Admiralty. How shameful that a woman, especially a woman, should be impoverishing herself to do what the Admiralty was failing to do: find her husband.

She was indeed impoverishing herself, and her family was not in the least happy about it. Early in 1849 John Philip Gell, who was Eleanor Franklin's fiancé, finally returned from Tasmania. Having been separated for years, the couple wanted to marry as soon as possible. Gell had a minimal income, enough to live on but not enough to provide Eleanor, who had grown up largely in the wealthy Griffin household, with the kind of life she was used to. Eleanor had not, says Jane Franklin's biographer Frances Woodward, "inherited her father's sweet disposition." The young couple wanted money from Franklin's first wife's estate— Eleanor's mother's money—to live on. If Franklin were dead she would inherit that money. If he had been home he would no doubt have granted them out of it enough of an income to make them comfortable. In his absence, however, and while the issue of Franklin's survival remained in doubt, Jane had power of attorney. It was up to her to decide what, if anything, to give them. "Jane was a generous soul—Gell had often had occasion to know it," writes Woodward; "but money had never been so precious to her as it was at this time." Other members of the family became involved, and it got nasty; it was one reason Jane left the family home for the apartment across from the Admiralty. Ultimately she paid a higher price than she could have expected. Her own father, John Griffin, now in decline, took Eleanor's side and disinherited Jane. She had money of her own, bestowed upon her as dowry when she married Franklin, and income from land she owned in Tasmania. But it must have been a terrible, hurtful blow. The world honored and respected her, and thought her heroic. Her own father thought she had lost her mind.

Indeed Jane must have seemed half mad to them—mad with anxiety and completely obsessed with the search. The family consensus was that it was up to the Admiralty to conduct the search, not to Jane Franklin. She was taking marital devotion to new extremes. And it was not as if the Admiralty was failing to take action, despite its sluggishness. On Arctic matters the Lords largely deferred to the Arctic knights— Beechey, Back, Richardson, Ross the younger, Parry, and Edward Sabine. Beaufort was also part of this group, even though he had never been in the Arctic. He was a personal friend of all of them and had served as a pallbearer at the funeral of Franklin's first wife. Most of all he was the Admiralty's grand old man, hugely respected for his work in the Hydrography Office, and certainly much more knowledgeable than any of the Admiralty lords about all things geographic. When both Ross and Richardson returned empty-handed in late 1849, it was Beaufort who conducted the official interviews with them. Beaufort could move the Admiralty if Jane Franklin could not, and it was thanks to Beaufort that the Admiralty sent James Ross's two ships, the *Enterprise* and the *Investigator,* back to the Arctic within three months of their return.

They left for Bering Strait in January 1850 under the overall command of Richard Collinson. Second in command, and captain of the *Investigator,* was Robert McClure, who had served with George Back on the *Terror* when it was beset in the ice of Hudson Bay off Southampton Island in 1836, and he had only just returned with James Ross from Barrow Strait. Markham tells a story about him that when the Admiralty was commissioning the *Terror* for Back's expedition, the first sea lord sent for him and said, "'M'Clure, you are just the man we want. There is an Arctic Expedition fitting out, will you join?' He could not make up his mind at once, and went to the waiting-room to think it over. The old porter asked him what was on his mind. M'Clure told him. 'Well,' said he, 'I saw Nelson sitting on that very chair, thinking what he would do, and he took what they offered him. Do you do the same.'" He did. Thus another Arctic hero was born.

On the eastern front, the approach from Baffin Bay, the level of activity was much higher. The U.S. Grinnell expedition sent two ships, the *Advance* and the *Rescue,* north to Lancaster Sound under the overall command of Lieutenant Edwin J. De Haven. The Admiralty was sending four ships under Captain Horatio T. Austin, whose Arctic experience dated to Parry's third voyage. Markham, who was on this expedition as a junior officer, describes Austin as short and fat and a first-rate organizer. The ships were cargo ships, the *Resolute* and the *Assistance,* which the Admiralty had bought and strengthened for Arctic service. Each was accompanied by its own steam tender, the *Intrepid* and the *Pioneer.*

The Admiralty also sent out two other ships under the command of a whaling captain named William Penny, with whaling ship crews. Penny was one of the most highly respected of the whaling captains of the day and he had ideas of his own as to where to look for Franklin. He had made friends with Lady Jane and she asked him to command her own privately financed expedition, then changed her mind and recommended that he apply to the Admiralty for a ship. It was another sign of the amount of pressure, both public and private, that the Admiralty was under that it gave him not one but two, and pay of double what a captain in the Royal Navy normally received. He named his two ships the *Lady Franklin* and the *Sophia*. Penny reached upper Baffin Bay before Austin. Theoretically they were going to cooperate, Penny being under Austin's titular command. But Austin had no time for a commercial fisherman. It was not a happy relationship, and Austin was much criticized for his snobbery and failure to work with Penny when all the ships returned in 1851.

Ten ships, then: two heading toward Bering Strait; four under Austin; two under Penny; two under the Americans. There were more. Sir John Ross, seventy-two years old, was determined to fulfill his promise to Franklin that he would come to his rescue. He applied once again to the Admiralty for financing, once again was refused, then turned to Sir Felix Booth, his old patron, who promised to help—and promptly died. So he tried the Hudson's Bay Company. In ordinary circumstances it is hard to imagine the HBC investing money in such an old codger as Ross, with a reputation such as his, but these were not ordinary circumstances, and they pledged five hundred pounds. Ross raised the rest from wealthy friends. On May 20 he left Scotland in a schooner he had bought for something over a thousand pounds, with a crew of twelve. He called his ship the *Felix*. The little *Felix* was towing an even smaller ship, Ross's own yacht, the *Mary*. The crew were dead drunk when they sailed. One of them, according to *The Shipping Gazette*, "had drank himself into a state of insanity, *delirium tremens*, and was in his bed." Ross had lost most of his initial crew to drunkenness in 1829.

Lady Jane's own ship completed the list. She too had help from friends and from public contributions, but the bulk of the financing came from her own funds. She named her ship, a small former pilot boat, the *Prince Albert* and gave the command of it to Charles Forsyth, a navy man who had served in Tasmania under Franklin and volunteered his services free of charge. Under the influence of the revelations from Weasy, she sent the ship to Prince Regent Inlet. Not mentioning Weasy, she wrote James Ross that if her husband were wrapped in the ice west of Boothia, she thought he might well have led survivors to Fury Beach via James Ross Strait. It was a reasonable theory, as good as anything the

Admiralty had in mind. Forsyth was instructed to sail not only to Fury Beach but as far south as John Ross had sailed in 1829, to the land of the Boothian Inuit. They were known to be friendly. They had helped save John Ross and his crew. If there were no survivors at Fury Beach, perhaps some of them had made their way there.

So it was a crowd that entered Lancaster Sound in August 1850, but more than a crowd was needed to find Franklin. They required some indication of where to look. Franklin's official written instructions from the Admiralty had come with the understanding that the course he chose would depend on the ice. He had been told, however, to proceed if he could through Barrow Strait to "that portion of land on which Cape Walker is situated," and from there "to penetrate to the southward and westward, in a course as direct towards Bhering's Strait as the position and extent of the ice, or the existence of land, at present unknown, may admit."

Cape Walker happened to be a small, high island standing just off the northwest corner of Prince of Wales Island, a fact that James Ross discovered in 1849. Parry had glimpsed, and named, Cape Walker from a great distance in 1819. To the south and west of it lie what would become known as Victoria and McClure Straits, and two large islands, Banks Island and Victoria Island. In the 1840s, right up to modern times, these two straits were permanently frozen.

Acknowledging the contingency of ice or land blocking his way, Franklin's instructions included one other option. "Should your progress in the direction before ordered be arrested by ice of a permanent appearance," they read, and if Wellington Channel, which divided Devon Island from Cornwallis Island, were free of ice, he was to try Wellington Channel. Wellington Channel led north, but if it offered a way out of the Canadian archipelago, "and a more ready access to the open sea, where there would be neither islands nor banks to arrest and fix the floating masses of ice," he was to take it. "The open sea": like the dream of an earthly paradise, the open polar sea was an idea that would not die.

Everyone who knew Franklin knew that he was a man who followed orders to the letter and would do everything in his power to follow these. But the possibilities remained endless. Wellington Channel was forty to fifty miles wide. Parry had seen and named it in 1819, but he had not sailed into it. Where did it go? Some speculated that it led to Jones Sound in Baffin Bay, others that it led north and west into that famous open polar sea. It was entirely possible that Franklin had sailed through

Wellington Channel into this sea and found it not open but clogged with ice, and that he was stuck in it, permanently beset. Or there might be yet more islands past Wellington Channel and he was among them, unable to find a way out, frozen into some harbor. Almost anything was possible. The high Arctic was unknown, and getting to know it was an extremely costly process. James Ross had crossed the top of North Somerset and added a water route to its west coast, Peel Sound, but was it a sound or a strait? Ross's men, and Ross himself, were sick with scurvy when he turned around on the west coast of North Somerset. Men would have died if he had gone on.

The expeditions of 1850 were yet another random foray into the heart of whiteness, darts thrown at the blank that was much more—and much less—than blank space on a map, that was vast and daunting, and also nothing, rock and ice and unfathomable cold, the ninth circle of Dante's hell, nothingness itself. It was 1850. Franklin had been gone for five years, on three years' worth of food. The distances were great, the conditions pitiless. In the winter of 1819–20 one of Parry's men had frozen his hands saving the instruments when the observation hut went up in flames. When the surgeon had plunged the man's frozen hands in water, the first step to defrosting them, the water in the bowl had immediately frozen.

The various expeditions were detained by the ice in Baffin Bay, often in sight of each other. In early August, while nearing Cape York, the top of Melville Bay on the east coast of Greenland, William Penny saw Inuit on the beach and went ashore with his interpreter, Carl Petersen, to find out whether they knew anything about Franklin and his ships. They knew nothing. The *Felix* was also in the area and sent its own boat with John Ross's captain, a Commander Phillips, and Ross's own interpreter, a half-Inuit, half-Danish Greenlander named Adam Beck. He questioned the same Inuit as Petersen had and came away with a totally different story. Four years earlier, they said, two ships "whose officers wore gold cap bands"—that is, Royal Navy ships—had stopped in Wolstenholme Sound, which was farther up the Greenland coast, where "their enfeebled crews had been massacred by the natives."

A bombshell, if it was true. But very little about the story was plausible. No one could imagine even weakened men who had firearms succumbing to bows and arrows, with their short range. Whalers regularly extended their cruises as high as Wolstenholme Sound, and no whaler had reported seeing ships there, or the wreckage of ships. Adam Beck insisted he had the story right and wouldn't back down. Sir John Ross, "always a one-man minority," took the story at face value and stood by Adam Beck. A conference was held in Captain Austin's cabin and Beck was interrogated more closely. Carl Petersen, meanwhile, talked to the natives again and determined that the story had to do with the *North Star,* the supply ship sent out to support James Ross in 1849. It had spent the winter at Wolstenholme Sound, where it lost a man who fell down a cliff.

When the story emerged in London a year later, Adam Beck's tale was added to a growing list of false leads and unfounded rumors. Then in December 1850 word spread all over London that Franklin was back safe. "People everywhere were elated, the offices of the Admiralty were besieged by callers during the night," notes W. Gillies Ross in *Polar Record.* The rumor, of course, was false. A whaler noticed a cairn in Jones Sound but did not get to shore to open it. When word reached London the papers assumed that Franklin had built it and left a message inside, and they covered the story like a breakthrough. Mysterious glass bottles were found on the north coast of Russia and sent to London. They turned out to be floats used by Norwegian fishermen. What toll these false reports took on Lady Jane one can only imagine.

Then suddenly there was a genuine lead. The configuration of the ice in Barrow Strait in the summer of 1850 funneled all the search ships to the mouth of Wellington Channel. There, at the southwest corner of Devon Island, stood Cape Riley, and just offshore lay a tiny island called Beechey Island, a knob rising out of the sea. On top of the knob somebody had built a cairn. A cairn stood on Cape Riley as well. On August 23 Captain Ommanney, Austin's second in command and in charge of the *Assistance,* reached Cape Riley and took the cairn there apart, to find nothing inside; but scattered around were broken bottles and other sorts of garbage, clear evidence of European occupation. On Beechey Island the cairn was also empty, but Ommanney found what had been the site of a tent—stones placed in a circle, the stones placed there to hold down the tent's sides. He left notes of his own in both cairns, then immediately sailed north into Wellington Channel, which appeared to be open.

Within a few days the ice had forced all the rest of the ships to the same site, all but Lady Jane's *Prince Albert.* Ten ships were there at once. William Penny was the first to find the remains of a garden on Beechey Island, then of a carpenter's workshop. The metallic debris of a metalworking or armorer's shop occupied another site. At yet another, six hundred empty tin cans were found carefully arranged on the ground, with limestone pebbles inside them to weight them down. Everywhere on the ground were, in Elisha Kent Kane's words,

> fragments of canvas, rope, cordage, sail-cloth, tarpaulins; of casks, iron-work, wood, rough and carved; of clothing, such as a blanket lined by long stitches with common cotton stuff, and made into a sort of rude coat; paper in scraps, white, waste, and journal; a small key; a few odds and ends of brass-work, such as might be part of the furniture of a locker; in a word, the numberless reliquiae of a winter resting-place.

Lieutenant Osborn, commanding one of the steam tenders, discovered "a pair of Cashmere gloves, carefully 'laid out to dry, with two small stones upon the palms to keep them from blowing away.' . . . The Arctic traveler they belonged to," Kane went on, "intended to come back for them." Most important were the graves, three of them, with headboards bearing the names of three of Franklin's seamen and dated in January and April 1846.

The conclusion was inescapable. The Franklin expedition had spent the winter of 1845–46 on Beechey Island. But the cairns were empty. He had left no message saying where he was heading next. He had left no message at all. And this was staggering. The whole purpose of a cairn was to protect the messages left inside it in watertight metal cans. Cairns were the principal means of communication in the Arctic. They were erected on clearly visible points of land or prominent beaches and marked the spot of buried food caches and the limits of exploration, and they contained messages—always messages. If the messages were not inside the pile of stones itself, they were buried a few agreed-upon yards away in an agreed-upon direction. Over the next few years Beechey Island would be put virtually through a strainer, but no message would ever be found. In the summer of 1846, when the ice broke, Franklin had moved on. But the searching expeditions had no more to go on than they had had two years before. The whole Arctic was still theirs to search.

Yet there was one clue. They had also found sledge tracks, an amazing survival in the ice after five years, leading up the east side of Wellington Channel, and traces of encampments along this track. Franklin had at some point during his stay sent a party to look into the possibility of Wellington Channel as a route, as per his instructions. Ommaney sailed up the Channel for a few miles, only to discover it blocked by ice. But he had seen a "water sky" ahead—the gray undersides of clouds that indicated water lay underneath. If there had been ice, the clouds would have been brightened by the reflection of light off the ice, a phenomenon known as "ice blink." Lacking any other indication of Franklin's route, the expedition leaders determined on Wellington Channel as a primary search area.

Cape Walker, incidentally, the other primary search area, forty miles away across Barrow Strait, was just visible from the highest point on Beechey Island. Franklin had been well placed to pursue his mission in 1846.

For the rest of August and into September ice determined the routes the ships took, and where they wintered. The Americans had not planned to winter over, were not prepared for it, and tried to escape Barrow Strait before being beset. Too late. Locked into the pack south of Wellington Channel, they were driven by a southerly wind up the channel in September for sixty miles. In October they drifted back down, still locked in the ice, into Barrow Strait. By late November they were in Baffin Bay, in the grips of a huge floe, and spent the winter trying to survive, sick with scurvy, without winter clothing. On February 22, Washington's birthday, Kane noted, "'hearts should be glad;' but we have no wine for the dinner-table, and are too sick for artificial merriment without it." At one point the crew put on a play called *The Irish Attorney.* "The ship's thermometer outside was at -46. Inside, among audience and actors, by aid of lungs, lamps, and housings, we got as high as 30 below zero, only sixty-two below the freezing point!!" Kane added that it was probably the lowest temperature in which a play had ever been acted.

The ice released them in June.

Frozen into the ice in Barrow Strait, Austin's ships spent the winter near Griffiths Island, just off the coast of Cornwallis Island, just west of the mouth of Wellington Channel. Penny and Ross were more secure, having found shelter in what they called Assistance Harbour, twenty miles away from Austin on the south shore of Cornwallis Island. That winter they split up the spring sledge journeys, sending Penny's crews up Wellington Channel while Austin sent parties west to Melville Island and south to Cape Walker and beyond. Lady Jane's ship, the *Prince Albert,* had sailed for home early, having been stopped by ice in Prince Regent Inlet. The only thing it accomplished was to take the news of the discovery on Beechey Island back to Great Britain. Lady Jane sent it out under a new captain first thing in the spring of 1851.

That winter was no different from the dozens of other winters men had spent in the Arctic since Parry. Lieutenant Sherard Osborn, commander of one of the steam tenders, was struck, as Parry had been struck, by the bleakness of the landscape and its "deadly white" uniformity; Osborn was as much a writer as a naval officer and the scenery filled him with flowery gloom:

> Talk of "antres [caves] vast and deserts idle,"—talk of the sadness awakened in the wanderer's bosom by the lone scenes, be it even by the cursed waters of Judea, or afflicted lands of Assyria,—give me, I say, death in any one of them, with the good sun and a bright heaven to whisper hope, rather than the solitary horrors of such scenes as these.

Osborn and the other officers filled the bleakness with more than the usual activity: "a theatre, a casino, a saloon, and two Arctic newspapers," which were handwritten. A sample entry: "What insect that Noah had with him, were these regions named after?—The arc-tic." Both a band and a glee club were formed; there was a fancy dress ball. But it was not all fun and games. They fired rockets into the sky in the vague hope of signaling some nearby Franklin survivor. They sent small balloons aloft too, made of oiled silk and filled with hydrogen. "To the base of the balloon," Osborn explained, ". . . a piece of slow match, five feet long, was attached, its lower end being lighted. Along this match, at certain intervals, pieces of coloured paper and silk were secured . . . , and on them the information as to our position and intended lines of search were printed." As the balloon caught the wind and sailed over the land, the match released these pieces of paper one by one and they "spread themselves on the snow, where their glaring colours would soon attract notice, should they happily fall near the poor fellows in the 'Erebus' and 'Terror.'" Osborn believed that the farthest away any of these pieces of paper was found was fifty miles. John Ross had brought carrier pigeons with him. One of them reportedly made it back to Scotland, but the messages it carried had fallen off.

In April fifteen sledges and 105 men left Austin's ships. Most of the sledges were support sledges, traveling with the lead sledge up to a certain point on the route, depositing provisions for the lead sledge's return, then themselves returning to the ships. All of them had names and even mottoes, some Latin, some English. Captain Ommanney's, with six men, was named the *Reliance,* its motto *Domine dirige nos:* Lord direct us. Osborn's, with seven, was the *True Blue,* its motto *Nil desperandum:* never despair. It was as if they were launching miniature ships, each with its own chain of command. Lieutenant McClintock was headed to Melville Island, three hundred miles to the west, Osborn and Omman-ney to the south—Cape Walker and beyond. The sledges were heavy, each carrying a small boat made out of gutta-percha, blankets, blanket bags, a tent, guns, a shovel, spare boots, knapsacks for every man—the total came to 440 pounds *before* the food was added. That weighed a lit-tle under a thousand pounds. In the end each man was dragging over two hundred pounds behind him.

Officers and men alike got into harness. They traveled by night to reduce the glare. When the wind was behind them, they raised a sail and that helped lighten the load considerably. It was intensely cold, often below zero, with a strong wind blowing, yet they all became soaked with sweat, and the sweat in their clothes froze at night, making them stiff and hard. It was simply brutal. Constant questions of "How are your feet?" were heard on all sides. They could not feel them; they did not know. Ommanney and Osborn found the ice piled up against the base of Cape Walker when they reached it to a height of fifty feet. They lifted and dragged the sledge over it and set up the tent at once; then every-body took his leather boots off to change into cloth boots made out of heavy flannel. "I shall not easily forget my painful feelings," wrote Osborn, "when one gallant fellow of my party, the captain of the sledge, exclaimed, 'Both feet gone, sir!' and sure enough they were, white as two lumps of ice, and equally cold."

Crippled or not, they struggled onward. "All was white, brilliant, and dazzling; the eye in vain turned from earth to heaven for rest or shade,—there was none; an unclouded sunlight poured through the calm and frosty air with merciless power, and the sun, being exactly in our faces, increased the intensity of its effects." One by one they went blind. "Those alone who have witnessed it," wrote Osborn, can conceive the pain of snow blindness. "Gradually," he added, "the film spread itself, objects became dimmer and dimmer, and at last all was darkness, with an intense horror of the slightest ray of sunlight." Sixteen men and one officer came down with it, out of thirty all told. A gale pinned them down and confined them to their tents. In a few days the blindness was gone. By May 6 they had covered sixty miles from Cape Walker. Osborn was full of praise for the men, who encouraged each other, cracked jokes, and passed off hunger with a smile. Often, he later remarked, he heard "a rough voice encouraging the sledge-crew by saying, 'Keep step, boys! keep step! she (the sledge) is coming along almost by herself; there's the "Erebus's" masts showing over the point ahead! Keep step, boys! keep step!'"

But the masts of the *Erebus* were not showing over the point ahead. Osborn and Ommanney climbed a tableland. They were on the western shores of Prince of Wales Island and could see only ice. "Landward, to the south, and far over the rugged and frozen sea, all was death-like and silent as the grave; we felt we might have been the first since 'creation's morn' to have looked upon it." They split up, Ommaney taking his men inland along the shore of a bay, Osborn continuing fifty miles farther south. He was three hundred miles from the ship when he decided to turn back. He reached it on June 12, crossing the thinning ice of Barrow Strait on a forced march. A week later only the parties led by McClintock that had sledged to Melville Island were still out. Parts of several seamen's feet had had to be amputated. One man had died. When McClintock did arrive, the melted water on top of the ice around the ships was four feet deep, so fast was the season advancing. McClintock had made Winter Harbour, where Parry had spent his first Arctic winter. In eighty days he had covered eight hundred miles. It was an extraordinary feat, and McClintock was from this time forward known as the father of Arctic sledge travel.

But no one had found any trace of the Franklin expedition.

So where had Franklin gone? No one knew. Any further course of action would be speculative, men and ships groping in the ice for clues. Captain Penny had sent six sledges north that spring, up both sides of Wellington Channel, far enough north to discover, at a place he called Point Surprise, that Wellington Channel opened into another strait and that, as early as May, it was not covered by ice. No trace of Franklin could be found on either side of Wellington Channel, but here was a clue—a strait of open water that went who knew where. Penny went back to his ship for a boat and spent late June and most of July exploring by boat more than three hundred miles of convoluted coastline. And the water was open! That was the exciting thing. Franklin's instructions had specifically mentioned Wellington Channel as an option. All other options seemed like dead ends. What looked like permanent ice filled up Melville Sound. The ice in newly discovered Peel Sound seemed from all appearances to have been there for years. The ice attached to the west side of newly discovered Prince of Wales Island was thick and rough and seemingly eternal. No ship, everyone who saw it assumed, could ever make it down those waters. Prince Regent Inlet was seldom, perhaps never, completely free of ice.

But here was a new strait and it was open. Perhaps the waters beyond it were open. Perhaps Franklin had gone that way, since certainly, it was only too natural to think, he could not have gone south and west. No thought was given to the possibility that the ice to the south and west was variable, that conditions changed season to season, that channels opened up one year that were closed in others. The sledging parties, first of James Ross's, then of Horatio Austin's, had found the routes to the south closed. So had Parry in 1819–20. Therefore they were always closed. Franklin must have gone up Wellington Channel.

Penny came back from his discoveries and told Austin he had found no trace of Franklin up Wellington Channel and there was no reason to look there further. Then he changed his mind and asked Austin for the use of one of the steam launches to break through the plug of ice that blocked Wellington Channel and explore further into the open strait beyond. Austin refused; he looked down upon this mere whaling captain. A hail of criticism for his attitude, and his refusal, greeted him when he returned to England shortly thereafter. Austin broke free of the ice on August 12; on August 13 he left Barrow Strait and sailed for Jones Sound in Baffin Bay, to see if that were open. Jones Sound, it was thought, opened into Wellington Channel farther north than anyone had been able to go. Where Jones Sound narrowed, it was frozen up. He did not find the cairn there that another whaling captain thought he had seen. He sailed to Wolstenholme Sound in Greenland and was nearly frozen in for the winter, but one of the steam tenders broke through the ice, and they escaped.

Back in England it was William Penny who was writing the epilogue to this particular stage in the Franklin search. Penny went to the Admiralty, told them his story, and applied for a steam tender of his own to take back to the Arctic that fall, right away, and push north into the open polar sea he had seen, or thought he had seen, beyond his farthest north. The Admiralty lords called in the Arctic knights and they, of course, advised the Admiralty to do no such thing. Navigation in the Arctic closed in early October at the latest. But they were open to the idea that Franklin might indeed have gone up Wellington Channel, or even backtracked out of Lancaster Sound to try Jones Sound. Parry thought Franklin might have tried to escape from the north through Jones Sound; Richardson agreed that Franklin might have attempted Jones Sound if he had been blocked in every other direction; and a Royal Navy captain named Robert McCormick was quoted in *The Nautical Magazine* in October 1851, shortly after Penny's return, to the effect that

> I then believed, and I do still, after a long and mature consideration of the subject, that Sir John Franklin's ships have been arrested in a high latitude, and beset in the heavy Polar ice northward of *Parry Islands*, and that their probable course thither has been through *Wellington Channel*, or one of the *Sounds* at the northern extremity of *Baffin Bay*.

The press and the public bought into the theory. *The Athenaeum*, for one, was shocked by Austin's refusal to lend Penny one of the steamers to try to break through the ice in Wellington Channel. W. Francis Ainsworth in *The New Monthly Magazine* reminded readers that people had scoffed at his suggestion that Franklin was in the north polar sea; now all the evidence pointed north. The well-known scientist David Brewster, writing in *The North British Review*, thought Franklin had sailed north and was somewhere close to the Pole. Brewster had his own well-thumbed theory about the Arctic to sell. He was convinced that the Pole was not its coldest point, that in fact there were two much colder areas, and that the waters around the Pole were relatively warm. Thus

> Sir John Franklin, in ascending Wellington Channel, would necessarily pass into a warmer climate, where an arctic winter would lose much of its horrors, and where a more genial temperature would foster animal life, and supply him, not only with materials for food, but even with the elements of luxury. Though barriers of ice or other causes may prevent him from retracing his steps by Wellington Channel, or by any other southward course, he may be carrying on his explorations in new regions . . . far to the east or west of the meridian in which he entered it.

The "elements of luxury" indeed: Brewster sounds uncannily like the would-be explorer Robert Walton in Mary Shelley's *Frankenstein*, dreaming of a paradise in the Far North.

Brewster was seconded by the German geographer and mapmaker August Petermann, then resident in England, who was touting his own theory of an open polar sea. Petermann wrote a book about the subject and suggested that people should be searching for Franklin in the waters above Siberia, where the Russian explorer F. P. Wrangel had found a polynya of unknown extent much like the area known as the North Water in Baffin Bay, which never froze. One of the more enthusiastic navy lieutenants engaged in the search, Bedford Pim, proposed in a talk to the Royal Geographical Society that he go by himself to Siberia, find a boat, and make the attempt. The members cheered him on—this was the spirit—and he went to the public to raise money by subscription. The Russian ambassador promised to help try to persuade his government. But the czar's government saw this for what it was, sheer romance, and turned Pim down. A Captain Beatson proposed something similar, a voyage straight north through Bering Strait. It too came to nothing. Pim went instead on the next Admiralty ships sent to Lancaster Sound.

In the meantime a new commander, William Kennedy, had taken Jane Franklin's ship, the *Prince Albert,* back to the Arctic in the spring of 1851 to finish the job she had sent it to do in 1850 under Forsyth—sail to Prince Regent Inlet, check out Fury Beach, spend the winter where John Ross had spent the winters of 1829 to 1832, and explore on foot the same area James Ross had explored on that ill-fated expedition—the area around the North Magnetic Pole and King William Island. Kennedy was an HBC man who had written Jane Franklin from Canada and volunteered his services. Since he was not much of a sailor, he took as his second another volunteer, a young French naval lieutenant named Joseph René Bellot, one of the most likable of the men who participated in the search for Franklin. He completely charmed Lady Jane; when she came to the Orkneys to see the ship off she went through Bellot's wardrobe and "observed that he still needed a mother." Bellot accepted the idea and told his diary that he would "seek my father with the inexhaustible devotion of a son."

Devotion would not be enough; luck was essential too, and the *Prince Albert* scored low on that count. The ship had more than the usual trouble getting around the ice in Baffin Bay and reached Lancaster Sound and Prince Regent Inlet late. Rapid freeze-up in the inlet forced them into winter harbor at Batty Bay, just thirty miles south of Port Leopold. In the spring they set out down the coast to Fury Beach and followed the coastline from there into the great arc of Brentford Bay, where they discovered, without quite realizing exactly where they were, a narrow strait that separates Boothia Peninsula from North Somerset, thus establishing the fact that North Somerset is an island. Moving through the strait, they found themselves on the shore of Peel Sound, looking across at Prince of Wales Island. To the north Kennedy thought he saw a land bridge connecting Prince of Wales Island to North Somerset, which, if it had existed, would have made it impossible for Franklin to have sailed through Peel Sound. In that case, Kennedy reasoned, there was no point in turning south, in accordance with Lady Jane's orders, because Franklin would have had to take some other route to the coast of North America. He decided to cross Peel Sound instead to Prince of Wales Island, then cross that to the coast Franklin would presumably have had to follow.

That was what they did, reaching the west coast of Prince of Wales Island at Ommanney Bay, tracing the coast north to Cape Walker, racing east to Port Leopold, where James Ross had cached provisions two years before, then making their way south to the *Prince Albert*. Lieutenant Osborn had already covered most of this route, so they added nothing to the knowledge of the Arctic. They had come in a great circle but they had not done what Lady Jane wanted them to do. If they had turned south they would almost certainly have reached the west coast of King William Island and discovered the truth. Kennedy had thrown away a great opportunity. Their single accomplishment was to solve one more of the Arctic's many geographical puzzles. A strait did, after all, exist between Prince Regent Inlet and the seas to the west. It now bears the name Bellot Strait. Until global warming it remained, like Hecla and Fury Strait, more or less permanently icebound.

One other expedition failed to reach the west coast of King William Island in 1851: John Rae's. Lady Jane had endeared herself to Rae by visiting his mother in the Orkneys in 1849 and getting to know her. He had asked for a leave of absence in 1850, only to receive from his superiors a letter requesting him to go out once again to the north coast of Canada, cross over to Victoria Land and Wollaston Land, and look for Franklin. At the same time Lady Jane wrote him to say that "it has been the custom of people to throw upon you everything that others failed to accomplish—'oh Rae's in that quarter, Rae will do that'—as if you and your single boat could explore hundreds of miles NSE & West and as if no obstacles of any kind could interfere." Mindful of other people as always, she had identified the trouble with having a reputation as a miracle worker. Under the circumstances, although Rae was beginning to feel he was too old for this kind of work, he could not refuse. In April, before he left, he wrote Simpson, "My whole toilet apparatus are a pocket comb, a tooth brush, towel and bit of coarsest yellow soap, with a wardrobe, which will boast of one flannel shirt (in addition to the shoes and socks absolutely requisite) besides my every day suit." No one before or since, perhaps, has ever traveled so light in the Arctic.

He took two men with him and three dogs, crossed the ice to Wollaston Land, discovered that Wollaston Land was part of the much larger Victoria Island, covered 413 miles of coastline, and found nothing. In June he went back, down the Coppermine by boat this time, traveled east along the coast to Coronation Gulf, crossed to Victoria Island on July 27, and in August reached the far eastern shore of the island. Rae was discovering new coastline and a new strait—Victoria Strait—which separates Victoria Island from King William Island. Rae would have gone on and crossed Victoria Strait, but the ice looked impassable, so he walked north instead, over ice so rough that his feet bled. For four days, August 15 to 19, Rae took to the water in his boat, hoping to reach the lee of Admiralty Island, which stood halfway between Victoria Island and King William Island, but he and his crew were forced to retreat every time. "A little before noon," he told Simpson, "the breeze increased to a gale and shifted two points more easterly, and there being a great accumulation of ice between us and Admiralty Island I sought shelter under the lee of a point." The next day even more ice had moved down the strait. He tried one last time. Too much ice. Had he made it, Rae would have solved the mystery of John Franklin and his expedition.

On the way home, however, Rae did find evidence of a sort. First was a piece of pine, resembling the "butt end of a small flagstaff." It was just short of six feet long, and there was a mark stamped on one side and a bit of white line "formed of a loop on it with two copper tacks. Both the line and the tacks bore the Government mark. The broad arrow being stamped on the latter, and the former having a red worsted thread running through it." These were Royal Navy marks. Farther to the west on the south coast of Victoria Island he found a piece of sawn oak three feet, eight inches long, evidently part of a stanchion. Rae was pretty sure, given the direction of the drift in the area, that these fragments had come down Victoria Strait. On his return he took them to England, where they were examined at the yards where the *Erebus* and *Terror* had been built, and also, in London, by Sir James Ross. Did they indeed belong to Franklin's ships? Ross thought it entirely possible, but he could not be sure about it.

Nor could anybody else. The bottom part of a flagstaff might have come from any British ship, and the *Fury* had been abandoned in Prince Regent Inlet and broken up. It could have come from the *Fury*. A stanchion was only a piece of a door. The Inuit whom Rae met on Victoria Island knew nothing of large ships in the area; nor had they seen white men. The Franklin searches were beginning to unravel the Arctic maze. Lands that had been known only to their native inhabitants before were filling in the blank spaces on British maps, British names were being tacked onto capes, harbors, bays, and islands—the royal family was honored at every turn of a strait. But Franklin was still lost. The public was still unsatisfied. The clock was running down on any hope of rescue.

CHAPTER NINETEEN

THE DISCOVERY OF THE NORTHWEST PASSAGE

W ere any of Franklin's men, in fact, still alive? Franklin had left London in the spring of 1845 with food for three years that conceivably, with a side order of terrible hardship, could have been stretched to five. But by the time Austin sailed home in the fall of 1851, they had been gone for more than six years. As early as October the year before, as another winter settled on the Canadian archipelago, W. Frances Ainsworth had written in *The New Monthly Magazine*, "Hope itself grows pale at the idea of our starving countrymen, if still alive, lingering in their icy prison for one more winter of cold, and darkness, and want!" *If still alive*—to more than a few it seemed highly unlikely. A year later, after the disappointing results of the Austin expedition—Austin himself thought further search was pointless—*The Times* editorialized that the country needed "some deliberate reflection on the course which it may befit the Government of this country to adopt." What, the paper asked, "has been the result of all our exertions? We speak without any wish to discourage when we say that it is almost nothing at all." Franklin's route was still an unknown. Not a single survivor and only the most meager of clues had turned up. "We are, in fact, no wiser than we were before."

The whole enterprise of the Northwest Passage, from *The Times'* point of view, should have been abandoned when it was discovered that Arctic ice was, in its word, "insuperable." Now pursuing this goal seemed even more foolish. We had entered the age of steam, the paper reminded its readers. Calcutta, thanks to the screw propeller and the Suez Canal, was only twelve days away. China could be reached in a fortnight. Except for the rescue efforts, which the national honor demanded, the "problem of the North-West passage is as obsolete as the quadrature [the squaring] of the circle, and we can only lament that so much has been staked on its solution."

The British public continued nevertheless to demand that the Admiralty send out rescue ships. The Admiralty, uncertain about what course to adopt, asked its Arctic knights what they thought about the chances that some, at least, of the Franklin expedition still lived. Their answers tended toward the positive. Sir John Richardson set the tone, pointing out that the Inuit had no trouble surviving in the Arctic. "Except practical skills in hunting seals, and the art of building snow-houses, that people have no qualifications that may not be surpassed by the intelligence, providence, and appliances of Europeans," he wrote. If the Inuit could do it, certainly British seamen could do it better. John Rae had been able to feed his party of thirteen men at Repulse Bay in the winter of 1846–47 by hunting caribou and ptarmigan and netting salmon and using nothing but the dried, withered stems of a shrub called *andromeda* for fuel. Someone had found in *The Annual Register* for 1774 the account of four Russian sailors who, marooned on Spitzbergen, had lived for more than six years on what the land offered up. It could be done. Food abounded in the Arctic, though not everywhere; some of the Arctic islands were completely barren. And if you had sailed into the ice, were locked in the pack far from land, God help you. Your only hope was the rare seal at the occasional seal hole, and there you needed the skills, the clothing, and the otherworldly patience of an Inuit to survive.

Richardson did not abandon himself completely to positive thinking. He understood that Franklin might be beset in the ice, in which case it was useless to speak of land animals as a resource. If the ships had been wrecked, the crew might not have saved enough in the way of supplies, clothing, and other necessities to live long. Fuel for cooking was another issue. It took the Inuit one pound of animal fat to melt enough snow to provide water for three men for one day. The Franklin expedition had 126 men. They would need a whale, or terrific luck hunting seals, or a steady supply of caribou, to do the same. "We ought also," Richardson went on, "to take into account the probable ravages of scurvy among the crews, in the course of so many years' seclusion in the north." As a doctor Richardson well knew that scurvy "always appeared in a greater or lesser degree in the discovery ships after the second winter, and it is likely to be severe and fatal, just in proportion to the scantiness of the diet on which the people feed."

This was a welcome note of realism, but it made no real difference to the issue of whether the search should be continued. The Admiralty did not hesitate long; even *The Times* had agreed that the search must go on as long as any hope remained. And hope did remain. Jane Franklin, for her part, fed on it. She too had acceded to the idea that her husband must have sailed up Wellington Channel, despite her earlier preference for the west coast of the Boothia Peninsula. If no one could possibly have sailed down that coast, as all the rescuers who had been there agreed, she could hardly argue otherwise, since the source of her own opinion to the contrary was a three-year-old girl who happened to be dead. Wellington Channel was the second choice in Franklin's orders; if the southwest was closed to him, he had been told to try the channel. He always followed orders. William Penny had found it open, once you got past its plug of ice. It was open when Barrow Strait was closed. Penny had found driftwood on its shores. Where could that have come from if not an open polar sea?

For more than four hundred years the belief in such a sea had survived; now, the feeling was, they were about to find it, and John Franklin and his crews with it. The Admiralty refitted the four ships that Austin had brought home and gave command of them to Sir Edward Belcher. He and his expedition left for the Arctic in April 1852, taking as his flagship the *Assistance*. The *Resolute* was under the command of Henry Kellett, formerly commander of the *Herald*, which had been resupplying the supply ship kept at Bering Strait for the last two years. Commanding the two steam tenders, *Pioneer* and *Intrepid*, were Sherard Osborn and Francis McClintock, the latter of whom had been promoted. Lieutenant Pullen, having proven himself on the Canadian coastline and now a commander, the rank below captain, was in charge of the store ship, the *North Star*, which was to settle at Beechey Island for the duration and replenish the other ships when necessary. They had another mission to fulfill in addition to finding Franklin. The two ships that had sailed for Bering Strait in 1850 under Collinson and McClure had not been heard from. No one knew where they were. The Admiralty, and the public, were becoming concerned about them. They too might need rescuing.

Belcher divided his flotilla into two divisions. He himself would take the *Assistance*, accompanied by Osborn in the *Pioneer*, up Wellington Channel and explore there. Kellett in the *Resolute* would sail west in Barrow Strait with the help of the *Intrepid* as far as they could manage;

their job was to explore the north shore of Melville Island and beyond it to the north, east, and west, fanning out from whatever harbor they would eventually find along the route to spend the winter. Kellett and McClintock ran into a streak of luck here; they were able to reach the south shore of Melville Island, under sail, for the first time since Parry had had the same good luck in 1819. Belcher had much less luck. He ran into the ice plug that was almost always to be found in Wellington Channel forty or fifty miles north of the entrance and found himself in winter quarters far sooner than he had anticipated.

In Belcher's case, luck might not have made much of a difference. He was not entirely incompetent. He had served in river wars with China that established the opium trade for British traders and had earned his knighthood there. He was an excellent surveyor, which endeared him to Sir Francis Beaufort. But otherwise Belcher was a disaster. Clements Markham called him "the very last man in the navy who should have been selected." Leslie H. Neatby in his book on the Franklin search compared him to Captain Bligh of the *Bounty* mutiny and described him as "coarse, meddling, tactless, and fearfully egotistical." To make matters worse, he had no experience with sea ice.

For Henry Kellett and Francis McClintock, however, Belcher's command hardly mattered. After a parting dinner at Beechey Island, they separated and began the next day to work west between the ice pack and the land, just as Parry had done, reaching Melville Island and Parry's Winter Harbour in early September. Six miles of pack ice blocked the entrance, so Kellett took his ships back east to a harbor called Bridport Inlet and sawed his way into winter quarters there behind Dealey Island. As soon as the ships were berthed, preliminary sledge parties were dispatched to set up depots for the main sledging explorations of the following spring. Spring sledging had become the MO in the Arctic; the ships were hardly more than warehouses, iced into harbors while the sledge parties did the work of exploring, mapping new land, searching for signs of the Franklin expedition and now of Collinson and McClure as well, and leaving dozens of messages behind in cairns advising whoever might come across them where food depots were to be found. In the spring of 1853 most of the crews of both ships would depart on sledges, leaving only skeleton crews behind.

Some of these sledge journeys were epic in scope, no less heroic for going in the wrong direction in the service of a hopeless cause. McClintock's was probably the hardest and certainly the longest. The sledge weighed 2,280 pounds, and there were ten men to drag it. They might make ten miles a day, but it took nine hours to make it. It was usually too cold to sleep. They slogged over ice and through snow and meltwater up to their knees. Like an overloaded pack animal, one man dropped dead in his traces. Over the course of three months, as winter morphed into spring, McClintock and his crew covered 1,408 miles on foot. To the west of Melville Island they discovered more land, an island they named Eglinton Island, then another, much larger, that McClintock named for one of Queen Victoria's sons, Prince Patrick. The discoveries came at a cost. Markham commented in his biography of McClintock that it "took more than a year for the sledge crew of 1853 to recover entirely." A marine who had to be carried back never did recover. To endure this work, wrote Markham, "youth and a perfectly sound constitution are essentials."

The sledge journeys were all this arduous; McClintock's was only longer than the others. Experiencing the conditions firsthand, most of the men must have understood that they were no longer searching for survivors, only for news; and indeed, they found no trace of Franklin. When McClintock returned from Prince Patrick Island in July 1853, the Franklin expedition had been in the Arctic more than eight years. Were any of them still alive? Hope needs more than hope to feed on. It needs at least a glimpse of something green, but this landscape was a solid white, covered only with snow and time.

Robert McClure, however, captain of the *Investigator,* and his crew were still alive in 1853, although they knew another winter in the Arctic would kill them all. The *Investigator* had made one of the most remarkable journeys to date into the Arctic, becoming the first ship in history to round Point Barrow under sail and penetrate the waters of the Beaufort Sea north of Alaska and the Canadian coast of North America.

McClure in the *Investigator* and Collinson in the *Enterprise* had sailed from Plymouth Harbour on the same day, January 20, 1850, but Collinson's ship was faster and they quickly parted company, with orders from Collinson, in overall command, to meet at the Straits of Magellan. McClure had on board a Moravian missionary who had spent years in Labrador trying to convert the natives to Christianity and who spoke fluent Inuit. He was along as an interpreter but he also kept a diary, and it provides a rare look at the internal dynamics of an Arctic exploration ship. Official accounts seldom say anything about bickering and complaints. Miertsching, the missionary, was under no such constraints. And it is clear that McClure was a complicated man, daring to the point of recklessness as a navigator, which can be a positive trait in the Arctic ice; a hard disciplinarian—one seaman got 48 lashes with a whip; yet capable of lying on his back on the quarterdeck with Miertsching at night, smoking a pipe and staring at the stars. McClure quarreled early on with his junior officers and put one under arrest with two armed marines standing outside his cabin door. The "devil of discord," wrote Miertsching, was in the ship. Not until they had passed through the Straits of Magellan did the junior officers make peace with McClure.

They found Collinson at the straits but the winter storms of the Southern Hemisphere drove them apart again. The next rendezvous was to be Honolulu; McClure got there to find that Collinson had left on July 4, a day before. The next rendezvous would be, Collinson had said, at the store ship *Plover*, stationed in Kotzebue Sound to wait for ships emerging from the Northwest Passage, should any get through. McClure thought Collinson was just as unlikely to wait for him there as he had been in Honolulu and would proceed directly into the ice, taking the *Plover* with him into the Arctic. McClure was ambitious. With the rewards being offered, definitive news about the fate of Franklin was worth quite a bit of money. The prestige of discovering the Northwest Passage was also well worth pursuing. Collinson, he knew, was taking the safe route to the Arctic, steering for Petropavlovska, on the Kamchatka Peninsula, to avoid having to sail through the fog-bound, poorly charted Aleutian Islands, with their tide races and the uncertain depths of the channels that divided them. It was much longer to go all the way around the Aleutians rather than through them, but it avoided the risk of shipwreck in dangerous waters. In Hawaii McClure heard about a route through the Aleutians, much more direct, that was relatively safe. McClure did not follow Collinson but sailed directly north. Sixteen days later the *Investigator* was "swept rapidly along in a tide race with a fair wind," catching sight of a headland, briefly, when the fog lifted a bit. That headland was all they saw of the Aleutian Islands.

It was a gutsy move that would of course have seemed stupid if they had run into the headland instead. In Kotzebue Sound McClure found the *Plover* but not Collinson. The *Plover* was under the command of T. E. L. Moore, the same officer who had spent the winter in her two years earlier on the Siberian coast. Moore was living openly with his interpreter, a young Inuit woman. Poor pious Miertsching was appalled, just as he had been earlier in the voyage by the behavior of British seamen generally—their propensity for swearing, their love of drink, and their incessant singing and dancing at night. McClure gave him permission to distribute religious tracts among them, telling him at the same time that it was hopeless. Now he found Moore, and others on the ship too, behaving "so shamelessly that here one will soon have an Anglo-Eskimo colony."

McClure cared only that Collinson was not there and had not been seen. He immediately sailed north toward Cape Lisburne, another rendezvous, leaving with Moore a letter to the Admiralty explaining his intentions. He believed, he told the Admiralty lords, that Collinson was ahead of him and had already proceeded beyond Cape Lisburne, and he did not expect to catch him. In that case, he wrote, it is "probable" that "this vessel may form a detached part of the expedition." He would go it alone. Some days later Captain Henry Kellett in the *Herald* came in view. It was Kellett's job to replenish the *Plover's* provisions once a year; otherwise the *Herald* was a survey ship, working along the western coastline of Central America. Kellett was a captain, one grade higher than McClure, and uneasy about McClure's decision to go ahead on his own. He tried to persuade McClure to wait for Collinson, but McClure knew an opportunity when he saw one. Collinson could have passed the *Herald* in the fog. It was foolish to wait for him, especially since open water waited to the northeast, around Point Barrow. Kellett was as reluctant to force McClure to wait as he was to let him go. In the end he chose the latter course, thinking better of it only at the last moment when he signaled to the disappearing ship, "Had you better not wait forty-eight hours?"

"Important duty," McClure replied. "Cannot upon my own responsibility."

McClure found the pack in retreat far enough from Point Barrow that he was able to round the point and sail east into the Beaufort Sea, skirting the same coast that Pullen was searching by boat. Collinson did not reach Cape Lisburne until mid-August, two weeks behind McClure. He too found open water about Point Barrow and could have sailed east, just as McClure did. But Collinson was an altogether different sort of sea captain from Robert McClure. Collinson wanted a minimum of fifteen miles between the pack and the land before he would try for an easting. George Back had told him the coast between Point Barrow and the Mackenzie River was so shallow that even small boats

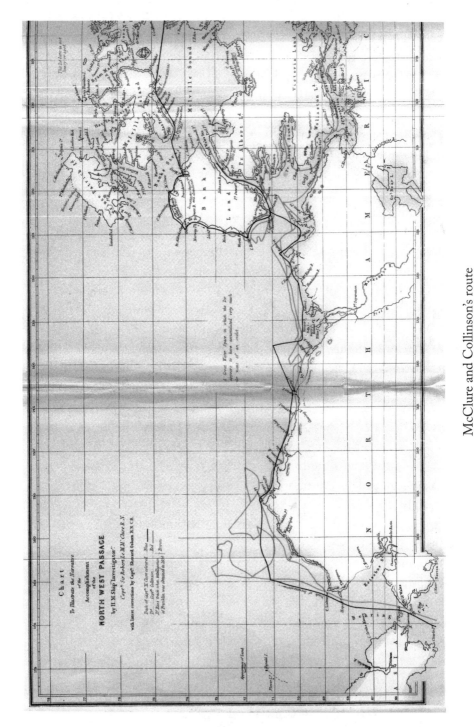

McClure and Collinson's route

(Source: Robert McClure, *Discovery of the North-West Passage*, 1855.)

needed two miles of water in some places to navigate. Two miles is not fifteen, however. McClure would later take the *Investigator* into channels between the pack on his port and steep cliffs on his starboard that were hardly as wide as the ship. It may be that Collinson was lazy, or afraid, or just not ready to spend the winter in the Arctic. Whatever the case, he ran. The *Enterprise* wintered in Hong Kong. It did not get back to the ice until the following summer.

The *Investigator* worked its way east, meanwhile, between the shallow coastline and the edge of the pack, generally aground in six or seven fathoms of water, which meant that the ice was thirty-five to forty feet thick. It was the height of summer but the pack was unbroken. As far as Miertsching could determine by talking to the natives, the Beaufort Sea ice pack was eternal. Occasionally they ventured up a vein of water but it soon came to an end. By the middle of August the ship had passed Franklin's turning point, Return Reef, and it had run aground on one of that coast's innumerable shoals and lost eleven casks of salted meat when, in order to lighten the ship, the men off-loaded it from the deck into one of the ship's boats, and the boat flipped. On August 19, tempted by a bight in the ice, McClure tried to steer for Banks Land to the northeast, only to run into a blind alley. He had to backtrack for seventy miles to avoid certain destruction when the pack closed.

On August 22 McClure passed Richards Island, east of the mouth of the Mackenzie River. On the same day Lieutenant Pullen was coasting Richards Island in the opposite direction, heading for the Mackenzie. Neither saw the other.

They were still under sail in early September. They had made their way past Cape Bathurst, where the Inuit were gathered in considerable numbers fishing and the native women were better looking than usual; Sherard Osborn, who wrote McClure's book for him from his journal, called the spot the Tahiti of the north. To the north lay Banks Island, and McClure steered for it, landing on its southwest corner. The shoreline trended to the northeast, and McClure followed it. Before long he found himself in a body of water thirty miles wide. The lane narrowed as they sailed, but it was heading northeast, toward Barrow Strait. If it were itself a strait, and not an inlet, if it opened into Barrow Strait, *voilà!* The Northwest Passage. They passed a couple of islands. The inlet, strait, whichever it was, narrowed to fourteen miles. They had very little time. The "season for navigation," Osborn wrote, "was now to be told in hours." On the ninth a sun sighting at noon made them a mere sixty miles from Barrow Strait. Could it be possible, McClure asked himself in his journal, that this water would lead him to the strait, and "prove to be the long-sought North-West Passage?"

Two days later the ice stopped them short of their goal. They spent the winter in the pack beset in what was indeed a strait, Prince of Wales Strait, as McClure named it, connecting the known coastal route of the Northwest Passage running along the shores of the North American continent to Barrow Strait. When the ice froze up hard enough to send out sledges McClure took a small party north along the strait and saw what the pack had denied him, the great ice-choked basin of Melville Sound. Cross that basin in the *Investigator*, sail east to Baffin Bay and home from there, and McClure would become the first man ever to complete the Northwest Passage. All he needed to achieve this extraordinary triumph was to force his ship through the ancient sea ice, thirty-five to forty feet thick, that clogged the basin and fed into channels like Prince of Wales Strait and Victoria Strait, Barrow Strait and Peel Sound, and made the dream of navigating the Northwest Passage seem, ultimately, foolish. McClure dreamed the dream nevertheless.

In the meantime he and his crew had to survive the winter. Until the ice froze solidly, immovably around them, the ship was in constant danger from shifting floes and tidal currents. Osborn reported that in his journal McClure "despairs of being able to convey to us even a remote idea of the harassing anxiety he underwent whilst his vessel was settling herself in her icy cradle. 'The crashing, creaking, and straining is beyond description,' he adds; 'and the officer of the watch, when speaking to me, is obliged to put his mouth close to my ear, on account of the deafening noise.'" The sledge party that went out to confirm that Prince of Wales Strait was a strait fell into their blanket bags at night too exhausted to eat. Over nine days, eight men consumed only eighteen pounds of pemmican, thirty-one pounds of ship's biscuit, and two pounds of oatmeal. That's a quarter of a pound of pemmican per man per day. Otherwise they ate fairly well. Musk oxen proved plentiful that winter, caribou were shot, and occasional hares and ptarmigans. In May McClure himself shot a polar bear. When they opened its stomach they found raisins, pork fat in small cubes, some pieces of tobacco leaf, and a bit of sticking plaster. The bear, they eventually discovered, had gotten into a can of preserved meat somebody had left on the ice nearby.

McClure sent sledging parties out in the spring and one of them went all around the north shore of Banks Island and determined that it was an island. Another went down Prince of Wales Strait to the south-west corner of Victoria Island and stood on the north shore of a deep sound that cuts into its southwest corner, even as John Rae was on its south shore, forty miles across the water. Men might not be meeting but geographical connections were being made; they were mapping the Arctic, step by step, sledge party by sledge party.

In mid-July 1851 the ice liberated the *Investigator*, and McClure did what he could to navigate up the strait toward Melville Sound and Bar-row Strait, but the ice was still so thick on the water he could do little but drift with it and hope not to be driven ashore, or against a cliff. At one point they were within twenty-five miles of the sound. However, the strait was jammed up beyond that point and McClure retreated. Now he would circle Banks Island to the west. For a while the sailing was easy. Banks Island had the same shallow sloping coastline as the North American continent west of the Mackenzie River, and he was able to find sailing room between the island and the pack. Then the geography changed. He rounded Prince Alfred's Cape on the west coast of the island and steep bluffs plunged straight down into the water. Now the pack was practically on the land; the lane of open water between the two was a mere two hundred yards wide.

Or even less. "In some places," Osborn wrote, "the channel was so narrow that the quarter boats had to be topped up to prevent them touching the cliffs on the one hand, or the lofty ice upon the other." Yardarms scraped the cliffs. It was insane to be there at all but they did not have room to turn around. They could only go on. The end of August found them stuck at the northwest corner of Banks Island. The officers went ashore and wandered a little way into the interior, to find fossil trees on the ground. McClure discovered a two-hundred-foot-deep ravine filled with wood to a depth of forty feet. No one could explain how it got there. Winter, meanwhile, was overtaking them. Whatever open water they could see was freezing up. To lie there all winter exposed to northwest gales, frozen into the edge of the Beaufort Sea in ice forty feet thick—that was an unpleasant thought. On September 10 the wind shifted to the south and drove the ice offshore, the *Investigator* with it. Desperate now, McClure used "enormous charges" of gunpowder to blow the ship out of its prison cell and worked his way east along the north shore of Banks Island. At night they sought shelter among grounded pieces of ice while the pack "rolled along the coast, pivoting upon the grounded pieces, and threatened, as it pulverized or threw masses thirty or forty feet thick high up on the beach, or a-top one another, to occasion a like catastrophe to their frail bark." Men prayed. McClure placed his hope in God. On September 22 they rounded a headland where the ice had been forced up a steep slope to the height of a seven-story building. Two days later they found a harbor. Bay of Mercy, they called it. That fall McClure put his men and officers on two-thirds rations.

Banks Island was full of caribou, as it happened—caribou and wolves. McClure was struck that winter by the fact that the caribou would move about unconcerned at the presence of wolves but would run when they saw human beings, which they had never seen before. The two species competed for the caribou that winter. When a hunter did manage to shoot one, the wolves often got to it first. If he left the carcass to get help from the ship in bringing it in, nothing would be left of it when he came back with his help. One man, the boatswain, Kennedy, advanced on the carcass of a deer he had shot, to find five wolves and several foxes fighting over it. He had a weapon but these were the old days, before breechloading guns. If he shot at one wolf he was afraid he would be dead before he could reload. So he shouted and waved his arms and was able to scare four of the wolves off. The fifth, a female, stood its ground. Kennedy picked up a leg of the dismembered deer and then grabbed one end of the entire carcass. The wolf grabbed the other and would not let go. Not until Miertsching, also out hunting, approached did the wolves give up the game.

Fresh meat was available, then, and they were able to shoot enough of it to have it three times a week. Usually fresh meat, which contains vitamin C, holds off scurvy, but it failed to do so this time. The men had not had fresh vegetables since they had left Hawaii two years before. It was usually the second season in the ice when scurvy began to appear, John Richardson had said, and here it was: blackening gums, weakening limbs, and the increasing lethargy that seems so much like depression that sea captains went to great lengths to keep their men occupied and cheerfully working. Osborn fails to tell us whether they had lemon juice on board. The Admiralty had lately taken to issuing lime juice, which has less vitamin C and is much less effective against scurvy; but they could not have known. Lemon juice was far more expensive.

On April 11, 1852, McClure left with six men across Melville Sound for Melville Island and Winter Harbour, where a depot was supposed to have been established. It was a rough crossing over the old ice in the sound, but McClure made it in two weeks, arriving at Winter Harbour on April 28. He found only a note left by McClintock the previous year. There was a depot, the note read, near Beechey Island, some three hundred miles to the east. The note also said that Sir John Ross had left his yacht, the *Mary*, near Beechey Island for survivors to use to sail out of the Arctic. Beechey Island was well out of reach. McClure left his own note at Winter Harbour and turned back across the ice. He had completed, after a fashion, the Northwest Passage with this trip, passing from Bering Strait to a point that another British expedition had once reached. But the journey had left him feeling that there was no help to be had. He was on his own. In fact he had just saved his life.

That summer the ice in Bay of Mercy did not melt. Into July it grew thicker instead. A man named Sergeant Woon killed two musk oxen in July. He had wounded the larger one with his last bullet, and the beast charged him. He killed it by firing his iron ramrod into its body. Wild sorrel eased the scurvy while the sorrel lasted, but they were unable to release the ship from Bay of Mercy, and the ice outside the bay, in Melville Sound, was immobile and impenetrable. In August a lane of open water did appear in the sound, but the temperature was already falling. Young ice was forming in the bay. Summer hardly came to the Arctic in 1852. The lane of water outside closed by August 24, and the remaining sorrel already lay under three inches of snow. Cloud cover was continuous and they had not seen the sun since May. The men, Miertsching wrote in his diary, "creep around with drooping heads and empty stomachs. . . . The captain, oppressed with anxieties, seeks comfort by wandering alone on the hill." One young sailor was going mad.

McClure was already hatching plans for the spring. He knew that another winter in Bay of Mercy meant reduced rations and more scurvy. On September 9 he called the crew together and told them that in the spring he would send thirty men away, half his crew. One group of eight would go to the Mackenzie River to look for help, the rest to Port Leopold, on North Somerset, where James Ross had built a hut and cached supplies in 1848 for possible Franklin survivors. In the meantime he would do everything he could to make their lives bearable. The men who remained with the ship in the spring, he added, would try to save her.

In October one of the officers went mad. His raving and babbling at night kept Miertsching awake.

They were on half-rations now. On October 18 the crew gathered en masse to ask the captain for an increase in rations. They could not sleep for hunger, they said. "I have at times . . . seen hungry people," Miertsching wrote, "but not until now had I personally felt what real hunger means—perpetual hunger; but I feel it now." And later: "My face and fingers have so often been frozen, and on healing have grown so tender that in the cold I can scarcely bear to handle my gun, so usually one of those sailors who are much attached to me carries my gun, and when a deer is killed they share the blood and the contents of the first stomach. A reindeer," he added, "has two stomachs." He does not mention what happened to the contents of the second stomach.

Breakfast that winter was "a cup of the weakest cocoa, and a small portion of the small allowance of bread." Dinner consisted of "the rest of the bread, and half a pound of salt meat, containing a good proportion of bone, with just enough vegetable to swear by." For supper? Weak tea. The list of men in sick bay grew longer. The situation grew more hopeless. By January 1, 1853, Miertsching knew his assignment for the following spring. He would accompany Lieutenant Cresswell and six "very sick seamen" on foot from Bay of Mercy and around Banks Island to Dolphin and Union Strait and from there along the American coast to the Mackenzie, then up the Mackenzie to the first HBC fort. From there they would head to England. He was clear about their chances. "There is not the faintest possibility," he wrote, "that any one of us should reach England." It was the same for the others, who were to try to make Port Leopold, five hundred miles away. There was no chance.

The two madmen continued to rave and howl that winter "day and night." The baker received two dozen lashes for stealing meat, flour, and dough. When they shot a caribou, they ate even the guts and the hide. "The hair is removed from the hide by boiling," Miertsching reported; "the latter is then cut into strips and eaten as *Sauerfleisch*." At the end of February a third of the crew was in the hospital. A few were close to death. Every single person on board showed signs of scurvy.

At the end of March the weather improved and Osborn wrote that the men did too, most of them being able to take a little exercise around the ship. That's where McClure and Miertsching were on April 7, walking on the ice talking about Miertsching's forthcoming effort to reach North America. "Sir," said McClure to the German, "if next year in Europe you neither see nor hear of me, then you may be sure that Captain McClure, along with his crew, has perished and lies unburied but wrapped in the fur coat which you gave me, enjoying a long and tranquil sleep until awakened on the Day of Resurrection by the Redeemer." It was a touching moment, a kind of good-bye, but just then one of the seamen approached to tell McClure that something was moving on the ice of Melville Sound, a "black moving point," maybe a musk ox. They went to look themselves and another seaman came up—"They are men—first a man, and then a sledge with men." Miertsching thought they must be Inuit, and a ray of hope burst upon him: "I thought that whence these come, thither we can go." They went out to meet them, hearts beating violently, unable to speak. They had not seen another human being for twenty-one months. They believed in their hearts that their lives were over. Then a voice greeted them in English: "'I am Lieutenant Pim of the ship *Resolute* in Winter Harbour.' The words came, said Miertsching, like an electric shock. They were saved.

It was McClure's sledge trip to Winter Harbour a year earlier that had saved them. The first thing that Kellett and McClintock had done when they reached Melville Island the previous fall had been to send out sledge parties to set up depots for the spring journeys. One under Lieutenant Mecham had passed through Winter Harbour, and Mecham had gone on ahead to the big sandstone boulder where Parry had inscribed his name and the names of his ships in 1820. It had become a kind of Arctic blackboard, a place where cairns were built to leave messages, and it was where McClure had left his message the previous spring. Mecham intended to carve the date 1852 on it. When he reached it he looked at McClintock's cairn, built in 1851, and "much to my astonishment," Mecham wrote in his report, "a copper cylinder rolled from under a spirit tin. On opening it I drew out a roll folded in a bladder, which being frozen broke and crumbled. From its dilapidated appearance I thought at the moment it must be some record of Sir Edward Parry, and fearing I might damage it laid it down with the intention of lighting the fire to thaw it." Curiosity, however, overcame prudence. He opened it gently with his knife.

> My astonishment may be conceived on finding it contained an account of the proceedings of H. M. Ship "Investigator" since parting company with the "Herald" in August 1850 in Behrins Straits. Also a chart which disclosed to view not only the long sought north-west passage but the completion of the survey of Banks and Wollaston Lands.

It was too late, Kellett and McClintock agreed, to send a sledge across that fall to Bay of Mercy. They sent Pim as early in the spring as men could travel. The meeting between Pim and McClure did not become as famous as Stanley finding Livingstone, but it is an iconic moment in Arctic history, and it saved a lot more lives. Not all, however. A man had died on April 5, two days before Pim showed up. Several of the seamen who traveled with Pim to Bay of Mercy wept when they saw the condition of the *Investigator*'s crew. Two more members of this crew died before the first of May.

After the meeting with Pim, McClure made his way to Dealy Island to see Kellett, the same officer who had urged him to wait for Collinson at Bering Strait in 1850, and told him what his plan of escape had been. Now he could bring his sick men to Kellett's and McClintock's ships and send them home with them later that year. But he still intended to stay with his ship with the healthier part of his crew and take her out, preferably by Barrow Strait. This plan changed when one of Kellett's surgeons, a man named Domville, made the trip back across the ice to Bay of Mercy and took a survey of the *Investigator*'s crew. All but two were scorbutic. Samuel Mackenzie, seaman, had been on the sick list for sixty-three days; his gums had ulcerated edges, and the slightest exertion exhausted him. James Williams had been on the list for 177 days, "123 with pneumonia, 36 pleuritis, and 18 with debility." And so it went. McClure had asked for volunteers that summer to help him try to get the ship out of its prison. All but one of the officers volunteered, but only four of the men. If he had stayed with his ship another winter there would have been few, probably no survivors. He gave the order to abandon ship. The crew hoisted the ship's flag to the masthead, then made their slow and painful way toward the *Resolute* and the *Intrepid,* some eighty miles away, and the first good meal they had had in years. Two dozen of the sickest had already made the journey across the ice with Lieutenant Cresswell. Captain Kellett singled Miertsching out and took him to his own cabin, where soap and water awaited. "They offer me coffee, real hot coffee," he wrote ecstatically. "What a delight is this also! I have not tasted it for two and a half years." Then he lay down on the floor and went to sleep.

Soon after they arrived, Kellett sent the most desperate cases among McClure's crew to Beechey Island with Lieutenant Cresswell, to be forwarded from there to England when the summer supply ship brought fresh food and other supplies to the *North Star*. Cresswell shipped out with them and took the news to England: the Northwest Passage had been discovered. The reaction in the press and among the public was mixed. The Admiralty promptly printed a chart of the Passage, which, according to *The Illustrated London News*, "has already had an enormous sale, and is in such request that it is impossible to keep pace with the demand of the public for copies." *The Athenaeum* noted that the discovery was "a great scientific triumph,—and adds fresh glory to the old and famous flag of England." Fresh glory was also on the mind of *Fraser's Magazine*: "We exult," wrote its author, "that our small island, ever in the van of civilization and human advancement, has added fresh glory to its history by this discovery."

But the news arrived when the press was distracted by more pressing news from the Middle East. Russia and Turkey had gone to war, and Great Britain, unwilling to see Russian power spread into the eastern Mediterranean, seemed ever more likely to be drawn into it. And no one could forget that none of these expeditions, McClure's or Belcher's or anybody's, had found a fresh trace of the Franklin expedition. The writer in *Fraser's* remarked, "We are painfully reminded that in all probability a gallant crew, headed by an officer who was Nelson's companion—his equal in courage, and as good as he was brave, have undoubtedly endured great hardships." Hardships as great as, the implication was, and greater than, what McClure's men endured. *The Athenaeum* struck the same note. It was now the general assumption that Franklin and his men were all dead. Only a stubborn few still thought they, or some of them, might be alive. Jane Franklin, of course, was one. Another was Sir Edward Parry. At a dinner in Lynn given for Cresswell, the aging explorer said that "there is that stuff and stamina in 120 Englishmen, that somehow or other they would have maintained themselves as well as a parcel of Esquimaux would."

Back in the Arctic things were not going particularly well for either of the two divisions of Belcher's expedition. After the spring sledge journeys came back, Kellett and McClintock could only wait for the ice to break up and release them from Bridport Inlet. They passed their time with athletic contests, including a race of three hundred yards in which Kellett carried McClintock on his back and still handily beat Lieutenant Pim. On August 18 the ice did break up and they made their escape, only to become beset again four days later to the south of Point

Griffith, the southeast corner of Melville Island. For the next two and a half months they drifted east, but not very far, to a point to the south of Bathurst Island. They were not going home this year. They spent the winter in the pack.

Belcher, for his part, was making life miserable for his officers. Osborn, in command of the steam tender *Pioneer,* came away from this voyage clearly hating the man; his contempt for him drips through the pages of the book Osborn wrote for McClure. Belcher did map the north shore of Devon Island, leading the sledge party himself, and he took the search by sledge and boat up Wellington Channel. In the process he became another true believer in an open Arctic sea. In the dispatches to the Admiralty that he sent back with Cresswell in 1853, he laid "so much stress on the existence of an open Polar sea," noted *The Athenaeum,* "that we are surprised that he does not state his intention of boldly entering it with his well-appointed ship and steam-tender." Instead Belcher left his winter perch in Wellington Channel and steered south that summer, for home, only to find the southern end of the channel clogged with ice. Osborn, experienced with ice navigation, claimed that he could have led the ships through the blockage, but Belcher refused to take his advice. They too would be spending another winter in the Arctic.

Belcher spent the winter bullying a Lieutenant May, the expedition artist, who objected to the captain's constant use of obscenities, and trying to bully Osborn, who refused the honor. Belcher was frequently drunk by this time. He relieved May of his duties and put Osborn under arrest. On the two ships under Kellett things were happier. Kellett was blessed with an officer named Krabbe who was adept at magic tricks, entertained the crew, and never failed to astonish Miertsching. He strung a wire between the *Intrepid* and the *Resolute,* which were embedded in the ice about a hundred yards apart, powered it with a battery, and the Arctic had its first telegraph line. Two more men from the *Investigator* died that winter. In the spring Kellett sent a small sledge party to find Belcher. It came back with orders from Belcher to abandon the ships.

This was staggering. Kellett and McClintock were frozen into ice only a year old, not into heavy, defiant "polar" ice. They had no reason to believe the summer would not release them. These were Royal Navy ships, and captains did not abandon them except under the direst circumstances. Under any circumstances they would face an Admiralty court-martial in London. Kellett sent McClintock back to clarify the orders and to explain their situation.

It made no difference. Belcher clearly wanted out of the Arctic. He was, he wrote in his account of the voyage, plagued with "carbuncles" in his head. He knew his officers hated him. He was, in fact, planning to abandon his own ships. While the ice was still firm in Barrow Strait and Wellington Channel, the men on all four ships made their way to the *North Star* and camped around it. When the annual supply ship showed up—the *Phoenix,* under Captain Inglefield—on August 26, the *North Star* was already under sail. Inglefield had orders, as it happened, for the Arctic ships to come home. In March the British had joined the fight against Russia, and the Crimean War was on. All naval personnel were needed for the war in the Baltic and the Black Sea. The Franklin search was over.

But the Admiralty did not anticipate that Belcher would simply leave his ships there; he was to bring them home if he could. In the court-martial that followed their return, McClure and Kellett were both acquitted with honor from any blame for the loss of their ships. Kellett's sword was returned to him with the words "Captain Kellett, I have much pleasure in returning you this sword, which you have so long worn with honour and credit and service to your country." McClure received the commendation of the court for his achievement of the Northwest Passage. To the public's dismay, Belcher also was acquitted. The court felt that he had acted within the range of discretion his original orders had given him. But the court returned his sword to him "without observation": that is, in silence. It was the end of Belcher's career.

A year after the Belcher expedition returned, Collinson sailed up the Thames in the *Enterprise.* It had been Collinson's peculiar fate to be second wherever he went. He spent one winter at the southwestern corner of Victoria Island; it was also the southern end of Prince of Wales Strait. He spent the next at a place called Cambridge Bay, toward the south-eastern corner of Victoria Island. John Rae had beaten him there. Like Rae, he tried to get across the bottom of Victoria Strait and reach King William Island. The ice there defeated him too. At one time or another he put every officer on board ship under arrest, proving himself an even worse commander of men than Sir Edward Belcher. Canadian Arctic historian William Barr called his book on the Collinson expedition *Arctic Hell Ship.* Collinson returned to find out that McClure had won all the honors for discovering the Northwest Passage. He wanted his officers court-martialed. That didn't happen. His officers wanted him court-martialed. That didn't happen either. But his career, too, was finished.

So was the search for Franklin, at least officially. On January 19, 1854, the Admiralty gave notice that "if intelligence be not received, before the 31st of March next, of the officers and crews of Her Majesty's ships *Erebus* and *Terror* being alive, the names of the officers will be removed from the Navy List, and they and the crews of those ships will be considered as having died in Her Majesty's service." Jane Franklin objected strenuously to the declaration, on the grounds that Belcher's expedition was still in the Arctic, and this was premature. Nevertheless no news was received before March 31, and it was done. The Admiralty would send no more ships in search of Sir John Franklin. England had declared war on Russia just a week before, and war news now absorbed the attention of the public. By the following fall Sebastopol was under its long siege. Lady Jane was entitled to a widow's pension. She refused to apply for it.

The Arctic, by the way, was not quite finished with the Belcher expedition. He published his own painfully defensive account of it in 1855, under the title *The Last Arctic Expedition*, which it was not. The reviews were less than enthusiastic. That same year, on September 10, while mired in the pack just above Davis Strait, an American whaling captain named James Buddington noticed a ship some miles distant, similarly beset, and apparently abandoned. Over the next few days they kept drifting nearer each other, until on the sixth day they were close enough for Buddington to send over four men to check out what ship it was. It was Henry Kellett's ship, the *Resolute*. Buddington left his own ship with the bulk of his crew and took eleven men with him, plus his young son, to sail the *Resolute*, a ship that normally required a crew of sixty, to his home port, New London, Connecticut, where after many difficulties he arrived on Christmas Eve. En route he met a British ship, told the captain what had happened, and gave him a pair of Henry Kellett's epaulettes he had found on board. The Admiralty subsequently forwarded them to Kellett, then in the West Indies.

The British waived all rights to the ship—she was salvage; in law they had no rights—and at the suggestion of Henry Grinnell, Congress bought her from Captain Buddington for $40,000 and repainted and refitted her down to the smallest detail, even to preserving the pictures in Captain Kellett's cabin. Then they gave her back to England. She arrived shortly before Christmas 1856, and huge crowds came to see her. The queen herself made a visit in the Royal Barge. For the next two weeks the *Resolute* stopped into various English ports while the crews of passing ships stood at attention on the yardarms, out of respect for this gesture of friendship between the United States and Great Britain. In 1880 Great Britain returned the favor. When the *Resolute* was broken up that year they made a desk of its timbers, a desk six feet by four, beautifully carved and weighing thirteen hundred pounds. It arrived at the White House in Washington in a large crate, unannounced, during the administration of Rutherford B. Hayes. As workers opened the crate Hayes himself stood by, fascinated, to see what was inside. The desk has been in the White House pretty much ever since. John F. Kennedy had it installed in the Oval Office. In 1966 it went on exhibition in the Smithsonian, but William J. Clinton brought it back to the Oval Office. As of this writing it is still there.

CHAPTER TWENTY

THE LAST DREAD ALTERNATIVE

In the final analysis perhaps the worthiest, and certainly the most heroic, accomplishments of the long and unsuccessful search for Sir John Franklin were the maps. For thirty years, from Sir John Ross's voyage in 1818 to Sir James Clark Ross's voyage in 1848 to Lancaster Sound looking for Franklin, surprisingly little progress had been made mapping the Arctic. But every grueling sledge journey from 1849 on added substantially to knowledge of the area's geography, and the maps of those journeys appear all through the thousands of pages of the Parliamentary Papers, the so-called Arctic Blue Books (for their blue paper covers), that the Admiralty began to issue in 1848 both for the information of Parliament and for the enlightenment of an anxious public. By 1854, when the search was called off, almost every corner of the Canadian archipelago below the 77th parallel had been traversed, drawn, and recorded on large maps carefully tipped into the papers. So fragile now they hardly bear touching, they are still in their spare precision beautiful and moving, the tangible result of the toes and fingers lost to frostbite, the starvation and profound exhaustion and sometimes the death of men dragging heavy sledges over rough ice or through deep snow, skirting the edge of human endurance.

By the spring of 1854 only a few diehards believed that any part of the Franklin expedition could still be alive. When the empire went to war with Russia that March, their voices became hard to hear in the clamor of war news and the jingoism that always accompanies it. Jane Franklin was still greatly respected in the kingdom, but no one in the Admiralty was going to listen to her. The Admiralty was finished with the Arctic. John Franklin and all his men were obviously dead. The one consolation, and it was not insignificant, was that the Northwest Passage, or at least *a* Northwest Passage, had been found. On that score, at least—mission accomplished. The nation, meanwhile, was at war. The Admiralty had done everything possible; it had gone to greater lengths than any other nation would or could have gone trying to find and recover its lost men, and it had spent an enormous amount of money to do so, well over £600,000, or close to $70 million in today's money. The more sensible, practical portion of the public seemed to agree. "No—we write it more reluctantly than we ever penned sentence," a writer in *Fraser's* put it, "—the time is now come when, with full hearts, we must bid adieu to HOPE, and turn to RESIGNATION."

John Rae had certainly given up. Of all the Arctic explorers, he was the one least likely to believe that Royal Navy personnel could survive as well as the Inuit. He was the only one among them to adopt Inuit means of survival until the quixotic American Charles Francis Hall went in search of Franklin survivors in the 1860s. When Rae proposed yet another expedition to the Arctic in 1853 to the Hudson's Bay Company, he did not have John Franklin on his mind. He was one of those who had found out straits and islands and inlets, he had chosen some of the names to put to them, he had won a measure of fame for his abilities as an explorer, and now he wanted to finish the job. He had no interest in looking for Franklin. His interest was in maps. *Almost* every corner of the Canadian archipelago had now been mapped, but blank spots did remain. The most important was that troubling patch of white between Simpson and Dease's farthest east on the lower coast of the Boothia peninsula, at the mouth of Castor and Pollux River, and Spence Bay to its north, where James Clark Ross thought he had seen land connecting King William Land with Boothia. For years the prevailing opinion in the Admiralty was that land did connect the two, while just below that land bridge lay a strait connecting the lower reach of Prince Regent Inlet with the open sea to the west. *That,* the late John Barrow had persuaded himself, was where the Northwest Passage was to be found. Rae knew better, but he had to prove it. In the spring of 1854, while the flappable Belcher was making plans to abandon his ships and go home, Rae was starting on his final expedition to the Arctic, to discover the last piece in the jigsaw puzzle and plug it into the map. As for the Franklin expedition, he told *The Times* in a letter, there was "not the slightest hope of finding any traces of them in the quarter to which I am going."

Rae left London in the spring of 1853 and reached York Factory in mid-June, leaving almost immediately for the North. He had two boats and thirteen men, but sent one boat back with seven of them and spent the winter at Repulse Bay, living in igloos and off the land. He had an Inuit interpreter with him, a man named William Ouligbuck. On the last day of March 1854 he set out with four men for Castor and Pollux River. Three weeks later, at Pelly Bay, the southernmost arm of Prince Regent Inlet, he came upon a group of seventeen Inuit, most of whom had never seen white men before. They urged him not to go any farther west—because, as Rae learned later, they had cached a great deal of food to the west and were afraid Rae and his party would steal it. Meanwhile they did their best to steal from Rae. Otherwise they were unforthcoming and Rae learned nothing from them about the lay of the land or anything else. The next day, however, Rae met two other Inuit who agreed to accompany him for two days and serve as temporary guides. Through Ouligbuck he asked them the question explorers now always asked Inuit when they met them: had they seen or heard of Kabloonas—white men—or seen any ships or boats? Did they know, in other words, of the whereabouts of the Franklin expedition?

For the first time in five years the answer was yes. The one named In-nook-poo-zhee-jook said he had never seen a white man before, but that "a number of Kabloonans, at least 35 or 40, had starved to death west of a large river a long distance off." The man was wearing a gold capband, the kind officers wore, around his head. Rae bought it from him and told him that he would buy anything else they had acquired of the same kind—European things, in other words—and to bring them to his winter quarters at Repulse Bay.

Rae was later much criticized for not immediately abandoning his plans and marching off "to the west of a large river a long distance off," but as he pointed out in his own defense, "a long distance off" could be a hundred miles or a thousand, and "a large river" could have been anything from the Great Fish River to the Mackenzie. He was not prepared for that kind of expedition. He had made plans, those plans were being financed by the HBC, and he had an obligation to fulfill them. The men had starved to death, the Inuit had told him, four years before. Rae continued west to Castor and Pollux River and from there north. He finished the puzzle that May—no land bridge connected Boothia Peninsula with King William Land. King William Land was King William *Island.* No strait connected the southern reaches of Prince Regent Inlet with the water to the west. Boothia was indeed a peninsula.

Simpson and Dease, George Back, and all those who had believed otherwise about the lay of the land had been wrong. They had not gone far enough. Now the map was complete.

On the way back to Repulse Bay, Rae set up camp on Pelly Bay and sent two of his men to look for the Inuit he had seen on the way north a month before. Ten or twelve showed up, and he bought a silver spoon and fork from them. On the spoon someone had scratched the initials F.R.M.C.: Francis R. M. Crozier, John Franklin's second in command, Sophy Cracroft's unsuccessful suitor. By the end of May, Rae had returned to his winter quarters, and he spent then until August questioning the Inuit who gathered around his camp what they knew about the Kabloonas who had died west of a large river many days' journey distant, and buying relics from them. None of these people had been on the scene, but they had talked to other Inuit who had. The story as Rae tells it is as follows:

> In the Spring, four winters past, (1850) whilst some Esquimaux families were killing seals near the north shore of a large Island named in Arrowsmith's Charts, King William's Land, about forty white men were seen traveling in company southward over the ice, and dragging a boat and sledges with them. They were passing along the west shore of the above named Island. None of the party could speak the Esquimaux language so well as to be understood, but by signs the Natives were led to believe that the Ship or Ships had been crushed by ice, and that they were then going to where they expected to find deer to shoot.

They were short of provisions, and thin, except for an officer who was tall, stout, and middle-aged. He was the only one not dragging the sledge.

Later that spring, before the breakup of the ice, Inuit found the bodies of some thirty men, along with a few graves, on the North American coast just to the south of King William Island and west of Chantrey Inlet. An additional five bodies lay on a small island nearby. "Some of the bodies were in a tent or tents," wrote Rae;

> others were under the boat which had been turned over to form a shelter, and some lay scattered about in different directions. Of those seen on the Island, it was supposed that

one was an Officer, (chief) as he had a telescope strapped over his shoulders, and his double barreled gun lay underneath him.

From the mutilated state of many of the bodies and the contents of the kettles, it is evident that our wretched Countrymen had been driven to the last dread alternative, as a means of sustaining life. A few of the unfortunate Men must have survived until the arrival of the wild fowl, (say until the end of May,) as shots were heard, and fresh bones and feathers of geese were noticed near the scene of the sad event.

Later explorers would learn much more over time, but Rae had heard the essence of the story. Franklin's ships had been crushed, or abandoned, near the west coast of King William Island—just where Weasy had said they were, and where Richard King had said they were, and the only place dozens of sledging parties had failed to look. These forty men had abandoned the ships and headed for the Great Fish River, precisely where George Back and John Richardson had said they would not go because everyone knew from previous expeditions that game was scarce there and, in the barren grounds beyond, nonexistent. And they had died, and those who had not yet died had resorted to the last dread alternative—they had eaten the bodies of their friends and fellow seamen.

Rae bought more silver tableware from the Inuit. Many of the pieces were decorated with crests or initials identifying them as belonging to the officers of the *Erebus* and *Terror*. Among them was a round silver plate marked on the bottom "Sir John Franklin K.C.B." There were pieces of instruments, of watches, metal boxes, a surgeon's knife and scalpel, coins. He also bought from the natives the ornate bronze star the British government had given Franklin in recognition of his services in Greece, when he had been made a Knight Commander of the Guelphic Order of Hanover. It was a metal object. All metal objects were in demand among the Inuit.

Rae left York Factory in September and wrote a letter to the secretary of the HBC from the Tavistock Hotel in Covent Garden dated October 22, 1854. He had rushed back to London not only to give the world the news, and to forestall any more now-pointless attempts to look for Franklin, but also to apply for the reward of ten thousand pounds that the Admiralty had offered to whoever discovered the fate of the

Franklin expedition. The siege of Sebastopol was on and news of the most dramatic event of the Crimean War, the "Charge of the Light Brigade," had just reached England; otherwise there might have been a serious uproar in the press. As it was, there was some. The popular American writer Hendrik van Loon, who was born in 1882, remarks in his autobiography that his father never forgot the "shock of horror that had swept across the civilized world" when Rae's report became known. The last dread alternative? Cannibalism? People were ready for news that the expedition, all 129 men, had died, but very few could accept the idea that members of the British military had resorted to eating the flesh of their companions.

The press did its best to deny it. No sooner did the news hit the papers than *The Athenaeum* declared that the charge of cannibalism was "absolutely unwarrantable on the evidence in court." The Inuit must have raided the empty abandoned ships to acquire the relics John Rae had brought back from Repulse Bay, and the rest of the story was mere lies. "We ask any one acquainted with the Arctic regions and with the Esquimaux, whether this story looks like truth? To us it seems incredible. . . . All who know the Esquimaux know that they have no sense of truth. Like all savages, they lie without scruple." As for the death of the crews, *The Athenaeum* insisted again on what so many before had insisted on—it was inconceivable that "Englishmen well supplied with clothing and ammunition should not be able to live where any other human beings can subsist." Maybe the Inuit killed them all. *The Times* for its part did not go quite so far as to make that accusation, and at first it seemed to accept Rae's report, out of respect for his abilities as an Arctic traveler, but a few days later *The Times* too was wondering whether the Inuit could possibly be telling the truth, since "like all savages, they are liars."

Those who did accept the news passed over it as quickly as possible, as something not to be spoken of. One man, the brother of an expedition member, wrote *The Times* criticizing Rae for not checking out for himself whether the report was true, then added that Rae should have kept silent about the evidence of cannibalism. Silence, in fact, quickly became general. Press and public tacitly ignored the charge of cannibalism as if it were no part of the story.

With one exception: Charles Dickens. Immersed in writing *Little Dorrit* at the time, which was going slowly, as well as editing and writing for *Household Words*, the magazine he founded in 1850, the great novelist was an "avid reader of volumes of voyages and travels," according to the Dickens scholar Harry Stone, and had been fascinated by the Arctic explorers since childhood. He was fascinated by cannibalism as well. Stone's book *The Night Side of Dickens* is subtitled *Cannibalism, Passion, Necessity,* and he offers abundant evidence for Dickens's morbid interest in the subject. Possibly at the suggestion of Jane Franklin—she sent for him; he went to see her—Dickens wrote two articles for *Household Words* on Rae's findings. He attacked not Rae so much as the Inuit testimony Rae had gathered, noting first that it was secondhand, none of Rae's informants having seen in person any of what they reported; then that the Inuit of different areas spoke different dialects and were unlikely to understand each other precisely; then suggesting that the Inuit had themselves set upon the starving survivors and killed them. "We believe every savage to be in his heart covetous, treacherous, and cruel," Dickens wrote, "and we have yet to learn what knowledge the white man—lost, houseless, shipless, apparently forgotten by his race, plainly famine-stricken, weak, frozen, helpless, and dying—have of the gentleness of Esquimaux nature."

Dickens, familiar with the story of Franklin's first expedition into northern Canada, went on to cite the horrors those twenty men had undergone under Franklin's leadership *without* resorting to cannibalism, quoting liberally from Franklin's book and focusing on Franklin's description of the most awful of what they had had to endure. The upshot of Dickens's argument was that in a similar situation, with dead bodies lying beside them, it had never occurred to Franklin or his starving companions to use them for food in order to save their own lives. Only Michel the Iroquois had resorted to cannibalism on that journey. It was therefore impossible, at the least "gigantically improbable," that any of these sailors or their officers, Christians all, had turned cannibal. Only savages did that.

John Rae was not easily intimidated. He had been forced to clarify the statements of other commentators in the press who objected to his findings and he did not hesitate to reply to Dickens. To the latter's credit he printed Rae's response in *Household Words.* His interpreter, William Ouligbuck, Rae explained, spoke English fluently and "more correctly than one half of the lower classes in England or Scotland." Franklin's interpreters, it was true, both from the Hudson Bay area, had only imperfectly understood the dialect spoken by Inuit from west of the Coppermine. But the eastern Inuit all spoke the same dialect, so there was no chance that Ouligbuck could have misunderstood the informants. Rae had checked into Ouligbuck's character and discovered he was "perfectly reliable." Dickens had assumed "that part of the information regarding cannibalism was conveyed to me by gestures." Not so, said Rae. Dickens thought there was no fuel in that area with which to cook meat. Rae pointed out that the first time the natives had seen the white men, they had sledges. There were no sledges where they died. Clearly they had used the wood from the sledges for fuel. He pointed out that bears, wolves, foxes, even wolverines, will not touch human bodies.

As for the Inuit killing the white men, that, he carefully explained, simply would not have happened. The Inuit to the east of the Coppermine seldom travel in parties larger than thirty because of the difficulty of finding food in that barren country. Sir John Ross had spent three winters in the same area where these Inuit lived; they had traveled in small parties that might have been overcome by violence if the Inuit had had any interest in killing them; and they had only been friendly and helpful. He cited his own experience when alone with Inuit men, at times when it would have been "an immense advantage" to the Inuit to have the things Rae had with him. "Last spring," he concluded, "I, with seven men, was almost in constant communication with a party four times our number. The savages made no attempt to harm us."

Rae goes on in this vein for some pages. The truth is that he knew his "savages," he had had a great deal of experience with them, and he understood something about their inclinations. Lying? He pointed out, a bitter tone creeping into his prose, that the information that Prince Regent Inlet was a dead end, with no outlet to the straits to the west, was first transmitted to Sir John Ross by just such savages, and that the Admiralty had refused to believe them and also himself when he said that same thing. Now he had proven otherwise: "where parties of high standing at home would insist on having nothing but salt water, I travelled over a neck of land or isthmus only sixty miles broad." The Inuit had all too much experience of their own with starving. He cited instances of Inuit men going mad watching their children starve. One of them went out and strangled himself. Another, unable to endure it, went into the open, stripped off his clothes, and let himself freeze to death. In extreme cases like that the Inuit have been known to eat their dead, but they abhorred it as much as anyone would. It was a last resort for them as for any human being, and rare in their culture, and these were a people who had a great deal more experience with starvation than the English.

Dickens responded by citing Franklin's description of the horde of Inuit living at the mouth of the Mackenzie who tried to steal his second expedition's goods and kill the men. He did not mention Rae's caveat, that the eastern Inuit and the western were different sorts of tribes. For Dickens, as for most of his countrymen at the time, it was impossible to conceive that a savage could have a sense of honor or compassion, or could restrain himself from stealing or lying or murder. Evidently it was not enough for the British that they were, in their own opinion, the most agreeably civilized people in the world. Others had to be subhuman.

Unfortunately for British amour propre, the account Rae had picked up from the Inuit at Repulse Bay was true in almost every detail. Bones found years later at the different sites of the final disaster had been sawn. Nobody saws the bones of dead men *except* to fit them into a kettle. In 1992 an amateur historian found a new Franklin site on a small island just off King William Island. Almost four hundred pieces of human bone lay scattered on the ground, comprising eleven individuals. A quarter of the bones had cut marks on them. "The cut marks," according to a scientific report in the journal *Arctic,*

> were easily distinguished from animal tooth marks by their sharper borders, narrower width, and wider spacing. In con- trast to cuts made by stone tools, the observed cuts, examined under a scanning electron microscope, exhibited features characteristic of cuts made by metal blades, namely straight edges, a V-shaped cross section, and a high depth-to-width ratio.

British seamen had indeed been driven to the last dread alternative.

John Rae called on Jane Franklin that November to offer his sympathies to the woman who had befriended his mother in the Orkneys. It could not have been a pleasant conversation. She too refused to believe that British seamen had done what the Inuit said they had done. Rae's news, furthermore, left a great deal unanswered. The Inuit spoke of forty men. What about the rest? Had other parties traveled in other directions? Where were the ships, and why had the men abandoned them? For Jane Franklin, and she had many allies, Rae's news brought little to an end except the fate of her husband, whom she could no longer believe was alive. The appearance in Inuit hands of the medal given him when he was made Knight Commander of the Guelphic Order of Hanover was proof positive that he was no longer alive. The medal had been precious to him; like Admiral Nelson, he wore his medals and decorations when he went on deck. If he were still somehow, miraculously, alive, he would have had it with him. The fact that he did not meant that he was dead.

But how had he died, and when, and what had happened to the journals, the log, the records of the expedition? How had it all happened? Had ice crushed one of the ships, or both, or were they frozen into a harbor on the west coast of King William Island? Lady Jane wrote James Ross in November asking for his opinion of Rae's findings, and his advice about the best way "of getting at the ships, if you agree with me & Sir J. Richardson & others in thinking that these are not crushed but only abandoned." She was already thinking about sending yet another expedition back to the Arctic, now that the site of the disaster was known, to find the ships, to refute the Inuit claims, and most of all to make sure that there were no survivors.

At the Admiralty's request the Hudson's Bay Company sent a small group of men down the Great Fish River in hopes of finding answers to some of the many questions that remained. Led by a chief factor named James Anderson, it left winter quarters in June 1855 in two birchbark canoes. It got as far as Montreal Island in Chantrey Inlet. The canoes were too frail to take them to King William Island. On Montreal Island they picked up a few relics from Franklin's ships, but they found no records, no graves, no bones. An early winter drove them back upriver to seek shelter.

Had not Jane Franklin been the woman she was, that might have been the end of it. It might have been a generation or more before men tried again to solve the Franklin mystery. The Admiralty was not going to send another expedition of its own to search for answers, and it had a war as an excuse. The war came to an end in 1856 but it changed none of the minds at Admiralty House. In June of that year Great Britain's leading scientists, led by Sir Roderick Murchison, then president of the Royal Geographical Society and one of the most influential men in the kingdom, petitioned Lord Palmerston, the prime minister, to send a final expedition to bury the human remains, to find and bring back relics, most of all to see whether there were written records in a cache somewhere that would explain what had happened to these men. The Arctic knights signed the petition as well. The public supported this last project, as did a number of other well-known men in and out of government. Much of the press was behind it. The issue was raised in the House of Lords.

For six months there was no response. In December Lady Jane wrote Lord Palmerston, the prime minister, herself. If the government did not respond favorably, she explained to him, she would not shrink "from the sacrifice of my entire available fortune for the purpose." Before she went so far, however, she went on, it was her duty "to entreat Her Majesty's Government not to disregard the arguments which have led so many competent and honourable men to feel that our country's honour is not satisfied while a mystery which has excited the sympathy of the civilised world remains uncleared." If no expedition is sent, she said, "the question will never die." New expeditions were being sent to Africa, she pointed out. Did not the Arctic have a prior and a greater claim?

> These 135 men of the Erebus and Terror (or, perhaps, I should rather say the greater part of them, since we do not yet know that there are no survivors) have laid down their lives, after sufferings doubtless of unexampled severity, in the service of their country as truly as if they had perished by the rifle, the cannon ball, or the bayonet. Nay, more; by attaining the northern and already surveyed coasts of America, it is clear that they solved the problem which was the object of their labour, or, in the beautiful words of Sir John Richardson, that "they forged the last link of the North-west Passage with their lives."

It was an eloquent plea, and Lord Palmerston tried to talk Sir Charles Wood, the first lord, into sending out another expedition. Wood could not be moved. The other members of the Admiralty Board were equally unenthusiastic. *The Times* thought the whole idea was absurd. "Another expedition in search of Sir John Franklin is now meditated," the paper thundered, "and while it is yet time we should invoke the aid of public opinion to put a stop at once to so outrageous a proceeding." Murchison wrote the paper and objected; Captain Collinson wrote that "we owe it to our national honour" to pursue an answer to the mystery; but *The Times* was as firm on the point as the government: "Have we not already done more than any nation in the world has ever done before us from tenderness to the feelings of those who have mourned for the crews of the Erebus and Terror? . . . There must be an end to all things; we have paid our debt."

So Jane Franklin used her savings and went out and bought another ship. A public subscription raised some three thousand pounds to help; the subscribers included the families of six of Franklin's officers and thirteen of the officers who had been part of the long Franklin search. The Admiralty released Francis L. McClintock, now a captain, from duty for eighteen months, and he took command. The ship was a yacht named the *Fox*, steam-powered, of 177 tons. McClintock took with him the half-Inuit interpreter Carl Petersen, who spoke the dialect of the eastern Inuit fluently; he took an old Arctic shipmate, W. H. Hobson, as his second. In a crew of twenty-five, seventeen were Arctic veterans. As had happened so many times before when an Arctic voyage was announced, offers to serve poured in from all over the country. McClintock could accept none of them, but he found them gratifying. They showed, he wrote, "that the ardent love of hardy enterprise still lives amongst Englishmen, as of old, to be cherished, I trust, as the most valuable of our national characteristics—as that which has so largely contributed to make England what she is."

The *Fox* sailed on July 1, 1857, entrusted with what McClintock described as "a *great national duty*." They were a "little band of heroes" in Jane Franklin's eyes, and she forbore to give them specific instructions, leaving everything in McClintock's hands. By the middle of August constant southerly winds had driven the ice up into the northerly reaches of Baffin Bay and the *Fox* was trapped in it, unable to reach the open water that was always to be found there in summer. The little ship spent the winter drifting south in its ice cradle toward Davis Strait, hunting seals, waiting for the sun. They spent 242 days in the ice. They had lost a year.

McClintock was not the kind of man to let this discourage him, however, and he was well used to the Arctic, where so much is out of anyone's control. They reached Beechey Island on August 11, 1858, sailed partway down Peel Sound, then turned around when they met the ice and sailed back north, around North Somerset, and pointed the *Fox* south in Prince Regent Inlet. After several tries they actually sailed through Bellot Strait, which is only a mile wide at its narrowest point, but ice to the west of it prevented them making any further progress in that direction, and they spent the winter in an inlet in the strait itself. They laid depots that fall for the coming spring sledge journeys to King William Island. One of them visited Fury Beach and found "an immense stack of preserved vegetables and soup," all of it still edible thirty-six years after Parry had stacked it there when the *Fury* could not be saved. On April 2 three main sledging parties left the ship to discover

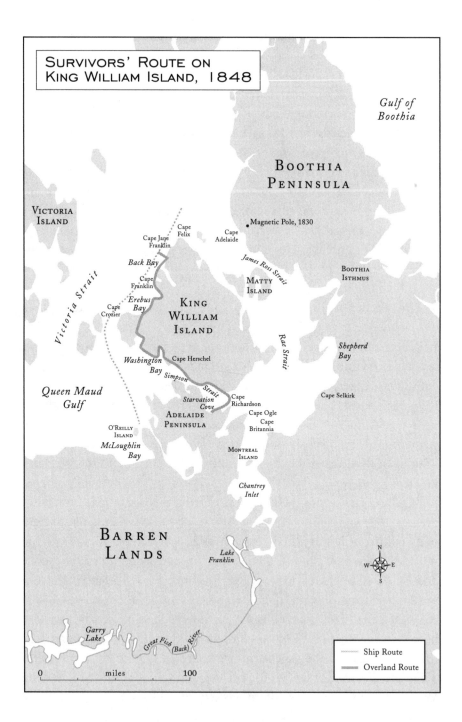

SURVIVORS' ROUTE ON
KING WILLIAM ISLAND, 1848

Gulf of
Boothia

BOOTHIA
PENINSULA

VICTORIA
ISLAND

Cape
Felix

Cape
Adelaide

• Magnetic Pole, 1830

Cape Jane
Franklin

Back Bay

Cape
Franklin

James Ross Strait

MATTY
ISLAND

BOOTHIA
ISTHMUS

Erebus
Bay

KING
WILLIAM
ISLAND

Cape
Crozier

Victoria Strait

Rae Strait

Shepherd
Bay

Washington
Bay

Cape Herschel

Simpson

Strait

Cape Selkirk

Queen Maud
Gulf

Starvation
Cove

Cape
Richardson

ADELAIDE
PENINSULA

Cape Ogle

Cape
Britannia

O'REILLY
ISLAND

McLoughlin
Bay

MONTREAL
ISLAND

Chantrey
Inlet

BARREN
LANDS

Lake
Franklin

N
W   E
S

Garry
Lake

Great Fish (Back) River

0   miles   100

·········· Ship Route

———— Overland Route

whatever they could of the remains of the Franklin expedition. Allen Young, a merchant marine officer with Arctic experience, set out for the west side of Prince of Wales Island, ground that William Kennedy had searched years before. McClintock sent Hobson to the west coast of King William Island while he headed down its east coast, traveling the shores of what was finally, thanks to John Rae, known to be a strait.

And now, at last, a Franklin search expedition reached the actual ground on which the final scenes of this sorrowful tale had been performed. It was Hobson who arrived first but McClintock who told the story, so we must hear him out. He had already met Inuit earlier that spring on a depot-laying journey who knew something of what happened to the *Erebus* and *Terror*. One of those Inuit had told him "that a ship having three masts had been crushed by the ice out in the sea to the west of King William's Island, but that all the people had landed safely." That ship sank. Now he met them again and obtained a more elaborate account. The second ship had not sunk. The massive ice of Victoria Strait had forced it ashore on King William Island—the same shoreline where James Clark Ross had seen ice floes driven half a mile inland. The Inuit had most of their wood from that ship. They had found the body of one man on it: "he must have been a very large man, and had long teeth." McClintock bought a few Franklin relics from this group and passed over the frozen strait to King William Island.

From there he traveled south, checked out Matty Island, then returned to King William Island, still heading south, until they reached a village of thirty to forty Inuit native to the island. McClintock bought more silver plates from them bearing the Franklin crests and those of other officers, then questioned them about the wreck. Little was left of it, they said; they and their countrymen had taken most of it. "There had been *many books* they said," all destroyed long ago by the weather. An old woman told them that "many of the white men dropped by the way as they went to the Great River [the Great Fish River]; that some were buried and some were not; they did not themselves witness this, but discovered their bodies during the winter following." They seemed to have no other information, and McClintock moved on. By May 12 they had reached the mouth of the Great Fish River. On Montreal Island they found a few scraps of metal and nothing else. McClintock was using dogs, so they made good time when they could travel, although often the weather pinned them down. Back on a gravel ridge on the south shore of King William Island they came upon their first body. It was the skeleton of a young man with what remained of his clothes, "the blue jacket with slashed sleeves and braided edging, and the pilot-cloth great-coat with plain covered buttons." Nearby lay his comb and a clothes brush, an odd touch, but poignant. He intended, it would seem, to stay neat to the very death. McClintock thought he was probably one of the ship's stewards. "This poor man seems to have selected the bare ridge top, as affording the least tiresome walking, and to have fallen upon his face in the position in which we found him.

"It was a melancholy truth that the old woman spoke when she said, 'they fell down and died as they walked along.'"

As McClintock and his men walked along, they opened every cairn they came across but found no records, no scientific journals, no evidence of any kind. They were all empty.

Twelve miles west of Simpson's Cape Herschel, they did finally come upon a cairn with a note in it. It was from Hobson. "He had reached his extreme point, six days previously, without having seen anything of the wreck, or of natives, but he had found a record—the record so ardently sought for, of the Franklin Expedition—at Point Victory, on the N. W. coast of King William's Land." It was a single piece of paper, one of the printed forms that navy ships were supposed to throw overboard in sealed copper cylinders listing their latitude and longitude. People who found these cylinders were asked to forward the contents to the Admiralty, giving the date and place where they were found. On this one, dated May 28, 1847, Lieutenant Gore, one of Franklin's officers, had written out their wintering latitude and longitude in the ice just off King William Island:

> Having wintered in 1846–7 at Beechey Island, in lat. 74 43' 28" N.; long. 91 39' 15" W., after having ascended Wellington Channel to lat. 77, and returned by the west side of Cornwallis Island.
>
> Sir John Franklin commanding the expedition.
> All well.
>
> Party consisting of 2 officers and 6 men left the ships on Monday, 24th May, 1847.

It was signed by Lieutenant Graham Gore and Charles F. Des Voeus, Mate. They wintered at Beechey Island not, in fact, in 1846–47 but the previous year. That was known from the dates on the headboards of the three bodies buried on Beechey Island in the spring of 1846. The date on the document itself, May 1847, demonstrated the error.

In any case Franklin had had a remarkable success. To have sailed up Wellington Channel and around Cornwallis Island was a major achievement. To have then penetrated Peel Sound—it must have been Peel Sound; the waters to the west of Prince of Wales Island were permanently impassable—as far south as they had come, six degrees of latitude, was also remarkable. Things had gone well those first two years. Had they known that King William Land was actually an island, they might have made it even farther south, through Rae Strait; from there they might have connected up with the straits that ran west along the coast past Chantrey Inlet, through the needle's eye of Simpson Strait, then Coronation Gulf, the narrow portal of Dease Strait, then Dolphin and Union Strait. After that it was an open run along the coast of North America and Collinson had made that run; he had made it home. *Erebus* and *Terror* might have made it home too.

But in 1830 James Clark Ross had looked south when he was crossing the ice from his trek to King William Island and thought he saw land, where there was only haze. The map Franklin had with him was the authoritative Arrowsmith map of the Arctic. It did not show a land bridge between King William Island and the Boothia Peninsula, only a dotted line, because the younger Ross had not been sure; therefore Arrowsmith could not be sure. But any line on a map is persuasive when you have not seen the landscape for yourself. So John Franklin had taken to the ice. He had authority for that too. It was one of John Barrow's pet theories that taking to the ice was perfectly safe. The drift would eventually spit you out where you wanted to go.

That was not the end of the document. Around its margins, eleven months later, in another hand, Captains Francis R. M. Crozier and James Fitzjames had written much grimmer news. The ships had been beset since September 1846; they had spent not just one winter, but the following summer and the subsequent winter, in the ice. They had been abandoned on April 22, 1848. There had been more deaths: nine officers and fifteen men. The document, brief, only a note with no explanations attached, was dated April 25. They were leaving the next day, it went on, for the Great Fish River, but without their beloved commander: "Sir John Franklin died on the 11th June, 1847." Of what it did not say, but it was sudden, for Lieutenant Gore had written "All well" on May 14, 1847. What all the others had died of, it also did not say. Lead poisoning was probably a factor. Recent analysis of lead levels in the bodies of the three seamen who died and were buried on Beechey Island during Franklin's first winter have shown that lead from the soldered seams of the canned

goods used on the expedition contaminated the food. But the real killer
was scurvy, which kills fast. They ought still to have had enough food in
April 1848. Just not fresh food. As Richardson had pointed out, when a
ship is beset in the ice, fresh food is nowhere to be found.

McClintock moved on, walking around the southwestern end of
King William Island. He named it Cape Crozier. He turned north up
the western shore, finding it low and barren and choked with ice. On
May 30 he and his party camped beside a large boat, twenty-eight feet
long, over seven feet wide, and mounted on a sledge. It was facing north,
strangely, back toward where the ships had been wrecked, and not south
toward the Great Fish River. McClintock took the measurements of the
massive sledge beneath it and calculated the whole weight of boat and
sledge at fourteen hundred pounds. Inside it were portions of two skeletons, each minus its skull. There were books too, all of them devotional
books, except for a copy of *The Vicar of Wakefield*. And besides that "an
amazing quantity of clothing" that included seven or eight pairs of
boots, silk handkerchiefs, "towels, soap, sponge, tooth-brush, and hair-
combs." McClintock must have stood there stunned:

> we found twine, nails, saws, files, bristles, wax-ends, sail-
> maker's palms, powder, bullets, shot, cartridges, wads, leather
> cartridge-case, knives—clasp and dinner ones—needle and
> thread cases, slow-match, several bayonet-scabbards cut
> down into knife-sheaths, two rolls of sheet-lead, and, in
> short, a quantity of articles of one description and another
> truly astonishing in variety, and such as, for the most part,
> modern sledge-travelers in these regions would consider a
> mere accumulation of dead weight.

Of food there was a little tea, and forty pounds of chocolate. No one
knows why they had taken with them so much useless stuff.

It did not escape McClintock's notice, incidentally, that James Clark
Ross had, so many years before, named two of the nearby capes along
this coast Cape Franklin and Cape Jane Franklin.

More was to be found. At Point Victory farther up the coast lay a pile
of abandoned clothing four feet high and other items it made no sense
for men with a major march ahead of them to try to take with them:
"four heavy sets of boat's cooking stoves"; "iron hoops"; "long pieces of
hollow brass curtain rods"; pick-axes; shovels; old canvas.

This was the gist of it—the skeletons, the boat, the things they carried. McClintock reached the *Fox* on June 19 to find Hobson sick with scurvy but recovering with the help of the lemon juice and fresh kills of meat. Hobson's illness was a demonstration of how quickly scurvy could destroy a man. He had started showing signs of scurvy ten days after they left the ship that April and had walked lame for a few weeks. Then he could no longer walk at all, and his men had put him on the sledge. Finally, the day he got back to the ship, he had been unable even to stand. His case bore strongly, McClintock believed, on "the last sad march of the lost crews." It was not just starvation that had killed them. The men of McClure's expedition had started to die of scurvy just as they were being rescued. The human body requires thirty milligrams of vitamin C a day. Ascorbic acid is fragile. Even in lemons it deteriorates over time. Without it, collagen in the body does not form, and collagen is what holds the body together. Men dying of scurvy cannot walk; they can barely get out of bed. Only the very healthiest of them made it so far as the Great Fish River. For the most part, the men of Franklin's expedition died on King William Island. Overweight, sedentary John Franklin himself died so soon after Graham Gore's "All well" that it is hard not to suspect that he died of heart failure. Gore himself died before they had abandoned the ships. That final note identified him as "the late" Graham Gore.

McClintock arrived in London on September 21, 1859, after a remarkably swift passage back from Greenland. A telegram announcing his arrival, and that he had discovered the fate of Franklin, reached Sir Roderick Murchison, the president of the Royal Geographical Society and Jane Franklin's great friend, in the midst of an afternoon garden party at Balmoral Castle in Scotland, the queen's summer residence. Murchison promptly sought out the queen in the crowd and told her.

The Admiralty, which had refused to send another expedition on the search, now reversed course and took the position that McClintock had in effect been serving on a Royal Navy ship, and it paid him his salary for the time he was in the Arctic. In time Parliament voted him and his men an award of five thousand pounds. The City of London gave McClintock the freedom of the city. Oxford and Cambridge both gave him honorary degrees; so did the University of Dublin in his native Ireland. The Royal Geographical Society gave him its gold medal. The nation gave him its thanks. McClintock had saved the national honor; he had written a conclusion of sorts to the Franklin drama that had occupied its thoughts for so many years. Moreover he had effectively buried, by ignoring it, the charge of cannibalism levied on the men of the Franklin expedition. Nowhere in McClintock's account does the word *cannibalism* appear, nor any of its euphemisms. McClintock was knighted soon enough for his work. John Rae, who had brought the terrible news of the "last dread alternative" home, and who was at least the equal as an Arctic explorer of any of those men who were knighted, never received that honor.

For the British, that was the end of it. For others the drama, the questions, the many remaining unknowns, would trouble them for years. Before McClintock had set sail the American doctor and adventurer Elisha Kent Kane had sailed north for the second time, again under the sponsorship of Henry Grinnell, with another expedition, this one aimed at Smith Sound at the top of Baffin Bay, to look for Franklin there. Kane endured incredible hardships, came back to write a second hugely successful book, and became a national hero in the United States. Inspired partly by Kane, a much more productive search was undertaken by the American Charles Francis Hall, a Cincinnati entrepreneur and hothead who became obsessed with finding Franklin survivors and left his wife and children in 1860 to take passage on a whaling ship to Baffin Bay. It was frozen in for two successive winters, and, an expedition of one, he lived off and on during that time with the Inuit of Frobisher Bay. Hall had hoped to travel by boat to Foxe Basin and thence overland to King William Island, but his boat was destroyed in an accident. Nevertheless his time with the Inuit was useful. He learned their language and found he could stomach eating raw meat and living in igloos. More important, he heard from an old woman who knew the tribe's stories about the Kabloonas who had come a long time ago in first two ships, the next year three, then many, and about the five men who had been left behind. A long time ago—in fact, nearly three hundred years. These were the Frobisher expeditions in search of the Northwest Passage. No one but a few whalers had been back to Frobisher Bay since that time. It was a remarkable example of the longevity and accuracy of Inuit oral traditions. The old woman even knew what had happened to the five men. They had lived with the Inuit that winter, then in the spring had built themselves a small boat and sailed for home. It was clear to Hall that if the Inuit could remember so much about something that happened so long ago, he could find out a lot more about the fate of Franklin's men from the natives of King William Island.

In June 1864 Hall returned to the Arctic, again on a whaling vessel but this time to Sir Thomas Roe's Welcome in Hudson Bay, where he was dropped off forty miles south of Wager Inlet. He spent the next five years in the area and made it to King William Island in 1869. The stories he heard from the Inuit on this second sojourn in the Arctic remain a major source of information on the Franklin expedition's last days. One repeated the story of finding a body on one the ships before it sank of a "very large kobluna." The Inuit had found a tent on shore:

> Three men first saw the tent. It had blankets, bedding & a great many skeleton bones—the flesh all off, nothing except sinews attached to them—the appearance as though foxes and wolves had gnawed the flesh off the bones. Some bones had been severed with a saw. Some skulls with holes in them. Besides the blankets, were tin cups, spoons, forks, knives, two double-barrel guns, pistols, lead balls, a great many powder flasks, and both books and papers written upon. As these last were good for nothing for the Innuits, the men threw them away.

In other versions the books and papers were given to Inuit children to play with. Children playing with a keg of powder—the Inuit had no idea what it was—in an igloo had accidentally blown it up; miraculously, the children had survived. On King William Island, Hall found one skeleton and took the bones back to civilization; in England, from a plug in one of the teeth, they were identified as being the remains of an officer from the *Erebus,* Lieutenant Le Vesconte. Hall was told that a small party of Inuit had encountered Crozier and some of the survivors near Cape Herschel, on the south shore of King William Island, and had fed them seal meat in their possession, but had abandoned them the next morning, despite Crozier's pleas that they stay, because there were too many Kabloonas, too few Inuit. The Inuit could sometimes be extremely kind, but they were always practical. No small band of Inuit could hope to sustain forty or fifty starving white men. Hall had heard earlier that certain Inuit had kept Crozier and two or three other men alive for several years after the others had died, long enough for Crozier to try to make it to Repulse Bay in a kayak. He came to discount this story, however, when the Inuit involved contradicted themselves under questioning.

American interest in Franklin's fate sparked another expedition in

1878–80, when a whaler came out of Hudson Bay with a story about a cairn on an island in the Gulf of Boothia that contained Franklin records. A spoon with Franklin's crest out of the same cairn was offered as proof. This expedition was led by a U.S. Army lieutenant named Frederick Schwatka. He and his companions, including an Inuit couple who had been Charles Francis Hall's friends and companions in his travels, made an astonishing sledge journey of over three thousand miles from the western shore of Hudson Bay to King William Island and back, the longest ever to that time. Not far from the Great Fish River Schwatka's party heard a story from an old Inuit about a ship some eight miles off Grant Point on the Adelaide Peninsula that contained the body of a white man in a bunk—yet another appearance for this particular corpse. The Inuit, not knowing how to get into the ship, had cut a hole in its side; when the ice melted the ship righted itself, but the water poured into this hole and it sank. The sea was shallow enough at that point that after it sank the masts were still sticking above the surface.

Schwatka found no cairn containing documents, but he heard plenty of stories: A tent filled with bones. A group of white men dragging a boat on a sledge along the south shore of King William Island who had nothing to eat. "They looked thin and worn out and their mouths were very dry, bleeding and black"—from scurvy, which blackens the gums. An old woman they met on King William Island told Schwatka's party that she had been present when a boat and skeletons had been found at a spot on Adelaide Peninsula that Schwatka came to call Starvation Cove. The boat was upright.

> Outside the boat they found a tin box about two feet long full of human bones. They came upon these in the summer time and the bones looked very fresh. One body had all its flesh on it. This was a tall man with light brown hair. Alongside of his head they found a pair of gold spectacles. . . . The Esquimaux thought that the white men had been eating each other, as some of the bones were sawed in two. They found one small saw and one large one.

Inside the boat they found a tin box full of books. Was it printing or writing? Schwatka asked, showing them the difference. They thought it was probably writing, but they weren't sure. The Inuit took the books out in any case and kept the tin box.

"The children took some of the books and used them for playthings," wrote Schwatka, "destroying them from time to time. Many of the leaves of the books were seen near the boat place, flying around in the winds, for quite a number of years afterwards, but they slowly disappeared." Schwatka was sure these were the journals and logs of the *Terror* and *Erebus*. What other books would they have preserved to the end? But it was in vain. No page of these records has ever been found. Only the bones, with their saw marks, survived to attest to the great and terrible suffering of these lost sailors, strung out over that brutal glaring landscape, empty of all life except their own. No words would have sufficed in any case to explain what they endured, and what they did. "There is," George Back had said as Franklin and the voyageurs descended the Coppermine in July 1821, on their way to their own starving time, "little compassion in the human frame I believe, when it is in a state of privation." The Yellow Knives had already explained to him that they knew how to starve and the white men did not. Whatever precisely they meant by that, in 1848 the Royal Navy had still learned no lessons about survival in the Arctic and could not, in fact, live wherever a native could live.

Schwatka's was the last of the Franklin search expeditions until the end of the twentieth century, although the Danish ethnographer Knud Rasmussen heard many of the same stories from Inuit in the area in the 1920s. Perhaps these stories are being told even today by the natives of Gjøa Haven, the Inuit village where Roald Amundsen spent two winters when he became the first to navigate the Northwest Passage end to end. These natives now run a modest resort, with a hotel, and will lead visitors along the Franklin Trail to the points on King William Island where the tragedy played out.

A couple of efforts have been made over the years to untangle the Inuit stories and create an accurate account of the final months of the expedition. The clearest is Richard J. Cyriax's, in his 1939 book *Sir John Franklin's Last Arctic Expedition*. Cyriax tried to answer some of the most obvious questions. One of them was why, after Franklin's death and the appearance of scurvy in the crew, Crozier did not lead his men to Fury Beach, where abundant provisions from the *Fury* still remained. From there he could have taken boats up Prince Regent Inlet to Lancaster Sound to look for the whalers who frequented it, instead of toward the Great Fish River. The distances were about the same.

Precisely because of the scurvy, Cyriax argued. The provisions at Fury

Beach were twenty-five years old and would have lost all their antiscorbutic value—even the lemon juice. At the time the Franklin expedition
left, in any case, rumors were circulating in England that whalers had
stolen the supplies cached there. At the mouth of the Great Fish River,
on the other hand, earlier explorers had seen large herds of caribou and
musk oxen. The estuary was full of fish. Birds abounded. Crozier had
told the Inuit he met on King William Island that he was heading south
to hunt, and the bones of geese were found with the bones of the dead at
Starvation Cove.

One could argue that it might have made sense nevertheless to send
part of the crew to Fury Beach, to increase the odds of somebody surviving. But they did not. One hundred and five men abandoned the
ships on April 22, 1848—Good Friday, Cyriax pointed out—and headed
for the Great Fish River. They landed at Sir James Clark Ross's Point
Victory, where they left the one written message that survived. After
discarding a great deal of unnecessary equipment and a pile of clothing
four feet high, Cyriax writes, they left for the Great Fish River on April
26 or soon thereafter. They marched south, dragging three boats overloaded with supplies and balanced on sledges, and men died all along
the march. Since they were probably marching on the sea ice, which
would have been smoother than the ice piled on shore, many of those
who had died no doubt dropped into the sea when the ice close to shore
melted that summer. At some point on the march they did after all split
up into smaller parties, and it may be reasonable to assume that this
meant leaving the weaker, sicker officers and men to their own fate. At a
point some sixty-five miles from the ships at least one group had been
sent back to the ships to replenish their supply of food; it was here that
McClintock found the boat with the two skeletons in it. The Inuit had
found a ship intact in the ice with at least one corpse inside, so it is probable that at least some of this party made it back, and then stayed with
the ships.

There can be no question that the march was slower than anticipated.
Cyriax refers us to a later expedition in which seemingly healthy men,
on a strenuous march toward the North Pole, had been attacked with
scurvy shortly after leaving their ship on April 3, 1876. On that occasion
the first signs of scurvy had appeared by April 14. By May 10 five men
had the disease and were incapacitated. By June 2 only six men out of
the original fifteen were able to do any work at all. Six days later a man
died. Heavy exercise, such as dragging two hundred pounds or more
over the ice, which is the load each of the men under Crozier's care

would have had to pull, only quickens the progress of scurvy. The boat with the skeletons obviously never made it back to the ships. The men who did almost certainly lacked the strength to ferry provisions back to the main body of men still traveling south with Crozier—who now had virtually no chance at all.

Sometime perhaps in July the remaining men made it to Cape Herschel on the south coast of King William Island and met Inuit there who sold them some seal meat, then decamped, fearful of starving themselves; for there were too many whites for the Inuit to feed. The party continued along the south coast, where McClintock found a skeleton in 1859, fallen face forward. Bones were later discovered at other places along the coast. Some of the bodies were buried, but not deeply; the permafrost allows only a light burial in the Arctic, usually under a pile of stone and gravel. At a point east of the Piffer River the remaining men left King William Island to make their way across Simpson Strait to the mainland. Bones were discovered on the small Todd Islands, which lie in the way. They reached Starvation Cove on the mainland. They still had a boat with them, guns, and inside a metal box, books and papers: the lost records. It was here that the Inuit gave the books and papers to their children as toys. An Inuit eyewitness to the scene said that he found thirty to thirty-five bodies here. The Inuit took the copper off the bottom of the boat and used it to make cooking pots. They broke up the boat for the wood. What they did not want or saw no use for, they threw away.

The Inuit told Charles Francis Hall that they had found a tent back on King William Island with some thirty bodies inside. Once again the Inuit took what they wanted from the bodies, then left them there. The Inuit did not bury their own dead, so there was no reason they should have buried the white men. No trace of this encampment has ever been found. The sea must have swept it away. They were all very thin, the Inuit said, except for one man. Cyriax concludes, "It is some consolation to know that lack of food, combined with exposure to cold, eventually produces a condition of apathy, stupor, and insensitiveness to pain, mercifully permitting the victims to pass away peacefully and without suffering."

Without suffering seems almost unconscionably anodyne. Cyriax was an astute and thorough scholar, but he never once mentioned cannibalism in his book, and evidence of cannibalism was abundant, both in the bones and in Inuit testimony; and surely the act of eating one's dead companions must entail a certain amount of suffering. It is a fearful thing to imagine what must go through the mind of a man reduced to eating the body of another, someone he has known personally, has broken ship's biscuit with. Did officers share in these desperate meals? How is it even possible to saw hands off arms, or to break into a skull for the brains inside? Very few of us have ever been hungry enough to know.

On December 31, 1859, a little piece appeared in *Once a Week* called "A Phase of the Arctic Mystery," written under the pseudonym "Voyageur." *Once a Week* was Charles Dickens's magazine, but there is no evidence that he wrote the piece. It is a tribute to Richard King, the Cassandra of this story, who knew or sensed that the Franklin expedition was doomed from the start and was himself doomed not to be believed. If King had been given the command of an expedition down the Great Fish River, he might have saved a few men, and the world would know what happened to the Franklin expedition, even what Sir John himself had died of. After detailing King's repeated proposals to make the trip, all of which the Admiralty ignored, the piece concludes with a story told by an Inuit woman. The ultimate source for it was the report that the HBC factor James Anderson brought back from the mouth of the Great Fish River in 1855. Anderson had talked to this old woman and she had told him about the last man.

"Englishmen must decide," Voyageur wrote,

> between Dr. King and the successive Secretaries of State and Admiralty Boards, who disregarded a proposal, by which it is now clear that this remnant might have been saved.
>
> "My Lords" were too official to entertain the right proposal; can they now be touched by the story of an Esquimaux woman who records the fate of the *last Arctic victim* . . . ? Let them listen:
>
> "One of the last crew died upon Montreal Island."
>
> "The rest perished on the coast of the Mainland."
>
> "The wolves were very thick."
>
> "Only one man was living when their tribe arrived."
>
> "Him it was too late to save."
>
> "He was large and strong, and sat on the sandy beach, his head resting on his hand; and thus he died."

Epilogue

The winter went, the summer went,
The winter came around;
But the hard green ice was strong as death,
And the voice of hope sank to a breath,
Yet caught at every sound.

—George Boker, "A Ballad of
Sir John Franklin"

The Hero

All that remained to do was erect the monuments. Jane Franklin made sure that happened. She enjoyed an enormous prestige in Great Britain now and hardly less abroad. Anywhere she went—and she managed in the early 1860s to circle the globe, her niece Sophy Cracroft always with her—people treated her as a great lady, and great men wanted to meet her and put themselves and their resources at her disposal. In 1860 she steamed to New York to see Henry Grinnell, then traveled to Canada, where the Prince of Wales was visiting; she toured Toronto in his carriage. From there she traveled to Brazil, where she gave the emperor, who granted her an audience of over an hour, a copy of Leopold McClintock's book. She sailed around the Horn and stopped in San Francisco and then Vancouver. From there she traveled up the Fraser River, spending part of the trip in a canoe manned by voyageurs, to give her a taste of how her husband had traveled in Canada. A contingent from Yale named a narrow pass in the river for her: Lady Franklin Pass. She sailed to Hawaii, where she made friends with the half-English, half-Hawaiian Queen Emma, tried to establish an Anglican mission there, and hoped to be able to use her considerable influence to bring the islands into the British Empire. From Hawaii it was on to a three-week stay in Japan, where she went on a shopping spree. When she returned to England, she decorated a room in her house in the Japanese style and caused a sensation in fashionable circles; she was ahead of the curve on the craze later in the century for all things Japanese.

She was seventy years old in 1862, but age seemed to have little effect on her passion for travel, or on her determination to see that her husband got what she believed to be his due. Her influence in Parliament, if not in the Admiralty, which was sick of Jane Franklin, was equaled by no woman of her time and by few men. The powerful Lord Palmerston was a friend and supporter, and she had known Benjamin Disraeli since he was a boy. Through them Lady Jane saw to it that McClintock received a monetary award for his services to the nation. At the same time Palmerston proposed and Disraeli seconded a motion to build a monument to Sir John. It passed without a dissenting vote. The Royal Geographical Society, of which her close friend Sir Roderick Murchison was soon to become president for the third time, voted her its Founder's Gold Medal. She was the first woman to receive the award.

This was all gratifying, but it was the wording on the monument to Sir John that really counted for her. For what had he done, after all, but die in harness? What were his actual accomplishments? He had mapped unknown coastline in northern Canada and led eleven men to a horrible death yet had come home a hero. He had mapped more coastline on his second expedition, this time without losing any of his crew, but had failed to reach his goal. Then he had taken two shiploads of men into the ice, and they had all died. Parry was almost certainly a better ice navigator. McClure's men had suffered nearly as much from hunger and disease. McClintock had mapped much more of the Arctic; so, for that matter, had Sir John Richardson. Yet it was Franklin who was to be immortalized in bronze because of Jane Franklin's insistence that it was he, and not McClure, who had discovered the Northwest Passage.

McClure, of course, had already received his award, and his designation, for discovering the Northwest Passage when he walked across the ice from Bay of Mercy to Melville Island and thereby completed a link, connecting his own remarkable achievement in reaching Banks Island by sail and Parry's equally remarkable achievement in reaching Melville Island by sail in 1819. But he had *walked* across ice that never melted. The passage that McClure had discovered was not navigable. Everybody conceded that, just as everybody knew now that this was only one of several passages across the top of North America. Lady Franklin had worked hard and successfully in 1854, after McClure returned to Great Britain, to ensure that he would not be designated as the man who had discovered *the* Northwest Passage, but only *a* Northwest Passage, one among several, and not the navigable one.

With the finding of the one scribbled record that the Franklin expedition had left behind, the pieces fell into place for her. The first message on that piece of paper had been from Lieutenant Graham Gore, who was clearly on a spring sledge journey when he wrote it, on his way to explore King William Island. Surely no one could dispute that he had reached the bottom of it, perhaps even seen Rae Strait and understood that King William Land was in fact an island. But even that wasn't strictly necessary to make the claim valid. He had only to walk down the western shore of King William island to where it met Simpson Strait, and thereby make that connection with a route already well known, to complete the Passage—or *a* Passage—and claim priority over McClure. The fact that Victoria Strait, where the ships were frozen in, was no more navigable than Melville Sound, which McClure had walked across, made no difference. Both parties had found water routes through the Canadian archipelago. It also made no difference that it was Lieutenant Gore, and not Sir John Franklin, who made this journey. Gore was acting for Franklin. The commander always had the glory. That was just in the nature of things. And he had made his discovery in 1847, not 1850.

Jane Franklin had too many friends and allies in Parliament and among the Arctic knights for anyone to argue seriously with this conclusion. The first of the monuments to Franklin went up in the center of Spilsby, not a hundred yards from the building where he was born. The inscription beneath the statue of Franklin read "Sir John Franklin," and then "Discoverer of the Northwest Passage." For the London monument Lady Jane had tried to secure a spot in Trafalgar Square, near Nelson's great pillar, but unsuccessfully. She settled for Waterloo Place, across from the Athenaeum Club, which her father had helped to found. That inscription makes it equally definite: "To the great Navigator / And his brave companions / Who sacrificed their lives / Completing the discovery of / The North-West Passage." The unveiling took place on November 15, 1866. Lady Jane watched from a window in the Athenaeum. A duplicate of this statue was raised in Hobart, Tasmania, not long after. The statue in Waterloo Place, it is worth noting, stands across the street from the monument to Robert Falcon Scott, that other martyr to polar exploration.

She wasn't done. She wanted a monument in Westminster Abbey as well, and she got one, a bust of Franklin under a sculpted Gothic canopy, the whole more than eight feet tall, placed against a wall. Beneath the bust is a bas-relief of a ship locked into the ice, and an inscription that honors Franklin "for completing the discovery of the North-West Passage." This was unveiled July 31, 1875. Two weeks earlier, at the age of eighty-three, Jane Franklin had died.

Monuments were only one step in the process of glorification. Sherard Osborn wrote the first biography of Franklin, a short book that reprints two pieces he had written for *Once a Week* about Franklin's last voyage in which he tried to imagine how it had gone, along with a panegyric on his life. Osborn compared him to the famous sixteenth-century hero the Chevalier de Bayard, "in all things and under all circumstances . . . *sans peur et sans reproche*," without fear or fault. "Thus, in this prosaic age, went forth again John Franklin, in true knightly mood, to endure, labour and accomplish much." The book was, in other words, a saint's life.

The culture followed suit. Children's literature held Franklin up as an example to follow. It was possible to buy pottery with Franklin's image transferred to the side. Players Cigarette Cards came with his image; so did Oxo Bouillon Trading Cards. Ballads about Franklin appeared in magazines:

> *Sir John, Sir John, 'tis bitter cold,*
> *The scud drives on the breeze,*
> *The ice comes looming from the north,*
> *The very sunbeams freeze.*

Longer, more serious poems also appeared. The minor poet Richard Blackmore, best known for his novel *Lorna Doone,* wrote something called *The Fate of Franklin.* Algernon Charles Swinburne wrote a long elegy to Franklin, one of his better poems, placing Franklin with Nelson and the Elizabethan sea dogs, imagining the satisfaction he and his men must have taken in serving England, and rendering him the highest praise:

> *This England hath not made a better man,*
> *More steadfast or more wholly pure of wrong*
> *Since the large book of English praise began.*

The three biographies of Franklin written after Osborn's brief life in the later nineteenth century were just as adulatory. In *Heart of Darkness* Joseph Conrad lists him with Sir Francis Drake among "the great knights-errant of the sea." Roald Amundsen confessed in his autobiography that he was moved by reading about Franklin to pursue the life he led as a polar explorer. He felt a strange desire to suffer, he said, as John Franklin had suffered. It was Robert Falcon Scott, however, not Amundsen, who suffered as Franklin had suffered, when he and his companions died of scurvy and starvation on their way back from the South Pole. A direct line connects Franklin and Scott. It was Clements Markham, a young officer on the Austin expedition in search of Franklin, who later, as president of the Royal Geographical Society, chose Scott to carry the national banner to the south. Markham was Francis McClintock's biographer. Markham had met Jane Franklin. His cousin wrote one of the Franklin biographies. It was a kind of apostolic succession. Their expeditions failed for similar reasons: because they would not learn the ways of natives who had spent their lives in the ice; because they refused to use dogs, thinking it nobler to pull the sledges themselves; because they were English gentlemen and Royal Navy officers and all too conscious of their own superiority.

For them it was a kind of warfare, man against nature, waged in a wilderness of ice and cold and all the more glorious for it. In 1910 J. Kennedy MacLean, the author of *Heroes of the Polar Seas,* put it this way:

> One generation of explorers after another fought their way through lonely wastes of snow and ice, and every page of the fascinating story is red with the blood of men who fell and died by the way. Heroism, glorious and undaunted even in death, and tragedy, grim and terrible, are twin-brothers throughout the whole of the long and weary struggle, the record of which is more romantic and wonderful than anything which the brain of the fiction-writer has ever conceived.

Not that they haven't tried. Between 1988 and 1998, according to one Franklin scholar, eight novels appeared with Franklin as their subject. In the spring of 2009 another one came out. Franklin is dead, but Franklin never dies. This pudgy, friendly, decent man remains a hero to this day. No revisionist historian has come along to deflate the image.

The search for him, meanwhile, continues. At the turn of the twenty-first century, over a period of several summers, a team of archaeologists sent a ship to Victoria Strait and its environs armed with sonar and a mobile underwater video device, trying to locate the wrecks of Franklin's ships. Parks Canada sends an archaeological crew to Queen Maud Gulf every summer to search for any surviving remains of the ships, "in a bid to assert its sovereignty over the waterways of the Arctic." Robert Grenier, the leader of the team, said in 2008 that "his expedition had been badly hampered by fog, snow and high winds" that August. It was another bad summer in the Arctic, evidently. So far they have found pieces of copper that might have come from the bottoms of Franklin's ships. The search will continue in subsequent summers, they say.

It is hard to know what Canada hopes to prove. The evidence that Franklin went that way is already abundant; bones and relics are plentiful. Who would question the fact? He risked everything to find his way through those icy straits. But was it indeed "romantic and wonderful" to have done so, as J. Kennedy Maclean would have us believe? Was it a transcendent expression of human daring, this long and painful quest for a largely useless geographical clarity? We live in much more ironic times. We can admire the courage, even the persistence of the quest. But if we respect history at all we must temper whatever admiration we may feel with the image of pieces of human arms and legs cooking in a kettle while starving men stare with deadened eyes at the ultimate consequences of this spectacular piece of folly.

Sources

Any history of the search for the Northwest Passage must rely primarily on the accounts of the officers and men who led or participated in the expeditions that made the search, and this book is no exception. I have also been concerned throughout to look at public responses to the expeditions and at the rise and fall of public interest in the Arctic, so my second main source has been the press, most notably in the years 1818–60, when this long search reached its climax. Since the book was always intended as a broad-brush approach to the search, I did not consult the manuscript resources available at the Scott Polar Research Institute in Cambridge, England, nor Admiralty records in the Public Record Office in London, nor other English manuscript depositories. To add that level of density to the book would have threatened to overwhelm the general reader, for whom the book was written.

One problem with this approach is that the expedition accounts were semiofficial, "published by the authority of the Lords Commissioner of the Admiralty." They do not, therefore, contain many voices from the lower decks; and they tend to ignore conflict among the crews. But such counterinformation seldom made it into Admiralty files in any case. The crews were usually barely literate. And in some cases, like Sir Clements Markham's biography of the great Arctic explorer Francis Leopold McClintock, we do get some insight into the interactions outside the captain's cabin. Markham himself participated in an Arctic voyage as a junior officer and knew McClintock personally. Older sources for this reason are sometimes better than modern; they are closer to the world they depict and give a richer taste of what life was like in the Arctic when wintering over in a ship, or trekking on snowshoes through temperatures that stood at forty or fifty degrees below zero. In some cases, too, like the first Franklin land expedition, which was so disastrous, every source of any interest has been published, and archives could add very little to the story.

The sources for individual chapters are listed in the chapter notes that follow and in the Bibliography.

INTRODUCTION

Parry describes the experience of looking out over the ice from Melville Island in Parry, *Journal of a Voyage*, chap. 10. For an in-depth view of the international dispute over the ownership of the Passage and the implications for Canada and the Inuit, see Griffiths, *Politics of Northwest Passage*. Up-to-date information can be found in *The Seattle Times* (October 3, 2007). *The New York Times* (August 29, 2004) reported on Canadian military exercises on Baffin Island; an account of more recent exercises is Funk, "Cold Rush." The *Financial Times* reported on the natural gas potential in northern Canada and offshore on August 23, 2006. A map in Borgerson, "Sea Change," shows the extent of sea ice deterioration in the Arctic. For ice core samples and temperatures in the nineteenth century, see E. T. Alt et al., "Arctic Climate During the Franklin Era" in Sutherland, ed., *Franklin Era in Canadian Arctic History*. On Franklin and the chivalric revival, see Girouard, *Return to Camelot*. Franklin's meeting with Tennyson is recorded in Levi, *Tennyson*, p. 135.

CHAPTER ONE: THE CROKER MOUNTAINS

The description of the send-off the ships were given comes from the assistant surgeon on Parry's ship, Alexander Fisher, in *Journal of a Voyage of Discovery*, a book not authorized by the Admiralty. For Franklin, a major source is Traill, *Life of Franklin;* the quote is from pp. 56–57. John Ross's expedition account is Ross, *Voyage of Discovery;* quotes are from this 1819 edition. On Scoresby in general, the essential source is Stamp and Stamp, *Scoresby, Arctic Scientist;* for this episode, see pp. 66ff and also Savours, *Search for Northwest Passage*, pp. 39ff. Scoresby's great book is *An Account of the Arctic Regions*.

For the mythical Strait of Anián, a convenient quick source is Morison, *European Discovery of America: Northern Voyages*, p. 515. Adams, *Travelers and Travel Liars*, discusses it at greater length. The 1566 map that shows the Strait of Anián is known as the Zalterius Map. For Barrow's map of the Arctic, see Barrow, *Chronological History*. The only account of the Buchan expedition to Spitzbergen is Beechey, *Voyage of Discovery Towards the North Pole*. The best source for John Ross's life is Ross, *Polar Pioneers*, a joint biography of John and his nephew James Clark Ross. For the remarks on cleanliness and the Inuit lack thereof, see Ashenburg, *Dirt on Clean*.

John Barrow's review of Ross's book appeared in *The Quarterly Review* (April 1819). Contributions to *The Quarterly* and its great rival, *The Edinburgh Review*, were anonymous, but most of the authors in these and a number of other Victorian periodicals where anonymity was standard practice have been traced and are available in Houghton and Slingerland, *Wellesley Index to Victorian Periodicals*. Ross replied to Barrow in a pamphlet, *Letter to John Barrow, Esq., or the Reviewer Reviewed*. I could not find a copy. Captain Edward Sabine's reply to Ross is another pamphlet, Sabine, *Remarks on the Account*.

CHAPTER TWO: THE SECOND SECRETARY

On ice cover in the Canadian Arctic and the Beaufort Gyre, see Thomas, *Frozen Oceans*. See *The Oxford Dictionary of National Biography* under "Moxon, Joseph," and

"Barrington, Daines," for brief lives of these men. For the history of the idea of an open polar sea, see Wright, *Human Nature in Geography*. Glyn Williams discusses Engel and his influence on Daines Barrington in Williams, *Voyages of Delusion*, a history of the quest in the eighteenth century. Barrington's ideas appear in his 1775 pamphlet, *Probability of Reaching the North Pole*. Scoresby discussed the issue in two pamphlets of his own, *On the Greenland or Polar Ice* (1815) and *On the Probability of Reaching the North Pole* (1828).

The pieces by Sydney Smith and John Leslie appeared in *The Edinburgh Review* in the March 1819 and June 1818 issues, respectively. The remark Halévy quoted appeared in Halévy, *England in 1815*, the first volume of his great history of England in the nineteenth century. Ann Parry's biography of her forebear, *Parry of the Arctic*, includes the number of signers to the visitor's book. On the Cruikshank print, see Spufford, *I May Be Some Time;* the best reproduction of it appears in Lehane, *Northwest Passage*, a surprisingly good Time-Life book. Barrow's article in *The Quarterly Review* came out in the January 1818 issue.

The source for the figures on Royal Navy manpower are from Rodger, *Command of the Ocean*, and Lewis, *Navy in Transition*. Halévy, *England in 1815*, is also an excellent source on the Royal Navy. On the act establishing the prize for discovering the Northwest Passage, the best source is Williams, *Voyages of Delusion*. For the African explorations run under the aegis of the Royal Navy, see Fleming, *Barrow's Boys*. And for the argument, which I adopt here, that the same attitudes that led British explorers into the ice were operating in the trenches in World War I, see Spufford, *I May Be Some Time*.

The most sympathetic source for Croker's career is Brightfield, *John Wilson Croker*. Christopher Lloyd, author of *Mr. Barrow of the Admiralty*, is a veteran naval historian. Barrow's autobiography is pretty much worthless with respect to the history of the Northwest Passage; he hardly mentions it. For the influence of Sir Joseph Banks on scientific exploration, see Mackay, *In the Wake of Cook*.

CHAPTER THREE: A PASSAGE TO INDIA

Standard sources for this period of exploration include Penrose, *Travel and Discovery in the Renaissance;* Morison, *European Discovery of America;* and for England, Quinn, *England and the Discovery of America*. For Mercator's views, a convenient source is Taylor, *World of Mercator*. Typically for the time, Mercator borrowed his depiction of the topography at the crown of the world from a fourteenth-century traveler who claimed to have been there. Richard Hakluyt printed Robert Thorne's letters; see Hakluyt, *Divers Voyages*, part 2. For Elizabethan geographical thought, see Taylor, *Tudor Geography*. For the Gilbert treatise, see Hakluyt, *Voyages* (the Everyman's Library reprint edition of Hakluyt), vol. 5. On Gemma Frisius, Taylor, *World of Mercator*, is useful; see also Quinn, "Northwest Passage," in Allen, ed., *North American Exploration*.

For Frobisher's life, the best source is McDermott, *Martin Frobisher, Elizabethan Privateer*. On the voyages of John Davis, see Markham, *Voyages and Works of John Davis*. On Henry Hudson's voyages, the best source remains Asher, *Hudson the Navigator*. For the impact all these explorations to the Arctic had on the literature of the period, see Cawley, *Unpathed Waters*, an old book but still useful. On Thomas James, see James, *Strange and Dangerous Voyage.* John Barrow's comment on it may be found in Barrow, *Chronological History.*

CHAPTER FOUR: AN OBJECT PECULIARLY BRITISH

Parry, *Trade and Dominion,* although published in 1971, is still a good source on the fluctuations in exploration during this period; Williams, *Voyages of Delusion,* covers Britain's continued search for the Northwest Passage in the eighteenth century very well. Dampier was a fascinating man—see Preston and Preston, *Pirate of Exquisite Mind.* For the voyage of James Knight to Hudson Bay, Williams, *Voyages of Delusion,* is the best modern source. Williams is also good on Arthur Dobbs, but a fuller treatment is Clarke, *Arthur Dobbs,* which details his life in British politics and affairs. On Middleton's voyage and the succeeding voyage organized by Dobbs, see Williams and Barr, *Voyages to Hudson Bay in Search of a Northwest Passage.* Croker's review of Mary Shelley's novel *Frankenstein* appeared in *The Quarterly Review* of May 1818.

CHAPTER FIVE: O CANADA

For Franklin's life, the best biography remains Traill, *Life of Sir John Franklin.* The most recent is Beardsley, *Deadly Winter;* others include Markham, *Life,* and Lamb, *Happy Voyager.* Markham's is the most thorough source for Franklin's role in the Flinders expedition to Australia. On the question of "interest" and how it worked in the Royal Navy, an enlightening book is Southam, *Jane Austen and the Navy;* he has a chapter on "Patronage and Interest." I took Nelson's well-known quote about the quality of Royal Navy officers from Gordon, *Rules of the Game,* a fascinating book. The definitive source for Arctic panoramas, and Arctic imagery generally, is Potter, *Arctic Spectacles.* Potter, based at Rhode Island College, maintains a Web site devoted to John Franklin: www.ric.edu/faculty/rpotter/SJFranklin.html.

The principal sources for the history of Franklin's first land expedition are Franklin, *Narrative of a Journey;* the remarkable Franklin, *Journals and Correspondence, First Expedition;* Richardson, *Arctic Ordeal;* Hood, *To the Arctic by Canoe;* and Back, *Arctic Artist.* The quotes are from these sources. For the geography of the area, Bone, *Geography of the Canadian North,* is a good summary. The most readable account of the history of the Hudson's Bay Company is Newman, *Empire of the Bay.* Newman is the source for the number of mosquitoes that the mathematician guessed occupied a cubic yard of air.

CHAPTER SIX: WINTER LAKE

This chapter continues the story of Franklin's first land expedition; its principal sources are the same as for Chapter 5. On the brilliance of the long polar winter night, Samuel Hearne remarked on the light from the stars and the aurora borealis compensating for the lack of sunlight; Hearne also thought he could hear the sound the aurora made, "a rustling and crackling noise, like the waving of a large flag in a fresh gale of wind." See Hearne, *Journey to the Northern Ocean,* pp. 144–45. On the duel between Back and Hood, see Bellot, *Memoirs,* p. 1:252. For the importance of

Richardson's work and his status as a scientist, see Levere, *Science and Canadian Arctic*, pp. 103–36. On George Back, see Steele, *Man Who Mapped the Arctic*. For the idea of Akaitcho as a businessman, trying to get the best deal for his people, see Franklin, *Journal and Correspondence, First Expedtion*, pp. ci—cii.

CHAPTER SEVEN: *DE QUOI À MANGER*

This chapter concludes the story of Franklin's first land expedition, and the same sources, the journals of those involved, were used. For Back's letter to Wentzel, the source is Masson, *Les Bourgeois de la Compagnie*, pp. 1:67–153.

CHAPTER EIGHT: A FINE ROMANCE

For Richard Davis's criticism of Franklin's performance in northern Canada, see his introduction to Franklin, *Journals and Correspondence, First Expedition*. For Simpson's comment on Franklin, see Simpson, *Journal of Occurrences*, p. 261. Wentzel's remarks can be found in Masson, *Les Bourgeois de la Compagnie*, and the skit put together by the fur traders is printed in Macleod and Glover, "Franklin's First Expedition." Barrow's review appeared in *The Quarterly Review* (January 1823); other quotes are from *The Gentleman's Magazine* (October 1822) and *The Times* (October 18 and 19, 1822, and November 9, 1822). On the publishing history of Franklin's book, see Davis, "History or His/Story?"

For the romance between Franklin and Eleanor Porden, the principal source is Gell, *John Franklin's Bride*. Mrs. Gell was married to a descendant of Franklin's daughter by Eleanor Porden and had access to their private correspondence. All quotes from their correspondence are taken from this book. The review of Eleanor Porden's poem appeared in *The Quarterly Review* 16 (1817), pp. 387–96.

CHAPTER NINE: FIVE THOUSAND POUNDS

William Edward Parry's son, the Reverend Edward Parry, wrote a biography of his father, stressing his piousness; see Parry, *Memoirs of Rear-Admiral Sir W. Edward Parry*. His great-great-granddaughter, Ann Parry, is the author of *Parry of the Arctic*, which depends on papers in the possession of the family and is the better, more detached book. For Parry's account of his expedition of 1819–20, see Parry, *Journal of a Voyage for the Discovery*. This Greenwood Press edition of 1968 is a facsimile edition in the same quarto size as the original.

Gosnell, *Ice*, goes deeply into its subject and is wonderfully entertaining as well; Pyne, *The Ice*, is about Antarctica but is extremely helpful on the action of ice. Scoresby's story from 1830 was reprinted in Mangles, *Papers and Despatches Relating to the Arctic Searching Expeditions;* on the experience of whalers generally, see Ross, *Arctic Whalers, Icy Seas*.

A convenient source for the history of canned food (and portable soup) is Davidson, *Oxford Companion to Food*, entries for "canning" and "portable soup." On *The Times* and the press in England generally, see Clarke, *Grub Street to Fleet Street*. *The Times* was opposed to the search for the Northwest Passage from the beginning. Quotes from the press reaction to Parry's voyage are taken from *Blackwood's Magazine*

(November 1820), pp. 219–23; *The Edinburgh Philosophical Journal* (January 1821), pp. 144–55; *The European Magazine and London Review* (February 1821), pp. 94–102; and, for Barrow, *The Quarterly Review* (April 1821), pp. 175–216.

CHAPTER TEN: FOREVER FROZEN

The two major sources for Parry's voyage to the upper reaches of Hudson Bay are Parry, *Journal of a Second Voyage*, and Lyon, *Private Journal*. All quotes from Parry and Lyon are from these two accounts. Fleming, *Barrow's Boys*, describes Lyon's adventures in North Africa. For the idea of a "Parry school" of Arctic explorers, see Markham, *Lands of Silence*.

CHAPTER ELEVEN: FURY BEACH

The Reverend Edward Parry describes his father's meeting with the king in Parry, *Memoirs of Rear-Admiral;* he and Parry, *Parry of the Arctic*, are the sources for other details about this period in Parry's career. The articles in the *New Monthly Magazine* and the *Mirror* appeared in, respectively, vol. 10, n.s. (1824), pp. 453–60; and vol. 2, Supplementary (November 1823), p. 428. Barrow's review came out in the October 1824 issue of *The Quarterly Review*. Cochrane's advice on pursuing the quest for the Passage is in *New Monthly Magazine* 10, n.s. (1824), pp. 393–403 and 549–59. The dinner party description is from Woodward, *Portrait of Jane*, p. 155.

Parry, *Journal of a Third Voyage*, is the source for the quotes here; his trip toward the North Pole is described in Parry, *Narrative of an Attempt*, while Lyon described his voyage in Lyon, *Brief Narrative of an Unsuccessful Attempt*. Barrow discussed Lyon's voyage and admits his mistake in Barrow, *Voyages of Discovery and Research*.

CHAPTER TWELVE: FOG

On the Brontë sisters and the naming of their toy soldiers, see Gérin, *Emily Brontë*, p. 12. John Ross's 1826 pamphlet was Ross, *Letter to John Barrow, Esq*. It was printed in London in 1826 "For Private Perusal Only." Barrow's *Quarterly Review* article on Parry's third voyage appeared in vol. 34 (1826), pp. 378–99.

The two sources for Franklin's second major expedition are Franklin, *Narrative of a Second Expedition*, Franklin, *Journals and Correspondence, Second Expedition*. Barrow's *Quarterly Review* article on this voyage appeared in Vol. 38 (1828), pp. 335–58.

CHAPTER THIRTEEN: WARMER WATERS

On Sir James Graham, see Erickson, *The Public Career of Graham*. For Barrow's side of the story of naval reform, see Lloyd, *Barrow of Admiralty*, but the best source will no doubt be the next volume of N. A. M. Rodger's history of the Royal Navy when it appears. For Barrow's writing career, Lloyd is also good, but the history of Barrow's *Mutiny of the Bounty* is best told by Gavin Kennedy in his introduction to the 1980 edition. The easiest-to-find history of the Royal Geographical Society is Cameron, *To the Farthest Ends of the Earth*.

For Beaufort's life and career, the indispensable source is Friendly, *Beaufort of the*

Admiralty. Rodger, *Admiralty,* covers the history of this branch of the British government as an administrative unit.

The great source for Jane Franklin, née Griffin, is Woodward, *Portrait of Jane.* McGoogan, *Lady Franklin's Revenge,* must also be consulted; McGoogan, a Canadian Arctic historian, has looked at the same sources and his interpretations are somewhat different from Woodward's. For Franklin's work in Greece, once again Traill, *Life of Franklin,* is the best source, however old-fashioned his style and approach, while Brewer, *Greek War of Independence,* is a good, up-to-date source for the conflict between the warring political factions in Greece.

Chapter Fourteen: Boothia

On John Ross, Jane Franklin's remarks are quoted in Woodward, *Portrait of Jane.* Ross, *Polar Pioneers,* is as good as one could ask of a joint biography of the two Rosses. On the transition to steam, a good short description can be found in David K. Brown's chapter on the subject in Hill, *Oxford History of Royal Navy.* The article on Ross's treatise on steam is in *Blackwood's Magazine* (April 1827), pp. 393–99. On the pamphlet war between Ross and Braithwaite, the two main pamphlets were reprinted as addenda in Ross, *Narrative of a Second Voyage.* Subsequent Ross quotes describing the voyage are from this Greenwood Press edition, which (except for the addenda) is a facsimile edition.

William Light's story is told in Huish, *Last Voyage of Capt. Sir John Ross.* The parliamentary committee assigned to investigate Ross's request for expenses published its findings as *Report of the Select Committee on the Expedition to the Arctic Seas,* House of Commons, April 28, 1834. James Clark Ross, it is worth noting, wrote those chapters of his uncle's book (Ross, *Narrative of a Second Voyage*) that pertained to his own explorations, and quotes from the younger Ross are from those chapters.

The press response to Ross is to be found in, among many other sources, *The Athenaeum* (July 21, 1832) and *The Gentleman's Magazine* (October 1833). Maginn's contribution appeared in *Fraser's Magazine* (January 1834).

Chapter Fifteen: The Question of Boothia

Desborough Cooley's review of John Ross's book in *The Edinburgh Review* is in the issue dated July 1836. For the story behind the attempt to rescue Ross that led to George Back's expedition down the Great Fish River, sources include Wallace's extremely useful *Navy, Company, and Richard King,* chap. 2; Ross, *Polar Pioneers,* and Steele, *Man Who Mapped the Arctic.* Back told the story of the run-up to the expedition, and the expedition itself, in *Narrative of the Arctic Land Expedition.* For King's account of this same expedition, see King, *Narrative of a Journey to the Shores of the Arctic Ocean.* The letters written from Back's winter quarters were printed in *The Athenaeum* in the issues of October 25 and November 22, 1834. Further articles appeared in the issues of August 22, September 12, and September 19, 1835.

Back told the story of his voyage to Repulse Bay and his winter in the ice in *Narrative of an Expedition in H.M.S. Terror.* On Richard King's proposals, the best source is Wallace, *Navy, Company, and Richard King.* The most reliable sources for Simpson and Dease's three years in the Arctic is Dease, *From Barrow to Boothia.* Editor

William Barr's objectivity corrects the boasting to which Simpson was prone. The quotes from Simpson are taken from this source, as are the quotes from Kenneth Coates.

John Barrow's comments on speculative mapping are from Barrow, *Voyages of Discovery*.

CHAPTER SIXTEEN: IN EXILE FROM THE LAND OF SNOWS

For John Barrow, Jr., see Lloyd, *Barrow of the Admiralty*. John Herschel's article on geomagnetism is in *The Quarterly Review* 66 (1840) pp. 271–312. For the science of terrestrial magnetism up to the magnetic crusade, the best source is Jonkers, *Earth's Magnetism,* and for the history of the magnetic crusade, see Mawer, *South by Northwest*. Charles Babbage, who was something of a crank on the subject, wrote a book in favor of the reform of scientific education; see Babbage, *Reflections on Decline of Science*. For the *Admiralty Manual,* see Levere, *Science and Canadian Arctic,* which devotes a chapter to it.

James Clark Ross's mission to rescue the Arctic whalers is the subject of a chapter in Ross, *Polar Pioneers*. For information on the maps produced by the voyage of the *Beagle* under Fitzroy, Friendly, *Beaufort of Admiralty,* is the source. The comment on Inuit mapping from *TLS* dates from the issue of January 4, 2008.

The indispensable source for Franklin's experience in Tasmania is Fitzpatrick, *Franklin in Tasmania*. Shakespeare, *In Tasmania,* gives figures for the size of the native population as it declined. For Jane Franklin's travels in Australia, New Zealand, and Tasmania, the best book remains Woodward, *Portrait of Jane;* for Jane Franklin's journal of the trip to Port Phillip and Sydney, see Russell, *This Errant Lady*. John Franklin's defense of himself is in Franklin, *Narrative of Passages in History of Van Diemen's Land*.

CHAPTER SEVENTEEN: THE GLORIOUS DEPARTURE

What is known of Franklin's last voyage has been thoroughly laid out in Cyriax, *Franklin's Last Arctic Expedition*. Cyriax went over the Admiralty supply records and correspondence with great care. Traill, *Life of Franklin,* is always a useful source on Franklin. Richard King's letters to *The Athenaeum* appeared on January 11, February 1, and March 15, 1845. On the positive attitudes of the early Victorian period, see Houghton, *Victorian Frame of Mind,* esp. chap. 2; Woodland, *Age of Reform;* Powell, *Nationhood and Identity*. The quotes about glory and hardship may be found in "First Half of the Nineteenth Century," *Fraser's Magazine* 43 (1851), pp. 1–15. For the light emanating from gas lamps, see Tristan, *London Journal 1840*.

The incident of the flag that Jane Franklin threw over her husband's legs may be found in Woodward, *Portrait of Jane*. James Fitzjames's descriptions of John Franklin and his fellow officers is in Fitzjames, *Last Journals of Fitzjames*. Ross, *Polar Pioneers,* describes John Ross's early offer to search for Franklin. Richard King wrote *The Athenaeum* with his own warnings and offers to lead an expedition in the issue of June 12, 1847. By the issue of November 13, 1847, *The Athenaeum* had changed its mind and become alarmed.

Dr. John Rae's most recent biography is McGoogan, *Fatal Passage*. But for his own voice, see Rae, *John Rae's Correspondence with the Hudson's Bay Company*. See also

Bunyan, et al., *No Ordinary Journey,* the catalogue of an exhibition of some of Rae's things.

Any number of books on the search for Franklin have been published. The chief ones, if not the most recent, are Neatby, *Search for Franklin,* and Owen, *Fate of Franklin.* Owen did not trouble the reader with any of his source material, which is too bad; he was a Franklin descendant and had access to family papers. Nevertheless both these books provide useful overviews of the subject. Isbister's letter to *The Athenaeum* appeared in the issue of December 18, 1847. The journals from the Pullen expedition are to be found in Pullen, *Pullen Expedition.* For the search by Richardson and Rae, see Rae, *John Rae's Correspondence,* and Richardson, *Arctic Searching Expedition.* James Clark Ross did not write a book about his abortive voyage of 1848–49, but Markham, *Life of McClintock,* is a good source; Markham was there.

The second letter from Isbister appeared in *The Athenaeum* on December 8, 1849. The articles by W. Francis Ainsworth came out in *The New Monthly Magazine* at intervals from March 1850 to November 1853. The quote from *The Illustrated London News* is from the issue of October 13, 1849.

Chapter Eighteen: Arctic Maze

Woodward, *Portrait of Jane,* details Jane Franklin's activities in the late 1840s as the search for her husband began. On the disputes about money between Jane and her stepdaughter, McGoogan, *Lady Franklin's Revenge,* is especially good. Jane Franklin's letter to President Zachary Taylor was printed in a variety of sources; one convenient source is Simmonds, *Franklin and the Arctic Regions,* a brief history of the events leading up to the Franklin search that reprinted many documents up to 1852 and kept current with the search in later editions. Elisha Kent Kane's quotes are from Kane, *United States Grinnell Expedition.* Kane was a doctor in the U. S. Navy.

For Jane Franklin's interest in clairvoyants, see Ross, "Clairvoyants and Mediums Search for Franklin." Both Woodward, *Portrait of Jane,* and McGoogan, *Lady Franklin's Revenge,* have sections on the subject as well. Clement Markham's book is *Life of McClintock;* the story about McClure appears on p. 51. On the numerous expeditions of 1850, Neatby, *Search for Franklin,* provides a good overview. For John Ross's part, the best source remains Ross, *Polar Pioneers.* John Franklin's official instructions were printed in, among other sources, Kennedy, *Short Narrative of Second Voyage.* W. Gillies Ross describes the numerous hoaxes and false leads in the search in "False Leads in the Franklin Search."

Simmonds, *Franklin and Arctic Regions,* prints many of the documents from the Arctic knights sent as advice to the Admiralty; so does Mangles, *Papers and Despatches,* including the speculations of August Petermann. Kennedy, *Short Narrative of Second Voyage,* tells the story of his expedition to Prince Regent Inlet. For Rae's 1851 journeys, *John Rae's Correspondence* is the best source.

Chapter Nineteen: The Discovery of the Northwest Passage

Ainsworth's comment in *The New Monthly Magazine* is in the October 1850 issue, p. 375. The *Times* editorial appeared October 7, 1851. For the replies of the Arctic experts, see Mangles, *Papers and Despatches.* For Markham on Belcher, see Markham,

Life of McClintock, p. 140; for Neatby's remark, see his *Search for Franklin,* p. 198. McClintock's journal of his sledge trip appears in Great Britain, Admiralty, *Further Papers Relative to Expeditions,* pp. 540ff.

The two principal sources for McClure's expedition are Miertsching, *Frozen Ships,* and McClure, *Discovery of North-West Passage.* For Collinson's voyage, the best source is Barr, *Arctic Hell-Ship.*

Lieutenant Mecham's account of finding McClure's message is in Great Britain, Admiralty, *Further Papers Relative to Expeditions,* pp. 496–97. Press reactions to the discovery of the Northwest Passage may be found in *The Illustrated London News* (October 29, 1853), *The Athenaeum* (October 15 and November 5, 1853), and *Fraser's Magazine,* November 1853. For Belcher's "carbuncle," see *The Athenaeum* (December 1, 1855). *The Times* reported on Belcher's court-martial (October 18, 1854). The notice announcing that the search for Franklin was over appeared in *The London Gazette* (January 20, 1854). The story of the ship *Resolute* has been well told in Sandler, *Resolute.*

Chapter Twenty: The Last Dread Alternative

The quote from *Fraser's Magazine* comes from the June 1854 issue. Ross's letter to *The Times* was printed on November 27, 1852. For Rae's journey and what he heard from the Inuit, see Rae, *John Rae's Correspondence,* pp. 274ff. The comment by Hendrik van Loon is from McGoogan, *Fatal Passage,* p. 208.

For the press reaction to Rae's news, see *The Athenaeum* (October 28, 1854), *The Times* (October 24, 26, and 30, 1854). Marlow, "Fate of Sir John Franklin," is enlightening. On Dickens, see Stone, *Night Side.* Dickens's articles on the subject appeared in *Household Words* (December 2 and 9, 1854), pp. 362–65 and 387–93. For Rae's response, see Dickens, *Uncollected Writings,* pp. 513–22. This was not the end of it. Dickens subsequently produced a play, written by Wilkie Collins and extensively rewritten by himself, called *The Frozen Deep;* it was put on at his London residence, Tavistock House, a number of times with invited guests who included the major drama critics. It proved to be so popular that the queen commanded a performance, and shortly after that it was staged with professional actors at a theater in Manchester. In the play the hero is an Arctic explorer who sacrifices his own life to save the life of his companion, who is also his rival for the affection of the heroine. The idea seems to have been to ennoble the reputation of Arctic explorers. People wept copiously at these performances. Dickens himself played the part of the self-sacrificing explorer. Shortly afterward he left his wife to live with his mistress, an actress he met when she joined the cast of the play in Manchester. See Brannan, *Management of Dickens.* For the cut marks on the bones of the Franklin crew members, see Keenleyside, "Final Days of the Franklin Expedition."

Jane Franklin's letter to Ross was quoted in Ross, *Polar Pioneers,* p. 353. Her letter to Palmerston was printed as an appendix to McClintock, *Voyage of the Fox.* The *Times* editorial opposing the voyage appeared on November 27, 1856, with further comment on December 2. For the lead level in the bones, the source is Beattie and Geiger, *Frozen in Time.* Scott Cookman, who has done extensive research in Admiralty provisioning records, argues that another source for the failure of the expedition was contamination of the canned meats supplied by a manufacturer named Goldner.

Goldner was investigated by the Admiralty for just this reason, sloppy work sealing cans, but since food supplies apparently remained in the ships that were abandoned, it may be that Cookman overstates his case.

For the reception of McClintock's news in England, see Markham, *Life of McClintock*. On Charles Francis Hall, an excellent book is Loomis, *Weird and Tragic Shores*. All quotes from Hall are borrowed from this book. For the Schwatka expedition, see Schwatka, *Long Arctic Search*. Cyriax's account is summarized from Cyriax, *Franklin's Last Expedition*. More recently David C. Woodman spent ten years visiting Franklin sites in the Arctic and studying the Inuit accounts from every source, in an effort to go beyond Cyriax and puzzle out exactly what happened after the ships were abandoned, but he admits that it is impossible to be certain about any of it. His book on the subject is Woodman, *Unravelling the Franklin Mystery*. B. J. Rule, a Franklin descendant who lives in Florida, has, finally, published an account of her conversations with Franklin, achieved through a medium; see Rule, *Polar Knight*. According to her, Franklin's spirit is most concerned that he be given credit for discovering the Northwest Passage. He claims to have been buried in the southeast corner of King William Island.

The story of the last man to die comes from "A Phase of the Arctic Mystery," *Once a Week*, December 31, 1859, pp. 13–15.

EPILOGUE: THE HERO

The best source for understanding Jane Franklin's quest for honors and memorials for her husband is McGoogan, *Lady Franklin's Revenge,* but it must be supplemented by Woodward, *Portrait of Jane*. The quote from Osborn appears in Girouard, *Return to Camelot*. The most bountiful resource for links to Franklin's story and his afterlife is the one maintained by Russell Potter, author of *Arctic Spectacles*, of Rhode Island College: www.ric.edu/faculty/rpotter/sjfranklin.html. For the latest on the Canadian effort to locate relics of Franklin's ships, and the hulls themselves, see *The Ottawa Citizen* (March 31, 2009).

BIBLIOGRAPHY

Primary Sources

[Anonymous.] "Scrutator." *The Impracticability of a North-West Passage for Ships, Impartially Considered.* London, 1824.

Back, George. *Narrative of the Arctic Land Expedition to the Mouth of the Great Fish River . . . in the Years 1833, 1834, and 1835.* 1836; reprint Elibron Classics, 2005.

———. *Narrative of the Arctic Land Expedition in H.M.S. Terror.* London: John Murray, 1838.

———. *Arctic Artist: The Journal and Paintings of George Back, Midshipman with Franklin, 1819–1822.* Edited by C. Stuart Houston. Montreal: McGill–Queen's University Press, 1994.

Beechey, F. W. *Narrative of a Voyage to the Pacific and Beering's Strait to Co-operate with the Polar Expeditions . . . in the Years 1825, 26, 27, 28.* 2 vols. London: Henry Colburn and Richard Bentley, 1831.

———. *A Voyage of Discovery towards the North Pole.* London: Richard Bentley, 1843.

Bellot, Joseph René. *Memoirs of Lieutenant Joseph René Bellot, . . . With His Journal of a Voyage in the Polar Seas, in Search of Sir John Franklin.* London: Hurst and Blackett, 1855.

Carter, Robert Randolph. *Searching for the Franklin Expedition.* Edited by Harold B. Gill, Jr., and Joanne Young. Annapolis: Naval Institute Press, 1998.

Dease, Peter Warren. *From Barrow to Boothia: The Arctic Journal of Chief Factor Peter Warren Dease, 1836–1839.* Edited by William Barr. Montreal: McGill–Queen's University Press, 2002.

De Bray, Emile Frédéric. *A Frenchman in Search of Franklin: De Bray's Arctic Journal, 1852–1854.* Translated and edited by William Barr. Toronto: University of Toronto Press, 1992.

Fisher, Alexander. *Journal of a Voyage of Discovery to the Arctic Regions . . . in his Majesty's Ship Alexander.* London: Richard Phillips, n.d. [1819].

———. *Journal of a Voyage of Discovery to the Arctic in His Majesty's Ships* Hecla *and* Griper *in the Years 1819 and 1820.* London: Longman, Hurst, 1821.

Fitzjames, James. *The Last Journals of Captain Fitzjames of the Lost Polar Expedition.* Edited by William Coningham. Brighton, U.K.: W. Pearce, n.d. [1859].

Franklin, John. *Narrative of a Journey to the Shores of the Polar Sea in the Years 1819, 20, 21, and 22.* 1823; reprint Edmonton: M. G. Hurtig, 1969.

———. *Narrative of a Second Expedition to the Shores of the Polar Sea in the Years 1825, 1826, and 1827.* 1828; reprint New York: Greenwood Press, 1969.

———. *Narrative of Some Passages in the History of Van Diemen's Land During the Last Three Years of Sir John Franklin's Administration of Its Government.* Hobart, Tasmania: Platypus Publications, 1967.

———. *Sir John Franklin's Journals and Correspondence: The First Arctic Land Expedition, 1819–1822.* Edited by Richard C. Davis. Toronto: Champlain Society, 1995.

———. *Sir John Franklin's Journals and Correspondence: The Second Arctic Land Expedition, 1825–1827.* Edited by Richard C. Davis. Toronto: Champlain Society, 1998.

Hakluyt, Richard. *Voyages [The Principall Navigations],* vol. 5. 1605. Everyman's Library No. 338. London: J. M. Dent, 1962.

Hakluyt, Richard, ed. *Divers Voyages.* 2 vols. Amsterdam: Theatrum Orbis Terrarum, 1967.

Hearne, Samuel. *A Journey from Prince of Wales's Fort in Hudson's Bay to the Northern Ocean, 1769, 1770, 1771, 1772.* Edited by Richard Glover. Toronto: Macmillan of Canada, 1958.

Hood, Robert. *To the Arctic by Canoe, 1819–1821: The Journal and Paintings of Robert Hood.* Edited by C. Stuart Houston. Montreal: McGill–Queen's University Press, 1975.

Huish, Robert. *The Last Voyage of Capt. Sir John Ross, R.N., to the Arctic Regions, for the Discovery of a North West Passage.* London: John Saunders, 1835.

James, Captain Thomas. *The Strange and Dangerous Voyage of Capt. Thomas James.* Edited by W. A. Kenyon. Toronto: Royal Ontario Museum, 1975.

Kane, Elisha Kent. *The United States Grinnell Expedition in Search of Sir John Franklin: A Personal Memoir.* New York: Sheldon, Blakeman & Co., 1857.

Kennedy, William. *A Short Narrative of the Second Voyage of the Prince Albert in Search of Sir John Franklin.* London: W. H. Dalton, 1853.

King, Richard. *Narrative of a Journey to the Shores of the Arctic Ocean, in 1833, 1834, and 1835; under the Command of Capt. Back, R.N.* 2 vols. London: Richard Bentley, 1836.

Klutschak, Heinrich. *Overland to Starvation Cove: With the Inuit in Search of Franklin, 1878–1880.* Translated and edited by William Barr. Toronto: University of Toronto Press, 1993.

Lyon, George F. *The Private Journal of Captain G. F. Lyon During the Recent Voyage of Discovery Under Captain Parry, 1821–1823.* Barre, Mass.: Imprint Society, 1970.

———. *A Brief Narrative of an Unsuccessful Attempt to Reach Repulse Bay Through Sir Thomas Rowe's "Welcome" in His Majesty's Ship Griper in the Year MDCCCXXIV.* 1825; reprint Toronto: Coles, 1971.

Masson, L. R., ed. *Les Bourgeois de la Compagnie du Nord-Ouest,* vol. 1. New York: Antiquarian Press, 1960.

McClintock, Francis L. *The Voyage of the 'Fox' in the Arctic Seas: A Narrative of the Discovery of the Fate of Sir John Franklin and His Companions.* New York: J. T. Lloyd, 1859.

McClure, Robert L. M. *The Discovery of the North-West Passage.* Edited by Sherard Osborn. Rutland, Vt.: Charles E. Tuttle Co., 1969.

Miertsching, Johann. *Frozen Ships: The Arctic Diary of Johann Miertsching, 1850–1854.* Translated and edited by L. H. Neatby. Toronto: Macmillan of Canada, 1967.

Osborn, Sherard. *Stray Leaves from an Arctic Journal; or, Eighteen Months in the Polar Regions, in Search of Sir John Franklin's Expedition in the Years 1850–51.* New York: George P. Putnam, 1852.

Parry, William Edward, *Journal of a Voyage for the Discovery of a North-West Passage from the Atlantic to the Pacific; Performed in the Years 1819–20, etc.* 1821; reprint New York: Greenwood Press, 1968.

———. *Journal of a Second Voyage for the Discovery of a Northwest Passage from the Atlantic to the Pacific; Performed in the Years 1821–22–23, in His Majesty's Ships* Fury *and* Hecla. 1824; reprint New York: Greenwood Press, 1969.

———. *Journal of a Third Voyage for the Discovery of a North-West Passage from the Atlantic to the Pacific . . . in 1824–25.* Philadelphia: Carey and Lea, 1826.

———. *Narrative of an Attempt to Reach the North Pole.* London: John Murray, 1828.

Peard, George. *To the Pacific and Arctic with Beechey: The Journal of Lieutenant George Peard of H.M.S. "Blossom," 1825–1828.* Cambridge, U.K.: Hakluyt Society, 1973.

Pullen, H. F., ed. *The Pullen Expedition in Search of Sir John Franklin.* Toronto: Arctic History Press, 1979.

Rae, John. *John Rae's Correspondence with the Hudson's Bay Company on Arctic Exploration, 1844–1855.* Edited by E. E. Rich. London: Hudson's Bay Company Record Society, 1953.

Richardson, John. *Arctic Searching Expedition.* 2 vols. London: Longman, Brown, Green, and Longman's, 1851.

———. *Arctic Ordeal: The Journal of John Richardson, Surgeon-Naturalist with Franklin, 1820–1822.* Edited by C. Stuart Houston. Montreal: McGill–Queen's University Press, 1984.

Ross, John. *A Voyage of Discovery, Made Under the Orders of the Admiralty, in His Majesty's Ships* Isabella *and* Alexander, *for the Purpose of Exploring Baffin's Bay, and Inquiring into the Probability of a North-West Passage.* London: John Murray, 1819.

———. *An Explanation of Captain Sabine's Remarks on the Late Voyage of Discovery to Baffin's Bay.* London: John Murray, 1819.

———. *A Letter to John Barrow, Esq. F.R.S. on the Late Extraordinary and Unexpected Hyperborean Discoveries.* London: W. Pople, 1826.

———. *Narrative of a Second Voyage in Search of a North-West Passage, and of a Residence in the Arctic Regions During the Years 1829, 1830, 1831, 1832, 1833.* 1835; reprint New York: Greenwood Press, 1969.

Ross, W. Gillies. *Arctic Whalers, Icy Seas: Narratives of the Davis Strait Whale Fishery.* Toronto: Irwin, 1985.

Sabine, Edward. *Remarks on the Account of the Late Voyage of Discovery to Baffin's Bay, Published by Captain John Ross, R. N.,* 3rd ed. London: John Booth, 1819.

Schwatka, Frederick. *The Long Arctic Search: The Narrative of Lt. Frederick Schwatka, U.S.A., 1878–1880, Seeking the Records of the Lost Franklin Expedition.* Edited by Edouard A. Stackpole. Chester, Conn.: Mystic Seaport, 1977.

Simpson, George. *Journal of Occurrences in the Athabasca Department by George Simpson, 1820 and 1821, and Report.* Edited by E. E. Rich. Toronto: Champlain Society, 1938.

Secondary Sources

BOOKS

Adams, Percy G. *Travelers and Travel Liars, 1660–1800.* Berkeley: University of California Press, 1962.

Anonymous. *Northern Regions; or, Uncle Richard's Relation of Captain Parry's Voyages for the Discovery of a North-West Passage, etc.* New York: C. S. Francis & Co., 1856.

Ashcroft, Frances. *Life at the Extremes: The Science of Survival.* Berkeley: University of California Press, 2000.

Ashenburg, Katherine. *The Dirt on Clean: An Unsanitized History.* New York: North Point Press, 2008.

Asher, G. M. *Henry Hudson the Navigator: The Original Documents in Which His Career Is Recorded.* London: Hakluyt Society, 1860.

Atwood, Margaret. "Concerning Franklin and his Gallant Crew." In *Strange Things: The Malevolent North in Canadian Literature.* Oxford, U.K.: Clarendon Press, 1995.

Babbage, Charles. *Reflections on the Decline of Science in England.* N.p: Dodo Press, 1830.

Barczewski, Stephanie. *Antarctic Destinies: Scott, Shackleton and the Changing Face of Heroism.* London: Hambledon Continuum, 2007.

Barr, William. *Arctic Hell-Ship: The Voyage of HMS* Enterprise *1850–1855.* Edmonton: University of Alberta Press, 2007.

Barrington, Daines. *The Probability of Reaching the North Pole Discussed.* 1775; reprint Fairfield, Wash.: Ye Galleon Press, 1987.

Barrow, John. *A Chronological History of Voyages into the Arctic Regions.* 1818; reprint Newton Abbot, Devon, U.K.: David and Charles, 1971.

———. *Voyages of Discovery and Research within the Arctic Regions, from the Year 1818 to the Present Time.* New York: Harper and Brothers, 1846.

———. *The Mutiny of the Bounty.* Edited by Gavin Kennedy. Boston: David R. Godine, 1980.

Bartlett, C. J. *Great Britain and Sea Power, 1815–1853.* Oxford, U.K.: Clarendon Press, 1963.

Beardsley, Martyn. *Deadly Winter: The Life of Sir John Franklin.* Annapolis: Naval Institute Press, 2002.

Beattie, Owen, and John Geiger. *Frozen in Time: The Fate of the Franklin Expedition.* Vancouver: Greystone Books, 1998.

Berton, Pierre. *Arctic Grail: The Quest for the Northwest Passage and the North Pole, 1818–1909.* New York: Lyons Press, 2000.

Black, Jeremy. *The English Press, 1621–1861.* Stroud, Gloucestershire, U.K.: Sutton, 2001.

———. *The British Seaborne Empire.* New Haven, Conn.: Yale University Press, 2004.

Bone, Robert M. *The Geography of the Canadian North.* Toronto: Oxford University Press, 1992.

Bown, Stephen R. *Scurvy.* New York: St. Martin's Press, 2004.

Brannan, Robert Louis. *Under the Management of Mr. Charles Dickens: His Production of "The Frozen Deep."* Ithaca, N.Y.: Cornell University Press, 1966.

Brewer, David. *The Greek War of Independence.* Woodstock, N.Y.: Overlook Press, 2003.

Briggs, Asa. *The Age of Improvement, 1783–1867.* London: Longmans, 1959.

Briggs, Sir John H. *Naval Administrations, 1827 to 1892.* London: Sampson Low, Marston & Co., 1897.

Brightfield, Myron F. *John Wilson Croker.* Berkeley: University of California Press, 1940.

Bulwer-Lytton, Edward. *England and the English.* 2 vols. New York: J. & J. Harper, 1833.

Bunyan, Ian, Jenni Calder, Dale Idiens, and Bryce Wilson. *No Ordinary Journey: John Rae, Arctic Explorer 1813–1893.* Montreal: McGill–Queens University Press, 1993.

Cameron, Ian. *To the Farthest Ends of the Earth: The History of the Royal Geographical Society 1830–1980.* London: Macdonald, 1980.

Canny, Nicholas, ed. *The Origins of Empire: The Oxford History of the British Empire,* vol. 1. Oxford: Oxford University Press, 1998.

Cawley, Robert Ralston. *Unpathed Waters: Studies in the Influence of the Voyagers on Elizabethan Literature.* 1940; reprint London: Frank Cass & Co., 1967.

Church, William Conant. *The Life of John Ericsson.* 1890; reprint Honolulu: University Press of the Pacific, 2003.

Clarke, Bob. *From Grub Street to Fleet Street.* Aldershot, U.K.: Ashgate, 1988.

Clarke, Desmond. *Arthur Dobbs, Esquire, 1689–1765.* Chapel Hill: University of North Carolina Press, 1957.

Colley, Linda. *Britons: Forging the Nation 1707–1837.* New Haven, Conn.: Yale University Press, 1992.

Colquhoun, Patrick. *Treatise on the Wealth, Power and Resources of the British Empire in Every Quarter of the Globe,* 2nd ed. London, 1815.

Conrad, Joseph. "Geography and Some Explorers." In *Last Essays.* New York: Doubleday Doran, 1926.

Cookman, Scott. *Ice Blink: The Tragic Fate of Sir John Franklin's Lost Polar Expedition.* New York: John Wiley and Sons, 2000.

Cooper, Paul Fenimore. *Island of the Lost.* New York: G. P. Putnam's Sons, 1961.

Crowe, Keith J. *A History of the Original Peoples of Northern Canada.* Rev. ed. Montreal: McGill–Queen's University Press, 1991.

Cyriax, Richard J., *Sir John Franklin's Last Arctic Expedition.* 1939; reprint Plaistow, U.K.: Arctic Press, 1997.

David, Robert G. *The Arctic in the British Imagination, 1818–1914.* Manchester: Manchester University Press, 2000.

Davidson, Alan. *The Oxford Companion to Food,* 2nd ed. Edited by Tom Jaine. Oxford: Oxford University Press, 2006.

Davidson, Peter. *The Idea of North.* London: Reaktion Books, 2005.

Day, Alan Edwin. *Search for the Northwest Passage: An Annotated Bibliography.* New York: Garland, 1986.

Dickens, Charles. *The Uncollected Writings of Charles Dickens: Household Words, 1850–1859.* Edited by Harry Stone. Bloomington: Indiana University Press, 1968.

Dodge, Ernest S. *Northwest by Sea.* New York: Oxford University Press, 1961.

———. *The Polar Rosses: John and James Clark Ross and Their Explorations.* London: Faber and Faber, 1973.

Eather, Robert H. *Majestic Lights: The Aurora in Science, History, and the Arts.* Washington, D.C.: American Geophysical Union, 1980.

Edinger, Ray. *Fury Beach: The Four-Year Odyssey of Captain John Ross and the* Victory. New York: Berkley, 2004.

Erickson, Arvel B. *The Public Career of Sir James Graham.* Oxford, U.K.: Basil Blackwell, 1952.

Fitzpatrick, Kathleen. *Sir John Franklin in Tasmania, 1837–1843.* Victoria, Australia: Melbourne University Press, 1949.

Fleming, Fergus. *Barrow's Boys.* New York: Atlantic Monthly Press, 1999.

Flinders, Matthew. *Terra Australis: Matthew Flinders' Great Adventures in the Circumnavigation of Australia.* Edited by Tim Flannery. Melbourne, Australia: Text, 2000.

Friendly, Alfred. *Beaufort of the Admiralty: The Life of Sir Francis Beaufort, 1774–1857.* New York: Random House, 1977.

Fry, Michael. *The Dundas Despotism.* Edinburgh: John Donald, 2004.

Gell, Mrs. E. M. *John Franklin's Bride: Eleanor Anne Porden.* London: John Murray, 1931.

Gérin, Winifred. *Emily Brontë: A Biography.* Oxford, U.K.: Clarendon Press, 1971.

Girouard, Mark. *The Return to Camelot: Chivalry and the English Gentleman.* New Haven, Conn.: Yale University Press, 1981.

Gordon, Andrew. *The Rules of the Game: Jutland and British Naval Command.* London: John Murray, 2000.

Gosnell, Mariana. *Ice: The Nature, the History, and the Uses of an Astonishing Substance.* New York: Alfred A. Knopf, 2005.

Great Britain. Admiralty. *Further papers relative to the recent Arctic expeditions in search of Sir John Franklin and the crews of H.M.S. Erebus and Terror.* House of Commons Sessional Papers. Accounts and Papers 35, no. 1898. London: George Edward Eyre and William Spottiswoode For Her Majesty's Stationery Office, 1855.

Griffiths, Franklyn, ed. *Politics of the Northwest Passage.* Montreal: McGill–Queen's University Press, 1987.

Gurney, Alan. *Compass: A Story of Exploration and Innovation.* New York: W. W. Norton & Co., 2005.

Halévy, Élie, *England in 1815,* rev. ed. London: Ernest Benn, 1949.

Hill, J. R., ed. *The Oxford Illustrated History of the Royal Navy.* Oxford: Oxford University Press, 1995.

Holland, Clive. "John Franklin and the Fur Trade." In Richard C. Davis, ed., *Rupert's Land: A Cultural Tapestry,* pp. 97–111. Calgary: Calgary Institute for the Humanities, 1988.

Houghton, Walter E. *The Victorian Frame of Mind: 1830–1870.* New Haven, Conn.: Yale University Press, 1957.

Houghton, Walter Edwards, and Jean Harris Slingerland. *The Wellesley Index to Victorian Periodicals.* Toronto: University of Toronto Press, 1989.

Jonkers, A. R. T. *Earth's Magnetism in the Age of Sail.* Baltimore: Johns Hopkins University Press, 2003.

Lamb, G. F. *Franklin: Happy Voyager.* London: Ernest Benn, 1956.

Lehane, Brendan. *The Northwest Passage.* Alexandria, Va.: Time-Life Books, 1981.

Levere, Trevor H. *Science and the Canadian Arctic: A Century of Exploration, 1818–1918.* Cambridge, U.K.: Cambridge University Press, 1993.

Levi, Peter. *Tennyson*. New York: Charles Scribner's Sons, 1993.

Lewis, Michael. *The Navy in Transition, 1814–1864: A Social History*. London: Hodder and Stoughton, 1965.

Livingstone, David N. *The Geographical Tradition*. Oxford, U.K.: Blackwell, 1992.

Lloyd, Christopher. *Mr. Barrow of the Admiralty: A Life of Sir John Barrow*. London: Collins, 1970.

Loomis, Chauncey C. "The Arctic Sublime." In U. C. Knoepflmacher and G. B. Tennyson, eds., *Nature and the Victorian Imagination*, pp. 95–112. Berkeley: University of California Press, 1977.

Loomis, Chauncey. *Weird and Tragic Shores: The Story of Charles Francis Hall, Explorer*. New York: Modern Library, 2000.

Mackay, David. *In the Wake of Cook: Exploration, Science & Empire, 1780–1801*. London: Croom Helm, 1985.

MacKenzie, John M. "Heroic Myths of Empire." In J. M. Mackenzie, ed., *Popular Imperialism and the Military, 1850–1950*, pp. 109–38. Manchester: Manchester University Press, 1992.

———. "The Iconography of the Exemplary Life: The Case of David Livingstone." In Geoffrey Cubitt and Allen Warren, eds., *Heroic Reputations and Exemplary Lives*, pp. 84–104. Manchester: Manchester University Press, 2000.

Mangles, James. *Papers and Despatches Relating to the Arctic Searching Expeditions of 1850–51–52*. London: Francis and John Rivington, 1852.

Markham, Albert Hastings. *Life of Sir John Franklin and the North-West Passage*. London: George Philip and Son, n.d.

Markham, Albert Hastings, ed. *The Voyages and Works of John Davis the Navigator*. London: Hakluyt Society, 1880.

Markham, Clements R. *The Life of Admiral Sir Leopold McClintock*. London: John Murray, 1909.

———. *The Lands of Silence*. Cambridge, U.K.: Cambridge University Press, 1921.

Mawer, Granville Allen. *South by Northwest: The Magnetic Crusade and the Contest of Antarctica*. Kent Town, South Australia: Wakefield Press, 2006.

McDermott, James. *Martin Frobisher, Elizabethan Privateer*. New Haven, Conn.: Yale University Press, 2001.

McGhee, Robert. *The Arctic Voyages of Martin Frobisher: An Elizabethan Adventure*. London: British Museum Press, 2002.

———. *The Last Imaginary Place: A Human History of the Arctic World*. New York: Oxford University Press, 2005.

McGoogan, Ken. *Fatal Passage: The Story of John Rae*. New York: Carroll and Graf, 2002.

———. *Lady Franklin's Revenge: A True Story of Ambition, Obsession and the Remaking of Arctic History*. Toronto: HarperCollins, 2005.

Morison, Samuel Eliot. *The European Discovery of America: The Northern Voyages*. New York: Oxford University Press, 1971.

Murphy, David. *The Arctic Fox: Francis Leopold McClintock*. Toronto: Dundurn Group, 2004.

Nanton, Paul. *Arctic Breakthrough: Franklin's Expeditions, 1819–1847*. Toronto: Clarke, Irwin & Co., 1981.

Neatby, Leslie H. *The Search for Franklin*, Edmonton: M. G. Hurtig, 1970.

Newman, Peter C. *Empire of the Bay: The Company of Adventurers That Seized a Continent.* New York: Penguin Books, 1998.

Nunavut Handbook. Iqaluit, Nunavut: Ayaya Marketing, 2004.

Officer, Charles, and Jake Page. *A Fabulous Kingdom: The Exploration of the Arctic.* New York: Oxford University Press, 2001.

Owen, Roderic. *The Fate of Franklin: The Life and Mysterious Death of the Most Heroic of Arctic Explorers.* Victoria: Hutchinson of Australia, 1978.

Parry, Ann. *Parry of the Arctic: The Life Story of Admiral Sir Edward Parry, 1790–1855.* London: Chatto and Windus, 1963.

Parry, Rev. Edward. *Memoirs of Rear-Admiral Sir W. Edward Parry.* New York: Protestant Episcopal Society for the Promotion of Evangelical Knowledge, 1858.

Parry, J. H. *Trade and Dominion: The European Overseas Empires in the Eighteenth Century.* New York: Praeger, 1971.

Penrose, Boies. *Travel and Discovery in the Renaissance, 1420–1620.* Cambridge, Mass.: Harvard University Press, 1967.

Picard, Liza. *Victorian London: Tale of a City, 1840–1870.* New York: St. Martin's Griffin, 2005.

Porter, Andrew, ed. *The Nineteenth Century: The Oxford History of the British Empire,* vol. 3. Oxford: Oxford University Press, 1999.

Potter, Russell A. *Arctic Spectacles: The Frozen North in Visual Culture, 1818–1875.* Seattle: University of Washington Press, 2007.

Powell, David. *Nationhood and Identity: The British State since 1800.* London: I. B. Tauris, 2002.

Preston, Diana, and Michael Preston. *A Pirate of Exquisite Mind: Explorer, Naturalist, and Buccaneer: The Life of William Dampier.* New York: Doubleday, 2004.

Pyne, Stephen. *The Ice: A Journey to Antarctica.* Iowa City: University of Iowa Press, 1986.

Quinn, David Beers. *England and the Discovery of America, 1481–1620.* New York: Alfred A. Knopf, 1974.

Quinn, David Beers. "The Northwest Passage in Theory and Practice," in John Logan Allen, ed., *North American Exploration,* pp. 1:292–343. Lincoln: University of Nebraska Press, 1997.

Rich, E. E. *The History of the Hudson's Bay Company 1670–1870.* 2 vols. London: Hudson's Bay Record Society, 1959.

Riffenburgh, Beau. *The Myth of the Explorer: The Press, Sensationalism, and Geographical Discovery.* Oxford, U.K.: Oxford University Press, 1994.

Robinson, Michael F. *The Coldest Crucible: Arctic Exploration and American Culture.* Chicago: University of Chicago Press, 2006.

Rodger, N. A. M. *The Admiralty.* Lavenham, Suffolk, U.K.: Terence Dalton, 1979.

———. *The Command of the Ocean: A Naval History of Britain, 1649–1815.* New York: W. W. Norton & Co., 2005.

Ross, M. J. *Polar Pioneers: John Ross and James Clark Ross.* Montreal: McGill–Queen's University Press, 1994.

Ross, W. Gillies. *Arctic Whalers, Icy Seas: Narratives of the Davis Strait Whale Fishery.* Toronto: Irwin, 1985.

Rule, B. J. *Polar Knight: The Mystery of Sir John Franklin.* New Smyrna Beach, Fla.: Luthers, 1998.

Russell, Penny, ed. *This Errant Lady: Jane Franklin's Overland Journey to Port Phillip and Sydney, 1839*. Canberra: National Library of Australia, 2002.

Sandler, Martin W. *Resolute: The Epic Search for the Northwest Passage and John Franklin, and the Discovery of the Queen's Ghost Ship*. New York: Sterling, 2006.

Savours, Ann. *The Search for the Northwest Passage*. New York: St. Martin's Press, 1999.

Scoresby, William. *An Account of the Arctic Regions*, vol. 1. 1820; reprint Newton Abbot, Devon, U.K.: David and Charles, 1969.

———. *The Polar Ice (1815); The North Pole (1828)*. Whitby, U.K.: Caedmon of Whitby Press, 1980.

Shakespeare, Nicholas. *In Tasmania*. Woodstock, N.Y.: Overlook Press, 2006.

Shelley, Mary W. *Frankenstein, or the Modern Prometheus*. 1818; reprint London: Oxford University Press, 1969.

Simmonds, Peter Lund. *Sir John Franklin and the Arctic Regions: With Detailed Notices of the Expeditions in Search of the Missing Vessels Under Sir John Franklin*. 1852; reprint Whitefish, Mont.: Kessinger, 2007.

Simpson, P. L. *Sir John Franklin and the Arctic Regions*. 1852; reprint Stroud, Gloucestershire, U.K.: Nonsuch, 2005.

Somerset, Anne. *The Life and Times of William IV*. London: Weidenfeld and Nicolson, 1980.

Southam, Brian. *Jane Austen and the Navy*. Greenwich, U.K.: National Maritime Museum, 2005.

Spufford, Francis. *I May Be Some Time: Ice and the English Imagination*. New York: Picador, 1999.

Stamp, Tom, and Cordelia Stamp. *William Scoresby, Arctic Scientist*. Whitby, U.K.: Caedmon of Whitby Press, n.d. [1975].

Steele, Peter. *The Man Who Mapped the Arctic*. Vancouver: Raincoast Books, 2003.

Stefansson, Vilhjalmur. *Unsolved Mysteries of the Arctic*. 1938; reprint New York: Collier Books, 1962.

Stone, Harry. *The Night Side of Dickens: Cannibalism, Passion, Necessity*. Columbus: Ohio State University Press, 1994.

Sutherland, Patricia D., ed. *The Franklin Era in Canadian Arctic History, 1845–1859*. Ottawa: National Museums of Canada, 1985.

Taylor, Andrew. *The World of Gerard Mercator: The Mapmaker Who Revolutionized Geography*. New York: Walker & Co., 2004.

Taylor, E. G. R. *Tudor Geography, 1485–1583*. 1930; reprint New York: Octagon Books, 1968.

Thomas, David N. *Frozen Oceans: The Floating World of Pack Ice*. Buffalo, N.Y.: Firefly Books, 2004.

Traill, H. D. *The Life of Sir John Franklin, R.N.* London: John Murray, 1896.

Tristan, Flora. *London Journal: A Survey of London Life in the 1830s*. London: George Prior, 1980.

Vale, Brian. *A Frigate of King George: Life and Duty on a British Man-of-War*. London: I. B. Tauris, 2001.

Vaughan, Richard. *The Arctic: A History*. Stroud, Gloucestershire, U.K.: Sutton, 1999.

Vaughan, Thomas, and Bill Holm. *Soft Gold: The Fur Trade and Cultural Exchange on the Northwest Coast of America*, 2nd ed., rev., Portland: Oregon Historical Society Press, 1990.

Wallace, Hugh N. *The Navy, the Company, and Richard King: British Exploration in the Canadian Arctic, 1829–1860.* Montreal: McGill–Queen's University Press, 1980.

Wiebe, Rudy. *Playing Dead.* Edmonton: NeWest Publishing, 1989.

Williams, Glyn. *Voyages of Delusion: The Quest for the Northwest Passage.* New Haven, Conn.: Yale University Press, 2002.

Williams, Glyn, and William Barr. *Voyages to Hudson Bay in Search of a Northwest Passage, 1741–1747,* 2 vols. London: Hakluyt Society, 1994, 1995.

Wilson, Ben. *The Making of Victorian Values: Decency and Dissent in Britain: 1789–1837.* New York: Penguin Press, 2007.

Woodman, David C. *Unravelling the Franklin Mystery: Inuit Testimony.* Montreal: McGill–Queen's University Press, 1991.

Woodward, Frances J. *Portrait of Jane: A Life of Lady Franklin.* London: Hodder and Stoughton, 1951.

Woodward, Sir Llewellyn. *The Age of Reform, 1815–1870,* 2nd ed. Oxford: Oxford University Press, 1992.

Wright, John Kirtland. *Human Nature in Geography: Fourteen Papers, 1925–1965.* Cambridge, Mass.: Harvard University Press, 1966.

ARTICLES

Borgerson, Scott. "Sea Change." *Atlantic* (November 2008).

Cawood, John. "The Magnetic Crusade: Science and Politics in Early Victorian Britain." *Isis* 70 (1979): 493–518.

Davis, Richard C. "History or His/Story?: The Explorer cum Author." *Studies in Canadian Literature* 16 (1991): 93–111.

———. " 'Which an Affectionate Heart Would Say': John Franklin's Personal Correspondence, 1819–1824." *Polar Record* 33 (July 1997): 189–212.

Funk, McKenzie. "Cold Rush: The Coming Fight for the Melting North." *Harper's* (September 2007), pp. 45–55.

Keenleyside, Anne. "Final Days of the Franklin Expedition: New Skeletal Evidence." *Arctic* 50 (1997): 36–46.

MacLaren, I. S. ". . . where nothing moves and nothing changes." *Dalhousie Review* 62 (1982): 485–94.

Macleod, Margaret Arnett, and Richard Glover. "Franklin's First Expedition as Seen by the Fur Traders." *Polar Record* 15 (1971): 669–82.

Marlow, James F. "The Fate of Sir John Franklin: Three Phases of Response in Victorian Periodicals," *Victorian Periodicals Review* 15 (Spring 1982): 3–11.

Ross, W. Gillies. "The Gloucester Balloon: A Communication from Franklin?" *Polar Record* 38 (2002): 11–22.

———. "Clairvoyants and Mediums Search for Franklin." *Polar Record* 39 (2003): 1–18.

———. "False Leads in the Franklin Search." *Polar Record* 39 (2003): 131–60.

———. "The Admiralty and the Franklin Search." *Polar Record* 40 (2004): 289–301.

———. "The Arctic Council of 1851: Fact or Fancy?" *Polar Record* 40 (2004): 135–41.

Russell, Penny. "Wife Stories: Narrating Marriage and Self in the Life of Jane Franklin." *Victorian Studies* 48, no. 1 (2005): 35–57.

Stone, Ian R. " 'The contents of the kettles': Charles Dickens, John Rae and Cannibalism on the 1845 Franklin Expedition." *Dickensian* 83 (1987): 6–16.

———. "The Franklin Search in Parliament." *Polar Record* 32 (1996): 209–16.

ACKNOWLEDGMENTS

The staff of the rare book division of Butler Library at Columbia University in New York, which has a remarkably comprehensive collection of Arctic books, pamphlets, and British government documents, was unfailingly polite and helpful, and I want to thank them. The rare-book staff at the New York Public Library research division on Fifth Avenue at 42nd Street was also helpful.

Particular friends were not only encouraging throughout this project but helpful in a material way. I want to thank Philip Spitzer, my agent and my friend, and his wife, Mary, for help and support throughout the project, not least for the use of their apartment when they were gone. I owe a similar debt to friends Lynn Langway and Jerry Edgerton, and Anne-Lise Spitzer, for the use of their apartments. I am deeply grateful to Ken Robbins for his help with reproductions of photographs and maps and for years of friendship. Thomas Harris, Pace Barnes, and Alexandra Leigh-Hunt got me through a number of crises and have been nothing but supportive throughout the three years it took me to write this book. All of these people are very dear to me. I don't know how I would have finished the book without them.

I owe many thanks to John Rasmus, editor of *National Geographic Adventure* magazine, and to his longtime associate, Steve Byers, my editor there, for their loyalty and encouragement. At the National Geographic Society, Lisa Thomas and Kevin Mulroy were very helpful. It is through them that I came to know about the long struggle for the Northwest Passage and John Franklin's role in it. My editor at Knopf, Andrew Miller, has been unusually patient and, through his close attention to the text, has saved me from numerous mistakes of emphasis and tone and helped me focus the book more tightly. I feel lucky to have him.

My wife, the writer Lorraine Dusky, knows better than anybody what it took to write this book. It is a pleasure to dedicate it to her.

Index

Page numbers in *italics* refer to maps.

A NOTE ABOUT THE AUTHOR

Anthony Brandt is the author of two previous books and has edited a number of others, including a new abridged version of the *Journals of Lewis and Clark*, published by the National Geographic Society. He was the general editor of the Society's Adventure Classics series. He has written for numerous national magazines and is currently a contributing editor at *National Geographic Adventure*. He is married and lives in Sag Harbor, New York.

A NOTE ON THE TYPE

This book was set in a modern adaptation of a type designed by the first William Caslon (1692–1766). The Caslon face, an artistic, easily read type, has enjoyed over two centuries of popularity in the English-speaking world. This version, designed by Carol Twombley for the Adobe Corporation and released in 1990, insures by its even balance and honest letterforms the continuing use of Caslon well into the digital age and the twenty-first century.

Composed by North Market Street Graphics,
Lancaster, Pennsylvania

Printed and bound by Berryville Graphics,
Berryville, Virginia

Designed by Wesley Gott